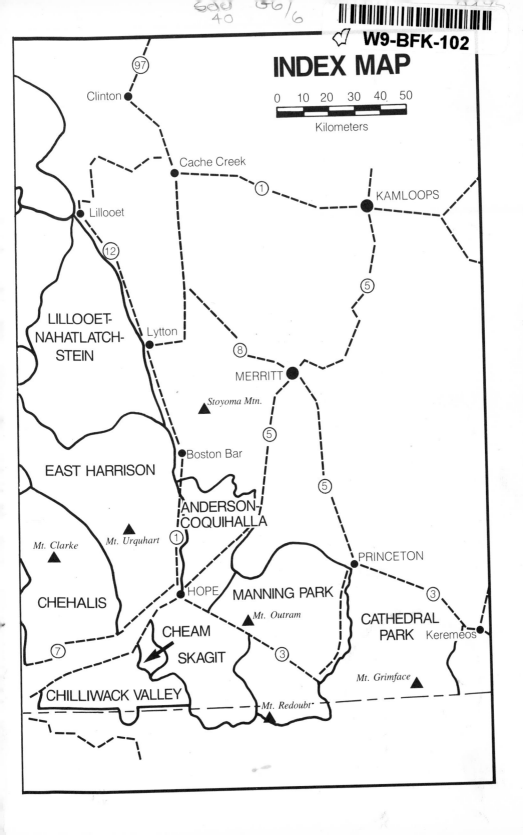

INDEX MAP

0 10 20 30 40 50
Kilometers

W9-BFK-102

97
Clinton

Cache Creek

1

KAMLOOPS

Lillooet

12

5

LILLOOET-
NAHATLATCH-
STEIN

Lytton

8

MERRITT

Stoyoma Mtn.

5

EAST HARRISON

Boston Bar

5

ANDERSON-
COQUIHALLA

Mt. Clarke

Mt. Urquhart

1

PRINCETON

3

CHEHALIS

HOPE

MANNING PARK

Mt. Outram

CATHEDRAL
PARK

Keremeos

CHEAM

7

SKAGIT

3

Mt. Grimface

CHILLIWACK VALLEY

Mt. Redoubt

A Guide to
Climbing & Hiking
In Southwestern British Columbia

BRUCE F. FAIRLEY

EDITORS:
Sheena Lambert
Dr. Tirthankar Bose
Dr. Glenn Woodsworth
Lori Thicke

Published by Gordon Soules Book Publishers Ltd., West Vancouver, Canada, in co-operation with the B.C. Mountaineering Club and The Alpine Club of Canada.

Canadian Cataloguing in Publication Data

Fairley, Bruce, 1951-
  A Guide to Climbing and Hiking in Southwestern British Columbia

Includes bibliographic references and index. ISBN 0-919574-99-8

1. Mountaineering – British Columbia – Guide-books.   2. Hiking – British Columbia – Guide-books.   I. Title.
GV199.44.C22B753 1986   917.11   C86-091305-8

Research assisted by a grant from Canada Works.

Gordon Soules Book Publishers Ltd.
1352-B Marine Drive
West Vancouver, B.C.
Canada
V7T 1B5

Designed by David Lim
Typeset by Joy Woodsworth and The Typeworks
Printed and bound in Canada by Hignell Printing Limited

Contents

This book is dedicated to W. Lee Wilks,
who gave me a push in the right direction,
and to the memory of Julian Harrison, my friend.

Acknowledgments

A guidebook is more than just a collection of routes; it bespeaks a mountaineering philosophy. While Dick Culbert took no part in the compilation of this guide, his influence lives and breathes on every page. "Culbert's Guide," as the precursor to this book has always been known, embodied qualities which characterized Dick's style of climbing: a relish for overcoming sticky approaches, a disdain of bureaucratic authority, and a love of the new and untried. For his generosity, egalitarianism and good humour, I first of all thank Dick Culbert, who has been more of an inspiration over the years than he could ever realize.

Next I must express a debt owed to three modern "prospectors," who together with me one season assayed the gold available in federal government contracts. Turned loose on the countryside of southwestern B.C. in the name of gainful employment in one of the wettest springs imaginable, my good friends Rob Driscoll, Kevin Haberl, Anders Ourom and I spent many hours checking and recording elusive access information in forest service offices and logging camps, trudging up boggy trails and dodging careening logging trucks. It was an atrocious year to be outdoors much of the time, but we had a lot of fun doing it. The chapters each of these three were mainly responsible for have been credited to them.

Glenn Woodsworth proved a bear for work when the going got rough towards the end and things seemed to be grinding down. He masterminded a complete tip-to-toe verification of the data, straightened out our geology, beefed up our history, edited the prose, and compiled the "Sources" section. Thanks also to Joy and Karen Woodsworth, who did a complete word processing and proof-reading of the manuscript, checked our metric conversions, and added much in the way of stylistic comment.

Other individuals deserve special comment for duty above and beyond the call. Chen Chih-Pien, our secretarial assistant in that far-off summer of 1984, somehow interpreted our scrawled notes to create a typed copy of them, and brewed endless cups of tea. Karl Ricker was merciless in his reviewing of our efforts, liberally sprinkling his extremely thorough editing with phrases such as "complete nonsense," "grossly inaccurate," "very deficient," and the like. Despite my feelings that these criticisms were at times too energetically expressed, in terms of raw information, no one has contributed more to this edition than Karl, and I thank him for all his work and for sharing his storehouse of knowledge with us.

Several others took the sort of personal interest in this project that is usually reserved for one's children. Don Serl and John Clarke come to mind as two who reviewed vast amounts of copy and who were better sticklers for detail than myself. John's knowledge of the outposts surpasses anyone's, and both he and Don were fastidious in keeping me up to date on the latest developments, and in sorting out my wooly language.

Others reviewed several chapters and gave liberally of their time and talent to improve the manuscript. Peter Jordan, John Howe, Maxim de Jong, Harold Redekop, Alan Dibb, John Baldwin, Bob Tustin, Steve Grant, Rob Richards and Michael Conway-Brown deserve special mention here. John Manuel phoned me weekly with a fresh supply of gossip, and proved to have a special talent for unearthing lost bits of history. Many corrections in first ascent records are due to his persistent sleuthing.

Others, not as involved in the entire project, were indispensable in filling gaps and verifying information in specific chapters. Here I must thank Grant McCormack, Roger Griffiths, Ed Zenger, Mike Feller, Esther and Martin Kafer, Syd Watts, Len Soet and Joe Bajan. On Vancouver Island, Martin Conder stage-managed meetings with Island climbers, and Jim Sandford, John Pratt, Rob MacDonald and Rick Eppler came and told us all they knew. Special kudos to Rick Eppler, who checked all the Island copy and wrote one chapter. David Harris stepped in at the last moments to donate his graphics arts expertise to the final polish. Moira Irvine deserves mention; she took time out from a busy schedule to assist with photography.

Thanks also to the ever co-operative forest service, to Pat Carney, M.P. for Vancouver Centre, who paved the way for our contract approval, and to Christine Vraine, project officer. Thanks as well to all those who sent letters, scribbled notes and made phone calls in an effort to keep me posted.

By way of a personal note, I would like to recognize the example and influence of Fred Beckey, whose guidebooks have set the standard for the genre, and whose meticulousness puts me to shame. Despite all the thousands of hours and hundreds of revisions, constantly changing conditions inevitably lead to a tentative final product; the ultimate and definitive guidebook for southwestern B.C. can never be written because each time we tackle a climb, weather factors, evolving abilities, changes in equipment, new techniques, and increased familiarity with the terrain make our experience of it different.

Lastly, a word of deep appreciation to my climbing friends with whom I have shared so many fabulous times, and especially to Harold Redekop. Much of what I know about southwestern B.C. I discovered with him. He was there on many of the finest climbs and has endured with me over the past six years more snow-choked, rain-soaked, bug-wrenching, mud-wracking, unprofitable bushwhacks than either of us will ever care to remember. Here's to many more!

Introduction

In 1974, Dick Culbert began his *Alpine Guide to Southwestern British Columbia* with the statement that "The Coast Mountains of British Columbia contain some of the least hospitable terrain on earth." While this remains true, they also happily contain some of the most attactive alpine regions on the planet. It is the purpose of this guide, based on Culbert's pioneering work, to describe access to and routes and climbs in this high country of the southwestern corner of British Columbia.

This book includes the Coast Mountains south of Toba Inlet, Toba River, the headwaters of the Lillooet River, and the plateau country of the Chilcotin, as well as the mountains of Vancouver Island. Also included is that part of the North Cascades which is most accessible from north of the American border (see Index Map). This is roughly the same area described in Dick Culbert's *Alpine Guide*, published in 1974. New areas in the present work are the Manatee Glacier and Clendenning Creek regions. The Squamish Chief and nearby rock climbing areas are not covered here, as they are well served by their own guidebooks (see Sources).

Based on the conviction that route finding is an integral part of the mountaineering experience, this guide is primarily intended for those who have the expertise to travel off trail and find their own routes. For such climbers and hikers, directions are given to locate each peak or route, with a short description of its difficulties. While not designed for the novice, this book does offer a great deal of information of use to the hiker and beginning mountaineer. This information has been kept brief enough to ensure that the spirit of exploration is not stifled. Two chapters (Lillooet-Nahatlatch-Stein and Duffey Lake Road Peaks) have been treated in wilderness fashion: access is completely described, but only minimal route information is given.

Discussions of climbing technique, such as how and when to use an ice-axe, are not included in this book. Novice climbers, or experienced ones who want to learn more, are encouraged to read *Freedom of the Hills*, an excellent sourcebook published by The Mountaineers, Seattle.

This guidebook is meant to be used in conjunction with the 1:50,000 topographic map series published by the federal Department of Energy, Mines and Resources. Other map series, listed later in this introduction, are useful for certain specific areas. Relevant maps are noted at the beginning of each chapter; sources for obtaining maps are included in the section on "Sources."

For descriptive purposes, southwestern B.C. has been divided into 32 self-contained areas, each of which is treated in one chapter. In general, these areas are defined on the basis of access, not geographic unity: for example, both sides of the Duffey Lake road are in the same chapter, even though they are in different mountain ranges. The easiest or most popular route on a mountain is listed first, with other routes following in either clockwise or counterclockwise order.

GEOGRAPHIC NAMES: WHAT IS A PEAK?

For the purposes of this guidebook an individual peak is at least 150 m/500 ft higher than the col which separates it from its neighbours. (This is one criterion used by the Canadian Permanent Committee on Geographic Names.) Outstanding pinnacles, such as The Witch's Tooth or Perkin's Pillar are legitimate exceptions;

however, the temptation to name or claim first ascents of spur ridges or subsidiary bumps should be resisted. Unofficial names are enclosed in quotation marks in this guidebook. Proposals for new names should be submitted to: Mr. D.F. Pearson, Surveys and Resource Mapping Branch, Ministry of the Environment, Parliament Buildings, Victoria, B.C. V8V 1X5. The articles on this topic in the *Canadian Alpine Journal* by D.F. Pearson (1983, pp. 52-53), and by Glenn Woodsworth (1980, p.84) are informative. Dr. Glenn Woodsworth, Geological Survey of Canada, 100 W. Pender Street, Vancouver, B.C. V6B 1R8, is always glad to give advice on appropriate names for features in southwestern B.C.

ACCURACY

This book is only a **guide**: it is not infallible and, no doubt, not without error. Guidebook users should keep in mind that changes may occur rapidly, especially after heavy rainstorms and during spring run-off. Undoubtedly some approach routes will change even as the book goes to press. However, this guidebook reflects the most recent conditions, with information updated through March 1986.

As distances have sometimes been measured using car odometers, or traced using map measuring wheels, accuracy is only claimed to within a quarter of a kilometre. Times given are for parties in good physical shape. If you've been watching the tube a lot recently, then you'd better add an hour or more accordingly.

LOGGING ROADS

Logging roads give the best access to most of the areas in this guidebook. Information on the state of disused logging roads can be obtained from the relevant companies; they are listed at the beginning of each chapter. Roads into areas being actively logged are often gated or otherwise barred. The public is usually forbidden from 6:00 a.m. to 6:00 p.m. on working days, as well as during periods of high fire hazard. Two or three companies may be logging the same valley; when you check in with one company make sure another outfit won't lock the gate while your vehicle is inside.

The most practical vehicle for logging road travel is one with good clearance, four-wheel or rear-wheel (rather than front wheel) drive, and snow tires. The vehicle should be in good repair and equipped to deal with mechanical problems, especially flat tires. Few logging roads are ploughed or otherwise maintained in winter.

WILDERNESS TRAVEL AND SAFETY

Travel in the Coast Mountains calls for care and self-reliance. Some guidebook users may come from areas where well-developed trail networks make approaches to the mountains less arduous. If you aren't used to log-walking, stream-crossing, and navigating through dense bush, you may want a few pointers.
Where to travel: Picking the best route through the bush is what wilderness travel is all about. Try to head for the ridge crests or the most mature timber, where undergrowth is least dense. Broad ridges are easy to spot on contour maps. Avalanche fans and slide alder—terrible for travel—are easy to spot in the field. These are indicated by light green bush below timberline, as are willow thickets, dwarf cedar and other undergrowth. Stay out of burns; they are messy and tend to be jigsaw puzzles of fallen timber. Moraine often means tedious travel because the debris tends to be unstable.

When backpacking in the bush, allow about an hour for every kilometre of travel plus about the same for every 150 m/500 ft of elevation gain. Timberline runs from about 1600 m/5200 ft to 1800 m/6000 ft on the coast, and is a bit higher in the Interior and somewhat lower on Vancouver Island.

As you travel, note landmarks and features, frequently looking back as you go. Familiar terrain can look totally different when you approach from the opposite direction. Above all, learn to use map and compass; it is not really very complicated to use them, and they are indispensable for safe wilderness travel.

Weather: Storms are very frequent in winter, and whiteouts over large ice sheets are common at all times of the year. Big, isolated summits tend to attract clouds and may host storms even when the surrounding country is calm and sunny. While the weather is more moderate and stable on the interior side of the ranges, it is extremely unpredictable along the coast. Take rainwear no matter what the forecast, and for camping carry a sturdy tent or bivouac sac. Recorded forecasts are available in most cities and large towns; they are listed under "Weather Information" in the telephone book.

Creeks and rivers: On the coast, creek beds and river valleys do not often make good routes for travel, even in winter. Many water-courses are criss-crossed by windfalls and constricted by deep gorges. If you follow an unknown stream down from timberline you may find that it plunges over bluffs or enters steep-walled canyons.

Waterflow can vary enormously from day to day in width and volume; one rainstorm can swell a shallow brook until it is impassable. If you doubt the wisdom of crossing a stream, try it first without your pack. If you are wearing a pack while crossing, always loosen its straps and be ready to throw it off. Wearing a rope is less useful than you might think; it may actually be dangerous if there is any chance of the rope becoming snagged.

The fast streams in this area make log walking an essential art in which crampons are occasionally useful. When moving across a log, always walk or crawl forward; do not shuffle sideways. Don't watch the water, because it will make you giddy. If you feel yourself falling off a log, try to land on the downstream side to avoid being trapped against branches by the current. For the same reason, when crossing a stream near fallen logs or logjams, always cross below them.

Avalanches and rockfall: Culbert noted that "novices in the mountains are afraid of falling, while experienced climbers are afraid of things falling on them." Snowslides, though most common in winter and spring, occur at all times of the year. All mountain travellers should know the signs of a possible avalanche and learn to recognize them. The most dangerous time for avalanches is during and after heavy snowfalls; high winds can severely intensify hazardous conditions, especially on the lee side of slopes. Spring and summer avalanches are usually triggered by weakening of the snowpack through warming and melting. Cornices are always a hazard and trigger many slides when they collapse.

Avalanches are a complex phenomenon and in order to travel safely, mountaineers must have some knowledge about their formation and behavior. The best starting point is a little book published by The Mountaineers called *The ABC of Avalanche Safety*. Courses in avalanche safety are now offered each winter by the Federation of Mountain Clubs of B.C. (listed in the Sources). John Baldwin's guide, *Exploring the Coast Mountains on Skis*, has a good introductory discussion on avalanches.

While not a universal hazard in the guidebook area, rockfall is common enough to call for precautions. Rockfall occurs most often when stones are dislodged either by melting or by heavy-footed climbers. The hazard can be minimized by seeking ridges and by travelling early enough to take advantage of the stability afforded by over-night freezing. Avoid travelling as a large party strung out over loose terrain; either diagonal up so as to eliminate any risk to those below or keep the party close enough together so that anything knocked off does not present a danger. Also, retrieval of rappel ropes requires care.

Glaciers: Glaciers and steep snow slopes are dangerous in several ways. Hazards in-clude hidden crevasses, ice avalanches in icefalls, and the unexpected difficulty of ar-resting a slip without an ice-axe. Icefall activity is not primarily determined by weather, but by the forward movement of the glacier, and seracs can collapse at any time. Only properly equipped, experienced mountaineering parties should venture over this type of terrain.

Emergencies: In case of emergency, contact the nearest R.C.M.P. station. An air-supported Armed Forces search-and-rescue unit is available, as are a number of local volunteer groups, but a sense of responsibility should keep parties with self-manageable problems from relying on outside intervention. Preparing yourself for emergencies and dealing with them are topics beyond the scope of this book; again, consult *Freedom of the Hills* for an excellent discussion of these matters.

Campfires: In the forest, accumulated dry debris can create a serious fire hazard, so dig through flammable humus to mineral soil before lighting a campfire. Near tree line attempt to choose fuel with the alpine aesthetic in mind; gnarled, dried branches are scenic as well as flammable. When you leave a campsite you should douse and dig out the fire area. Use your hand to ensure that a fire is dead out. Permits are not usually necessary, but the forests are often closed entirely due to fire hazard during summer dry spells.

ETHICS

No one will be looking over his or her shoulder at you as you climb in most areas of the Coast Mountains. Here you have the freedom to climb a route in the manner you choose without having to meet someone else's standards of performance. None-theless, and partly because the Coast Mountains represent one of the last accessible realms for exploratory climbing, strong ethical guidelines as to what is acceptable be-havior have emerged and are respected by even the most ambitious climbers.

The alpine regions of the Coast Mountains have never been all that easy to reach, and the struggle to get to the base is part of the mystique of coastal mountaineering. There are some who hope it will remain that way. As John Baldwin has said, "The helicopter is by far the most powerful tool developed by man for removing the veil of remoteness from a wilderness area." The over-use of air support is the most con-tentious of the ethical issues that coastal mountaineers debate. To be blunt, helicopter parties are not welcome at cabins which have traditionally been approached on foot. This category includes most of the cabins within range of this guidebook. Moreover, parties that make use of the helicopter to capture important new climbs must always consider whether they are acting within the accepted traditions which prevail in this area. Virtually all the important ascents documented here have been made without the use of this overbearing aid.

Rock ethics are a simple matter; whenever possible we should use protection that does not damage the rock. Generally speaking, chocks work well on most of the climbs described in this book. In my view, it is quite acceptable to carry a few pitons on the more technical routes. Coast Mountains rock is not all flawless granite as found in such areas as California's Sierra Nevada, and a number of the harder routes in southwestern B.C. may require knifeblades, horizontals or one or two thin pegs. Larger angles, on the other hand, have been replaced by chocks and Friends and should not be necessary.

Litter and defoliation are unacceptable and are clearly environmentally destructive. Pack out what you pack in. In my opinion, however, the prohibition against campfires that some would advocate is unnecessary in most parts of the range. We are still well-endowed with firewood, and those who exercise self-restraint will not damage the environment as long as fires are not built in sensitive alpine areas.

Ethics is ultimately a matter of respecting the values and traditions of the sport and of conserving the environment by restraining the power that we have to destroy and deface it.

FIRST ASCENTS

Climbers should be cautious in claiming first ascents of peaks, as prospectors, packers and survey parties climbed more peaks in southwestern B.C. in the early part of the century than many people realize. In addition, some Vancouver climbers who explore the outer fringes of the guidebook areas choose not to record their activities or to leave cairns to mark their passage. There are also those who believe that it is vain and pointless to record first ascents. I do not agree. A few carefully arranged stones on the summit cost little effort, and prevent embarrassing claims by later parties. First ascent records also provide an invaluable tool for securing information about peaks and climbs. As well, a historical record helps maintain perspective. It is salutary for modern climbers, who tend to think of themselves as better alpinists than the pioneers, to be reminded that Basil Darling climbed the north buttress of the West Lion solo with only the cedars for protection, that the first ascent of Mt. Pitt was made before the concept of air support was even thought of, and that Tom Fyles soloed The Table in Garibaldi Park before most of us were born.

WINTER ASCENTS

Accumulated snowfall, low temperatures, short days and difficult access are the really critical factors that make winter climbing a challenge. In this guidebook, winter ascents are taken to mean only those made between December 19 and March 22. While "winter conditions" can be encountered in spring and fall, the most formidable combinations occur during winter. Limiting winter ascents to the calendar winter means that climbers must meet the mountain on its own terms; you can't always wait for better weather.

Ratings

This guidebook uses the Yosemite Decimal System for rating climbing difficulty. The system is as follows:

Class 1 Hiking

Class 2 Scrambling

Class 3 Some use of handholds for balance, but rope not required

Class 4 Most parties will rope up and either travel together or put in belay stations at the start of each pitch

Class 5.0-5.4 Easy roped climbing, requiring occasional use of protection such as chocks

Class 5.5-5.7 Moderate roped climbing, requiring good technical skills and considerable protection for most climbers

Class 5.8 Many mountaineers regard 5.8 as the limit of what can be climbed in mountain boots

Class 5.9 & up Difficult, strenuous roped climbing requiring strong technical skills and considerable protection

A1-A4 Aid climbing, where it is necessary to put weight on one's protection in order to move up

breviations

 abbreviations are used in this text. Directions (north, northwest, etc.) are ab-
ted (N, NW, etc.) when they are used as compass directions. Others are:

    no technical difficulty
    first ascent
    first winter ascent (see Introduction, Winter Ascents)
    first recorded ascent; other parties may have preceded the recorded party
 : first recorded winter ascent

breviations of clubs and journals, see ''Sources.''

Sources

MAPS

The 1:50,000 series of federal topographic map sheets has long been the most popular among mountaineers. This series is the only one that covers the whole of the
guidebook area on a large scale. Be wary when using these maps, as they do sometimes overlook glaciers and lakes or misrepresent the contours of peaks. Some sheets
have elevation mix-ups and assign names to the wrong feature. On the whole, however, these maps are extremely good. They are available from:

Geological Survey of Canada
100 West Pender Street
Vancouver B.C. V0B 1R8

Dominion Map Ltd.
541 Howe Street
Vancouver B.C. V6C 2C2

Worldwide Books and Maps
949 Granville Street
Vancouver, B.C. V6Z 1L3

The Provincial Ministry of the Environment also publishes a series of map sheets.
Most of these are on a scale of 1:100,000 or 1:125,000 and those currently available
cover the regions closest to Vancouver. They tend to show more land status detail
and are often more accurate with regard to cultural features such as roads. These are
available from Worldwide Books and Maps (see above) or:

Surveys and Mapping Branch
Parliament Buildings
Victoria, B.C. V8V 1X5

These maps are also available from Government Agents in the various municipalities
(but not in Vancouver).

Specialized recreation maps on a scale of 1:100,000 are published by the Outdoor
Recreation Council of B.C. These maps emphasize trails, visitor services and so
forth. They are available from:

Outdoor Recreation Council
1200 Hornby Street
Vancouver B.C. V6Z 2E2

Currently issued maps relevant to this guidebook are: *Whistler/Garibaldi*; *Princeton-
Manning-Cathedral*; *Chilliwack-Hope-Skagit*; and *Campbell River*.

The provincial government also publishes specialized map sheets for some of the
provincial parks, including Manning and Garibaldi, and the Parks Branch prints
simple pamphlet maps of all provincial parks, which, although short on detail, are
often accurate in terms of nomenclature.

The *Recreation Map of the North Cascades*, by Fred Beckey and Al Cardwell,
and published by The Mountaineers, covers much of the area south of the Fraser
River and Highway 3.

BOOKS

The following is a selection of the current guidebooks covering this region. Some are a bit out of date and some are better than others. No guide, this one included, should be taken as the last word!

Baldwin, John. *Exploring the Coast Mountains on Skis*. 1983. Vancouver: the author. Similar in approach and philosophy to this book; covers much the same area from the ski mountaineering viewpoint.

Beckey, Fred. *Cascade Alpine Guide: Climbing and High Routes, Rainy Pass to Fraser River*. 1981. Seattle: The Mountaineers. The standard reference, with excellent illustrations and much historical material, to the area south and east of the the Fraser River.

Campbell, Jim. *Squamish Rock Climbs*. 1985. Vancouver: the author. A topo guide, particularly good for the Little Smoke Bluffs area.

Darvill, Fred T. *Hiking the North Cascades*. 1982. San Francisco: The Sierra Club. Thorough coverage of trails south of Manning Park.

Freeman, Roger and David Thompson. *Exploring the Stein River Valley*. 1979. Vancouver: Douglas and McIntyre. Excellent guide to all aspects of the Stein River drainage. Much of the introductory material applies to other parts of the Cascades and eastern Coast Mountains.

Freeman, Roger and Ethel. *Exploring Vancouver's North Shore Mountains*. 1985. Vancouver: Federation of Mountain Clubs of British Columbia. Meticulous trail descriptions for the North Shore mountains.

Harcombe, Andrew and Robert Cyca. *Exploring Manning Park*. 1979. Second edition (revised). Vancouver: Douglas and McIntyre; Seattle: The Mountaineers. Trails and natural history in Manning Park, now a bit outdated.

Harris, R.C. and H.R. Hatfield. *Old Pack Trails in the Proposed Manning Park Extension*. 1977. Summerland: Okanagan Similkameen Parks Society. Pamphlet with good descriptions of trails in the region just north of Manning Park.

Macaree, Mary and David. *103 Hikes in Southwestern British Columbia*. 1980. Second edition (revised). Vancouver: Douglas and McIntyre; Seattle: The Mountaineers. Comprehensive guide to non-technical trails and routes in the Lower Mainland.

Mathews, W.H. *Garibaldi Geology*. 1975. Vancouver: Geological Association of Canada, Cordilleran Section. Fine, non-technical account of the geology of the Garibaldi Lake area.

Ourom, Anders. *A Climber's Guide to the Squamish Chief*. 1980. Vancouver: B.C. Mountaineering Club. Good photos and route descriptions.

Page, Jay, Alan Dibb, Paul Phillips, and Bruce Blackwell. *A Guide to Ski Touring in the Whistler, Garibaldi Park, Squamish, and Pemberton Areas*. 1984. Vancouver: The Varsity Outdoor Club. Particularly good for Garibaldi Park.

Roberge, Claude. *Hiking Garibaldi Park at Whistler's Back Door*. 1982. Vancouver: Douglas and McIntyre. Good for the Diamond Head-Black Tusk and Whistler areas.

Shewchuk, Murphy. *Exploring the Nicola Valley*. 1981. Vancouver: Douglas and McIntyre. Useful for the Coquihalla side of the Anderson River area.

Whitney, Stephen. *A Field Guide to the West Coast Mountains*. 1983. Vancouver:
Douglas and McIntyre; Seattle: The Mountaineers. An excellen[t]
of the Cascades, Coast Mountains, Vancouver Island and the Olym[pics]

JOURNALS

The following journals and newsletters may be ordered from their
Back issues of most of these journals are available at the Vancouv[er]
and at the University of British Columbia.

American Alpine Journal: Published annually by the America[n]
New York. Commonly contains notes on significant climbs
cades.

Avalanche Echoes (*AE*): Published monthly by the Vancouver Sec[tion]
Club of Canada. An excellent source for new climbs in the g[...]

The B.C. Mountaineer (*BCM*): Published monthly by the B.C.
Club, Vancouver. An ''annual'' issue with the same title is
Both contain route information pertinent to the guidebook are[a]

Canadian Alpine Journal (*CAJ*): Published annually by the Alpine
Banff. The primary reference for mountaineering in Canada.

Island Bushwhacker (*IB*): Published monthly by the Vancouver Isl[and]
Alpine Club of Canada, Victoria. The best source for new
couver Island.

The Mountaineer: This annual volume by The Mountaineers, Seat[tle]
useful information on the North Cascades.

Varsity Outdoor Club Journal (*VOCJ*): Published annually by th[e]
Club at the University of B.C., Vancouver Over the year
wealth of information on southwestern B.C.

CLUBS

The following are the main mountaineering clubs in the are[a]
guide.

Alpine Club of Canada, Vancouver Section (ACC)
Alpine Club of Canada, Vancouver Island Section, Victoria
B.C. Mountaineering Club, Vancouver (BCMC)
Island Mountain Ramblers, Nanaimo
Varsity Outdoor Club, University of B.C., Vancouver (VOC)

All may be contacted through:

Federation of Mountain Clubs of B.C.
1200 Hornby Street
Vancouver, B.C. V6Z 2E2

Climbing In Southwestern British Columbia: A Brief History

Anyone who travels extensively on foot in the mountainous country around Vancouver quickly gains an admiration for the hardiness and enthusiasm of the early explorers who first contended with the deep valleys and glacier-draped summits of this province. No veteran of Coast Mountain travel, no matter how seasoned, can avoid gritting his teeth just a little before leaving the road or the trail behind and plunging into the bush. Sudden gorges, thorns and slide alder, raging creeks, and omnipresent devil's club, often combine to make valley travel a gymnastic chore.

Who were the mountaineers to first confront these challenges? For the most part, their names are lost forever. We have no way of knowing if the native Indian people of the province climbed any of its many summits before the arrival of white men, and much of the activity of prospectors, trappers, and surveyors can only be guessed at, although here at least there are some scattered records to go by. A few mountain areas were thoroughly prospected even before the turn of the century. Records of heavy claim-staking in the Sky Pilot, Gun Creek and Lillooet regions suggest that the high ridges and gentler peaks in such neighbourhoods were visited by prospectors as they blanketed the terrain with mineral claims.

In addition to these prospectors, surveyors made forays into unknown areas, and sometimes made first ascents. From 1857 to 1862 the British and American parties surveying the International Boundary explored the Skagit and Chilliwack valleys. Henry Custer, the most vigorous of the surveyors, claimed the first ascent of Shawatum Mountain in 1859 and planned an attempt on Hozomeen, which failed to materialize. Although they didn't climb many peaks, these parties frequently described the steep, dangerous, and dramatic summits they found in the ranges along the International Boundary. Later, during the second boundary survey between 1901 and 1908, first ascents were made on Whitworth Peak and Mount Spickard.

Details of other early forays into the Coast Mountains have also been preserved, but none of them can compare with the traverse made in 1893 by Stanley Smith and a companion identified only as "Mr. Doolittle of Maple Ridge." Little is known of the character or achievements of Stanley Smith beyond this one journey, but it appears that, like the explorers Waddington and Downie before him, he was interested in discovering a viable overland route through the Coast Mountains to the Pacific Ocean. In 1893 he was dispatched by the Superintendent of the Provincial Police to search for two men named Clark and Braden, an engineer and his artist companion, who had set off up the Squamish River to discover if its drainage would make a good route for the proposed Alaska and Peace River Railway.

Stanley Smith left from the town of Squamish (little more than a logging camp at that time) and proceeded up the Squamish River by Indian canoe for four days, before taking to the bush on foot. Several days later he halted and spent two days building a canoe to get across the Elaho River, a major tributary of the Squamish. Once across, he and Doolittle shouldered hundred-pound packs and continued on foot. On August 12, while crossing a rock slide, Smith found a gray tweed cap, the only evidence of the lost men he ever discovered.

It took Smith twenty days to reach the head of the Elaho; then, rather than turn

back, he plunged ahead into the completely unknown country of the Lillooet Icecap region. As Don Munday put it:
Smith's instructions seem to have included investigation of a report that Indians had found bodies of the missing men near Chilko Lake, and he simply went on through the unknown heart of the Coast Mountains, seemingly fully confident of being able to find it though distant fifty miles as the crow flies (*CAJ* 1940, p. 163).

The men reached Chilko Lake on September 13 and built another canoe for the lake crossing. They then travelled overland to Tatla Lake before exiting by way of the Klinaklini River and Knight Inlet, building yet another "cottonwood" canoe to speed their travel. They reached Knight Inlet on the eighteenth of October, having covered a distance of well over four hundred kilometres! The entire journey was made without benefit of maps or mountaineering equipment, while provisions consisted of anything the two could scavenge along the route. In his account Stanley Smith mentions feasting on goat, porcupine, groundhog and muskrat. By the time the pair arrived in Chilko Lake their clothes were in rags: "One suit," observed Smith, "will not stand a trip like this."

Stanley Smith had not set out to explore mountains, and in fact may have climbed only a single peak on his journey. In similar fashion early ascents around Vancouver were often made by parties who went into the mountains for reasons other than climbing. Peaks along Howe Sound, such as Harvey, Brunswick, and The Lions fell to hunting parties. Typical of such ascents was that of the West Lion in 1889, made by a party who followed goats to the summit. The group included the Indian chief Joe Capilano, who later that evening asked Dr. Bell-Irving, another member of the party, to time one of his Indian youths in a race from the base to the top. According to Bell-Irving, the youth, stripped naked, completed the ascent and descent in twenty minutes!

It was perhaps the allure of The Lions, prominent landmarks on the North Shore skyline, which ultimately initiated recreational mountaineering in the Vancouver area. They were rumoured to be impossible to climb, but once the West Lion had been scaled it was inevitable that someone should try to set the rumour completely on its head by climbing the East Lion as well. So it was that in 1903 the three Latta brothers set out up the Capilano River. Ostensibly their purpose was a goat hunting expedition, but along with their "empty lard pail, three pounds of bacon, two pounds of beans, one pound rice and quarter pound of tea" they carried fifty feet of half-inch manilla rope. The account of their subsequent climb makes amusing reading, for in fact they had no knowledge of roped climbing technique at all, and found the security afforded by bush on the route more to their liking. John Latta wrote, "It is amazing what a feeling of security you get when hanging on to a friendly bush, rather than risking your safety on a projecting piece of rotten rock that may come away in your hand." In addition to the first ascent of the East Lion, this party also made the third ascent of the West Lion.

It did not take long for the new interest in climbing to gain impetus. In 1907, a group of Vancouver climbers founded the Vancouver Mountaineering Club, which soon became the B.C. Mountaineering Club (BCMC). Virtually all the best Vancouver climbers were club members, and they organized a vigourous schedule of weekend hikes and summer camps, which took parties into the mountains in larger numbers than ever before. In 1908, BCMC parties recorded first ascents on Seymour, Bishop, the Lynn Peaks, The Needles, Mt. Burwell and Cathedral Mountain.

It was also in this year that H. Hewton first gained the hump of The Camel, a rock blade mounted to the east of Crown Mountain, which became the first focus of rock climbing in the Vancouver area.

The equipment of these early enthusiasts was primitive, and their understanding of modern climbing techniques was almost nonexistent. For food they carried "iron rations:" a can of beans, a can of sardines, chocolate, and prunes. Their shelters were canvas tarps or tents, carried on wooden packboards. Often they lacked stoves and had to carry firewood to higher elevations. To some extent, they also laboured under a suspicion that their activities were only marginally socially acceptable; Phyllis Munday, the outstanding female climber in the province in the first half of the century, spoke of wearing the proper skirt across on the ferry from Vancouver to the North Shore mountains, then ditching it in the bushes and changing into more practical knickers! Apparently this subterfuge allowed her to escape the censure of those matrons of the time who did not approve of women in trousers.

A mystique of heroism and mortal danger came to be associated with some of these early ascents, even though the climbs were not difficult by any standards. The newspapers of the time, and some early climbers themselves, tended to encourage this attitude by exaggerating the difficulties on a number of ascents. The second party to climb the West Lion, for example, reported camping "on the edge of a precipice" and spoke of each climber being "compelled to press his fingers into a depression and hang on until the blood almost came." This ascent was challenged by an article in *The Province* of August 24, 1903, when an unsuccessful party claimed on returning from their attempt that climbing either of The Lions was impossible. This prompted Atwell King, who had led the previous ascent, to return to the peak and, at a selected time, light a bonfire on its summit. The fire was witnessed by (among others) the Deputy Registrar of the Supreme Court, all the way from the Court House in Vancouver!

Also notable from this period was the coveted first ascent of Mt. Garibaldi in 1907, then believed to be more than ten thousand feet high. Again, the account of the climb seems a trifle exaggerated. The phrase "any slip now would have meant certain death" was especially popular among these early climber-journalists. The scarcity of visiting climbers from Europe or the Rockies prevented locals from comparing their achievements with what was happening elsewhere.

One man whose activities from this period cannot be underrated, however, is Basil Darling. Like Tom Fyles, who came on the scene a few years later, Darling was undoubtedly one of the outstanding mountaineers in all of North America in his time. He made many notable ascents, including the north buttress of the West Lion, and first ascents of Sky Pilot, Golden Ears, Cathedral, and other peaks in the Vancouver area. Darling also made early winter attempts on The Lions, ascending the frozen Capilano River in the wee hours by lantern light. He later climbed high on the Wishbone Arête of Mount Robson, a line that was not completed until 1955, and which, even at that time, was considered a fine achievement.

Darling's greatest contributions in southwestern B.C., however, were made in the Tantalus Range. Early trips had nibbled away at the minor summits of the area, mostly on the southern fringes, but Darling stormed the main challenges of the range. In 1911, on his first visit with Allan Morkill and Stanley Davies, he negotiated the difficult glacial approach on the east side of Mt. Tantalus to make the coveted first ascent of the peak; his descent along the north ridge also gave him the first traverse.

Subsequently, Darling climbed Serratus, Alpha and The Red Tusk; he also made the second ascent of Tantalus.

If Darling was the outstanding mountaineer of the early years, there is no doubt that Tom Fyles was the rock-climbing genius. Fyles was remarkable in many ways; he seems on the surface to have been a mild, self-effacing man, yet his ascents demonstrate great courage, drive, and self-confidence. Unlike some of the present generation of climbers, Fyles was also a highly sociable climber; his willingness to lead BCMC trips seemed unquenchable. As one club member once put it, "In the old days, Tom **was** the club. He led every trip."

One anecdote about Tom Fyles neatly summarizes his personal qualities. Sometime in the 1920s he was leading a group up The Camel. The group had all made the summit, and Fyles decided to investigate a new descent route. Noticing a gully, he descended, unroped, to its base, then climbed back up again to report to the party whether or not the route was feasible. On reaching the summit, he shook his head and said, "Nope. It won't go."

Tom Fyles did not view rock climbing and mountaineering as separate sports, and a number of his finest ascents remain respected today because of the rotten rock he climbed. Among such ascents are the remarkable solo climbs of The Table and the north peak of The Black Tusk, in the area that later became part of Garibaldi Park.

Conquering peaks was by no means the sole aim of the early B.C. climbers. One of the great mountaineering themes in southwestern B.C., down from earliest times to the present, has been the urge to explore. To the early members of the BCMC, marching into unknown country was just as exhilarating as climbing a new peak. As Phyl Munday once said of her many exploratory trips into the Waddington area: "We didn't go into the Waddington country just to climb one mountain and run out and leave it. We went into the Waddington country to find out all we possibly could about glaciers and mountains and animals and nature and everything about that particular area." Tom Fyles shared this desire to discover new ground, and in the early years he consistently ventured farthest into the wild, unexplored corners of southwest B.C. Many of the routes credited to a BCMC party were climbed on trips led by him, his historic climb of Judge Howay in 1921 being one of the most remarkable. It was his fourth attempt and typified the determination Fyles brought to his sport. To this day the peak has been climbed only a handful of times. Fyles is also now believed to have made the first complete winter ascent of The Lions, in 1922.

Despite the difficulties Fyles must have encountered on his many trips, his reports rarely dwelt on the horrors of approach through jungles of slide alder and devil's club. Yet it is well to remember how forbidding the mountains of the province were until extensive logging pushed back the forest barriers. On one two-week trip up the Toba River in the 1930s, for example, Fyles's group managed only one climb, even though the party, which included Neal Carter, Alec Dalgleish, and Mills Winram, was exceptionally strong for its time. Their achievement did not lie in conquering a summit so much as in persevering through the discouragingly bushy, tangled approach along the Toba River before they even reached the high icefields they wanted to explore.

These early climbers did not particularly dread approach difficulties; they looked upon them as simply part of the climb. They were old-fashioned for the 1930s in that they seemed to enjoy general exploration of glaciers and valleys as much as scaling serious mountain routes. In the Canadian Rockies at this time, and certainly in

Europe, where approaches were more developed, a shift from exploratory climbing to more difficult, technical mountaineering was taking place. However, if the coastal pioneers were old-fashioned in their non-technical attitudes, they were modern in disdaining the use of guides. Guided climbing simply never got started in the Coast Mountains; indeed, to this day Coast Mountain exploration has remained the province of amateurs.

Mountaineering in southwestern B.C. has produced several unique partnerships, but one that never had a chance to completely mature was that between Tom Fyles and Alec Dalgleish. Popular among Vancouver climbers, Dalgleish was a young man who felt a sense of wonder and joy in the mountains, which is rare even among seasoned climbers, but perhaps not surprising in a man who wanted to pursue an artistic career. Like Fyles, he enjoyed climbing alone on occasion, and was interested in training and developing his technical abilities. He was the first Vancouver climber to use The Camel as a crag for practicing rock climbing. Dalgleish had the drive and endurance that good coastal mountaineers of his day required; he and Eric Brooks, for example, once made an ascent of The Old Settler, a high peak east of Harrison Lake, in only one day.

Tom Fyles saw something in Dalgleish which he liked, for the two made three very significant exploratory trips together: up Bute Inlet in 1930, to the Meager Creek peaks in 1932, and up the Toba River in 1933. Dalgleish had just begun to come into his own as a rock climber, however, when he was killed at the age of twenty-seven in an unexplained fall on the south face of Mount Waddington. He was probably the one climber in Vancouver at the time who could have matched Fyles's ability on rock; in any case, one cannot help but notice that Fyles's own record of achievement comes to an end about this time.

Of all the partnerships that coastal mountaineering has produced, none is more celebrated, or more important, than that between Don and Phyllis Munday. Don Munday, an officer in the Canadian army, had been wounded during World War I. On returning to Vancouver following the war, he quickly resumed his passionate exploration of the mountains around Vancouver. In the BCMC he met fellow enthusiast Phyllis James; the two were soon inseparable on the rope—or indeed elsewhere, and were married in 1920. Over the next twenty-five years the Mundays dominated the exploration of the big ranges in the Coast Mountains north of the Bridge River; they made scores of first ascents in the Waddington, Queen Bess, Homathko, and Klinaklini areas, and they also confirmed beyond all doubt the existence of Mount Waddington and established its claim over Mount Robson as the highest peak completely within B.C.

The influence of the Mundays on climbing within southwestern B.C. is more difficult to evaluate; they were not as dominant around Vancouver as they were in the great glaciated ranges to the north. Don and Phyl nonetheless garnered a number of important first ascents, including Blanshard Peak in the Golden Ears group, and Foley Peak. The Mundays also helped to popularize the climbing in the Cheam group of peaks, where they must have felt at home among the glaciers and snowfields of Mount Stewart and Welch Peak. Their comparative neglect of rock climbing was very likely due to their interest in glaciology, which may explain the surprisingly few rock ascents they made in southwest B.C. The Mundays were the most important of the early ski mountaineers in the southwest, and were among the first to extend the climbing season into winter. During the 1930s and the 1940s, they laid ski tracks through the Coquitlam Range and Garibaldi Park, making ski ascents of a number of the peaks around Garibaldi Lake.

Garibaldi Provincial Park was established in 1920, partly through the efforts of the BCMC, who had used the area for summer camps since before the First World War. Don Munday produced the first guidebook to the Park in 1922, with beautiful photographs. Neal Carter, a Vancouver oceanographer and chemist, and a good friend of the Mundays', drew the first topographic map of the area. Later he kept records of the park's history and of the naming of its features.

Himself an accomplished climber, Neal Carter made a number of first ascents in the park, notably in the group of summits to the east of Garibaldi Lake, including Mt. Davidson. He also made many climbs in the Tantalus Range, producing the first topographical map of the area, and he was the first person to climb Grimface Mountain to its summit, in the region that is now Cathedral Park. When mapmakers produced the first guidebooks to southwestern B.C., they relied heavily on Neal Carter's knowledge of alpine geography and place names.

Valuable as it was, Carter's Garibaldi map had not completely covered the area; so in 1927 and 1928 the A.J. Campbell survey party of the provincial government carried out an extensive survey, and in the course of collecting their data, they climbed many peaks. The map that resulted contained a spate of politically inspired names, such as Mt. Sir Richard and the McBride Range. However, Tremor Mountain, in the Spearheads, was named because an earthquake rocked the surveyors even while they stood on the summit!

With accurate maps available, exploration in the park proceeded more rapidly than elsewhere in the province. The Mundays' ski trips in the Wedge area in the 1930s culminated in a ski ascent of the highest peak in the park, Wedge Mountain. The Mundays capped their Garibaldi activities in 1937 with a ski ascent of the remote Mt. Sir Richard.

A year later a second twosome made one of the outstanding trips of the thirties — the first ascent of Mt. Pitt. Using a route unrepeated to this day, Charlie and Ernie Jenkins left from Garibaldi Lake, traversed the headwaters of the Pitt River, ascended Pitt by way of its north ridge, and returned to the lake again — all in five days, a fast trip even by today's standards. The second ascent of the peak was not made until 1959, and then the climbers used a floatplane for access.

During the war years climbing and hiking naturally decreased in B.C., and original routes were not recorded again until the 1950s. Although by this time mountaineering in Europe and the United States had taken a technical direction, Canadian climbers still continued in the old traditions. As late as 1953 (fifteen years after the north face of the Eiger had been climbed using modern techniques), John Dudra still felt it necessary to defend the use of piton protection ("In Defence of a Piton," *CAJ* 1953, p. 150). The influence of British climbers like Frank Smythe, who disdained pitons as "an unfair advantage," was felt strongly in Canada, especially among members of the Alpine Club.

One of the best climbers of this period was Howard Rode, who explored the Chehalis area and made first ascents of the west summit of Robie Reid and the central tower of the Hozomeens. In 1950, when he and John Dudra scaled the final pitch leading to easier ground on the north ridge of Mt. Ratney in the Chehalis, they made what was probably the best mountain lead on a new route of any Vancouver climber since the days of Tom Fyles.

John Dudra was a prominent climber of this period and had important connections in American climbing circles, where technical mountaineering was appreciated. He amassed an enviable record of climbs, including the second ascent of Monarch Mountain. His first winter ascent of Slesse Mountain, made with Fips Broda in 1955, was the outstanding climb of the decade in southwestern B.C. He also did some fine climbing with Fred Beckey in the Chilliwack River valley. In 1958 John Dudra died piloting his own light plane. His premature death, like Alec Dalgleish's before him, likely slowed down the exploration of challenging routes in southwestern B.C.

Fred Beckey had appeared on the scene during the 1940s, and although he made most of his climbs south of the border, his importance as an innovator and technical mountaineer was felt by everyone in southwest B.C. who followed climbing development. Beckey was a brilliant mountaineer and a driven climber, and early on he staked out the entire Cascades as his own special bailiwick. Not surprisingly then, his most important routes in the guidebook area are found in the Chilliwack valley and Skagit regions, and include such classics as the northeast face of Redoubt, one of the finest mountaineering routes in all of southern B.C. Beckey moved Class five climbing into the mountains of the Pacific Northwest with determination and the reports of his achievements helped to stimulate locals into activity. When he scaled the south peak of Hozomeen in 1948, he overcame what was considered "the last great problem" of the North Cascades. North of the border his routes on Slesse Mountain were milestones.

Also of note during the period of the late 1950s was a group organized around Roy Mason, a well-known amateur bush pilot of the Coast Mountains. The Mason group explored three important alpine areas: the Snowcap Lake area in eastern Garibaldi Park, the Rutledge Glacier area south of Kwoiek Creek, and the Joffre area southwest of Duffey Lake. All these locations later saw visits by club camps or climbing schools.

During the 1950s the Varsity Outdoor Club, mainly under the leadership of Karl Ricker, became an important force in exploring the mountains of southwestern B.C. Early postwar trips went into Garibaldi Park and explored the James Turner area and the peaks to the east of Singing Pass. Cheakamus Mountain and Mt. Neal were first ascended during these campaigns. In 1954 the first Spearheads traverse in northern Garibaldi Park was made by a VOC group, although several peaks were missed. This first party through the range cut across Cheakamus Lake to finish their trek at Garibaldi Lake via Castle Towers Creek. Later in 1964 a VOC party completed the entire horseshoe traverse of the Spearheads in nine storm-laden days.

As the 1950s drew to a close, most of the summits near Vancouver had been explored, and the most ambitious climbers of the BCMC and the Alpine Club were heading north to explore the uncharted mountains north of the Homathko River. For a short period Fred Beckey and his American friends had the field to themselves when it came to putting up the hard climbs in the mountains of the southwest. Then the younger generation produced Dick Culbert, whose enthusiasm for new routes rivalled Beckey's and whose personality and style set the tone for the Vancouver mountaineering community for the next fifteen years. In the first half of the century, the greatest climbing challenge was to make a first ascent. But by Culbert's time, the number of untouched peaks had dwindled, so Culbert and his friends challenged themselves by putting up imaginative, difficult new routes on familiar mountains.

The opening of a paved highway to Squamish in 1961 also opened new opportunities by providing access to the granite walls of the Squamish Chief which became for the VOC group a focus and a field on which to develop their technical expertise. Over the next decade a small group of rock-climbing mountaineers, including Culbert, Glenn Woodsworth, Alice Purdey, Bob Cuthbert, Fred Douglas, and Paul Starr, used Squamish as a training ground to hone their mountaineering skills. They began with the smaller problems—pinnacles and short faces in places like the Sky Pilot area—but soon moved out onto the big faces. Unfortunately, being first on the scene, they were sometimes disappointed by what they discovered; routes on Panther Peak and Rideout, for example, proved to feature poor rock, bush, and uninteresting climbing. However, by the end of the 1960s, this group, with assistance from a cadre of BCMC members such as Martin and Esther Kafer, and unaffiliateds such as Jack Bryan had greatly increased the stock of entertaining climbs available to local mountaineers. The north face of the West Lion, the Nose Route and Gambit Grooves on Mt. Habrich, and new routes on Alpha, Niobe, Dione and Tantalus in the Tantalus Range were all discovered by climbers of this period, and are still considered exciting climbs today. Culbert capped his program in southwestern B.C. with two exceptional routes: the elegant southwest buttress of the north peak of Hozomeen (with Alice Purdey), and the poorly protected east face of Mt. Colonel Foster (with Starr and Douglas).

Although women had been active in Vancouver mountaineering circles since the earliest times, the 1960s were an especially productive time for female mountaineers. Esther Kafer and Joyce Davies, prominent members of the BCMC, laid ski tracks through many new areas, including the Manatee Glacier, North Creek and Pemberton Icefield regions. Esther Kafer was also a strong technical climber, and pioneered new routes in several areas. Elfrida Pigou, however, was the strongest female climber of the 1950s. She discovered the remains of a famous plane crash on Slesse Mountain, and made a couple of winter ascents in an era when almost no one climbed anything in winter. Her career was cut short when she disappeared with her party under an avalanche on the Bravo Glacier of Mount Waddington.

Of the later generation, Alice Purdey stands out as the most outstanding technical climber among the women. She climbed, often with Dick Culbert, important routes on such peaks as Hozameen, Habrich, the Squamish Chief, Alpha, Dione, and Tantalus; and her many new ascents included most of the important peaks lying to the north of North Creek. She also made the first Canadian ascent of Mt. St. Elias, and was a member of the first party to complete a traverse of the Pemberton Icefield. There are a number of vigourous female rock climbers on the Vancouver scene today, but none has yet been able to match Alice Purdey's energy and enthusiasm for alpine adventures.

The Culbert era lasted till 1974. By this time Culbert, and a number of the mountaineers associated with him, had essentially retired from active climbing. The traverse of the Hozomeens by Paul Starr and Fred Douglas in 1974, culminating in the first ascent of the intimidating north ridge of the south peak, marked the close of almost fifteen years of dominance by this closely linked group friends. Coincidentally, this was also the year that the *Alpine Guide to Southwestern British Columbia* came out. It was as though Culbert had summarized the achievements of his circle and passed the mantle on to a new generation.

Of this new generation of climbers, the first to be mentioned must be John Clarke.

Already by 1974 Clarke had bagged many first ascents, and he has continued to add more to his tally every year since then. In 1972 Clarke began a routine that continues to this day. He studies the 1:50,000 map sheets (often just newly released) spotting high alpine areas which have rarely been visited. He then plots a traverse route through the maze of unclimbed peaks and untrodden glaciers, often beginning in remote inlets and ending in even remoter logging camps. These trips typically involve multiple air drops, and some have been plagued by violent storms. On one traverse in the Klinaklini country, clouds moved in just as Clarke stepped out of the plane. He was pinned down, unable to move, for eleven days while a storm blanketed the area with enormous piles of snow. Clarke later said, "I read *The Valley of the Dolls* through twice from cover to cover."

To most, John Clarke remains an enigmatic character: an intense enthusiast of the mountains who is indifferent to the goals that motivate most North Americans. He stands completely outside the mainstream of modern technical climbing, preferring the solitude of the quiet, serene ranges where modern life does not intrude. His travels really hark back to an older exploratory tradition; he seems motivated by the same values that moved the pioneer coastal climbers, such as Darling, Fyles and the Mundays. Certainly Clarke has seen more of the distant alpine corners of southwestern B.C., and has made more first ascents, than any other individual.

In recent times, two trends have emerged which indicate where modern mountaineering in southwest B.C. is going. The first is towards discovering new, technical routes that can be climbed in good style; aesthetics in rock climbing have become increasingly important. The second trend is towards winter mountaineering. Spurred on by articles in the *CAJ* by Robin Barley, who made the first winter ascent of the northeast face of Mt. Redoubt and reawakened Vancouver climbers to the delights of winter crag climbing on The Lions, interest in winter mountaineering was further accelerated by the development of ice-climbing tools and protection, which only began a dozen years ago. The winter of 1978–1979 demonstrated how popular ice climbing had become, when for the first time in many years Shannon Falls froze solidly; it hosted several dozen ascents, with three or four parties on the climb at one time during weekends. Shades of Ben Nevis! The powerful drive towards winter climbing is best exemplified, however, by the recent ascent of the northeast buttress of Slesse Mountain by the Washington climbers Jim Nelson and Kit Lewis. Their eight day ascent would have been unthinkable only a dozen years ago, but in 1986 many climbers winced at not having made the climb themselves. This brilliant and tenacious effort certainly eclipsed every other winter ascent to date in the mountains of southwestern B.C.

Most representative of these new trends is the Vancouver climber Don Serl, who has developed many fine, new alpine rock climbs in southwestern B.C., and has extended the boundaries of winter climbing. Unquenchable enthusiasm for the long and sometimes bushy approaches of the Chehalis (an inexplicable craving!) has brought Serl and his friends some of the finest climbs of the 1980s in this part of the world. Especially notable are the north ridge of Mt. Clarke, the Tuning Fork buttress on Mt. Bardean, the Opus Route on Viennese Peak, and several routes on Grainger Pk. These climbs involve many leads of high-angle rock climbing; usually they are climbed free with rock shoes and sizeable racks.

Two other climbers who have pioneered bold new alpine routes are Scott Flavelle and John Howe, both of whom have made major new ascents of one and two-day routes in the Chehalis, Anderson River, and Chilliwack valley areas. Their dramatic line on the northwest buttress of Steinbok Peak in the Anderson River group is one of the most distinctive and clean technical lines ever to be climbed in southwestern B.C. The two also knocked off one of the "Great Problems" of the Chehalis: the north face of Viennese Peak. John Howe scaled the graceful "Pillar of Pi" in the Chilliwack valley (with Joe Buszowski), and Flavelle climbed the northeast face on Mt. Joffre (with Dave Lane), and the Flavelle-Beckham route on Mt. Bardean (with Perry Beckham). Recently the Vancouver climber Maxim De Jong has been especially active in the Chilliwack and Skagit areas, and has pioneered some important new routes, including a winter ascent of the north face of Mt. Cheam.

In the Vancouver mountaineering community, a democratic spirit still prevails, as does a belief in the traditions that have made mountaineering in the Coast Mountains unique. Professional and novice mountaineers have always mixed in the same circles, and support is given by expert climbers to such endeavours as the annual climbing courses run by the Federation of Mountain Clubs of B.C. (an umbrella organization founded in the 1970s to promote and protect the concerns of mountain lovers). The adventurous spirit of the community is reflected in the unstated code of ethics, which frowns upon practices such as using aircraft to approach peaks easily accessibly by foot, skis, or snowshoes.

Through the past century the techniques and interests of B.C. climbers may have changed, but not their attitude. The same spirit of joy in nature and thrill in a personal encounter with some of the most challenging mountains in the world drives today's climbers as it drove such pioneers as Basil Darling, Phyl Munday or Tom Fyles. Coastal mountaineers have always considered themselves a unique breed. In the early days climbers were isolated from the mainstream of climbing development and technology; Vancouver climbers were a happy band of eccentrics, who never fitted into the pattern of established international or national mountaineering. In the 1960s this isolation broke down, as younger climbers, visiting places like Yosemite Valley in California, became imbued with the new spirit of technical mountaineering. Today, the Coast Mountains are the homeland to some of the best climbers in Canada. The immediate future promises a strong, continued emphasis on developing long, difficult alpine rock climbs, and more exploration of the remote, unfrequented nooks and corners of this varied alpine region. The future remains exciting: there is lots of exploring still to be done in southwestern B.C., and enough intriguing alpine country to satiate the most voracious of mountaineers.

Geology

by Peter Jordan and Glenn Woodsworth

The popular image of climbing in the Coast Mountains is of flawless granite on the Squamish Chief or on the peaks in the Chilliwack or Chehalis areas. In fact, less than half the area covered by this guide consists of granitic rocks; most of this is mediocre in quality, and little is true granite. A brief summary of the geology of southwestern B.C. helps explain why the rocks in the region are so varied, and what the different varieties are.

Some 200 million years ago, the west coast of B.C. lay along a line running roughly northwest through the middle of the province. All the area to the west had either not formed yet, or lay far to the south, at the latitude of California or still farther. Since that time, much of the floor of the east Pacific Ocean was driven beneath North America. In the process, continental fragments and pieces of ocean floor were added to the western edge of the continent. As ocean crust is swallowed beneath the continent (a process called subduction), heat generated beneath the edge of the continent causes rock to melt. This molten rock, called magma, erupts as volcanoes or is injected beneath the surface to form plutonic ("granitic") rock. In the last 50 million or so years, stresses set up by subduction compressed the new additions to the continent into mountain ranges.

In the eastern part of the area covered by this guide, the Fraser and Yalakom rivers mark important faults along which the Coast Mountains moved northwestward as much as 200 kilometres. Along these fault systems, large areas of ocean floor composed of sedimentary and volcanic rocks are mixed with huge pieces of the interior (mantle) of the earth. These mantle rocks are found in the Shulaps Range, near Skihist Mountain, and near the lower Coquihalla River, among other places. The rock varies from orange-weathering varieties, which offer fairly good climbing, to slippery green serpentine, which is among the rottenest of rock.

The Manning Park and Chilcotin areas consist mainly of 45 to 200 million year old sedimentary and volcanic rocks. In general, the rock is very rotten and tends to form gentle scree ridges and debris-filled valleys, good for backpacking but of little interest to climbers. However, peaks in the Anderson River, Needle Peak, and Cathedral Park areas are formed of young (40 million year old) granitic rocks and offer some of the best rock climbing in the entire region.

The Chilliwack, Cheam, and Harrison east areas have more in common with the North Cascades of Washington than with the Coast Mountains proper. The rocks are mainly volcanic, sedimentary, and metamorphic (altered) rocks offering poor to excellent climbing. These are disrupted by bodies of granitic rock which range from fairly old, such as Slesse Mountain, to young (20 million years), such as Mt. Rexford.

The Coast Mountains proper form the region west of Harrison Lake and north of the Fraser River, as far west as the Strait of Georgia. The Coast Mountains consist of one of the world's greatest masses of granitic rocks, called the Coast Plutonic Complex. This complex consists of a complicated series of granitic bodies of various ages, composition, and climbing quality. Mixed in are volcanic and sedimentary rocks which were altered and partly mixed with the granitic magma. Rocks of the plutonic complex began to form some 150 million years ago and continued to form until about 55 million years ago. The actual mountains themselves are much younger, perhaps less than 20 million years old.

Granite, a rock composed largely of light-coloured minerals, is relatively rare in the Coast Mountains. Far more common are granodiorite, quartz diorite, and diorite, which tend to be progressively darker than granite. Gabbro, a very dark rock, is relatively rare but is present on The Lions and elsewhere. In general, the older rocks tend to be darker and offer less solid climbing than the younger, generally lighter rocks. For example, much of the diorite and quartz diorite in northern Garibaldi Park is highly fractured, whereas younger granodiorite near Squamish, in the Chehalis area, and elsewhere is sparsely fractured and offers superb climbing.

Many areas of the Coast Mountains consist of the altered remains of the rock into which the granitic rocks were injected. These are commonly rusty in colour due to the presence of small amounts of pyrite ("fool's gold"). Climbing quality varies from good (e.g. Sky Pilot area) to poor (e.g. Singing Pass area).

Vancouver Island differs from the Coast Mountains mainly in that it contains much more sedimentary and volcanic rock and much less granitic rock. Most of the ranges on the Island consist of basalt, greenish-black volcanic rock laid down under water some 210 million years ago. Unlike much of the volcanic rock on the mainland, that on Vancouver Island is generally firm and offers good climbing. There are also areas of older volcanics and sediments, on the Golden Hinde, for example. Younger granodiorite bodies (about 180 million years old) are present in some areas, western Strathcona Park, for example.

During the period from 1 to 2 million years to about 8 thousand years ago, the mountains on both the mainland and Vancouver Island were dissected by a series of glacial advances. Ice covered all but the highest summits in the eastern part of the area. Glacial activity was most intense in the coastal areas, where valleys were deepened and steepened, and most glacial debris was carried into the lowlands or out to sea, leaving a much greater proportion of bare rock than in the other areas. The Squamish Chief, the huge walls in the Anderson River area, and the smooth, rounded ridges above Princess Louisa Inlet, for example, are all results of glacial action. In the drier regions, glaciation was less intense and many valleys are floored with thick, glacial deposits.

Glaciation is still extensive. Large icefields are present in areas such as the Squamish Icefield. Elsewhere, smaller cirque glaciers are common, particularly in the western and central Coast Mountains. In the eastern parts of the region, the remaining glaciers are in sad shape: many have only vestiges of ice under a thick mantle of rubble.

Aside from glacial and river deposits, the youngest rocks in the guidebook area are volcanic rocks in the Garibaldi, Cayley, and Meager areas. These volcanoes are the extension into Canada of the Cascade volcanic chain (St. Helens, Rainier, Baker, etc.). They formed within the last million or two years in a line roughly parallel to the zone along which subduction is taking place off the west coast of North America. The Canadian volcanoes have been dissected by glaciation and are, therefore, less shapely than those south of the border. The rock generally offers very poor climbing. Many interesting features were formed as the lava erupted under and into ice, including the Table, the lava flows near Brandywine, and the Touch and Go Towers.

Several post-glacial lava flows came from Opal Cone and from Mount Price. One of these forms the dam ("The Barrier") which holds back Garibaldi Lake.

Plinth Peak in the Meager Creek group is the most recently active volcano in the Canadian part of the chain. About 2400 years ago, a huge explosion on the north side of Plinth created a conspicuous bend in the Lillooet River and spread volcanic ash as far east as Edmonton. Ash from this explosion can be found in a broad band running northeast of Plinth, including the Ash Pass, Athelney Pass, Mount Sloan, and lower Gun Creek areas. The well known hotsprings in the Meager area indicate that magma is still present at depth.

The most obvious and spectacular signs of continuing geologic activity are the rockslides and debris flows that periodically close the Squamish highway. These are natural and ongoing phenomena, although their effects are magnified by bad logging and road-building practices. A much larger landslide occurred in the winter of 1855–56 in the Garibaldi area. An enormous landslide from the Barrier travelled down Rubble Creek to the Cheakamus River and downstream for some distance. The slide reached a velocity of about 30 m/100 ft per second, and swept away all of the trees in its path. The Barrier remains unstable, geologically speaking. In a 1973 legal battle, development of a subdivision near the mouth of Rubble Creek was disallowed for long-term safety reasons. The next time you drive up the road to the Barrier parking lot, look at the Barrier and the landslide debris around you, and think about it.

Chapter 1

North Shore And Howe Sound

BOUNDARIES:
North: North boundary of G.V.R.D Watershed
East: Indian River, Indian Arm
South: Burrard Inlet, English Bay
West: Howe Sound

FOREST SERVICE OFFICES:

Maple Ridge Forest District
22747 Selkirk Avenue
Maple Ridge, B.C. V2X 2X9
467-6971

Squamish Forest District
P.O. Box 1970
Squamish, B.C. V0N 3G0
898-9671

MAPS:
Federal:
92 G/6 North Vancouver   92 G/7 Coquitlam
92 G/11 Squamish
Provincial:
92 G/SE   92 G/SW
92 G/NW

Introduction

The North Shore mountains are well loved by Vancouver hikers. Many popular trails on Seymour, Hollyburn, Black Mountain, and other peaks in the area lead to small lakes set in deeply forested basins. Easy trails from Cypress Bowl wander over the broad summit plateau of Black Mountain, while the longer Howe Sound Crest Trail also leaves from the Cypress Bowl ski development. This latter trail follows the crest of the divide along the eastern side of Howe Sound. One day it will lead to Squamish, although at the moment it ends at The Lions, and then begins again in the Deeks Lake area.

Almost all of the peaks in this area can be easily reached by a fit individual with sturdy footwear, and there are always fine views of Vancouver and the Howe Sound region to be had. Although mountaineers are less attracted to these summits today than they were fifty years ago, there are some fine rock crags sprinkled here and there throughout the group. The Camel, a blocky formation on the east side of Crown Mountain, was once popular as a rock-climbing practice cliff, and recently a new generation of climbers have been rediscovering its appeal. You can also find rock climbs on The Lions and Mt. Harvey. Soon the Lynn Creek area will be opened to the public as a regional park, and a new series of trails will give access to the rock-climbing area at the head of Lynn Creek.

Winter mountaineering on the coast got its start in the North Shore mountains. Mount Seymour often sports good one-pitch ice climbs, and over the last few years winter climbing on The Lions has surged in popularity.

One word of caution: trails on these peaks tend to wander about, and it is easy for a hiker to get turned around or confused. Making a mental note at key intersections and landmarks can avoid the embarrassment of having a mountain rescue party called out on your behalf. It is also a good idea to carry a compass; these mountains are well known for their fog, especially in winter. Many trails in this area are well described in *Exploring Vancouver's North Shore Mountains* and *103 Hikes in Southwestern British Columbia*.

Approaches

A. FROM INDIAN ARM
The easiest but least popular way to approach the North Shore mountain's eastern side is from the head of Indian Arm. To get there you need to take a boat. A water taxi runs from Deep Cove (Deep Cove Water Taxi, 2890 Panorama Drive, North Vancouver, B.C. V7G 1V6, 929-3011), and Harbour Ferries runs a commercial service up Indian Arm from Vancouver (north foot of Denman St., Vancouver, B.C. V6G 2W9, 687-9558).

B. FROM HIGHWAY 1 (UPPER LEVELS)
Most North Shore mountains can be reached from roads in North and West Vancouver which branch from the Upper Levels (Highway 1). Many peaks in this area have well-developed trails associated with them, so although roads are described here under "Approaches," most trails up the North Shore mountains are described under each peak.

1. Mt. Seymour roads: Take the first turnoff at the N end of the Second Narrows Bridge and follow well-marked roads to the park entrance. From there, drive the steep road 13 km/8 mi to parking lots at the downhill ski development.

1a. Seymour River road: This road, which ascends the west side of the Seymour River, is a continuation of Lillooet Road in North Vancouver. Because it runs through the Seymour watershed, the entrance is gated and guarded. The road runs E around Seymour Lake and continues in deteriorating condition to the headwall below Loch Lomond (see Sky Pilot chapter). From here, a rough trail runs up beside Clipper Creek and then crosses to Furry Creek (*C6*).

2. Lynn Creek: New trails are currently being constructed in the Lynn Creek watershed; this whole drainage is now open to hiking and climbing. These new routes give access to peaks that have been stranded in watershed land for eons, and a resurgence in popularity is likely. The trail presently under construction goes N along the east side of Lynn Creek to Norvan Creek, and plans are to push this trail further up Hanes Creek. The FMCBC can supply up to date details (687-3333).

3. Grouse Mountain roads: Three roads lead to Grouse Mountain. The first, Mountain Highway, turns off the Upper Levels Highway at a posted junction just past Lynn Creek, climbs through a residential area and ends at a locked logging road (limited parking). The second, Skyline Boulevard, is most easily reached from upper Capilano Road in western North Vancouver. Turn right on Montroyal and after about 1.5 km, turn left onto Skyline; it zigzags steeply to a small parking area just above powerlines. The third road, Nancy Greene Way, extends from the top of Capilano Road to the Grouse Mountain gondola base (Skyride).

4. Cypress and Hollyburn roads: Two roads can be taken to reach Cypress Bowl. To get to the first, Eyremount Drive, follow Taylor Way from its junction with the Upper Levels. At Taylor Way's top, turn left onto Southborough Drive, then, after about 1 km, turn left again onto Eyremount Drive. Follow it to a rightward switchback (limited parking) and a gated road, signposted for Cypress Park Resort. A trail climbs northward from this road to Cypress Park Resort and "First Lake." The resort is an easy 2–3 hour hike. The second road, Cypress Bowl Highway, leaves the Upper Levels in West Vancouver and climbs to the ski area in Cypress Bowl. At a marked parking lot (and cross country ski area), the road levels out. Further up, a parking lot at the road's end services the downhill ski area.

4a. Howe Sound Crest Trail: Begin at the upper end of the Cypress Bowl downhill parking lot. The trail is well marked and contours around the west side of Mt. Strachan for 2 km. It then follows a wooded ridge N to a bump at 1360 m/4460 ft. After descending, it climbs again to **"UNNECESSARY MOUNTAIN"** at 1520 m/4990 ft; a trail drops NE from here towards the base of The Lions. Takes three hours; NTD.

No trail through the Lions area has yet been built. The northern section from Deeks Lake to "Harvey Pass" E of Mt. Harvey is described below.

C. FROM THE SQUAMISH HIGHWAY (HIGHWAY 99)

This highway runs N from Horseshoe Bay along Howe Sound. All distances are measured from Horseshoe Bay.

1. Sunset trail (4.5 km/2.8 mi): Leads to Yew Lake. Park opposite the marina entrance and take the second road running uphill to the right (likely gated). Continue past a private driveway to near a small water tower, where the badly marked trail begins. The trail follows the south bank of the creek, and fades out in marshy ground around Yew Lake. Takes 2 hours to Cypress Bowl.

2. Old Lions trail (11.5 km/7.1 mi): Leads to "Unnecessary Mountain." Take the Lions Bay turnoff before crosssing Harvey Creek and continue to the highest switchback S of the creek. Trailhead should be marked. Steep and boring. Takes 3–4 hours to the ridge.

3. The Paul Binkert Trail (New Lions Trail) (11.5 km/7.1 mi): Leads to Unnecessary Mountain. Turn into the Lions Bay subdivision on Centre Road and go left on Bayview. Park well off the road (Sunset Drive) at the end of the pavement when you reach the gate: here the old Harvey-Brunswick logging road begins. At about 600 m/2000 ft take the right fork and bear right at the second fork a little later on. After about 2 km, the Binkert Trail branches to the right from the logging road and drops into Harvey Creek. It is 3–4 hours to the summit of the West Lion via this trail, and there is no water once past the creek. Some of this area is in the Lions Bay watershed —caution with personal sanitation is necessary. Claims by Lions Bay residents that the trail is "closed" or off limits should be ignored.

3a. Brunswick trail: Take the first fork to the left on the Binkert Trail approach road (see above). Shortly after crossing Magnesia Creek, take the right branch of the road which climbs steeply uphill. At the end of the road a trail begins in the logging slash and leads to a steep and exposed summit ridge. The trail is intersected by the Howe Sound Crest Trail about 1.5 km from the end of the road.

3b. Mt. Harvey, north side: Take the second fork to the left on the Binkert Trail approach road. An old road leads up to below the north face of Mt. Harvey. At a further junction, go left again, continuing up Magnesia Creek. Bushy.

3c. Mt. Harvey: Go left at the marked second fork on the Binkert Trail approach road as for Mt. Harvey, north side, above. At the next junction, an overgrown spur goes right and climbs onto the west flank of Harvey. Just beyond its end, pick up an indistinct trail; it leads steeply onto a ridge which leads to the summit. Takes 4 hours from parking spot. Alternatively, continue along the approach road past the second fork; the start of the trail can be found in a minor road cut on the left shortly before you come to Alberta Creek.

3d. Harvey Creek road: The "third fork" on the Binkert Trail approach is really the continuation of the old road up Harvey Creek. It climbs up the north side of the creek to near Harvey's summit ridge. Some of the ugliest logging slash in the whole world is the main feature of this route.

4. Old Deeks Lake trail (16 km/10 mi): Park in a viewpoint area on your left as you approach from Horseshoe Bay. The trail, which climbs steeply at first, follows up the west side of Deeks Creek. Ignore all spurs to the left.

5. New Deeks Lake trail (21 km/13 mi): Preferable to the old Deeks trail. Shortly before reaching Porteau Cove, park in a large viewpoint area on the west side of the highway. The trail (signposted) begins across the road; much of it follows old logging grades. Turn right when the logging road is reached, and then go straight ahead at the first fork. The left branch cuts back into the valley of Kallahne Creek, climbing to 1220 m/4000 ft. Go left at the next fork and continue on the main road avoiding righthand forks. The trail stays on the north side of the creek and climbs into the valley of Deeks Creek. About a 4-hour pack to the lake.

5a. Mt. Hanover trail: This recently constructed trail connects the Deeks Lake area to the Brunswick Mountain area. It will eventually form part of the Howe Sound Crest Trail. The trail follows the west and south shores of Deeks Lake, then heads S past two small lakes ("Middle Lake" and "Brunswick Lake"), eventually climbing SW to the col between Brunswick and "Hat" mountains. Here the trail meets the Howe Sound Crest Trail which crosses the west flank of Brunswick and swings into the headwaters of Magnesia Creek, eventually reaching "Harvey Pass" to the E of the summit of Mt. Harvey. There are two small emergency shelters en route.

6. Furry Creek road (28 km/17.4 mi): Leads to Capilano Mountain and Mountain Lake. This road cuts back from the Squamish Highway about halfway up a long and steep hill located just past Furry Creek. The gate which bars the road here is locked routinely so don't drive in without making arrangements to get out. The road follows the north side of the creek; at 8 km/5 mi there is a major fork. The right branch leads to Phyllis and Marion lakes; the left branch extends to the head of the Furry Creek valley. At 7 km/4.4 mi along the left branch, a trail to the right leads to Beth Lake and beyond that to Capilano Mountain. Furry Creek road has been used as a route into the southern Sky Pilot area and Mountain Lake. Spurs climb northward along Cyrtina Creek to 1220 m/4000 ft and come within 1.5 km of the Mountain Lake cabin.

Routes

SIWASH ROCK 13 m/40 ft
A famous sea-stack adjacent to the western shore of Stanley Park in Vancouver. A seawall walk along the shoreline from Third Beach gives access to Siwash Rock, but something less than a 1.8 m/6 ft tide is required to reach the rock without wading. Many routes have been put up on all sides, the easiest being a stiff Class 4 on the face opposite the shore. The prominent overhang on the corner farther left is a shorter line, requiring only one low Class 5 mantleshelf from a cave onto a protruding shelf. A sign has been placed on the southwest face threatening climbers with prosecution. The sign is cemented on and makes a good foothold. The Rock is popular among the midnight mountaineering set (see *VOJC* 1968, 1971). The first ski ascent was by Dick Culbert.

MT. SEYMOUR 1450 m/4766 ft
Named for Frederick Seymour, Governor of B.C. from 1864 to 1869.
FRA: C. Chapman, B. Darling, W. Gray, G. Harrow, R. Mills—1908.
Although moderate in height and easy of access, Seymour is the site of more mishaps than any other mountain in B.C. It is roamed extensively by hikers taking advantage of the all-weather highway, which rises to 1000 m/3300 ft, and by skiers using the chairlift facilities. The mountain is characteristic of coastal peaks: it has much rugged terrain, and sudden unpredictable changes in the weather. Hypothermia victims are not uncommon, and it is wise to carry rain gear in your pack even on a day hike.

The trails on Seymour have been somewhat improved of late, but maps available from the park authorities are poorly drawn and of little use. Like most broad ridges, once you get off a trail Mt. Seymour can be confusing, especially in poor visibility. Trails tend to run along the ridges, so if you do get confused **go up**, not down. If you are unfamiliar with the mountain, you should carry a compass.

Reach Seymour's main peak by following a trail which begins from the upper parking lot and strikes out to the left (W) of the chairlift *(B1)*. The marked trail climbs toward the top of the lift (Mystery Peak), then runs along the ridge, around the first (**PUMP PEAK**) to the right *(E)*, and back to the ridge, which is followed past the second peak to the summit. Takes 2 1/2 hours; NTD. Some rock scrambling is possible here.

In winter, ice routes are possible on some of the steeper bluffs of Seymour. One area is the bluffs reached by traversing NE from the top of the chairlift for 20 minutes. Other routes may be found in the vicinity of the second peak. These routes are typically only 1 pitch but some are challenging. The region of the Pump, or first peak, has also been used for training in snow craft and affords good practice slopes for this purpose.

Another hike in the Seymour area follows a marked trail WNW from the parking lot. It contours past First Lake to a disused fire lookout at **"DOG MOUNTAIN"** (1000 m/3280 ft) overlooking the Seymour River. Takes 1 hour; NTD.

RUNNER PEAK 1340 m/4400 ft
A small rock horn immediately N of Mt. Seymour. You can reach it easily and quickly by scrambling up from the ridge connecting Runner with Mt. Elsay. It can also be reached from the summit of Seymour: drop down to the Seymour-Runner col

(Class 4), then scramble to the summit. Takes 1 hour return from Seymour.

MT. ELSAY 1418 m/4653 ft
FRA: BCMC party of twenty—1923.
Follow the main Seymour trail until it forks just before it re-ascends to the ridge between first (Pump) and second peaks. At this point, go right and follow a well-marked trail for 2 km to "Canadian Pass" (920 m/3020 ft) on the divide between Gopher Lake and the south fork of Elsay Creek. A flagged route leads from here to the summit, which is approached from the SE. There are plans to complete the trail to the peak. Takes 4 hours; NTD. A small shelter sits on the shore of Elsay Lake to the N of the peak.

MT. BISHOP 1508 m/4946 ft
FRA: BCMC party—1908.
Named for the first president of the BCMC, killed in an avalanche on Mt. Baker. You can reach this peak most easily by bushwhacking N from Mt. Elsay. NTD; 5 hours from parking lot. Alternatively, bushwhack up and E from Seymour River (an illegal approach through the watershed (*B1a*) or ascend from Indian Arm (*A*) via old logging roads in Bishop Creek, then climb up through bush on the south side of the creek until you reach the southwest ridge. NTD.

LYNN PEAKS 1000 m/3300 ft
Two minor summits on the S end of the Lynn-Seymour divide.
FRA: C. Chapman, R. Mills, F. Perry—1908.
The summits are entirely forested. They may be reached from the Lynn Creek road (*B2*), although this trek has little to recommend it.

THE NEEDLES 1250 m/4090 ft
Three minor summits on the Lynn-Seymour divide.
FRA: C. Chapman, R. Mills, F. Perry—1908.
All routes and approaches are illegal, as the Needles are in the watershed. Ascend from the Seymour River road (*B1a*) or off Lynn Creek trail to Norvan Creek (*B2*) up an indistinct ridge to the minor southern peak, then head N along the divide. Neither difficult nor interesting. All routes an easy day return.

MT. BURWELL 1530 m/5025 ft
A friendly, open summit E of the head of Lynn Creek.
FRA: W. Gray, Heney, R. Mills, F. Perry—1908.
Follow the Seymour River road (*B1a*) about 8 km/5 mi beyond the guardhouse and climb timbered slopes to the Needle-Coliseum col. Hike N along the open divide, then over **COLISEUM MOUNTAIN** (1437 m/4714 ft) to Burwell. A more logical approach soon will be via the Lynn Creek trail to Norvan Creek (*B2*), then over Coliseum to Burwell. NTD, but route finding is tricky in fog. You can also easily reach Burwell either from its col with Cathedral Mountain (see entry below) or from the ridge N of Cougar Creek.

CATHEDRAL MOUNTAIN 1732 m/5683 ft
Located 4 km W of Seymour Lake.

FRA: B. Darling, F. Hewton—1908.

The most interesting mountaineering objective in this group of peaks. Approaches from the E are currently illegal. Cross Seymour Lake (*B1a*) by boat to Burwell Creek, then ascend to the Burwell-Cathedral col either by climbing over Burwell or by climbing up the north side of Burwell Creek (old trail). From here, the south ridge is NTD. Another line goes from Burwell Lake up the prominent gully on Cathedral's south face. From the ridge above, traverse around to approach summit from the NW. (The ridge, if ascended directly, is steepish on top). You can also reach Cathedral by coming up Eastcap Creek from Capilano Road in North Vancouver (watershed territory).

MT. FROMME 1177 m/3861 ft

The old Grouse Mountain Highway (*A3a*) is reached from Lynn Valley Road in North Vancouver; it traverses the mountain's southwest flank. Ascent from here is neither difficult nor attractive.

GROUSE MOUNTAIN 1211 m/3974 ft

FRA: R. Parkinson, S. Williams—1894.

The climb up Grouse is most easily accomplished by taking a gondola from the end of Nancy Greene Way (*B3*) to the restaurant and ski slopes at the summit. This approach will appeal to those schooled in the European teleferique tradition. Coastal purists can either hike up under the old chairlift, which leaves from the top of Skyline Drive, or hike up the old Grouse Mountain Highway (*B3*), which is a continuation of Mountain Highway. Unrewarding, except for the views, unless you are continuing on to Crown or the Camel.

A nicer hike follows the Baden Powell Trail E from the Skyride parking lot, then follows another trail to the old BCMC cabin site at 600 m/2000 ft, and from there continues on to the ski area.

GOAT MOUNTAIN 1319 m/4327 ft

FA: G. Edward, Knox, R. Parkinson, S. Williams—1894.

An abrupt rock and heather knoll N of Grouse Mountain. From the Grouse Mountain chalet at the top of the skyride (*B3*), a well-defined but unmarked trail skirts the west side of the summit of Grouse and wanders to the top of **DAM MOUNTAIN** (1340 m/4400 ft). The trail follows the ridge N from here over **LITTLE GOAT MOUNTAIN** (1319 m/4327 ft) to Goat Mountain, which is an easy scramble from the trail.

CROWN MOUNTAIN 1503 m/4931 ft

Located above the Capilano River on the Vancouver skyline.

FRA: G. Edward, Knox, Musket, R. Parkinson (all good men and true!)—1895.

From the saddle between Goat and Little Goat, a trail drops NW into "Crown Pass" at the heads of Crown and Hanes creeks. The trail skirts the cliffs of Crown's east face on the left, and ends on the summit of Crown itself after crossing some slabs on the way. Looking back to the SE, you can spy the jagged arête of the "Crater Rim" which provides some Class 4 scrambling. Plans call for a trail up Hanes Creek from the Lynn Creek system (*B2*) sometime in the near future, which would open up climbing on the interesting north flank of Crown.

The Camel   1.) 5.9 top rope   2.) 5.0 face   3.) 5.6 off width   4.) 5.7 corner   5.) 5.6 exposed chimney   6.) 5.9 hunk   7.) 5.2 regular route   8.) rap block   9.) hind leg route   Maxim de Jong

"THE CAMEL" 1495 m/4900 ft

A small, abrupt rock peak on the north side of Crown's highest summit, visible from Vancouver.

FRA: H. Hewton—1908.

Turn the summit of Crown on the left (NW) via an incredibly exposed but easy ledge which ends in 20 ft of Class 4 downclimbing. Although a mere half-pitch high, the Camel is a veritable circus ground of practice rock climbs. The regular route is a scramble from the northeast corner with one low Class 5 move in a tight vertical crack. Climb straight up from a dead tree near the base. A traverse to a second tree farther right gives a low Class 5 route with more exposure.

Reaching the Camel's head elegantly has always been the main allure of the beast. The usual method is to rope down into the so-called "neck nape," pop up to the top of the head (5.0), then rap out of the neck to the ground. Two corners offer tricky climbing into this nape from the platform below. See photographs for further rock routes.

The Camel, East Face   1.) 5.0 face   2.) 5.9 top rope   3.) 5.7 exposed corner
4.) 5.7 corner   5.) 5.6 off width   6.) 5.9 finger   7.) 5.6 exposed chimney   8.) 5.9 hunk
9.) rappel block   10.) rap anchor   11.) hind leg route   Maxim de Jong

Widowmaker Arête: *FA: H. Mathers, L. MacDonald—1960s.* This buttress drops
from the Camel NE into Hanes Creek; mixed Class 4 and 5. Inexplicably unpopular,
but new access may spark renewed interest.

HOLLYBURN MOUNTAIN 1324 m/4345 ft
The standard approach to this rounded summit is from the Cypress Bowl cross-
country ski area (*B4*). A broad trail leads NE from here, near or under powerlines.
After 1 km it flattens out; turn left at a warming hut, and continue N to the summit.
Takes 2 hours; NTD. Hollyburn is also accessible from the Cypress Bowl downhill
ski area (*B4*). Follow ski runs NE to the pass between Strachan and Hollyburn; it is a
short hike SE from here to the summit. Presently private developers are charging
park users a fee to climb Hollyburn; the mountaineering community is justifiably
fighting this attempt to alienate historic access to a popular climb.

MT. STRACHAN 1454 m/4769 ft

Pronounced "Strawn." Reach the pass between Strachan and Hollyburn by ascending NE from the downhill parking lot along the ski run (*B4*). From the pass, climb to the top of the lifts. Pick up a trail just N of here which leads to the south summit. Descend to the gap to climb the higher north peak. This gap can also be reached from the Howe Sound Crest Trail by ascending a broad couloir. Takes 2 hours; NTD.

BLACK MOUNTAIN 1217 m/3992 ft

The peak is easily approached from the Cypress Ski area via a short trail which begins as an old road climbing from the lift area (*B4*). Alternatively, drive to Horseshoe Bay. To park, turn left onto the overpass bridge leading to the upper townsite and sharp left again after the bridge: you will see a large parking area below highway level here. The Black Mountain trail begins back on the other side of the bridge, where Highway 99 forks to Squamish, and at first it follows an old logging road. Take the left branch at the T junction (the right branch comes down from the Highways Department yard at the top of Eagle Ridge Drive). The trail is obvious and well marked; branches higher up join near the summit, although the left alternative is steeper. Takes 3 1/2 hours; NTD.

THE LIONS 1646 m/5401 ft; 1599 m/5245 ft

Two conical rock summits which are prominent landmarks when viewed from Vancouver. The western summit is the higher and more popular.
FRA of West Lion: H. Bell-Irving, J. Capilano and an Indian companion—1889.
FRA of East Lion: W. Latta, J. Latta, R. Latta—1903.
Winter climbs on The Lions were reported by Basil Darling in the 1910 *CAJ*. It is unclear if Darling reached either summit. Some reports credit the first winter ascent to Tom Fyles in 1922.

WEST LION 1646 m/5401 ft

Tourist Route: Approach via "Unnecessary Mountain" (*B4a, C2, C3*). A sharp gap (usually with a fixed rope) isolates the peak; a steep gully descends from this gap, and the first part of the climb from this point is distinctly exposed. Cross the gap and make an eastward traverse across a downsloping ledge which leads right to a bushy and well-marked route beyond. **Slippery when wet!** Inexperienced climbers should not underestimate the difficulty of this seemingly innocent route—a couple of fatal accidents have occurred here. If you are not properly psyched or equipped, do not go beyond the gap.
North face: *FA: R. Culbert, A. Purdey—1968. FWA: K. McLane, D. Serl—January 21, 1979.* Drop from the road (*C3d*) near the head of Harvey Creek and continue up along this creek until you can double back through bluffs to the base of the face. Alternatively, approach via the Paul Binkert Trail (*C3*) and traverse below the west face of The Lions. This alternative is preferable, although steep snow and a rock rib must be crossed. The lower face is slabby, but the upper part is on rough, firm gabbro. This route lies mainly on the western part of the main wall, but it keeps well to the left of the major corner bordering this face. Takes 7 hours up from the road. Class 5.7. Many parties have had troublesome route finding problems

North face of the West Lion   1.) Northeast buttress   2.) North face   Dick Culbert

on this climb. Large, unstable blocks in the upper regions increase the seriousness of the route. (Ref: *VOJC* 1983, p. 14.)

Northeast buttress: *FA: Probably by Basil Darling—1913.* Approach via the Harvey Creek road (*C3d*) as for the north face. The buttress is interrupted by a shoulder and has unstable rock in places. Bushes close by on the east face and on parts of the route make it less than aesthetic. Climbing to Class 5.3. Takes 6 hours up from road. The first winter ascent party (*R. Barley, G. Shannon—January 1977*) traversed

North face of Mt. Harvey   1.) approach ramp from road   2.) Pup buttress   3.) Cuthbert-Rowat
route   4.) Culbert-Purdey route   Dick Culbert

across from a ramp 2 pitches up the north face in order to gain the arête, which may
also be gained by making a 2-pitch ramp traverse across the east face. Beware of
avalanches in this area. (Ref: *CAJ* 1977, p. 61.)

Southeast gully: *FWA: R. Barley, P. Rowat—January 1974.* A prominent 3-pitch gully line leading to the summit snowslopes, and featuring good ice in winter. Gain the base of this route by traversing the northeast side of the peak, approaching as for the north face climbs.

EAST LION 1599 m/5245 ft

As this peak is in watershed territory, it is illegal to approach or climb it, although this has not been enforced. It is somewhat more difficult than its twin.

"The Great Thrash": To reach the East Lion, leave the approach ridge W of the West Lion and drop E to skirt below the bluff which rims the divide. Continue traversing until you reach the East Lion, and cross between the two Lions to reach the bush route on its east side. The bush line is beyond the col and although fairly obvious, it is steep and unpleasant. While not technically difficult, many parties prefer to rappel rather than downclimb it. Takes 1 1/2 hours up from the base of the West Lion. The peak can also be reached by descending from the gap at the base of the tourist route on the West Lion.

Southern routes: The East Lion has been climbed from many angles; most routes are short, Class 5 climbs on variable rock. There are at least two lines, however, which are largely on rock rather than bush, and which need not get above a stiff Class 3. One ascends from the southeast face, the other traverses upwards across the south face from snow and scree at the southwest corner of the peak. Most parties, however, encounter some Class 4 rock.

West face: *FWA: R. Barley, P. Rowat—April 1975.* Begin at the highest point of the col. Two pitches of steep ice lead to easier slopes above. Descend by rappel. (*CAJ* 1977, p. 61.)

MT. HARVEY 1703 m/5590 ft

FA: H. Bell-Irving, J. Capilano, and an Indian companion—1889.

There are two easy ways to climb this peak: the first is via its western flank (*C3c*), the second from Harvey Creek to the southeast (*C3d*). The most notable aspect of Mt. Harvey is its impressive north face, which is easily reached from the end of the logging spur in Magnesia Creek valley (*C3b*). Scramble up a short scree slope to the prominent ramp which makes an ascending traverse under this face. (It was climbed in 1969 by R. Cuthbert and P. Rowat, who started from this ramp just beyond the gut which separates "Harvey's Pup.") Head for the main pocket or ledge on the western side of the face, following lines of weakness up low Class 5 rock. Continue next to a second prominent ledge on deteriorating rock, the final lead being 5.7. Route now runs up a 40 m/130 ft loose chimney (Class 5.5) without protection. Takes 6 hours up—not recommended.

A shorter route has been put up from further up the ramp (*R. Culbert, A. Purdey—1970*). This starts at an attractive dihedral somewhat before the ledge ends at the wooded shoulder. Climb the dihedral until you are forced to the right along the rim of the overhang, then up again for another lead. Route here becomes easier and looser. Class 5.6; 3 hours.

"HARVEY'S PUP" 1520 m/5000 ft

A small rock tower on the west ridge of Mt. Harvey.
FA: Large BCMC party—1923.

From the north: A short Class 3 climb runs from the uphill notch. Reaching this notch is messy, however. You can either make a descending traverse through bushy bluffs from Harvey's more southerly west ridge, or climb from spurs above the Magnesia Creek road up an unpleasant gully S of Harvey's Pup (*C3b*).

Pup buttress: *FA: R. Culbert, R. Cuthbert, G. Kozel, A. Purdey—1969.* The Pup's major north buttress drops to the ramp beneath the north face of Mt. Harvey and is the only recommended climb yet reported on this complex. Start from where the ramp is intersected by the gut isolating Harvey's Pup, then climb a short overhang, swing down to right under a roof, then around into the prominent chimney, which you then ascend to slabs. Climb an overhanging crack in the corner beyond slabs and continue up the corner. A mossy exit-pitch 30 m/100 ft higher may be avoided by an aid crack to the right. Four more leads on easier rock complete this route, which is enjoyable when dry. A fairly full day. Class 5.7; minor aid in the corner.

BRUNSWICK MOUNTAIN 1785 m/5855 ft
Highest peak in the North Shore group.
FRA: H. Bell-Irving, J. Capilano, and companion—1889.
From the south: A trail to the summit of Brunswick runs up from the left fork of the Harvey-Brunswick logging road (*C3a*). Keep right at the next two forks after crossing Magnesia Creek. From the end of the road, pick up the trail at the edge of the timber. Trail ascends Brunswick's west ridge, and is steep and rough. About 5 hours up from highway.
From Deeks Lake: Approach via the Mount Hanover trail (*C5a*) to the uppermost (third) lake. A cornucopia of gullies and snowfields leads to the summit. About 2 hours of scrambling from the upper lake.

"HAT MOUNTAIN" 1653 m/5425 ft
Located NW of Brunswick Mountain. The Brunswick trail (*C3a*) intersects the newest section of the Howe Sound Crest Trail at the 1520 m/5000 ft elevation. Follow this trail NE to the col between Mt. Brunswick and Hat Mountain. NTD. The peak is also easily climbed from the Mt. Hanover trail (*C5a*), or directly from the outlet of Deeks Lake via a ribboned route.

MT. HANOVER 1747 m/5730 ft
A rock and scrub summit located 2.4 km SE of Deeks Lake.
FRA: H. Bell-Irving, J. Capilano and an Indian companion—1889.
From Deeks Lake: From the lake (*C5*), take the Mt. Hanover trail to the second lake ("Middle Lake"). Ascend to the divide between Hanover and the unnamed peak to the N. Descend into a snow basin tucked in behind the northwest ridge. Use snow to gain the northeast ridge, which is easily followed to the summit. An ice-axe and rope may be required. Alternatively, take the trail as far as the third lake, and then gain a prominent gully (snow in spring) which is climbed to the divide adjacent to the summit of Hanover. From here, scramble easily to the summit.
Northwest ridge: *FA: K. Hunt, K. Ricker—July 1984.* Gain the divide between Hanover and the unnamed peak to the N as for the first route from Deeks Lake. Ascend the northwest ridge until you reach a steep gap. Descend slightly to the right (W) into a steep snow gully. Regain the ridge by climbing the opposite gully wall (Class 5). Alternately, downclimb a steep Class 3 gully to a snow basin on the left

and regain the northwest ridge on steep snow. The summit is a scramble from this point.

From the southwest: From the Hanover-Brunswick col, contour into the basin on the southwest side of the peak. Skirt minor bluffs to gain the summit. NTD.

PEAK 5400 1650 m/5400 ft

An elongated summit located between Windsor and Hanover. From Deeks Lake (*C5*), ascend the creek as for Windsor or Deeks Peak. Bear SE to reach the col between Peak 5400 and Mt. Windsor, then follow the north ridge to the summit. You can also reach the north ridge in winter or spring via steep gullies from Deeks Lake. This peak has also been climbed from the divide N of Mt. Hanover via gullies and ribs. Descent on this last route is confusing, and the divide can easily be overshot on either its west or east sides. Be cautious when visibility is poor.

MT. WINDSOR 1680 m/5500 ft

Located NE of Deeks Lake.

From Deeks Lake (*C5*), ascend towards the Deeks-Windsor col, keeping close to an intervening creek valley bottom, which leads into Deeks Lake at a favoured camping spot. Just below the col, ascend right to the west ridge of Windsor and scramble to the summit. Alternatively, approach from the road which runs to 1220 m/4000 ft on the north fork of Kallahne Creek (*C5*). From the cirque here, ascend W to gain the divide N of Deeks and Windsor peaks.

DEEKS PEAK 1673 m/5490 ft

Located above Howe Sound, S of Furry Creek.

From Deeks Lake: From Deeks Lake (*C5*), ascend directly to summit. This is NTD and about 2 hours up.

From Kallahne Creek: Deeks Peak can be gained easily from roads in either fork of Kallahne Creek (*C5*). From the south fork, swing around to approach peaks from the W. From the cirque at 1220 m/4000 ft on north fork, gullies can be used to avoid bluffs, or the north divide can be gained by ascending W. For the latter approach, skis are best.

CAPILANO MOUNTAIN 1685 m/5529 ft

Located E of the head of Capilano River.

FRA: Survey party—1920.

From the west: Walk up the road to within 1.2 km of Marion Lake (*C6*), then head left on an overgrown logging track; this is followed to the highest point in old logging scar. Ascend directly through bush and forest to the open summit. Takes 1 day return from cars. Spring snow helps subdue bush.

From Beth Lake: From the main road on Phyllis Creek, another road runs up the south side of Furry Creek valley (*C6*), and a trail from this climbs up toward Beth Lake (1070 m/3500 ft) on the north side of Capilano Mountain. The trail swings W around the lake and continues to the summit.

Chapter 2

Sky Pilot

by Glenn Woodsworth and Bruce Fairley

BOUNDARIES:
North: Stawamus River
East: Mamquam River
South: Furry Creek
West: Howe Sound

FOREST SERVICE OFFICE:
Squamish Forest District
P.O. Box 1970
Squamish, B.C. V0N 3G0
898-9671

MAPS:
Federal:
92 G/10 Pitt River   92 G/11 Squamish
Provincial:
92G/NE   92G/NW

Introduction and History

The Sky Pilot area deserves to be more popular. It has all the necessary attributes: proximity to Vancouver, reasonable approaches, a closely packed cluster of peaks, and some gentle terrain ideal for ski touring. Some of the rock in the area is not outstanding, but Mt. Habrich is almost unique in the guidebook as a peak which offers half-a-dozen challenging alpine rock climbs, each of which could be completed in a day by fast parties. The hike up the Shannon Creek road to Habrich provides an unusual view of the backside of the Squamish Chief, and there are even a few crags en route with very difficult looking cracks and corners in them. Sky Pilot (highest peak on the east side of Howe Sound), Ledge, and Habrich are obvious objectives for winter ascents; yet they seldom seem to be attempted, and careful scrutiny will even show that a route or two in the area may still be waiting to be put up.

The Sky Pilot area has much to offer advanced hikers and is a popular training ground for beginning mountaineers. There are some fine alpine lakes, open meadowland, and easy rambles on Red Mountain. Routes to timberline from the Stawamus River offer some of the quickest ways for Vancouver alpine enthusiasts to get above tree line and onto rolling ridge systems.

Skiing the basins to the east of the main peaks was once popular with the old Mt. Sheer Ski Club, which disbanded when the mines in the area shut down in the 1960s. Still, the area holds many attractions waiting to be rediscovered by today's skiers.

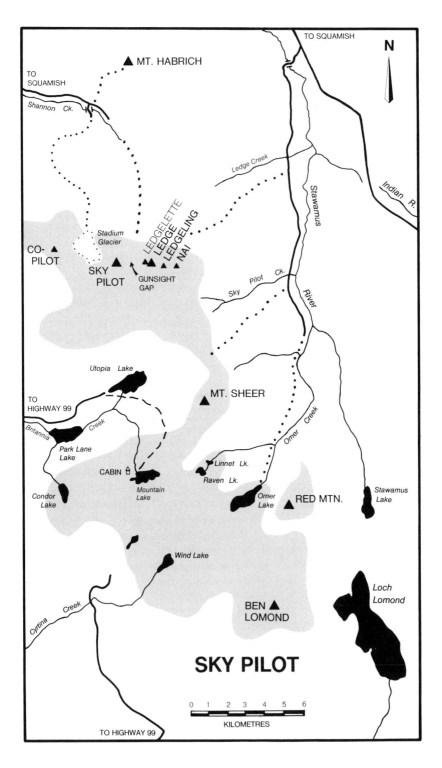

SKY PILOT

There is good ski touring both in the Loch Lomond basin and in the series of basins at the head of Omer Creek, while scenic Marmot basin has always been popular among those Vancouver skiers who value its proximity to the city and its easy approach. The ski trip from the gate at Britannia to the Mountain Lake Hut, a small cabin maintained by the BCMC, should take 6–8 hours. Skins are advised as some of the terrain is steep, and often the snow conditions vary greatly. Parties should be wary of avalanches; a slide on Mt. Sheer killed a young hiker only a couple of years ago.

Prospectors were probably the first to seriously explore the Sky Pilot area; old records indicate that they staked large areas on Goat Ridge, Red Mountain, and Mt. Baldwin before World War I. Britannia was once an important copper mining town and operated into the early 1970s.

Most of the recorded first ascents in the Sky Pilot area were made by climbers who figure prominently in the development of mountaineering in southwestern B.C. Basil Darling made the first ascent of Sky Pilot; Don Munday first stood on the summits of Mt. Habrich and Ledge Mountain; and Dick Culbert and Glenn Woodsworth accounted for most of the pinnacles and towers that remained.

The Sky Pilot massif was traversed from east to west in August 1975 by Bob Paul and Karl Boerner. They began by ascending The Nai, then climbed all the peaks between it and The Copilot. They bivouaced on Ledge Mountain and made their exit by Shannon Creek. This trip is one of the finest alpine traverses in the Vancouver area.

Approaches

All practical approach routes lead from the Squamish Highway.

A. FROM FURRY CREEK ROAD
Shortly after the Squamish Highway crosses Furry Creek, about halfway up the long, steep hill, a road cuts back from the highway (28 km/17.4 mi from Horseshoe Bay). A gate bars the road. Follow the road on foot as it climbs the north side of Furry Creek. At 8 km/5 mi the road forks. The right branch leads to Phyllis and Marion lakes; the left branch extends to the head of the Furry Creek valley. A trail branches to the right 7 km/4.4 mi along this left branch; it leads to Beth Lake and beyond that to Capilano Mountain. The Furry Creek road can be used to reach Mountain Lake and the southern Sky Pilot area. Spur roads climb northward along Cyrtina Creek to 1220 m/4000 ft and come within 1.5 km of the Mountain Lake cabin.

B. FROM BRITANNIA TOWNSITE
The main road through the Britannia townsite crosses Britannia Creek and climbs for about 150 m/500 ft to a locked gate. Park here and follow the road as it climbs to the abandoned Mt. Sheer townsite at 670 m/2200 ft (only a few skeletal buildings now stand). Continue along the road as it ascends the north side of Britannia Creek to Park Lane Lake (1100 m/3600 ft) and Utopia Lake (1310 m/4300 ft). After it leaves the Mt. Sheer townsite, the road degenerates and becomes overgrown in parts. Skins may be useful if travelling in winter. It is just over an hour's hike to the Mt. Sheer townsite, and it is 2 hours more to Utopia Lake.

1. Marmot Creek trails: About 2 km past the Mt. Sheer townsite, just past Marmot Creek, a little-used trail branches left. It climbs N, then E in the Marmot Creek valley, eventually reaches alpine country, and then ascends to the south shoulder of Sky Pilot at 1735 m/5700 ft. It is the quickest route to Sky Pilot and Copilot from the old Mt. Sheer townsite, but is prone to avalanches in winter.

2. Sky Pilot basin: A steep gully leads directly from Utopia Lake to an open basin SE of Sky Pilot. This gully can be climbed quickly when snow-filled in spring. At other times it is easier to climb the forest just E of this gully.

C. THE MOUNTAIN LAKE HUT

There are two ways to reach this hut. The first way is to cross the dam at Park Lane Lake, ascend 370 m/1200 ft through steep bush, a prominent gully, and finally an open snowslope, to a bluff to the SE, on which the cabin sits. The second way is to cross the dam at Utopia Lake and traverse the slopes W of Mt. Sheer, including one steep, timbered slope just beyond the lake crossing. This route takes longer but is easier. To find the cabin, turn right when you emerge from the western slopes of the long traverse ridge; the cabin sits at the 1460 m/4800 ft level, about 100 m/330 ft to the W of Mountain Lake. The hut may be locked; ask the BCMC for keys before you go. When in this area, keep on the lookout for any signs of a possible avalanche; a mountaineer was killed by one here in 1982.

D. FROM PETGILL LAKE

A trail begins on the right of the Squamish Highway, 0.5 km N of Murrin Park. It climbs steeply through bluffs and then through open forest (in part via old logging roads) to the lake, which lies in a pleasant basin at the base of Goat Ridge (760 m/2500 ft). This approach takes 2 hours.

E. FROM THE STAWAMUS RIVER

The Mamquam River road leaves the Squamish Highway immediately before the bridge over the Stawamus River and runs along the northern side of the Squamish Chief massif. It joins the Mamquam River further up the valley. There are many spur systems which constantly open up, then wash out. Mamquam River road access is described under Garibaldi Park. Distances are from the Squamish Highway.

1. Stawamus River road: This road branches right off the Mamquam River road just after the 5 km marker. The road crosses to the west side of the river and follows power lines SE to roads in the Indian River drainage.

1a. Shannon Creek road: This four-wheel drive road branches right about 200 m/660 ft after the Stawamus River road crosses the river to the west side part way up a steep hill. It heads roughly SW and provides views of the backside of the Chief (6 km/3.7 mi). Ignore the spur road which switchbacks left to run under the north side of Habrich. After climbing a major hill, bear right at a fork; the road descends slightly, then flattens out, eventually climbing to 820 m/2700 ft in the Shannon Creek valley. The road forks before reaching the valley head. The left fork leads to Mt. Habrich and the pass between Habrich and Sky Pilot; the right fork crosses Shannon Creek and climbs into a basin on the north side of Goat Ridge. Approach the Sky Pilot massif from this fork by ascending to the prominent shoulder immediately to the S, and then traversing eastward to the "Stadium Glacier" below the Sky Pilot group. About half the road is in good four-wheel drive condition.

2. Sky Pilot spur: The entrance to this spur is overgrown, and the spur itself is undriveable. It branches right off the Stawamus River road about 3 km after that road recrosses to the east side of the river. The spur crosses the Stawamus River to the W after 100 m/330 ft and runs generally S past Sky Pilot Creek to a spot about 0.4 km before Omer Creek. A number of important but unmarked routes strike off from the spur up the slopes to the W.

2a. North Ledge basin: About 2 km along the Sky Pilot spur, reach a creek descending from the W. Ascend the south side of the creek through open forest. There are small bluffs near timberline. This leads into an open basin N of Ledge Mountain; from here, you can climb Sky Pilot, Ledge and Habrich.

2b. Sky Pilot Creek: Take the Sky Pilot spur road for about 3 km. This route begins here, about 1 km before the end of the road. In spring, it is marked by an open snow gully leading up to large timber. You can see The Nai immediately above (if you are not completely enclosed in foul and pestilent vapours). You may occasionally come across the remains of a flagged route. Ascend through light bush and easy bluffs S of the creek to the basin between the Sky Pilot group and the north shoulder of Mt. Sheer, where there is plenty of camping space.

2c. Omer Creek: This route gives access to the large basin between Red Mountain and Mt. Sheer, and is a good approach in spring when snow still covers the ground. The climb to Linnet or Omer lakes is surprisingly quick and painless, and this is a fast route to Red Mountain, Sheer or Ben Lomond. It may also be a feasible alternative route for reaching the Mountain Lake hut, although you would have to cross the high ridge forming the western rim of the basin at an elevation of almost 1520 m/5000 ft.

Routes

GOAT RIDGE 1770 m/5800 ft
A long, gentle summit W of the Sky Pilot group.
FA: Probably by prospectors before the turn of the century.
You can gain Goat Ridge's north ridge from Marmot Creek, but the common approach to the summit is to ascend the steep flanks of the mountainside directly from the Britannia Creek road before it crosses Marmot Creek. The approach is messy, but the summit is pleasant. One branch of the Shannon Creek road leads around almost onto Goat's north ridge at about 1070 m/3500 ft and makes another obvious approach route (*E1a*), although the ascent of the ridge is Class 4. The summit can also be reached from Petgill Lake (*D*).

"SKY PILOT GROUP"
A compact ridge of craggy peaks at the head of Britannia Creek. Contour maps of this group are very poor; as far as the map is concerned, Ledge and the other summits E of Sky Pilot do not exist. Rock is metamorphosed volcanic and reasonably firm.

SKY PILOT MOUNTAIN 2025 m/6645 ft
Highest of the summits E of the head of Howe Sound.

FA: B. Darling, H. Dowler, A. Morkill, J. Huggard, and a companion named Grubbe—1910.
FWA: A. Ellis, A. Shives, G. Woodsworth—December 30, 1960.

South ridge: The most popular route. Most parties gain the base of the ridge from the head of Marmot Creek (*B1*). Alternatively, from the scree basin SE of Sky Pilot (*B2*), head N toward Gunsight Gap, which separates Sky Pilot from Ledge Mountain to the E. Just before entering the final scree funnel, turn left and make an ascending traverse to a notch in Sky Pilot's south ridge. Scramble up the ridge, bypassing the gendarme just before the summit to the right or left. Class 2–3; 1 1/2 hours up from basin. Inexperienced climbers should use this route. The gendarme is is mid-5th if climbed directly.

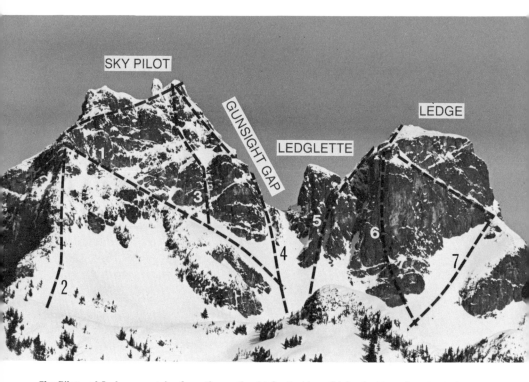

Sky Pilot and Ledge mountains from the south   1.) South ridge   2.) South ridge, alternate start
3.) Southeast face   4.) Northeast route   5.) West shoulder   6.) South face   7.) The Ledge

Peter Jordan

From the northwest: Ascend Stadium Glacier (*E1a*) and either scramble up the west nose of Sky Pilot (steep at bottom) or traverse back to left on snow ledge to upper north ridge. Either is a simple Class 3. The entire north ridge is Class 4–5.
North Face: *FA: K. Barnard, E. Butler—November 1984.* From the Stadium Glacier (*E1a*), begin at an obvious tongue of snow which narrows down into a couloir. This couloir is directly below the summit of the gendarme. From the couloir, 4 leads over mixed ground lead to the west ridge, where 1 steep Class 5 pitch gains the summit of the gendarme. It is possible to skirt the gendarme to the S to gain the main

summit. This face is somewhat featureless and it is quite likely parties will get lost en route if not careful.

From the northeast: From the scree basin SE of Sky Pilot (*B2*), climb to the abrupt Gunsight Gap, which separates Sky Pilot from Ledge Mountain to the E. On the north side of the gap, traverse around to right over steepish, exposed snow, or along inside marginal crevasse, until you are able to double back up the prominent scree ledge to Sky Pilot's east shoulder. Continue in bush and easy rock to peak. Class 2, with minor 3; about 1 1/2 hours up from basin. Gunsight Gap can also be reached from the N (*E1a, E2, E2b*) via a steep snow couloir which is easily gained from the Sky Pilot-Habrich col.

Southeast face: *FA: M. McCuaig, S. McMeekin, H. Mutch—September 19, 1965.* Start in the prominent gully directly below the summit. Climb 2 pitches up the gully (Class 4), then traverse left 3 m out of the gully (5.4). Ascend grassy ledges to a beautiful pink groove which you follow to the summit. Recommended.

Southwest face: *FA: J. Archer, A. Parke—1958.* From Marmot basin, climb the centre of the face to a conspicuous ledge beneath the summit. Use ledge to reach easy ground, or climb directly to summit. Probably low Class 5 on somewhat greasy rock.

THE COPILOT 1860 m/6100 ft

A steep rock horn 2 km NW of Sky Pilot Mountain.

FA: B. Darling, H. Dowler, A. Morkill, J. Huggard, and Grubbe—1910.

East gully: The easiest route is unfortunately on poor rock. From the Stadium Glacier basin, which may be reached from Shannon Creek (*E1a*), by descending from Sky Pilot, or by ascending from Marmot Creek basin (*B1*), ascend to the shallow gully on the east side of Copilot. This provides 2 leads of Class 3 on stained and somewhat loose rock.

West ridge: *FA: R. Culbert, G. Woodsworth, R. Woodsworth—1965.* Approach is from Shannon Creek (*E1a*) and the ascent is a none-too-inspiring Class 3–4 on fairly good rock. Keep to the right on the final buttress.

North face: *FA: R. Culbert, R. Cuthbert, T. Hall—1968.* Start on the west corner of the north face and climb up and left to a small basin, then straight up. There is a Class 5.5 chimney on the final lead. Three leads; 3 hours from base. Surprisingly firm rock.

LEDGE MOUNTAIN 1920 m/6300 ft

An impressive, block-shaped summit immediately E of Sky Pilot Mountain.

FA: C. Field, D. Munday, F. Smith—1912.

FWA: A. Shives, G. Woodsworth—1963.

The Ledge: From the scree basin SE of Sky Pilot Mountain (*B2*), traverse scree or snow to the southeast corner of Ledge Mountain. Ascend the broad scree shoulder on this corner until it peters out, then double back to left on a hidden ledge traversing the south face. From the west end of the ledge, scramble up directly to summit. Class 2–3, 1 1/2 hours up from basin.

West shoulder: From scree basin SE of Sky Pilot Mountain (*B2*), ascend gully leading toward the west shoulder of Ledge Mountain. Keep to left of Tombstone Tower here and continue to the head of the gully, where a window leads through to the north face. This split, which is fitted with a large chockstone, separates Ledge Mountain

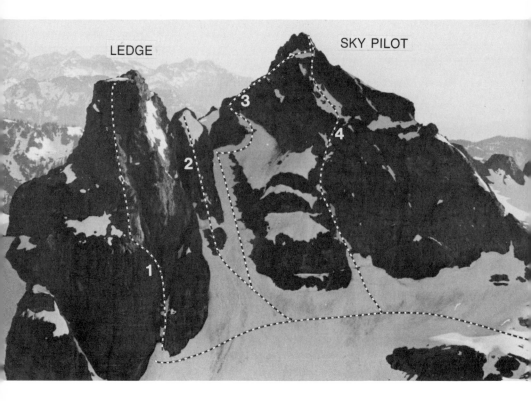

Sky Pilot and Ledge mountains from the north   1.) North face   2.) North face of The Ledgelette   3.) Northeast route   4.) North face   Dick Culbert

from Ledgelette on the W. You can reach the top of this chockstone by climbing (Class 5) around either side of the window (rock a bit loose). One long lead of stiff Class 4 and some scrambling lead to the summit of Ledge. This is an unusual and interesting route which takes 2 1/2 hours up from basin.

North face: *FA: G. Walter, E. Zenger—1969.* This wall is easily reached from the pass between Sky Pilot Mountain and Mt. Habrich (*E1a, E2a*). Begin in a prominent central cleft which is climbed to an overhang. Step right to the crest and surmount a steeper wall, aided on the first ascent. Above this 4th pitch, go straight up over large blocks, then up a difficult chimney. Swing to right of a prominent pocket, then left to gain summit on easier rock. A full day and a good climb on reasonably sound rock. Most pins (soft) were left in place. (Ref: *BCM* 1969; *CAJ* 1970, p. 65.)

South face: *FA: F. Douglas, P. Starr—1969.* This is the broad buttress rising above the scree basin SE of Sky Pilot Mountain (*B2*). Climb the shallow chimney to the right of Ledge's southwest corner. The route is about 250 m/800 ft, and the crux, an overhang about two-thirds of the way up, was aided on the first ascent. Protection is thin in places but the belays are good and the line recommended. Class 5.6; A2. (Ref: *VOJC* 1969, p. 103.)

"THE LEDGELETTE" 1860 m/6100 ft

A separated, western buttress of Ledge Mountain.

FA: R. Culbert, A. Shives, T. Stevens, G. Woodsworth—1962.

East notch: Gain the chockstone between The Ledgelette and Ledge Mountain as you would for Ledge's west shoulder. From here, there is one awkward move with a long reach.

West buttress: *FA: F. Gratwhol, T. Kempter—1965.* This follows the steep rib from Gunsight Gap between Sky Pilot and the Ledge massif. There are 3 short leads, involving in turn a Class 5.5 chimney, a rotten 5.6 overhang, and a 5.4 traverse. Rock is generally poor.

North face: *FA: M. Lopatecki, G. Woodsworth—1967.* From the pass between Sky Pilot Mountain and Mt. Habrich (*E1a, E2a*), traverse to the gully which drops N from Gunsight Gap. Ascend face to left of this gully; Class 4 and 5 for 2 hours on generally good rock.

"TOMBSTONE TOWER" 1800 m/5900 ft

A 30 m/100 ft tongue of rock splitting the gully which drops S from between Ledge and Ledgelette.

FA: R. Culbert, J. Owen, E. Pigou—1958.

Reach this pinnacle from the scree basin SE of Sky Pilot Mountain (*B2*) by hiking up the scree gully which drops from the southwest side of the Ledge massif. The original route traversed onto outer (south) arête where an overhang was forced by a delicate shoulder stand (and a few aid pins). The more popular north edge (*P. Thompson, G. Woodsworth, R. Woodsworth—1962*) ascends directly from uphill notch up the 30 m/100 ft Class 5.8 arête. Recommended.

"THE LEDGELING" 1800 m/5900 ft

A rock tower immediately E of Ledge Mountain.

FA: R. Culbert, W. Sharpe—1958.

FWA: A. Shives, G. Woodsworth—December 29, 1960.

East side: From the scree basin SE of Sky Pilot Mountain (*B2*), traverse under Ledge Mountain and follow a ledge across Ledgeling's south face to its east ridge. Scramble up this, then left under cliffs. One Class 3 pitch leads to bush and the summit.

West arête: *FA: A. Ellis, G. Woodsworth—1963.* Reach the gap between Ledgeling and Ledge from the scree basin (*B2*) or from the N (*E1*) via steep snow. From the gap there is one long Class 3–4 lead on good rock. The preferred route.

"THE NAI" 1740 m/5700 ft

Two rock tusks terminating the ridge E of Ledge Mountain.

FRA and FWA: A. Shives, G. Woodsworth—December 28, 1960.

Reach the gap between these peaks via the easy but loose gully which drops S towards the scree basin (*B2, E2*). Both summits are short scrambles from the gap. Some pinnacles in the gully offer short Class 3–4 climbs (*FA of all pinnacles: F. de Bruyn, A. Shives, G. Woodsworth—1961*). The west Nai may also be climbed from the gap between The Nai and Ledgeling in one Class 3 pitch.

North face couloir: *FA: H. Boschman, R. Charters—August 1983.* This short route gains the gap from the north side (*E2a*). Snow to 45° with a couple of mixed moves in the final pitch. From the gap, scramble up either of The Nai's summits. The preferable route.

MT. HABRICH 1700 m/5600 ft

A lovely granite horn above the Stawamus River, N of Sky Pilot.
FA: D. Munday, F. Smith—1912.
FRWA: J. Howard, K. McLane—late 1970s.

Approach: The Shannon Creek approach (*E1a*) to Habrich is almost exclusively used now. Gain the southwest face and cols on either side of the summit from the end of the road on Shannon Creek via a gully which leads to the col immediately NW of the peak. This takes about 1 1/2 hours up from the road. It is best to enter the gully just above the logging slash, scramble up it about 60 m/200 ft, then transfer right to ascend open timber. Bluffs farther up are avoided by entering the gully again. In winter, going straight up the gully is fastest. Some parties have used the next gully to the N, then crossed the rocky knob on the divide to reach Habrich. It is easy to reach the divide S of Habrich by swinging under the southwest face.

West face: *FA: B. Hagen, G. Woodsworth—1965. FWA: J. Howard, K. McLane—late 1970s.* Climb from the divide NW of Habrich. Work up through non-descript Class 3 ledges and bluffs, with the odd Class 4 move. Most problems are near the bottom where route finding is tricky. Takes 2 hours from base. An easy day climb in winter requiring a couple of ice screws and some slings.

Cooper-Shellborn chimney: *FA: C. Cooper, R. Shellborn—October 15, 1980.* Approach as for the west face. From the base of the face on its western side, ascend an obvious chimney system for 2 leads (5.8). Another 2 leads up a gully gain a final headwall blending into the Initial Route. Finish on exciting faceholds and a flaring crack. Last belay is poor. (Ref: *CAJ* 1983, p. 69.)

Initial Route: *FA: B. Hagen, S. Pilkington, A. Purdey, D. Tate—1965.* This goes up the broken bushy zone on the west side of the southwest face. Climb a crack to ledge then a groove system to right of a tree up to a large bush and crack area. This is ascended angling left. From the top, climb the chimney which narrows to a crack (5.6). Continue up this until you can traverse left to easier ground.

Drug Stabbin' Time: *FA: W. Robinson, C. Thompson—1983.* The party which first climbed this route could not remember most details. The following description is a reconstruction. Climb an obvious sloping ledge in the centre of the southwest face, which ends at a Class 5.8 crack. Climb the crack to a gravelly ledge. Walk to the west end of the ledge and ascend cracks for two pitches until able to move to and climb the left side of a prominent overhanging block. From a bush belay, climb straight up a wide crack, which flares into a very difficult off-width (5.9). There is a two bolt station at the top of this off-width. From here, pendulum or traverse left into another crack system, which leads to easier ground. The "Diachronous Variation" climbs straight up from the right side of the gravelly ledge for three excellent pitches, rejoining the main route just past the overhanging block (*FA: R. Driscoll, B. Fairley, K. Legg, A. Ourom—1984*).

Gambit Grooves: *FA: R. Culbert, R. Cuthbert, T. Hall—1968.* This route runs to the left of the Nose, which forms the lowest rock at the base of the southwestern

South face of Mt. Habrich   1.) West face   2.) Cooper-Shelborn chimney   3.) Initial   4.) Drug Stabbin' Time   5.) Diachronous variation   6.) Gambit Grooves   7.) Solar System   8.) The Nose   9.) Southeast ridge
Bruce Fairley

walls. Take a chimney to the left at the Nose. The second lead is also up a chimney with a 5.6 exit. Continue up and left on slabs and cracks, then nail a 10 m section (overhanging corner block) and continue up gully beyond. Final lead is 5.7 up a thin groove and slab system. Climb is continuously interesting and aesthetic; 8 leads; 6 hours. (Ref: *BCM* 1969.)

Solar System: *FA: R. Barley, D. Serl—August 1976.* Begin on a clean crack system immediately left of the Nose and climb leftward to gain a series of flakes. Three bolts then lead to a large, suspended flake which is crossed to an obvious ramp leading up to slabs. A mixed pitch of slabs, liebacks, and face climbing leads to the base of a large dihedral. The crux on the final pitch is an overhanging flake crack, exiting to a grubby chimney. This route is 6 pitches; 5.9, A1. (Ref: *CAJ* 1977, p. 42.) G. Walter and E. Zenger apparently climbed the upper part of Solar System (reached from Gambit Grooves) in 1969.

The Nose: *FA: R. Culbert, F. Douglas, A. Purdey, P. Starr—1969.* You can begin this route in two ways. Either start at the lowest extent of the southwestern walls on thin 5.10 cracks which peter out, or move right about 15 m to where a continuous easier crack system leads to a prominent ledge. From the ledge, work left onto the main nose. Above this area the route is more distinct. Climbing is somewhat easier in the shallow gully to the left (5.6). To complete the climb, gain a sloping ledge which is followed up and right, intersecting a major cleft at the top of the wall. A direct route on the Nose has not yet been finished. An enjoyable and popular line. (Ref: *BCM* 1969.)

Southeast ridge: From the divide S of the peak, scramble up over slabs, ledges, and bluffs. Some Class 4 and considerable route finding. A continuous wall runs just below the main bush ledge on this side; avoid it by stepping across the chasm on the extreme left. Follow bush ledge left to easier ground, or continue up near south ridge for 2 pleasant Class 4–5 pitches to summit.

Northeast ridge: This is the easiest line (Class 3). Sometimes reached by thrashing directly up from the Stawamus River road (an ugly approach, especially after snow leaves). It can also be reached via a descending traverse from the Shannon basin col. Limited popularity.

MT. SHEER 1680 m/5500 ft
A rock and heather knoll at the head of Britannia Creek.
FRA: C. Chapman, W. Gray, C. MacDonald, F. Perry—1909.

South ridge: Just before the Mountain Lake route via Utopia Lake (*C*) reaches Mountain Lake, ascend E up the basin toward Mt. Sheer. Hike into the notch SW of peak and scramble up summit ridge. There is one exposed gap to be negotiated.

Northeast buttress: *FA: M. Lassere, A. Shives—1963.* This extremely obscure climb follows a buttress on the north side of Sheer for 2 low Class 5 pitches ending on the summit.

BEN LOMOND 1620 m/5300 ft
A tusk of dark rock located W of Loch Lomond; an attractive snow pyramid in winter.
FRA: C. Chapman, W. Gray, C. MacDonald, F. Perry—1908.

North ridge: From Mountain Lake (*C*), cross the broad divide which leads S to Ben Lomond. Alternatively, drop eastward down a gully toward Omer Lake (1310 m/4300 ft) and then up an open valley to the col NW of the summit tusk. Ascend this by scrambling up its north ridge which is only Class 2–3, but loose and exposed. Ben Lomond is generally done from the Mountain Lake cabin; meadows and lakes abound in the region between Ben Lomond and the cabin, and the area is excellent for hiking and ski touring. Route finding can be tricky in bad weather.

Southeast face: *FA: R. Driscoll, B. Fairley—June 12, 1982.* The route begins with solid face climbing and ascends a bush-free apron towards the central gully of the face in a long rightward traverse (5.2), then straight up a faint nose to the left of the gully for 3 pitches to 5.7, ending in a further, easier gully of loose rock, situated between two ribs. The route gained the right hand rib, which was Class 3 to the summit; the left rib appears to offer a further pitch of Class 5 climbing. Although the face seems bushy from the ground, the greenery is avoidable and does not spoil the climbing. Rock is reasonable; 2 1/2 hours. (Ref: *CAJ* 1983, p. 69.)

MT. MULLIGAN 1620 m/5300 ft; MT. BALDWIN 1465 m/4800 ft
Two minor summits located on the divide between the Stawamus River and Raffuse Creek. The name Mt. Mulligan is incorrectly placed on map 92 G/11. It should be moved to the summit 1 km S.

FA: Probably by prospectors.

Old logging roads climb some distance up Mt. Mulligan's north flank. From the end of the road, you can either contour to the W around the false north summit or traverse over the summit to the col with the main summit. From here, follow the easy north ridge to the peak.

MT. ALPEN 1703 m/5588 ft
Located on the ridge E of Raffuse Creek. The central summit of the three is the highest.

FA: Probably by prospectors.

Branch "P" of the Mamquam River road (*E*) has spurs to near timberline on the west side of the most northerly summit. NTD from here. Alternatively, from the upper end of the road in Raffuse Creek (E branch), ascend to the col between the east peak and lesser summits to the S and E. From here, it is an easy scramble to any of the summits (*FRA: BCMC party—April 1980*).

PINECONE LAKE PEAKS
This gentle, pleasant group of summits is located E of Squamish, between the headwaters of Crawford Creek and the Mamquam River. Approach via the Mamquam River road system (see Garibaldi Park section). Spurs lead from this system near the mouth of Crawford Creek to over 900 m/3000 ft on the shoulder SE of Crawford's mouth. Hike up the ridge through easy bush to "Knothole Lake" (1675 m/5500 ft), then cross E through the 1765 m/5800 ft col to Pinecone Lake. From here, you can easily reach the 1980 m/6500 ft summits N and S of this col. The peak farther NE is best ascended by dropping S and skirting the divide to approach from the E.

Alternatively, use the "M-4" branch of the Mamquam logging road as an approach from the SW. Leave the road near the boundary of TL 3228 to 4794 (on 92 G/10) and ascend wooded slopes to gain the crest of the northwest ridge which leads to **PEAK 5700** (1735 m/5700 ft). From the ridge, you can easily gain the basin N of this summit. The unnamed lake just to the E of this basin sits on a striking platform; from here, you can easily ascend **PEAK 6600** (2010 m/6600 ft) (*FA: K. MacKenzie, K. Ricker—October 1976*), and **PEAK 6500** (1980 m/6500 ft), both SW of Pinecone Lake.

Chapter 3

Garibaldi Park

by Anders Ourom

BOUNDARIES:
North: Lillooet River
East: Lillooet Lake, Lillooet River
South: Mamquam River
West: Highway 99

FOREST SERVICE OFFICE:
Squamish Forest District
P.O. Box 1970
Squamish, B.C. V0N 3G0
898-9671

MAPS:
Federal:
92 G/9 Stave River
92 G/14 Cheakamus River
92 G/16 Glacier Lake
92 J/7 Pemberton
Provincial:
92 G/NE

92 G/10 Pitt River
92 G/15 Mamquam Mountain
92 J/2 Whistler

92 J/SE
PSG 3 Garibaldi Park
Outdoor Recreation Map of B.C. #3: Whistler-Garibaldi

Introduction

Anyone who has never made the 8 km hike up the Rubble Creek trail to the Black Tusk Meadows in Garibaldi Park has missed seeing a landscape which has held the affection of mountaineers since the earliest days of climbing activity in the province. Garibaldi Park contains some of the most stunningly beautiful alpine terrain in all of British Columbia. From the immense lava cliffs of the Barrier, the huge natural dam which impounds Garibaldi Lake, to the isolated icefields of Mount Pitt and Mount Sir Richard, the park unfolds scenic wonder after scenic wonder. There is the famous profile of the Black Tusk jutting up and above the meadows; the splintered pillars of granite on Crosscut Ridge, Phyllis' Engine, or Mount Luxor; the exquisite turquoise of Garibaldi Lake; the wide open carpets of heather and flowers in the upland of Helm Creek, Singing Pass or Taylor meadows; and the high, glaciated ridges of the Spearheads or McBrides. No matter whether you are a hiker, climber, skier or naturalist, you cannot claim to have fully experienced the mountains of southwestern British Columbia until you have visited Garibaldi Park.

While climbers have never neglected Garibaldi Park, it is the skiers who have most completely made it their home. Hundreds of ski tourers have had their first introduction to the sport in Garibaldi Park. Today you can drive a well-maintained road from Squamish to the Diamond Head parking lot, then follow old, wooded roads into Red Heather meadows and over Paul Ridge into the Elfin Lakes. A cosy lodge built during the Second World War once stood here, but it has now been replaced by a commodious cabin run by the Parks Branch. The slopes of Paul Ridge or Columnar Peak, just beyond the Elfin Lakes area, offer some of the best powder snow to be found anywhere north of Squamish during the winter months, and the area is popular with telemark schools. And certainly few sights anywhere can compare with the view of Atwell Peak to the north on a crisp winter day when the sun is shining.

Garibaldi Lake, Black Tusk Meadows, the Black Tusk microwave site, and the Helm Glacier are all well-loved touring destinations. More ambitious skiers relish the classic horseshoe traverse of the Spearhead Range, which begins on Blackcomb Mountain, and takes one into the gentle alpine country of the Singing Pass area, where the BCMC maintains a rustic cabin at Russet Lake.

Hikers and climbers generally do not go to Garibaldi Park in search of technical challenge. The well known summits in the western half of the park are like old friends: easy to get along with—and they don't throw many surprises at you. But some of the more remote summits are not nearly as well known. To approach the solitary sentinels of Mt. James Turner or Mt. Pitt on foot and still claim the summit is the mark of a dedicated mountaineer. Garibaldi Park was also the scene of some of the first winter ascents to be done in southwestern B.C. It is probable that more peaks have been climbed in winter than are indicated in this guidebook.

A mention should be made of the tight group of summits surrounding the east end of Garibaldi Lake. These are usually approached on skis, in the spring when Garibaldi Lake is frozen. Climbs on Castle Towers, Davidson, Sphinx, or the peaks just east of Gray Pass can be recommended for their solid rock, which always yields sufficient cracks and holds to make the climbing fun. But Garibaldi Park is so big that it is difficult to recommend any one special area without slighting other equally beautiful spots. Mountaineers who return here again and again will develop their own favourite haunts. The best advice is to take the map and the guide, and just go where the spirit of adventure leads you.

Approaches

A. FROM THE MAMQUAM RIVER ROAD

Turn right off Highway 99 just before it crosses the Stawamus River at the base of the Squamish Chief, 1 km S of Squamish. A complex series of roads leads S and E. Locating the routes up Mamquam Mountain from these roads can be confusing, so allow time for sorting out access. The following guidelines may be helpful. Keep to the main road for 6 km/3.7 mi (from the highway) where you will pass a gate that is usually unlocked. A further 1 km will bring you to a fork; go left. At 9 km/5.6 mi there is a bridge across Raffuse Creek and a B.C. Forest Service campsite. Take another left fork at 9.8 km/6 mi, then at 13.1 km/8.1 mi again bear left and take the bridge over the Mamquam River to the north side. At 13.4 km/8.3 mi keep right, then take all left forks again until 22.2 km/13.8 mi, at which point go right. In another 1 km you should reach the bridge across the east fork of Skookum Creek. The last couple of kilometres of this road system are complicated and variations on the pattern may emerge. However, aim for GR 054130 on 92 G/15 and park somewhere in the area of the Skookum Creek bridge.

B. FROM HIGHWAY 99 (WHISTLER MOUNTAIN HIGHWAY)

Distances are measured from the first Squamish traffic light on Highway 99, reached just after crossing Mamquam Slough.

1. Diamond Head road (4 km): Leads to Paul Ridge and Elfin Lakes. Turn right off the highway onto the Diamond Head road (signposted) about 1 km past the Mamquam River bridge. Take the left fork 4.5 km from the highway. Park in the parking lot at 1010 m/3300 ft, then follow the jeep track and trail up the northeast side of **PAUL RIDGE** and **ROUND MOUNTAIN** (1675 m/5500 ft) to a hut by the Elfin Lakes at 1460 m/4800 ft. This roomy shelter is run by the provincial Parks Branch and presently costs $5.00 per night. In winter, to avoid the serious avalanche hazard in the areas above timberline to the NW and NE, take a route which climbs right to the ridge crest (usually marked by the Parks Branch) and follow the crest to the shelter.

2. Alice Lake Park and roads (8.4 km/5.2 mi): Turn right off the highway and follow signs to the park entrance. To reach Alice (Cheekye) Ridge, take the road to the left at the park entrance and drive toward the park headquarters, but angle right again at forks before reaching headquarters. The road (presently two-wheel drive) switchbacks to S, then swings to E and climbs the nose of the ridge to a 1400 m/4600 ft shoulder. Keep left at all major forks. The road was graded and the trail flagged in 1983, but washouts must be anticipated. A marked trail runs up the ridge to the divide S of Mt. Garibaldi.

3. Brohm Ridge road (14 km/8.7 mi): This road branches to the right just before Brohm Lake, a narrow swampy pond on the west side of the highway. The Forest Service can give you current information about its condition. The best road at present goes via Cat Lake. Go right after crossing the bridge just off the highway, and follow the rugged two-wheel drive road (bulldozer graded in 1984) for 4.5 km to "midstation" at 1120 m/3700 ft. This road may be gated, but a key is available from the Forest Service. A second road, which cuts left about 1 km from the highway, rejoins the Cat Lake approach at "midstation" and is two-wheel drive to about 750 m/2400 ft. The crest of Brohm Ridge is very scenic, and offers good access to the north side of Mt. Garibaldi. This is a designated snowmobile area and is used extensively for that purpose.

4. Culliton Creek (25 km/15.5 mi): Little remains of the flagged route beyond the short road ascending the north side of this creek; parties who attempt this entrance into Garibaldi Park may find it takes 2 days to reach Garibaldi Lake. The road may be gated. Beyond the road, expect jungle.

5. Black Tusk trail (33 km/20.5 mi): A signposted road leads E to a parking lot at 610 m/2000 ft beside Rubble Creek; from there a parks trail climbs to a junction at 1370 m/4500 ft. Follow the right fork to reach Garibaldi Lake and the left to reach Taylor meadows. Expect company. Rustic winter shelters are maintained at both locations by the Parks Branch; these are little more than open sheds, and tents are probably preferable. There is now a $5.00 fee in the summer to stay at either meadows or lake.

When there is spring snow, some travellers still prefer to walk up Rubble Creek from the parking lot to the Barrier at its head, then climb steepish snow on the left side, looking up, to Barrier and Lesser Garibaldi lakes. This is direct and fast but loose footing after the snow leaves, and there is the danger of avalanches and falling rocks. Ski parties usually travel from Garibaldi Lake to the Mimulus Lake area via Mimulus Creek, swinging left at the headwall.

A public cabin (Burton Hut) has been placed by the VOC near the lakeshore at the mouth of the valley holding Sphinx Glacier. Small glaciology huts at the tongue of the Sentinel Glacier are also left open in winter for emergency use. These are difficult to reach if the lake is not frozen over, and are employed mainly for ski touring, to which this area lends itself admirably. Ski parties require about 6 hours to pack to Burton Hut and another 2 1/2 to climb to upper Sphinx Glacier. After the lake thaws, the few parties that do trek S to Sentinel Glacier usually keep well up on the flank of Mt. Price. The upper Sphinx Glacier is reached by following the main trail across Black Tusk Meadows past Mimulus and Black Tusk lakes and beyond to Helm Glacier just S of the interesting volcanic vent called **CINDER CONE** (1860 m/6100 ft). Ascend S up the east portion of the glacier and across **GENTIAN RIDGE** at its head, dropping to Gentian Pass beyond, where there is a good campsite at 1830 m/6000 ft. An easy day's pack from cars. Climb S to **POLEMONIUM RIDGE** and cross snow (ice in late summer) beyond Castle Towers and Mt. Carr to the main portion of Sphinx Glacier. Sentinel Glacier can also be reached by climbing Brohm Ridge and crossing the Warren Glacier.

6. *Cheakamus Lake trail (51 km/31.7 mi):* Turn right off the highway, then go left at 0.8 km. This road goes 8 km/5 mi to the park boundary, then a good, marked trail leads the remaining 3 km to Cheakamus Lake.

6a. *Helm Creek trail:* About 1 km before reaching the lake, a trail branches right to the river. The Park Service has established a cable car across the river; from there, a good park trail runs up Helm Creek past Helm Lake to Black Tusk Meadows. This approach has the advantage of less traffic, but two people are required to operate the cable car.

6b. *Black Tusk microwave site:* Go right at the fork 0.4 km from the highway. The main branch crosses to the south side of Cheakamus River, takes the next left fork, then climbs to the S, leading to microwave relay tower at 1830 m/6000 ft on the shoulder NW of The Black Tusk. This road is rough but maintained, and gives the shortest summer access to the summits E of Garibaldi Lake.

6c. *Whistler microwave:* A road climbs E from just S of the Whistler gondola, taking first a left and then a right fork. Shortly before the microwave tower (at 1430 m/4700 ft), a trail branches left. It leads to timberline on the west side of Whistler Mountain.

7. *Singing Pass trail (56 km/34.8 mi):* Take the main entrance into Whistler Village and go straight ahead, following signs to trailhead. A good two-wheel drive road runs for 3.8 km, beginning just outside the town where the paved road ends. The trail is well marked and well worn from here. A small public cabin (Himmelsbach Hut) has been placed by the BCMC at Russet Lake (1890 m/6200 ft). This hut is NOT intended for the use of helicopter parties. It may be reached from the pass by making an ascending traverse SE to swing around the east side of a 2010 m/6600 ft knoll at the 1950 m/6400 ft level, and then dropping NE beyond to the lake. Shelter is W of the lake's outlet. It is a 3 hour pack to Singing Pass from the road and another hour

to Russet Lake. Singing Pass may also be reached in about 3 hours from the top of the Whistler lifts. In summer, parties can follow the divide back over the minor summits of the "Musical Bumps:" **PICCOLO** (2010 m/6600 ft), **FLUTE** (1980 m/6500 ft), and **OBOE** (1920 m/6300 ft), but usually prefer to traverse from the top of the Red Chairlift across Harmony basin on upper bench at about 1830 m/6000 ft, crossing the ridge beyond at a small notch and gaining the main divide behind Piccolo Summit, or even beyond Flute Summit. Ski parties tend to depart by the ridge crest and return by the lower route, with a deviation in Flute basin to pick up the skier collector trail to the base of the Blue Chairlift in Harmony bowl. The divide is a pleasant route to Singing Pass, but it is difficult to follow if visibility is poor.

7a. Spearhead Range approach: For winter traverses, a ride up the chairs at Blackcomb can save much time and energy, though the cost may be discouraging. A walk up under the lift in any season gives good access to the alpine terrain beyond. There are also powerline roads on the east side of Green Lake which might be a starting point for trips to the Phalanx Mountain area.

8. Wedgemount Creek road (67 km/41.6 mi): A bridge crossing to the east side of the Green River gives access to the northwestern section of Garibaldi Park. However, the road is gated just before the bridge and vehicles are usually prohibited. Call Sabre Sand and Gravel in Whistler for more information on this road and gate. Cross the bridge, then stay left at all major forks except the first until you reach Wedgemount Creek. The log bridge across the creek was washed out and has been replaced with a new bridge in an obscure upstream location, found along a rough trail leading 100 m/330 ft up the south side of the creek. After crossing, follow the trail on the north side; it is steep but in good shape. It takes about 4 hours from the road to reach the public cabin placed by the BCMC at Wedgemount Lake (1890 m/6200 ft). Add 1 more hour if you are skiing up, or if the road cannot be driven. To reach Weart Glacier from the shelter on the northwest side of the lake, climb E up the glacier from the head of the lake, avoiding the first crevasses by moving to the right or left and the next set by moving to the left. Follow snow S then E onto the lowest point in the divide N of Wedge Mountain, and cross here to Weart Glacier.

8a. Rethel Creek route: After crossing Green River and passing through the gravel pit, take all right forks to the highest spurs at about 1200 m/3950 ft. From here, a rough track leads up onto the west ridge of Wedge Mountain. The lower west ridge of Wedge is bushy and rarely used, while the old Wedge Creek trail is now overgrown and difficult to follow. This creek valley offers a good winter approach route to the Wedge area, however.

8b. Mystery valley route: From N of Wedgemount Creek, it is possible to climb E in this valley or the next valley S into either of the basins N of Mt. Weart.

C. FROM LILLOOET RIVER
A new bridge crosses to the west side of Lillooet River at Little Lillooet Lake. The roads on the west side of Lillooet River are in much better condition than those on the east side.

1. Lillooet Lake and Ure Creek approach: A bridge is expected to be built across the Green River just E of Pemberton. Long range plans call for a road to be pushed E on the south side of Lillooet Lake to the Ure Creek area, which will then be logged.

2. Tuwasus Creek roads: Roads on the west side of the creek climb to the park boundary, with spur roads climbing to 400 m/1300 ft. Good access to the eastern McBride Range.

3. Snowcap Creek approach: Just N of where Snowcap Creek flows into the Lillooet River, a four-wheel drive logging spur ascends to a logging cut. Gain the high, rolling ridge running down from the Greenmantle-Three Bears area to the W. There are some pleasant meadows along this ridge, and it can be skied to Snowcap Lake, although there is some avalanche danger in winter on the west side of Greenmantle, when you descend to the valley. Likely 2 days to Snowcap Lake.

4. Fire Creek roads: Roads climb on both sides of the creek to within about 2 km of the park boundary. On the creek's south side, the highest spur reaches an altitude of 640 m/2100 ft, giving good access to the Fire Spires area.

5. Sloquet Creek roads: Only the first few km of this road system is easy hiking; the rest is very overgrown, although a party did walk out from Glendinning via North Sloquet Creek in summer 1984 in 1 1/2 days. They had to make a tricky ford of the creek above some falls. The climb up into the hanging valley N of Mt. Glendinning is very steep.

D. VIA PITT RIVER ROADS

The ferry which used to make regular runs up Pitt Lake no longer operates here, so to reach the head of the lake you must either use a private boat or make arrangements with B.C. Forest Products. Roads leading from the head of Pitt Lake do not provide outstanding access to alpine country, but they are useful for exiting from regions such as the Misty Icefield.

1. Pitt River main line: This road begins from a wharf at the head of Pitt Lake. It runs N on the east side of Pitt River to a logging camp at Alvin (8 km/5 mi) and then continues about 14 km/8.7 mi to a major bridge. From here, roads on both sides ascend almost to the southern boundary of Garibaldi Park.

2. Corbold Creek roads: Roads up both forks of this creek already extend to near the boundary of Golden Ears Park. At present, branches go up the south side of the south fork to 760 m/2500 ft and up the southeast side of the north fork to 490 m/1600 ft, 4 km W of Remote Peak. A branch also climbs up the west side of Corbold Creek to 730 m/2400 ft, where it forks. The left fork traverses N into Shale Creek; the right fork splits again, its right branch going to 910 m/3000 ft, and its left going to 1190 m/3900 ft on the divide SW of Stave Glacier.

3. Shale Creek roads: From the bridge at the end of the main line, a road ascends the south side of this creek to 1070 m/3500 ft. It then contours S into the Corbold Creek system. The road on the north side of Shale Creek switchbacks to 1070 m/3500 ft.

4. Bucklin Creek road: From the end of the main line, cross to the west side of Pitt River. A road climbs to 400 m/1300 ft in Bucklin Creek, then contours NW for several kilometres to 980 m/3200 ft.

5. Pinecone Creek roads: From the bridge at the end of the main line, head S on the west side of the river. The first creek encountered is Steve Creek. The road climbs W and forks at 370 m/1200 ft. The right fork, encompassing both Steve and Pinecone creeks, has branches which climb northward to 980 m/3200 ft and southward to 1220 m/4000 ft on the divide between the creeks. The left fork leads S into Homer Creek, with parallel branches reaching about 760 m/2500 ft on its north side.

6. Boise Creek roads: Cross Pitt River at a bridge 4 km N of Alvin. Roads are presently being planned to reach 700 m/2300 ft in the north fork and 580 m/1900 ft in the south fork of Boise Creek, which is located to the NE of Meslilloet Mountain.

Garibaldi Traverses

Several overland treks and traverses have been done in the park. The most popular is the trip from Diamond Head shelter over Garibaldi Névé to Garibaldi Lake. It is especially popular as a ski trip when the lake is frozen. The traverse takes 1–3 days and is famous for whiteouts. When you cross Garibaldi Lake, beware of thin ice near creek outlets, and of dark areas of surface water. From Garibaldi Névé (see Mt. Garibaldi), cross the divide below The Tent on the east ridge of Mt. Garibaldi, continue N down névé across the head of Warren Glacier (pass E of the Sharkfin), and reach the 1890 m/6200 ft pass W of Glacier Pikes. Descend the steep slopes of Sentinel Glacier and cross Garibaldi Lake to usual exits at its west end. There are shelters at Garibaldi Lake in Sentinel and Sphinx bays.

Two other fairly short popular trips (3–4 days) are the circuit around Fitzsimmons Creek through the Spearhead and Fitzsimmons ranges, and the trip down the divide from Wedgemount Lake to Mt. Currie. More serious treks include one that starts from Garibaldi Lake, and goes through the McBride Range and around the headwaters of the Cheakamus River to Singing Pass. For variations on this route, start from Tuwasus Creek on the east side of the park, or finish via the Spearhead Range. (Ref: *VOCJ* 1969, p. 83; 1977, p. 15.) The routes are briefly described in this guide under approaches to Mt. Sir Richard.

Parties have also traversed the Misty Icefields, and in 1972 K. Haring and P. Olig trekked from Wedgemount Lake to Alouette Lake in 16 days. In summary, they went across the south slopes of Wedge Mountain to Wedge Pass, then traversed Shudder, Shatter, Ripsaw, and Naden glaciers to Naden Pass. They then dropped down Diavolo Creek and crossed Cheakamus River, ascending Ubyssey Glacier and dropping beyond onto upper Tuwasus Creek. They used the north and south forks of Tuwasus Creek to bypass Mt. Pitt, then traversed the Misty Icefields to Remote Peak. They continued S along, or to the E of, the Pitt-Stave divide across the head of Thomas Lake to the head of Tingle Creek. Next they packed E of Osprey Mountain, dropped into Osprey Creek, crossed the southeast fork of this over the ridge into Gold Creek, and from there, reached Alouette Lake. Many ski traverses are described in John Baldwin's guidebook.

Routes

MAMQUAM MOUNTAIN 2595 m/8515 ft

A nest of glacial summits on the south side of Mamquam Icefield to the E of Skookum Creek. A surprising number of parties routinely fail to climb this summit.

FA: B. Gray, C. Chapman, H. Korten, F. Perry, F. Smith, W. Taylor—1911.

Via Mamquam Lake: This lake can be reached in 4 hours from Diamond Head Shelter (*B1*). Take Garibaldi Névé approaches to S of Opal Cone, cross E over the open valley of Zig Zag Creek to Rampart Ponds, then drop to Mamquam Lake (1300 m/4300 ft). From the lake, drop S down Skookum Creek until it forks at Eanastick Meadows. Ascend the ridge S of Skookum's northeast fork, bearing up and right near the top to cross onto the icefield at the Tyee Glacier at the 2100 m/6900 ft notch. You can also reach the icefield from Eanastick Meadows by swinging SE into the high valley W of Mamquam, then climbing NE onto the divide at the 2100 m/6900 ft pass just S of Darling Peak about 1.5 km NW of **DELUSION PEAK** (2700 m/8200 ft). Bypass Delusion Peak on the E; the final peak is not difficult by its northwest ridge. Strenuous day from Mamquam Lake.

From the Mamquam River: Mamquam River and Skookum Creek roads (*A*) lead to a bridge across the east fork of Skookum Creek at 880 m/2900 ft. Begin from N and W of here; climb NE through forest into the valley trending NW/SE which drains the basin W of Mamquam. Before reaching the lake mapped at GR 082130, climb NE to the 2100 m/6900 ft pass and icefield. Swing around the north side of Delusion Peak and gain Mamquam from the N. Mt. Mamquam is possible as a long day trip by this approach if the roads are driveable. Various parties have flagged routes into the valley over the years, and some parties have started at the bridge and climbed straight up onto the ridge to the NE to reach the valley. (Ref: *VOC Ski Guide*, p. 48.)

From the south: This disused route relies on roads in Crawford Creek to reach the 1740 m/5700 ft pass S of Mamquam. Ascend glacier on the southwest side of the summit, then climb to the final northwest ridge. The direct upper south rib is Class 3 (*FA: T. Rollerson, S. White—1971.*). The 1980 m/6500 ft summits on the divide S of Mamquam can also be reached by this approach. Logging roads which climb high in Martin Creek from the Mamquam system lead to the SW summits. In 1975, J. Clarke climbed the rugged 6500 ft peak W of the 3300 ft level in Bucklin Creek via its 1500 ft south ridge. Class 3 mixed rock and brush.

DARLING PEAK 2469 m/8100 ft

Located 1 km W of Mamquam Mountain. An easy ascent from the Mamquam Icefield.

PEAK 7400 2260 m/7400 ft

Located 2.5 km NW of Mamquam Mountain.

PYRAMID MOUNTAIN 2130 m/7000 ft

The rock summits on the ridge immediately E of Mamquam Lake. From the northeast side of Mamquam Lake (see Mamquam Lake approach to Mamquam Mountain), ascend slopes to northwest ridge of the central of the three western summits. Scramble easily to the peak and reach the other two from there, the northeast summit being Class 3. The southwest ridge of this massif is also a Class 3 rock climb. The two higher summits of **SPIRE PEAK** (2260 m/7400 ft) further NE are most easily gained from the 2040 m/6700 ft col at the head of Skookum's northeast tributary.

MT. GARIBALDI 2678 m/8787 ft

You can get a good view of this prominent volcanic peak by looking NE from Squamish. Garibaldi (named after the famous Italian patriot) is 14.5 km/9 mi away. Because the mountain is composed of loose, young volcanic material, routes keep to the glaciers where possible. Despite the poor rock, it is still a very popular mountain. The sharp southern summit is named Atwell Peak, but it is widely referred to as "Diamond Head" due to its shape. (The name "Diamond Head" has been officially given to a 2070 m/6800 ft shoulder further S, although it is known unofficially as "Little Diamond Head.")

FA: A. Dalton, W. Dalton, A. King, T. Pattison, J. Trorey, G. Warren—1907.
FWA: V. Brink, R. McLellan, H. Parliament, J. Rattenbury, F. Roots—1943.
An all female ascent (*A. Dalgleish, E. Fee, E. [Brooks] Milledge*) was made in 1932.

The following aproaches may be used:
From the Elfin Lakes shelter: From this shelter (*B1*), follow a rough track which contours N to the head of Ring Creek. At forks, cross to the east side of creek and continue N to Garibaldi Glacier (following cairns), which leads onto névé. There is often high avalanche hazard on this route in winter and spring. Alternatively, ascend to saddle (described below) and descend to Ring Creek; longer, but safer and more aesthetic.
From Alice (Cheekye) Ridge: An approach often used in winter. From the Elfin Lakes shelter (*B1*), climb NW to cross the saddle between **COLUMNAR PEAK** and **THE GARGOYLES** (both 1830 m/6000 ft). Drop to divide beyond, a point which can also be reached from Cheekye Ridge road (*B2*) in 3 hours. Next, make a descending traverse through the valley NE, crossing Ring Creek below bluffs W of the creek head. Join Elfin Lakes shelter route (above). The Cheekye Ridge approach features exceptional views of the steep and rotten southwest bowl of Atwell Peak—a sight to terrify even the most hardened mountaineer. From Cheekye Ridge, a higher route can also be taken when conditions are good. From a point about 300 m/985 ft below Little Diamond Head, traverse NW and drop steeply to glacier, then make an ascending traverse, crossing the east-southeast ridge of Atwell at about 2200 m/7200 ft to gain the upper slopes of Garibaldi Névé below The Tent. This is tricky country in fog or whiteout; map and compass are essential.
Brohm Ridge: From the end of the Brohm Ridge road (**B3**), follow the ridge E onto the Warren Glacier. This offers direct access to the north side of Garibaldi. You can also continue NE to the Sentinel Glacier area, passing W of the possibly unclimbed **SHARKFIN** (2195 m/7200 ft) or continue E onto the Garibaldi Névé.
Sentinel Glacier: This glacier leads up from the southeast side of Garibaldi Lake (*B5*) to the Warren Glacier SW of Glacier Pikes. Access is then as in Brohm Ridge approach. This route is most commonly used in spring, when the lake is frozen.

GARIBALDI ROUTES
East face: From Garibaldi Névé, climb the glacier which descends from between Garibaldi and Atwell, then up summit glacier to between Mt. Garibaldi and Dalton Dome, Garibaldi's west peak. An easy ledge and short couloir lead to the northwest ridge and the summit. Crevasses can cause problems late in the season. Takes 6 hours up from Elfin Lakes.
Northeast face: From the névé contour NW onto the east ridge ("Pringle's Ridge") of Garibaldi below The Tent. Climb W to the head of Warren Glacier below final steep slopes. Alternatively, approach via Brohm Ridge. Climb the Warren Glacier headwall past a bergschrund, which must often be outflanked using the rotten rock of the northeast or northwest ridges. There is more poor rock on the summit ridge. A nice winter objective, requiring only an ice-axe. **THE TENT** (2440 m/8000 ft) is a NTD snow slog by way of its southwest ridge.

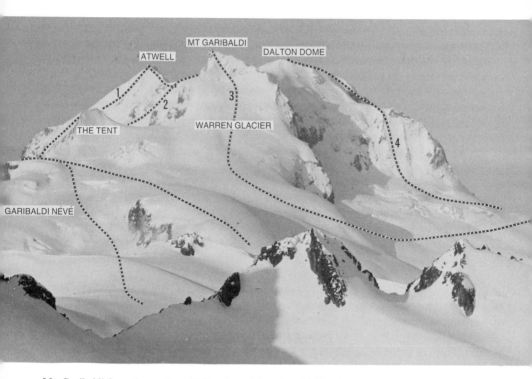

Mt. Garibaldi from the north   1.) East face of Atwell   2.) East face of Garibaldi   3.) Standard Warren Glacier route   4.) North face of Dalton's Dome

Bruce Fairley

DALTON DOME 2620 m/8600 ft

North face: *FA: D. Jones, D. Serl—1979.* The route follows the thin snow gully right of the hanging glacier on the Warren Glacier headwall. It then climbs 55° snow, then up terribly shattered rock to a slight snow rib on the left leading to the northwest shoulder. Class 4.

Northwest face: *FA: I. Brown, R. Chambers, E. Kafer, M. Kafer, E. Larsen, B. Richardson—1963.* This climbs the dirty, indistinct shoulder from Brohm Ridge to its top on the upper rim of Warren Glacier. A more distinct ridge and snow rib then lead to the top. Class 4 on snow and bad rock.

Southwest ridge: *FA: F. Douglas, N. Varco—1966. FWA: P. Beckham, J. Howe—January 23, 1985.* This is the prominent crest dropping SW from Dalton Dome. Reach it by traversing S from the head of Brohm Ridge (exposed to falling ice and rocks). The ridge is Class 3–4 on mixed rock and snow. Takes 7 hours, and is reportedly a sporting winter climb.

ATWELL PEAK ("DIAMOND HEAD") 2620 m/8600 ft

The sharp southern summit of Garibaldi. Usually climbed in winter or early spring, when snow can be used instead of loose rock.

FA: A. Armistead, B. Darling, J. Davies, F. Hewton, A. Morkill—1911.

North ridge: Climb to saddle N of the peak as in east face route for Garibaldi. Atwell's north ridge is rotten rock, but not very difficult. Not for novices or the nervous.

East face: When Don Munday published his guidebook to Garibaldi Park in 1922, he reported that the east face of Atwell had been climbed, but further details of these ascents are not known. Several broad couloirs on the face provide snow and ice routes of moderate challenge, and are good winter climbs. Descents of Mt. Atwell are sometimes made down the east face.

South ridge: *FWA: J. Bryceland, B. Hagen, L. Patterson, G. Woodsworth —February 1966.* The route is obvious. There are 2 rock bands, one halfway up and one near the summit. The last pitch is at times unprotectable. Descend via a couloir on the east face. One of the most notable winter routes in the guidebook, and a perennial frigid favourite.

Northwest face: An imposing 1000 m face that offers alluring winter lines. Considerable rockfall hazard.

Siberian Express: *FA: P. Beckham, J. Howe —January 30, 1985.* An open couloir and rib system leads to immediately left of the summit tower. Mostly 35–40° snow, with the top 100 m/330 ft at 55–60°. Done as a 21 hour single push up Brohm Ridge, traversing the west slopes of Dalton Dome (avalanche danger), crossing the gut beyond (high icefall danger), and descending via the north side of Dalton Dome. Sure to see lots of repeat ascents.

Armenian Express: *FA: C. Zozikyan —February 2, 1985.* Soloed only 3 days after the preceding route, with an unequipped bivy on the summit. Route follows narrow righthand couloir (35°), then angles right to gain the south ridge just below the summit section (65° at top).

VIKING RIDGE 2070 m/6800 ft

A triple summit standing N of Bishop Glacier E of Mt. Garibaldi. The northeast side features ferocious ice gullies and glaciers, which few people have ever seen, let alone thought of climbing. From Opal Cone trek NE across snowfield to Viking's easy southwest side.

THE BLACK TUSK 2315 m/7598 ft

A picturesque horn of dark, volcanic rock rising N of Mt. Garibaldi.
FA: W. Gray—1912.

A striking peak in a popular area, the Tusk has been host to occasional mob scenes and a track has been worn from Black Tusk Meadows (*B5*) to the base of a route near the southwest shoulder. The usual summer route through the rock step here is a wide chimney which intersects a prominent diagonal gully near the summit scree ridge. It is a Class 2–3 climb and not particularly aesthetic, although the high rate of use has now stripped off most of the loose rock. Most novices have no trouble on this climb, but the rock is steep and nobody should be urged by pride or companions onto terrain where they are uncomfortable. Aptitudes for climbing vary enormously and getting down is always the hardest part for novices. The diagonal gully mentioned above is difficult at the bottom, but it is sometimes preferred by early season parties when snow covers this part. The Tusk is a quick ascent from the microwave towers.

The Tusk has a north peak which is actually a shade higher than the main one and is isolated by a difficult gap. When this is climbed (which is rarely), the best method is to rappel 9 m into the gap and bypass the gendarme here on the west side. The

The Black Tusk

Bruce Fairley

north peak is a Class 4 climb and loose, and it is more difficult still to regain the main summit. (*FA: T. Fyles—1917.*) A peak known as **"THE BISHOP'S MITRE"** on the outer part of the Tusk's northeast ridge appears to be unclimbed.

EMPETRUM PEAK 1992 m/6536 ft
An open ridge NE of The Black Tusk.
Walk around the west side of Helm Lake (*B5*) and ascend Empetrum's easy south ridge. A pleasant hike with spectacular views of the Tusk. The Helm Creek trail (*B6a*) is also a viable approach, as is contouring to N of the Tusk from microwave towers (*B6b*).

PANORAMA RIDGE 2100 m/6900 ft
Located immediately above the north shore of Garibaldi Lake.
Take the trail through Black Tusk Meadows (B5) to Black Tusk Lake, then hike up north ridge of Panorama Ridge. This is an easy summit with fine views, and may be done as a day hike from the road or as an afternoon stroll from the meadows. In spring, the northeast ridge and the northwest slope make good ski routes, preferable to the north ridge.

GENTIAN PEAK 2199 m/7216 ft
A minor peak at the head of the east arm of Helm Glacier.
The easy summit may be reached by traversing ridges from Panorama, or by ascending from Helm Glacier (B5). Ski parties operating from the east side of Garibaldi Lake can first ascend to Gentian Pass and then continue up slopes to W.

CORRIE PEAK 2262 m/7423 ft
A nondescript summit NE of Helm Glacier and Gentian Ridge.
From the east lobe of Helm Glacier (B5), climb to Gentian Ridge and continue NE along Corrie Ridge to climb Corrie from the SW. Not difficult.

HELM PEAK 2145 m/7038 ft
Located NE of the snout of Helm Glacier.
From Black Tusk Lake (B5), hike down Helm Valley past Helm Lake and the Cinder Cone and climb slopes to the divide S of Helm Peak. Pass around the east side of the summit to climb Class 2–3 couloir on the northeast side. Takes 5 hours return from meadows. There is some nice skiing in this area.

CASTLE TOWERS MOUNTAIN 2675 m/8778 ft
Highest of the summits E of Garibaldi Lake. Composed of quartz diorite.
FA: H. Korten, T. Park—1911.
FRWA: BCMC party—1979.
West ridge: From Gentian Pass (B5), ascend SE to crest of Polemonium Ridge, W of Castle Towers. (Spring ski parties can ascend this ridge from Garibaldi Lake.) Bypass the minor 2290 m/7500 ft summit and climb the west ridge of Castle Towers. This is quite easy, except for a gap before the main centre summit, which is steep and loose (Class 3–4). Beyond the gap, avoid difficulties via ledges left of the divide. Takes 4 hours return from Gentian Pass. For the climb of the summit you can camp in the pass, in Black Tusk Meadows, at the head of Helm Glacier or at the east end of Garibaldi Lake. Rope advised.
South side: The glacier S of Castle Towers Mountain can be reached from Gentian Pass (B5) by traversing around the top of Polemonium Ridge at about the 2130 m/7000 ft level—crampons advised late in the season. This area may also be reached by spring ski parties by traversing from the head of Sphinx Glacier. From ice, ascend couloir to gap mentioned in the west ridge route. This gives a Class 3 line of ascent. Near the bottom of this couloir, a prominent shelf runs to the right, and two routes have been recorded from this ledge. The first of these (*J. McGhee, K. Ricker—1957*) ascends a broad crack system slanting to the W of Castle Tower's summit visible overhead. Follow this weakness to the upper west ridge; an easy Class 4. The second variation (*J. Bryett, S. Fall, K. Hunt, I. Leaming—1957*) goes

up and to the east to the block and slab system on the southeast corner of the face about 60 m/200 ft below summit. Follow corner to the top, using the left face where necessary. A stiff Class 4.

East side: From Sphinx Glacier (*B5*), cross the divide NW of Mt. Carr and adjacent to the north or south stack of Phyllis' Engine, then traverse over Cheakamus Glacier to ascend Castle Towers' east peak on steep eastern snowslopes. To reach the main summit, a Class 4 notch must be negotiated. The east side has also been approached from Gentian Pass by ascending steep Castle Towers Glacier and crossing the col in the massif's long north ridge, then walking the rim of a windcirque and traversing on Cheakamus Glacier.

Northwest face: *FA: T. Hall, C. Oloman—1970.* The glaciated northwest face is directly accessible from Gentian Pass (*B5*). Climb snow up centre of face to bergschrund, which may be outflanked or crossed directly in sporting style. Above this comes 4 leads on 50° snow and ice, then the Class 4 true summit (which is the peak appearing on the right). Alternatively, depending on condition of bergschrund, cross well left of summit area and climb directly up 50° snow and ice, through a short rockband, and finish up 65° slope onto snow E of east summit. It is best to climb this route early in the season before the icefall opens up too much. Still awaits a winter ascent.

PHYLLIS' ENGINE 2560 m/8400 ft

A group of granitic spires on the divide S of Castle Towers. Named in honour of Phyllis Beltz, a staunch BCMC member, who first likened the pinnacle to the profile of an engine.

FA: F. Gratwhol, T. Kempter—1966.

The northern spire (smokestack of engine) is the highest. From the head of Sphinx Glacier (*B5*), and to the NW of Mt. Carr, climb up and to the right on the obvious ledge system, then traverse smaller ledge back across the face. Climb Class 5 jamcrack and enter cleft leading completely through massif. Stem this to ridge just S of the smokestack. Final lead is a short but exposed Class 5.7 jamcrack to the right of the arête. Rock is excellent and lower pinnacles are presently unclimbed. The second ascent of this spire came two days after the first.

MT. DAVIDSON 2500m/8200 ft

A steep granitic summit across Cheakamus Glacier from Castle Towers.

FA: N. Carter, E. Milledge—1925.

South-southwest ridge: The Cheakamus Glacier is usually gained from Sphinx Glacier (*B5*) via the pass to the W of Mt. Carr, but might be approached more conveniently in summer directly from the camp in Gentian Pass (*B5*) by way of steep Castle Towers Glacier. From Cheakamus Glacier, ascend Davidson's south-southwest ridge, passing gap by using the ledge on the south side. Class 4 on good rock, but a very strenuous weekend objective.

Northwest ridge: *FA: K. Cover, B. Gavin—September 1, 1985.* From the Cheakamus Glacier gain the northwest corner above a badly broken section of the glacier. Class 4 to low Class 5 rock leads to the south-southeast ridge shortly before the summit.

Northeast ridge: *FA: R. Driscoll, B. Fairley, K. Haberl, K. Legg—June 1, 1984.* The Cheakamus Glacier may be approached via Mt. Carr or by traversing E from

Gentian Pass (*B5*). It is possible to descend the east side of the glacier on steep snow to gain the ridge at the 1830 m/6000 ft elevation. The ridge is quite narrow and at times heavily corniced. Several rappels are necessary, with climbing to Class 5.7. The major wall on the route is bypassed by rappelling to the east face. The ridge is regained higher up. Minor aid was used just below the summit. A long and interesting alpine climb, calling on a variety of techniques. Takes 18 hours return from bivy on Sphinx Glacier. (Ref: *CAJ* 1985, p. 48.)

MT. CARR 2590 m/8500 ft
Located on divide 2 km SE of Castle Towers.
FA: Large BCMC party—1911.
FWA: Likely by the Mundays in the 1930s.
Northwest ridge: From Sphinx Glacier (*B5*), gain the easy northwest ridge by using a short snow couloir. Alternatively, use the pass between Phyllis' Engine and Carr, crossing E to Cheakamus Glacier and Carr's easy northern slopes.
South ridge: *FA: A. Fall, J. Fall, S. Fall—1978.* Beginning at the col between Bookworms and Carr, climb rock and snow of the south ridge. Class 3.

THE BOOKWORMS 2350 m/7700 ft
Three rock spikes on the divide E of Sphinx Glacier.
FA: N. Carter, C. Townsend—1922.
From Sphinx Glacier (*B5*) all summits are short Class 3 or 4 rock climbs. The southwest Bookworm is climbed up northeast arête, with a chimney on the southwest face providing an alternative line. The middle peak is climbed by a layback on the southwest arête and the northeast one via its south arête and southeast face. Short Class 5 routes could be done on the northern exposures.

THE SPHINX 2410 m/7900 ft
Located on the divide SE of Sphinx Glacier.
FA: Large BCMC party—1911.
Southwest ridge: Ascend Sphinx Glacier (*B5*) to col southwest of The Sphinx and climb a steep headwall (ice-axe required) to the easy southwest ridge. The col may also be reached from the head of the glacier E of Guard Mountain by swinging S of Deception Peak.
Northwest face: *FA: R. Carter, P. Kindree—1978.* Begin 60 m/200 ft S of the north ridge. Four pitches to 5.8 up a prominent crack system lead to the summit.
West pillar: *FA: R. Carter, P. Kindree—1978.* A prominent pinnacle on the north side of The Sphinx, just left of a snow gully leading to southwest ridge. It is climbed from the gap between it and the main face; 5.7.
North ridge: *FA: A. Ourom, L. Soet—1973.* This is the finest route on the peak. It involves 6 leads of fairly sustained climbing on excellent rock to Class 5.8. The crux is a small overhanging section on the top pitch.
East face: *FA: B. Fairley, J. Manuel—1982.* Approach via Sentinel and Phoenix glaciers, which requires a 240 m/800 ft descent. The climb involves 3 rock bands separated by snow. Excellent rock with a variety of possible lines. A few nuts are sufficient for the rock steps, the second of which is 2 pitches. Definitely not as good as the west face of the Dru.

The Sphinx from the north   1.) East face   2.) North ridge   3.) Northwest face   4.) West Pillar

Bruce Fairley

DECEPTION PEAK 2230 m/7320 ft
A group of rock spikes on the divide S of Sphinx Glacier. Also called the "Deception Pinnacles."
FA: N. Carter, C. Townsend—1922.
Reach the divide W of Deception from the west side of Sphinx Glacier (*B5*), or by ascending the glacier E of Guard Mountain, or from Sentinel Glacier. There are five or six peaks, and these may be traversed from the W without much difficulty, except for the easternmost spike which is better ascended from E or SW.

GUARD MOUNTAIN 2185 m/7170 ft
An attractive rock peak rising E of the south end of Garibaldi Lake.
Southeast ridge: Like its eastern neighbours, Guard is seldom climbed except in spring when Garibaldi Lake is frozen. The col in the divide to the SE is usually reached from the cabin at Sphinx Bay by climbing the valley and glacier E of Guard, but it can also be gained by traversing from Sphinx Glacier (*B5*) or by ascending from Sentinel Glacier, both of which are more useful summer approaches. Scramble up Guard's southeast ridge to the south summit. The slightly higher northern peak is isolated by a small but loose gap. Class 4; 3 1/2 hours up from lake. One sometimes sees gymnastic goats on this route ambling up loose 5.10 death traverses.

West face: Ascent of Guard's west face directly from Garibaldi Lake need be no more difficult than Class 4, but is loose and not recommended.

North ridge: *FA: R. Culbert, A. Purdey, M. Warr—1967.* The base of this ridge is easily reached from lower parts of the glacier to the E. There are three steps of Class 4–5 on good rock.

GLACIER PIKES 2130 m/7000 ft

Located at the head of Sentinel Glacier.

FA: Large BCMC party—1911.

It is a 2–3 hour hike up Sentinel Glacier to the col between the summits, neither of which is difficult. The southeast peak is higher. The Diamond Head-Garibaldi Lake traverse passes through the col on the west side of the Pikes.

THE TABLE 2020 m/6625 ft

FA: T. Fyles—1916.

Because of its climbing history, The Table has a mystique which few summits in Garibaldi Park can match. The mountain, a volcanic mesa, has an arresting and dramatic shape, but because of the exceptionally loose, dangerous rock the climb is seldom attempted. Soon after Fyles' ascent, Neal Carter repeated the route, but Dick Culbert's ascent in 1959 was the first in about 40 years. The next day Sev Heiberg and Karl Ricker repeated the feat, and easily removed Culbert's top rappel pin by hand.

The east ridge of The Table is usually reached by ascending from Table Bay on Garibaldi Lake. Ascent is just S of the east ridge, with the first pitch (Class 3) on the south flank. The next 2 follow the ridge and are a loose, dangerous Class 5. Descent is difficult due to the lack of good rappel placements. This is a serious and un-aesthetic ascent. Hazards include terrible rock and heli-picnickers. Attempts via the west ridge ("Teacup Handle") have so far been unsuccessful.

MT. PRICE 2049 m/6721 ft

A gentle, isolated summit on the west side of Garibaldi Lake.

FRA: Large BCMC party—1912.

FWA: D. Munday, P. Munday—1930s.

You can gain this summit from any side, although some exposures are bushy or bouldery. One standard route is to proceed from the outlet of Garibaldi Lake (*B5*) to the first prominent northwest ridge, follow adjacent gullies to the col W of the summit, then continue up the southwest slopes. NTD. Takes 3 hours up from lake. Ski parties may prefer to gain this col via the basin to the N directly from Garibaldi Lake (avalanche danger). The lava flows which created the Rubble Creek barrier and Culliton canyon topography originated from Mt. Price. The minor **CLINKER PEAK** (1980 m/6500 ft) on its west shoulder is a volcanic vent.

PARAPET PEAK 2470 m/8100 ft; ISOSCELES PEAK 2530 m/8300 ft

Two of a knot of heavily glaciated peaks SE of Gray Pass at the head of Pitt River.

FA: N. Carter, D. Munday, P. Munday, H. O'Connor, C. Thompson—1922.

Reach Gray Pass (2010 m/6600 ft), which isolates this group, from the top of Sphinx Glacier (*B5*) by crossing the col N of Bookworms, traversing the snowslopes beyond, then dropping into the pass. You can climb directly up Parapet's northwest ridge, or you can traverse at 2200 m/7200 ft to reach the easier northeast ridge. Climb Isosceles most easily by traversing S on the western snowslopes, then by ascending to either its col with Parapet or its easy eastern side. The col can also be reached by traversing Isosceles. Beware of avalanches on the northern exposures.

Crosscut Ridge and Mt. Luxor   Peter Jordan

MT. LUXOR 2320 m/7600 ft
FA: H. Angus, K. Carter, N. Carter, D. Hossie, B. Martin, W. Martin—1926.
To the S of Isosceles is **CROSSCUT RIDGE**, a jagged line of sharp corners, blocky pillars, and myriad cracks. It would be a popular area for high-standard rock climbs if located near a road, but as it is, no climbs have yet been reported on this fine collection of granodiorite. To the S of Crosscut Ridge is Mt. Luxor. Traverse S on snow from the flank of Parapet to the bowl on Luxor's north side; from here, climb the peak easily on snow or Class 3 rock. The ridge SE of Luxor was climbed on skis in 1972 (*J. Clarke, B. Samson*).

TUTANKHAMEN PEAK 2290 m/7500 ft
An easy summit 1 km SE of Mt. Luxor.

HOUR PEAK 2350 m/7700 ft
FA: D. Etches, P. Starr, S. White—1970.
The abrupt summit on the ridge SE of Isosceles. Reach it by crossing the divide N of Luxor or by traversing around the north and east sides of Parapet and Isosceles. A

short Class 3 climb. The **"MINUTE HAND"** on its northeastern side remains un-climbed. The four gentle summits on the ridge E of Isosceles Creek were traversed on skis in 1972 (*J. Clarke, B. Samson*).

FITZSIMMONS RANGE

WHISTLER MOUNTAIN 2190 m/7200 ft
A summit and ski development at the W end of Fitzsimmons Range. From the top of the alpine T-bar of the ski development, reach the summit in an hour's hike to the S up the ridge, then W along the divide. Not difficult. A less populated solution is the Whistler microwave road (*B6c*) and trail. There are some nice rock routes on Whist-ler's north and east sides, and short rock and ice climbs around the cirque to the N (beware of kamikazi downhill skiers). The area would have considerable potential as a training ground if it were not for the atrocious prices of the lift. In summer you can use a mountain bike to gain access to this area.

SINGING PASS AREA
Thanks to the BCMC cabin (Himmelsbach Hut) at Russet Lake, and the excellent access either by trail from Whistler Village (*B7*) or through the alpine terrain from Whistler Mountain, the summits of the eastern Fitzsimmons Range are popular climbs in summer and winter. These peaks are heavily glaciated and thoroughly al-pine, but they present few technical difficulties.

From Russet Lake (*B7*), reach the Overlord Glacier either by descending ENE, or climbing SE to gain the glacier's head at the Fissile-Whirlwind col. Two main lines now continue to the Overlord-Benvolio saddle. The first goes across the north slopes of Whirlwind to the divide beyond, then traverses over **REFUSE PINNACLE** (2500 m/8200 ft) and across the south slopes of Overlord Mountain to the saddle. Traversing Refuse Pinnacle is easy although in summer it is exposed, and in winter there are large cornices and the serious danger of avalanches. The second route climbs the north side of Overlord Glacier and swings over the north shoulder of Overlord Mountain to the saddle. Reach the col between Diavolo and Benvolio easily by making a descending traverse from the saddle or by climbing from the south slopes of Overlord Mountain. Reach the Diavolo Glacier by dropping down steepish snow from Mt. Benvolio, from the Benvolio-Diavolo pass, or by swinging N to the Fitzsimmons-Benvolio col.

An icefall covers the lower parts of Diavolo Glacier. Naden Pass to the NE is reached either by dropping down Detour Ridge to Diavolo Creek and ascending N to the pass; or by climbing the glacier to the shoulder E of Mt. Iago and going down the rather crevassed Iago Glacier. The head of Naden Glacier can be reached from the head of Iago Glacier by traversing up Macbeth Glacier on the west side of interven-ing **COULOIR RIDGE** (2470 m/8100 ft). Naden Pass or Glacier are a fairly short day's pack from Russet Lake (*B7*). For a slightly faster route to Macbeth and Naden glaciers, swing N of Fissile Peak from Russet Lake (*B7*) and ascend Overlord Glacier, crossing the 2190 m/7200 ft col to the E and dropping onto dirty Fitzsim-mons Glacier. From there, you can climb to Macbeth Glacier, or you can descend the Fitzsimmons and swing E on moraine to Curtain Glacier and Platform Glacier of the Spearhead Range.

FISSILE PEAK 2440 m/8000 ft

A reddish peak of poor rock rising SE of Russet Lake.
FA: Likely by prospectors.
From the west: From Russet Lake *(B7)*, the summit can be reached by scrambling up the west buttress to the ridge above, or by going first to Fissile-Whirlwind col and then ascending the loose rock of the southeast ridge. Between these two lines, snow and rubble on the southwest side offer the easiest access to the summit.
Northwest face: *FA: J. Byers, C. McNeil, T. Rollerson—1969.* Reaching this face directly from the hut involves 270 m/900 ft of Class 4 ice or snow gully followed by scrambling along the ridge above. Late in the season, poor rock becomes exposed in the gully. **WHIRLWIND PEAK** (2440 m/8000 ft) to the SE is easily ascended from its col with Fissile Peak, if you avoid the large ice wall in the col.

OVERLORD MOUNTAIN 2634 m/8641 ft

A high, gentle summit at the head of Overlord Glacier.
FRA: D. Munday, P. Munday—1923.
Overlord Mountain and the neighbouring **MT. BENVOLIO** (2620 m/8600 ft) to its SE are both easily ascended from the high saddle between them. These constitute an easy 3 hour trip from Russet Lake *(B7)* or a rather full day return from cars.

DIAVOLO PEAK 2590 m/8500 ft

A rock summit on the divide SW of Diavolo Glacier.
FA: N. Carter, C. Townsend—1923.
From the Diavolo-Benvolio col, Diavolo's north ridge is a rock scramble of Class 3–4 difficulty, but loose on top. A white dyke leading to the ridge crest is somewhat firmer. **ANGELO PEAK** (2560 m/8400 ft) immediately S is a short ridge walk from the summit of Diavolo. Very loose rock. *(FA: N. Carter, C. Townsend—1923.)*

CHEAKAMUS MOUNTAIN 2588 m/8490 ft

Located above Cheakamus River on the south rim of Diavolo Glacier.
FA: R. Hooley, J. Kilborn, I. Kirk—1950.
From Diavolo Glacier, climb the steep snow gully on the northwest side of Cheakamus Mountain into the col E of the highest peak. Follow ridge crest to summit. A low Class 3 climb. The more difficult east peak *(FA: VOC party—1968)* may be climbed from the same col. Bypass first gendarme on the S and traverse base of pinnacles beyond to gullies leading to east summit. Cheakamus Mountain is a moderate day trip from Russet Lake *(B7)*.

MT. FITZSIMMONS 2650 m/8699 ft

On the divide between Fitzsimmons and Diavolo glaciers.
FA: Large BCMC party—1924.
South face: From Diavolo Glacier, climb snow gully until just below the col between the main and western summits, then veer right on Class 2–3 rock. Takes 5 hours up from Russet Lake *(B7)*.
West ridge: *FA: B. Port, K. Ricker—1964.* From the Fitzsimmons-Benvolio col, climb Class 3 rock to the western summit. Descend rib on southeast face into gully,

traverse ledge to reach the col beyond, and from there continue to peak.
North face: *FA: S. Fuller, C. Guest, D. Serl—August 9, 1981.* From Fitzsimmons Glacier, reached by dropping steeply E from the north shoulder of Overlord Mountain, scramble up and left to base of main snow face. Face is 370 m/1200 ft high and about 45°. Some loose rock scrambling is necessary to gain the summit.

MT. IAGO 2500 m/8200 ft
Located on the north rim of Diavolo Glacier.
FA: E. Buss, M. Dempsey, B. Ellis, K. Ricker—1968.
The couloir between the two highest summits may be reached from Diavolo Glacier by crossing steep snow. From the couloir, climb S to the summit on Class 2–3 rock. Takes 8 hours return from Russet Lake (*B7*).

MT. MacBETH 2620 m/8600 ft
Located E of the head of Fitzsimmons Creek.
FA: E. Buss, B. Ellis, P. Macek, P. Starr—1969.
From Naden Glacier, Macbeth is a fairly easy ascent over snow on the east side, although the bergschrund here may cause problems. South and southwest faces are also NTD, although steep. **THE RIPSAW** (2650 m/8700 ft) is also easy from the E.

THE SPEARHEAD RANGE
Despite its name, the range N of Fitzsimmons Creek is largely of a gentle, if icy, nature. The traverse of Spearhead and Fitzsimmons ranges around the watershed of Fitzsimmons Creek is a recommended trip. It is usually done on skis and requires 3–4 days, although it has been completed from the top of Blackcomb in 1 long day without climbing summits and by bypassing the Diavolo Glacier, using instead the Fitzsimmons Glacier. The easiest way into the Spearhead Range is to start from the top of the downhill ski lifts at Blackcomb Mountain (*B7a*) and climb SE onto northwest shoulder of Blackcomb. From here, drop N onto the Blackcomb Glacier, then ascend SE to the Spearhead-Blackcomb col. You can also approach from Horstman Creek or from the divide between Blackcomb and Wedge creeks. (Ref: *VOCJ* 1964; 1978, p. 5.)

BLACKCOMB PEAK 2440 m/8000 ft
Located on the west end of the Spearhead Range.
FRA: D. Munday, P. Munday—1923.
This summit can be climbed by its easy northeast slopes from the Blackcomb-Spearhead col (see above) or from Blackcomb Glacier. Alternatively, you can climb up the ridge E of the lake located W of Blackcomb Peak. This line provides several leads to Class 3–4 on reasonably good rock. **THE SPEARHEAD** (2440 m/8000 ft), an abrupt summit located immediately NE of Blackcomb, can be reached by scrambling up from the intervening col. (*FA: A. MacDonald, B. Port, K. Ricker—1964.*) The sharp summit of **PHALANX MOUNTAIN** (2440 m/8000 ft), about 1.5 km farther N, was climbed in 1922 by N. Carter and W. Wheatley. An easy climb over snow from Phalanx Glacier on the N, or a steep scramble from Blackcomb Creek basin.

MT. TROREY 2470 m/8100 ft; MT. PATTISON 2500 m/8200 ft

Located at the head of Trorey Glacier in central Spearhead Range.
FRA: A.J. Campbell Garibaldi survey party—1928.
To reach the Trorey-Decker col, traverse SE from the Blackcomb-Spearhead col across the Decker Glacier; from here it is an easy climb up to the col. Mt. Pattison has been climbed from the divide via its short, easy south ridge and Trorey by its northeast and southwest snowslopes and its northwest shoulder. All are steep snow. The more gentle **DECKER MOUNTAIN** (2410 m/7900 ft) to the W is NTD from the NW, S or E (*FA: VOC party—1954.*) These are now reasonable day trips from Blackcomb.

TREMOR MOUNTAIN 2650 m/8700 ft; SHUDDER MOUNTAIN 2680 m/8800 ft; QUIVER PEAK 2680 m/8800 ft

The main eastern summits of the Spearhead Range.
FRA: A.J. Campbell Garibaldi survey party—1928.
This area can be reached from the Decker-Trorey col; from Saucer Lake by following the B.C. Hydro powerline road and the prominent topographic shelf above Wedge Creek, and then dropping to Wedge Creek and ascending Tremor Glacier; or from Singing Pass via the Naden Glacier and the Platform Glacier. The northeast ridge of Tremor is not difficult in summer from the Tremor-Shudder col, but winter trips require a traverse to the south or southeast ridges at the summit. Both Shudder and Quiver can be ascended from the Platform Glacier. Quiver has two peaks, the southern being higher and easily attained from the N. It can also be reached and climbed directly from The Ripsaw. The peaks received their names from an earthquake which attended the first ascent party while they were making surveys from the summit of Tremor.

NORTHERN GARIBALDI PARK

The highest summits in the park, and the best weather, are found N of Wedge and Billygoat creeks. The peaks tend to be rubbly, but some of the faces are good granite. Except for the mountains on the north and east fringes, the best approach is via Wedgemount Lake (*B8*).

WEDGEMOUNT LAKE BLUFFS 2410 m/7900 ft

A prominent series of bluffs on the south side of Wedgemount Lake offer rock climbs of up to 460 m/1500 ft relief on good rock. These are the north buttresses of **RETHEL MOUNTAIN** (2560 m/8400 ft), whose summit can be reached by scrambling up over scree ledges to a col separating Rethel from Parkhurst Mountain and then by following the divide. The Rethel Creek valley can also be used. Ribs and gullies cover the bluff and offer lines from a stiff Class 4 to aid. Rock is generally firm, with excellent holds. A few routes have already been put up; enough that the record is confused. One of the few features on this bluff sufficiently distinctive to describe is a series of three small towers on a ridge directly across from the cabin on the lake. This ridge is an enjoyable half-day climb along the crest to the central tower (*FA: J. Oswald, E. Zenger—1972*), with difficulties up to moderate 5th Class. The face of this tower E of the ridge, involving moves up to Class 5.5, was also climbed in 1972 (*R. Barley, P. Koedt, P. Rowat*). The highest tower on this ridge is best reached by a short rappel from the main divide. (Ref: *CAJ* 1973, p. 62.)

Wedge Mountain   1.) North arête   2.) North face variation   3.) North couloir   4.) West ridge
variation   5.) West ridge

Dick Culbert

WEDGE MOUNTAIN 2904 m/9527 ft

Highest summit in Garibaldi Park.

FRA: N. Carter, C. Townsend—1923.

West ridge: Reach the col between Wedge and easy **PARKHURST MOUNTAIN** (2500 m/8200 ft) to the NW by hiking up the glacier from Wedgemount Lake (*B8*), or by climbing from Rethel or Wedge creeks (*B8a*). Parkhurst is a pleasant hike from the col. To reach Wedge, swing S to the main divide and ascend steep, loose talus on its southwestern slopes to level summit ridge. Takes 4 hours up from cabin. Unless you are a real scree freak choose another route for ascending and take advantage of the spring glissading possibilities on the west ridge for descending.

North couloir: *FRA: R. Driscoll, K. Legg—February 1981.* This is the first long couloir on the western end of the north face. It involves steep snow climbing to 55°.

North arête: *FRWA: D. Fox, R. Thomich—December 28, 1985.* From Wedgemount Lake, ascend glacier to the low point in main Weart-Wedgemount divide, or if bergschrund permits, climb Wedgemount Glacier directly to the col at the toe of Wedge's north ridge. Ascend steep snow or ice to just W of summit. Difficulty depends on conditions; the climb is reasonably easy in spring and Class 4 when icy. Takes 4–5 hours up from cabin. As snow lines go, this one is hard to beat.

North face: *FA: G. Mumford, E. Zenger—August 1974.* The steep face to the left of the north ridge, it features steep snow with the occasional mixed move and involves 7 pitches of climbing. Approach via Weart Glacier. First ascent party also climbed the snow gully immediately right (W) of the north face.

Northeast side: From Weart Glacier, climb to and up Wedge's Class 3 east ridge. On the upper part, swing onto the glacier on the northeast side. The northeast arête has also been used.

South side: The south side of Wedge can be reached either from Wedge Pass or by traversing from the west ridge. As a route, it has little to recommend it. A few yahoos have been known to ski down the south face, a rather serious 1520 m/5000 ft drop, getting to 35–40° in places. To return, head back to Wedgemount Lake via the Parkhurst-Wedge col NW of Wedge Mountain.

LESSER WEDGE MOUNTAIN 2710 m/8900 ft

From the west: Ascend via the Weart Glacier to the col between Wedge and Lesser Wedge, and from here scramble to the summit. May be Class 4 under spring conditions.

Northwest face: *FA: D. Adshead, S. Oates—July 8, 1984.* Reach the base by crossing the head of Weart Glacier. Snow and ice to 45° lead directly to the summit. A bergschrund must be negotiated at the base.

MT. WEART 2870 m/9400 ft

A sprawling summit above and NE of Wedgemount Lake.

FA: B. Cook, P. Tait—1932.

Southeast ridge: From Wedgemount Lake (*B8*), ascend the east arm of Wedgemount Glacier overlooking Weart Glacier, then climb Weart by its southeast shoulder and south ridge. Neither very difficult nor inspiring. Takes 3 hours up from cabin.

Southwest ridge: The Armchair Glacier on the west side of Weart is gained directly from Wedgemount Lake. Ascend the glacier to reach the gap behind the 2710 m/8900 ft summit on Weart's southwest ridge. You can also reach this gap by traversing over the glacier from the southeast ridge route, or by traversing the 2710 m/8900 ft summit, but the latter is tricky and not recommended. Ascent from the gap is Class 2–3. Takes 3–4 hours up from Wedgemount Lake.

West face: Gain Armchair Glacier on the west side of Weart from Wedgemount Lake (*B8*). Several routes have been put up on the headwall of the west face. These are largely Class 4 on reasonable rock, although loose in places. The central rib leading directly to summit (*FA: T. Clayton, P. Glennon, G. Kozel—1971*) is Class 4 and requires 4 hours.

Northwest ridge: Ascend from Wedgemount Lake (*B8*) to the col isolating Mt. Cook on the main ridge NW of Weart. From here, climb SW over a minor summit (not difficult) and continue along Weart's north ridge. There are some short Class 3–4 steps involved in gaining the middle peak of Weart, and some climbing on loose rock to continue to south summit. A fairly full day.

THE OWLS 2710 m/8900 ft
Two stubby pinnacles on the east shoulder of Weart.
FA: K. Carpenter, T. Stafford—1966.
These have been climbed without much difficulty by their south sides from Weart Glacier (*B8*).

MT. MOE 2680 m/8800 ft
Located on the divide N of Mt. Weart.
FA: C. Jennings, J. Nairn—1967.
From Wedgemount Lake (*B8*), climb to the 2620 m/8600 ft saddle on the ridge between Mt. Weart and **MT. COOK** (2680 m/8800ft), and continue NW to Mt. Moe's south ridge, a Class 3 rock scramble. Mt. Cook itself is easily climbed from its col with Weart. The easy summits SE of Mystery Glacier may be reached by traversing around Moe's east flank, but they are a longish day return from cabin.

EUREKA MOUNTAIN 2530 m/8300 ft
Located N of the pass between Weart and Needles glaciers.
FA: Large BCMC party—1968.
From Weart Glacier, climb to the col between Eureka and the 2560 m/8400 ft **OASIS MOUNTAIN** to the N and follow the divide to the summit. Oasis can also be reached without difficulty from this col. (*FA: C. Fenner, D. Lazenby—1957.*)

MT. JAMES TURNER 2686 m/8812 ft
A jagged summit S of the Chaos Glacier and SE of Wedge Mountain.
FA: N. Carter, C. Townsend—1923.
Cross Weart Glacier (*B8*) and traverse E to the head of Chaos or Needles Glacier. Head S, then swing around the south side of jagged Fingerpost Ridge. The peak may be reached from the Turner Glacier by loose gullies in the southwest face leading to upper south ridge (Class 3), or by the less attractive route up to northwestern arête (Class 4). Rock is poor. This is a strenuous 2 day trip, and parties are advised to camp near the divide W of Weart Glacier.

MT. NEAL 2530 m/8300 ft
A glaciated summit at the head of Carter Glacier, 5.6 km/3.5 mi E of Mt. Weart. Named after Dr. Neal Carter, an early mapmaker and mountaineer in the Coast Mountains.
FA: A. Ede, F. McConnel, B. Nicholson—1949.
From Weart Glacier (*B8*), cross the divide to E and descend the northern part of Needles Glacier. From the broad pass at the head of Ure Creek, climb up the west face of Mt. Neal to its south ridge. Not very difficult, but a 3 day trip from roads. (Ref: *CAJ* 1968, p. 199.)

MT. CURRIE 2596 m/8518 ft
The prominent summit rising S of Pemberton.
FA: A.J. Campbell Topographical Survey—1920s (lower northwest peak).
Once a popular hike with Pemberton district residents, Mt. Currie has been climbed less frequently since the Green River bridge was washed out. The best approach now is probably overland from the Mt. Weart area, although this would take 3 days

return. Another option is to use a boat to get across the Green River.

From the west: Ascend old logging spurs to the basin under the northwest ridge of Mt. Currie. Ascend the west branch of the ridge bounding the basin, reaching more open country at 1520 m/5000 ft and continuing on to summit. The 6 hour hike from the valley is not particularly aesthetic, but there is a good view.

Northwest face: After crossing Green River (boat necessary) keep left. Roads climb to 850 m/2800 ft, and from where they end, you can hike around the ridge to the E into the cirque under the northwest face. Climb timber to W of stream here to basin at its head. The northwest face is Class 3 on poor rock. The main north buttress is also loose with one steep section. A long day return from river, so parties usually camp in basin.

Northwest ridge of northeast peak: *FA: D. Jones, K. Kraft, D. Serl, G. Shannan—June 3, 1979.* This ridge drops steeply towards the Green River from the 2470 m/8100 ft minor summit 1 km NE of Mt. Currie. The ridge bounds the north face on the W. Go left after crossing the Green River (boat needed) and get across the creek draining the northwest face of Currie as soon as possible. Climb directly uphill, staying somewhat to right. The route is 760 m/2500 ft long and reaches a stiff Class 4. To reach the high but gentle summits on the divide SE of Mt. Currie, take the route from the W (listed above), and swing around the south flanks at about the 2000 m/6560 ft level, traversing into the high basin W of divide. In 1974, G. Woodsworth traversed all summits on the Currie massif and descended to the Lillooet River via the long northeast ridge (minor Class 3).

North face: *FA: P. Kindree, W. Robinson—late 1970s.* This climb has one of the most spectacular vertical rises of any route in the guidebook. Take the large couloir dropping from the summit area and just crampon right on up, keeping to the left. Do some calf raises before you go. A fine winter workout.

GUNSIGHT PEAK 2380 m/7800 ft

A notched summit rising W of Little Lillooet Lake.

FA: J. Clarke—1967.

From the road on the west side of Little Lillooet Lake, ascend to the S of the unnamed canyonous creek flowing into the head of the lake. From the pass NNW of Gunsight Peak, traverse into the col at 2160 m/7100 ft on its W and climb slopes to E to gain southwest ridge, traversing the notch between summits. Class 3 and rotten. The 2380 m/7800 ft summit W of Gunsight, and peaks further N, can be climbed easily from the intervening col.

McBRIDE RANGE

MT. SIR RICHARD 2710 m/8900 ft

A remote, sprawling and heavily glaciated massif at the head of Cheakamus River. The summit is easy to ascend, but difficult to approach. Named for an early B.C. premier. Most ascents in this range are made by ski touring parties.

FA: P. Brock, D. Munday, P. Munday—1937.

From the Cheakamus River and Lake: The first ascent party skied up the Cheakamus Lake and River (*B6*) to the Ubyssey Glacier in spring. After snow leaves and the lake breaks up, the river valley is very bushy and the north side of the lake is not only unpleasant but blocked by a tricky cliff band near its northwest end. (Ref: *CAJ* 1936, p. 71.)

From Tuwasus Creek roads: First used by J. Clarke in 1968. From roads in lower Tuwasus Creek (*C2*), climb SW to open country. From 1800 m/5500 ft, follow the divide SW, swing S of 2370 m/7800 ft peak and drop to the glacier beyond. The 2650 m/8700 ft **NIVALIS MOUNTAIN** 4 km NE of Sir Richard can then be traversed, and the glacier crossed, to reach the summit of Sir Richard without difficulty. The long ridge starting SW of the mouth of Billygoat Creek was also used in 1968. Takes 4 days return.

From Singing Pass: In 1971, J. Clarke returned to this area via the Fitzsimmons Range and Naden Pass (*B7*). He climbed peaks E of the pass, then traversed the slopes beyond, dropping to the snout of McBride Glacier. (This route might also be done from the snout of Diavolo Glacier.) The glacier leads directly to Mt. Sir Richard. Strenuous 3 days.

From Garibaldi Lake: In 1969, a VOC party climbed Mt. Sir Richard from Garibaldi Lake (*B5*) via the McBride Range. The ascent was easy from The Gatekeeper while the descent went down the McBride Glacier.

TENAS PEAK 2260 m/7400 ft
Located 6.4 km/4 mi NE of Mt. Sir Richard and E of The Orphans. *FA: J. Clarke—1968*. The peak can be easily climbed via west or southwest ridges.

PEAK 7800 2380 m/7800 ft
Located 2 km ESE of Tenas Peak. *FA: J. Clarke—1968*. A pleasant scramble via the south-southeast ridge.

THE ORPHANS 2190 m/7200 ft
Twin summits 5 km NE of Mt. Sir Richard on the north side of "Nivalis Glacier." *FA: J. Clarke—1971*. NTD all the way.

NIVALIS MOUNTAIN 2650 m/8700 ft
Located 3 km NE of Mt. Sir Richard. *FA: J. Clarke—1968*. NTD. This mountain was traversed en route from Tuwasus Creek to Mt. Sir Richard.

TALON PEAK 2410 m/7900 ft
Located 4 km due E of Mt. Sir Richard. *FA: J. Clarke—1971*. This peak can be easily traversed from the N en-route to **ADIEU MOUNTAIN** (2350 m/7700 ft) to the SSW, which is easily climbed along the connecting ridge. (*FA: J. Clarke—1971*.)

THE LECTURE CUTTERS 2560 m/8400 ft
Three rock peaks on the ridge NW of Mt. Sir Richard and across the Ubyssey Glacier from Veeocee Mountain. *FA: J. Clarke—1971*.
These summits can be climbed from the ridge which connects them to Mt. Sir Richard (see entry this chapter), and they have been entirely traversed from the N

without meeting difficulties higher than Class 3. Many names in this area memorialize the long association the Varsity Outdoor Club has had with this corner of Garibaldi Park.

THE GATEKEEPER 2350 m/7700 ft
About 2.5 km SW of Sir Richard. *FA: VOC party—1969.* NTD.

VEEOCEE MOUNTAIN 2380 m/7800 ft
An easy summit on the west side of Ubyssey Glacier. *FA: R. Burton, P. Macek, P. Thompson—1966.* Approach col to the S from Ubyssey Glacier, then climb the south ridge.

"FORGER GLACIER PEAKS"
This name appears to include **PEAK 7700** (2350 m/7700 ft) just E of Drop Pass (*FA: VOC party—1969*) and **PEAK 7900** (2410 m/7900 ft) SW of Snow Bowl Glacier (*FA: J. Clarke, B. Samson—1972*). Neither is a difficult ascent.

OUTLIER PEAK 2440 m/8000 ft
Located 6 km/4 mi E of Naden Pass. *FRA: J. Clarke—1971.* From Naden Pass, traverse E over **PEAK 7600** (2320 m) and 2260 m/7400 ft **CARCAJOU PEAK**, and descend beyond to the west ridge of Outlier. This is a scramble. A 3 day return trip from cars.

SNOWCAP LAKE AREA

MT. PITT 2500 m/8200 ft
A remote summit standing W of Snowcap Lake. Pitt is one of the grand sentinels of Garibaldi Park, and a noble objective for non air-supported parties.
FA: C. Jenkins, E. Jenkins—1938.
From the west: The mountain was originally approached in a 5 day blitz from the Garibaldi Lake area. This route involves following the divide around the head of Pitt River watershed, crossing two deep breaks in the divide running SE from Forger Glacier Peaks. Traverse on snow under the west face of the north peak and climb a gully to the notch between the two peaks. The final ridge is loose but not difficult.
East ridge: *FA: J. Hutton, D. McLaurin—1959.* Approach from Snowcap Lake (*C3*) via Roller Coaster Ridge and the Solitude Glacier. A 20 m/70 ft downclimb off the east summit can be avoided by traversing S into a snow-gully, which leads to a loose couloir, which is followed to the highest summit. The final climb is Class 3. A 1 day return trip from the lake.

GREENMANTLE MOUNTAIN 2375 m/7800 ft
Located NE of Snowcap Lake.
FRA: W. Dean, J. Roddick—1955.
The summits NE of Snowcap Lake (*C3*) are easy and pleasant ascents from the lakeshore. Greenmantle has also been climbed from the Lillooet River by following the divide N of Snowcap Creek and traversing over 2345 m/7700 ft **THREE**

BEARS MOUNTAIN (*K. Haring—1978*). **TUWASUS MOUNTAIN** (2165 m/7100 ft) is possibly unclimbed. A ski ascent of **GREYMANTLE MOUNTAIN** (2345 m/7700 ft) was made in June 1984 (*A. Frid, S. Sheffield, B. Waddington*). This may have been the first ascent. The glacier between these peaks is correctly designated the Icemantle Glacier, not the Snowcap Glacier as shown on some topographic sheets.

SNOWCAP ICEFIELD
This is the large glacier S of Snowcap Lakes between the heads of Snowcap Creek and Iceworm Creek. Best access to the icefield from Snowcap Lakes (*C3*) is either up the rocky ridge immediately S of the causeway between the lakes, or via the Glacier de Fleur des Neiges (longer but easier). All the summits of this group are easily ascended from the icefield. (Ref: *BCM* 1982, p. 18; *CAJ* 1979, map p. 60, p. 72.) The highest, **SNOWCAP PEAK** (2410 m/7900 ft), was climbed in 1955 by W. Dean and A. Nutting.

MISTY ICEFIELD
This is the glacial complex straddling the divide between Pitt and Lillooet rivers and S of Snowcap Lake. For convenience, the region S to Remote Peak is described under this heading. The icefield is one of the closest glacial complexes to Vancouver. This area was named and geologically mapped in 1955 by a Geological Survey party under J. Roddick, but seldom visited prior to 1971 when a party of four (R. Burton, J. Frizell, S. Golling, B. Narod) traversed the area (Ref: *VOCJ* 1971, p. 141). Later that year J. Clarke made a solo trip through the southern complex picking off most of the unclimbed summits. (Ref: *CAJ* 1972, p. 70.)

The easiest approach to the northern icefields is by flying into Snowcap Lake, while the southern part may be reached in a day via logging roads extending up the ridge N of Corbold Creek from Pitt Lake. These roads are described in the Coquitlam/Pitt section. The lake at the snout of Stave Glacier has also been used for floatplane landing. (Ref: *VOCJ* 1971, p. 141; *CAJ* 1984, p. 78.) Weather can be very, very bad in this area—take *Gone With the Wind* or equivalent for reading material.

STAVE PEAK 2350 m/7700 ft
Located N of head of Stave Glacier.
FA: J. Clarke—1971.
Stave Peak may be ascended by scrambling up the north ridge (gained by couloir from W) or by climbing up the east ridge. **MISTY PEAK** (2230 m/7300 ft), which stands to the W, displays a row of rock needles when seen from NE. From the Stave-Misty col, cross bergschrund to the northeast side and climb steep snow to between needles and summit; then climb Class 3 rock up ridge to peak. The 2290 m/7500 ft summit NE of Stave Peak has been traversed from the N without difficulty, and has also been climbed by the southwest rock ridge.

KATZIE PEAK 2320 m/7600 ft
The highest of summits SW of the head of Stave Glacier.
FA: J. Clarke—1971.

Katzie may be climbed from the N over easy snow and adjacent (to NE) **HALKOMELEM PEAK** (2290 m/7500 ft) via its east ridge. **NIMBUS PEAK** (2190 m/7200 ft) 2.4 km WNW of Katzie is likewise an easy ascent, and minor **SKAKALA** (2130 m/7000 ft), which is immediately SW of Katzie, is climbed on the north side. **STALO PEAK** (2230 m/7300 ft), located 1.6 km SE of Katzie at the head of Shale Creek, is climbed from the NW over snow.

NEBULA PEAK 2260 m/7400 ft
The highest summit S of Stave Glacier but E of the Katzie group.
FA: J. Clarke—1971.
Reach all summits in this group over snow from the Stave Glacier. None are difficult. The 2130 m/7000 ft summit on the ridge to the S, however, is Class 3 on good rock on its north ridge (*J. Clarke—1972*). The prominent intervening **BETSTEL PINNACLE** is unclimbed at the present.

PEAK 7000 2130 m/7000 ft
Located S of Stave Glacier at the northeast corner of the head of Corbold Creek.
FA: R. Culbert, A. Ellis, G. Woodsworth—1963.
The summit is reached from Stave Glacier by swinging around the west side of the southwest ridge, or by climbing the south ridge from glacier W of the head of Corbold Creek.

PEAK 6700 2042 m/6700 ft
Located 3 km SE of Peak 7000.
FA: R. Burton, J. Frizell, S. Golling, B. Narod—1972.
Easily ascended via west face, though more interesting scrambles have been done.

PUKULKUL PEAK 2100 m/6900 ft
An isolated summit on Stave-Corbold divide 3 km S of head of Corbold Creek. This and the summit S to Remote Peak are in northern Golden Ears Park.
FA: R. Culbert, A. Ellis, G. Woodsworth—1963.
North face: The first ascent route. From glacier to the N, climb the north face on ice, bypassing bergschrund by Class 3 rock on the right. The tower on the north side was climbed by the first ascent party by Class 4 rock on its east face. The summit is easily ascended from the S.
East ridge: *FA: J. Cicero, L. Suchy, M. Thompson—1983.* Climb over the east gendarme (Class 3) and thrash to the summit. The false summit to the W offers a short lead of Class 5.

OLD PIERRE MOUNTAIN 2190 m/7200 ft
Located on Stave-Corbold divide, 3 km NNW of Remote Peak.
FA: J. Clarke—1971.
The summit was gained by its southeast buttress, described as sinuous and rotten, composed of black, slatey rock. Class 3. Gullies on the south side have also been climbed; the bergschrund may present a problem late in the season. Old Pierre has also been climbed from the E, swinging around onto the north face to reach the western summit. A rugged route with bergschrund problem. (*K. Haring, P. Olig—1972.*)

SKAYUK PEAK 2010 m/6600 ft
Located 2 km ENE of Old Pierre. *FA: J. Clarke—1971.* An easy ascent from the western side.

REMOTE PEAK 2100 m/6900 ft
Located 9 km/5.5 mi NE of Alvin. *FA: Topographic survey party.* This peak is easily ascended from the NW.

PILUK PEAK 2070 m/6800 ft
Located 2 km WNW of Remote Peak. *FA: J. Clarke—1971.* Scramble up snow to the S of the east ridge. The east ridge itself is reported to be Class 5.

FIRE SPIRES
This group of reddish rock peaks stands E of the head of Stave River. It is most easily approached from the end of the highest spur road on the south side of Fire Creek (*C4*). Ascend through moderate bush to a lake at 1430 m/4700 ft, and from there climb over and around the ridge to the lake below Spark Peak. This area could also theoretically be reached from the road in the north fork of Sloquet Creek valley, but the approach would be a horror show (*C5*).

MATKW PEAK 2100 m/6900 ft
Located about 2 km ESE of Terrarosa Lake.
FA: P. Adam, B. Edmonds, W. Frank, B. Gabriel, D. Joseph—July 16, 1984.
Ascend snow on the south face, then finish via the narrow southeast ridge. Class 3. The name means "to play with fire" in the language of the Lil'wat Indians.

FLICKER PEAK 2260 m/7400 ft
A steep summit about 1 km SE of Matkw Peak.
FA: R. Culbert, A. Ellis, G. Woodsworth—1963.
From Terrarosa Glacier, climb scree ramp on face of Flash to col between Flicker and Flash, and scramble up a gully to the summit.

FLASH PEAK 2230 m/7300 ft
Located immediately SE of Flicker and marked by 4 summit gendarmes.
FA: R. Culbert, A. Ellis, G. Woodsworth—1963.
From Terrarosa Glacier, scramble up south ridge of Flash. Bypass the eastern (highest) summit gendarme on the north face and climb it from SW. Class 4. The farthest western gendarme is of nearly equal height and is reached by traversing over intervening peaklet.

THE FLAMES 2200 m/7200 ft
A triple rock summit rising E of Pyrotechnic Pass, which forms the height of land for Terrarosa Glacier. The western summit is the highest.
FA: J. Clarke—1972.
From Terrarosa Glacier the western Flame is a scramble via its west face. The central peak (*FA: R. Culbert, A. Ellis, G. Woodsworth—1963*) and eastern peak are scrambles on poor rock from the S.

EMBER PEAK 2260 m/7400 ft
The highest and southernmost summit of the Fire Spires, located on the north side of Terrarosa Glacier.
FA: H. Genschorek, I. Kay, J. Lintott—1950.12b
Scree slopes on the south side provide an easy route from Terrarosa Glacier. A narrow snow gully on the east side is a more sporting line.
North ridge: *FA: P. Adam, B. Edmonds, W. Frank, B. Gabriel, D. Joseph—July 17, 1984.* A short route of low Class 5 difficulty.

SPARK PEAK 2040 m/6700 ft
A reddish summit about 1 km NE of Ember.
FA: R. Culbert, A. Ellis, G. Woodsworth—1963.
Swing to S of Ember Peak on snow and descend NE down glacier to the south side of Spark. Scramble up loose rock on the southwest side to summit.

ASHES PEAK 2100 m/6900 ft
Located 2 km S of Ember across the Terrarosa Glacier.
FA: M. Feller, M. Force, P. Parrotta—1979.
Climb the northwest side from the glacier. NTD. Reportedly has an impressive east face.

MT. GLENDINNING 2040 m/6700 ft
Located S of the Fire Spire group.
FA: R. Culbert, A. Ellis, G. Woodsworth—1963.
This rock peak may be approached either from the Fire Spires group to the N or through bush from the main fork of Sloquet Creek (*C5*) to the SE. The highest summit is one of the peaks on the north end. It is easily approached over snow to N. The south summit is a rock scramble from the pass to the S.

Chapter 4
Squamish River and Pemberton Icefield

BOUNDARIES:
North: Meager Creek, Lillooet River
East: Highway 99
South: Ashlu Creek
West: Elaho River, Ashlu Creek

FOREST SERVICE OFFICE:
Squamish Forest District
P.O. Box 1970
Squamish, B.C. V0N 3G0
898-9671

LOGGING COMPANIES:

Empire Logging Division (Weldwood)
3150 Cleveland Street
Squamish, B.C. V0N 3G0
892-5244
(Squamish, Ashlu, and Elaho drainages)

Malloch and Moseley Logging
2610 Sooke Road
Victoria, B.C. V9B 1Y2
932-5435 (Whistler)
(Brandywine Creek, west Callaghan)

Harnor Logging
Box 1160
Squamish, B.C. V0N 3G0
892-3613
(Roe Creek)

Valleau Logging
Box 1160
Squamish, B.C. V0N 3G0
894-6612
(Ryan River)

Pacific Forest Products - Blakey Logging
Box 357, Pemberton, B.C. V0N 2L0
(Rutherford Creek)

MAPS:
Federal:
92 G/14 Cheakamus River
92 J/4 Princess Louisa Inlet
92 J/7 Pemberton
Provincial:
92 G/NW
Outdoor Recreation Map of B.C. #3
(Whistler-Garibaldi)

92 J/3 Brandywine Falls
92 J/5 Clendenning Creek
92 J/11 North Creek

92 J/W half

Introduction

The Squamish River and Pemberton Icefield region is a four season alpine adventure land. In spring, Tricouni and Brew meadows are attractive for hiking, while the ever-popular Rainbow Lake trail now boasts almost a kilometre of boardwalk, so that even the most reluctant hikers can now be assured of keeping their feet dry.

Peaks in this area are some of Vancouver's most popular ski-touring objectives. Sproatt, Rainbow and Ipsoot receive plenty of attention from the bindings and boards crowd. Since 1974 improved access into the area around Brandywine Mountain, and the building of a cabin near Brew Lake have brought increasing numbers of people to the high divide between Callaghan Lake and Tricouni Mountain, where large snowfalls accumulate each winter. The complete trip down the divide makes a nice miniature "Haute Route," and takes one past the craggy towers of Mount Fee.

The traverse of the Pemberton Icefield, first done in 1969, has been repeated several times. It offers a more remote traverse than several of the favourites in Garibaldi Park, passing through country which is surprisingly little known, despite its proximity to Vancouver.

There is some good general mountaineering potential in the Squamish region. The elegant north ridge of Cayley is a good spring climb on snow, Tricouni is a popular scramble, and Mount Fee is an unusual ascent on large, loose, exfoliating slabs. Some of the climbs are difficult because of poor rock quality. The Vulcan's Thumb is the most notorious of the unclimbed problems; plans to waterbomb the tower and make the ascent with ice gear have so far not materialized.

Improved access in the northern part of this area has focused attention on the climbing potential of granitic peaks, such as Mount Ashlu, and one exceptional route has already been climbed there. It seems likely that over the next few years this northern section of the region will excite the most attention from the more exploration-minded of the mountaineering fraternity.

Approaches

A. FROM HIGHWAY 99

Highway 99 leads N from Squamish, first along the Squamish River and then along the Cheakamus and Green rivers. It eventually reaches the town of Pemberton on the Lillooet River. The highway is a major access route for the eastern and northern parts of this section. All distances are measured from the Squamish traffic light.

1. Roe Creek (32.3 km/20.1 mi): Drive left over the Cheakamus River bridge, then left again immediately after you cross the railway tracks. This bridge is sometimes locked but a key should be available at the lodge. Follow the logging road around a switchback to the right to a gate at 2.7 km. Harnor Logging (Squamish) has keys to the gate but they may be reluctant to give them to you during the fire season. The road forks immediately after the gate. The right fork goes 7.5 km/4.7 mi beyond the gate to 1130 m/3700 ft (two-wheel drive condition to 1000 m/3300 ft). A trail up to Tricouni Peak starts at "Cabin Lake" (GR 867359) about 2 km beyond the gate. The left fork goes up Chance Creek to an elevation of 730 m/2400 ft (stay right at next fork). This road nearly reaches the divide, which can be easily gained from the west side via High Falls Creek (*C3*).

2. Mt. Brew trail (41.4 km/25.7 mi): Park in Brandywine Provincial Park lot and walk S along the railway tracks. After about 2 km, the tracks turn right, then left again; the trail starts just near the end of the left bend. The lower portion of the trail runs through forest, but higher up it crosses talus slopes. It leads to "Brew Lake" at 1430 m/4700 ft. Roe Creek provides safer access in winter.

3. Brandywine Creek road (43.9 km/27.3 mi): This two-wheel drive road climbs high in the Brandywine Creek valley. It was formerly locked, but the gate has recently been taken down. If it reappears, the key is available from Mallock and Mosely Logging, Whistler and Squamish offices. Proceed past an old sawmill building and take the first right, which is a switchback ascending a hill. If proceeding to Brew or Brandywine, continue up the valley. The first right branch after this switchback ascends the flank of Metal Dome to a pass, then drops into Callaghan Creek. The first left fork, after about 4.5 km, crosses Brandywine Creek and climbs up the north side of Brew. For Brew, take the first left fork after the bridge; for Mt. Fee go right. Yet another branch road (Branch 12) climbs right 5 km from the highway: it climbs to 1370 m/4500 ft on the southeast flank of Metal Dome.

4. Callaghan Creek roads (Northair Mine road) (46.3 km/28.8 mi): At 4.2 km on the Northair Mine road, a marked fork to the left leads to Callaghan Lake (17 km/10.6 mi). Mt. Callaghan can be reached from the north side of the lake. The Callaghan Creek valley is a confusing jumble of logging roads which lead to most corners of the drainage. The right fork of the Northair Mine road climbs to Northair Mine at 1000 m/3300 ft and provides alternate access to the Mt. Sproatt area, and beyond to Rainbow Lake.

5. Alpha Road and Rainbow Lake trail (54 km/33.6 mi): Alpha road turns left off the main highway and swings around to run along the west side of Alta Lake. Go past the Youth Hostel (4.5 km from highway turnoff) to a parking area where Twentyone Mile Creek crosses the road. The trail here (which follows old logging roads in some early stretches) is well signposted and, although muddy in spots, has recently been upgraded with 1/2 km of boardwalk. The trail eventually leads to Rainbow Lake, a lovely basin at 1460 m/4800 ft. At 1370 m/4500 ft the trail crosses to the north side of the valley, and just before this a rougher trail climbs S up the side valley to "Gin and Tonic Lakes" at 1430 m/4700 ft.

5a. Nineteen Mile Creek roads: Old roads begin in the Alpine Meadows subdivision and ascend both side of the creek, giving access to the steep bowls on the west side of Rainbow Mountain.

5b. Sixteen Mile Creek road: This old road is used by cross-country skiers to gain the rolling ridges N and W of Green Lake.

6. Soo River road (76 km/47 mi): This new road crosses to the north side of Soo River and follows it for several kilometres. May provide access to eastern Pemberton Icefield area in the future.

7. Rutherford Creek road (84.6 km/52.6 mi): This road goes W just N of the Rutherford Creek bridge, climbing to 1130 m/3700 ft on the southwest side of the valley, W of Mt. Ipsoot.

B. FROM ASHLU CREEK

The Ashlu main line has advanced a considerable distance up Ashlu Creek since 1974; it now continues some 64 km/40 mi up the north side of the creek. The main road is mostly two-wheel drive but is impassable 1 km before crossing Shortcut

Creek, which drains Rugged Lake. It deteriorates to four-wheel drive condition for about 3 km before that point, though road work allowed two-wheel drive passage in July '84. There is a gate at the start of the Ashlu main line which Weldwood generally does not lock. On occasion, Osprey Mines, which also uses the road, will lock the gate. A key is available from Weldwood (Empire) in Squamish. During high fire-hazard periods the gate is locked and the key is unavailable. In winter 1984, the road was plowed to milepost 29. At present the main trunk road crosses the creek at mileposts 22, 25, 32; major branch roads are described below. All distances are measured from the Squamish townsite and agree with those posted on the logging roads.

1. Branch A-100 (34.6 km/21.5 mi): Climbs to about 1100 m/3600 ft on the divide N of Ashlu Creek.

2. Branch A-300 (37.5 km/23 mi): Joins Branch A-100 above.

3. Branch A-600 (40.2 km/25 mi): Crosses Ashlu Creek and runs along the south side of the creek to the Osprey Mine about 1 km beyond Roaring Creek. From Branch A-600 there are two spurs.

3a. Pokosha Creek road: Climbs S to about 850 m/2800 ft on the slope W of Pokosha Creek and to 760 m/2500 ft on the eastern flank.

3b. Marten Creek road: Climbs to about 1040 m/3400 ft on slopes E of Marten Creek (W of Coin Creek). Road graded to 820 m/2700 ft in 1984.

4. Branch A-700 (40.9 km/25.4 mi): After crossing Ashlu Creek at milepost 25, this branch may be followed to about 910 m/3000 ft (towards ''Stuyvesant Creek''). The road continues past Pykett Creek to almost 1250 m/4100 ft on the broad ridge SE of Pykett Peak.

5. Branch A-800 (45.1 km/28 mi): Climbs to the 610 m/2000 ft level on Pykett Creek.

6. Tatlow Creek road (51.5 km/32 mi): The road crosses to the south side of Ashlu Creek. At this point, however, it gains little elevation on the east side of Tatlow Creek. Weldwood has no plans at this time to push farther up Tatlow Creek. A road presently runs to 1040 m/3400 ft. on the north side of Falk Creek.

C. FROM THE SQUAMISH RIVER ROAD

Distances are again measured from Squamish townsite and agree with those posted on the road.

1. Ashlu Creek road (33.8 km/21 mi): See B above.

2. Branch 100 (35.1 km/21.8 mi): Before the power station, a rough road (currently four-wheel drive) climbs E, then traverses S behind a microwave relay on the 910 m/3000 ft shoulder on Cloudburst Mountain. It is currently quite overgrown.

3. High Falls Creek road (38.5 km/23.9 mi): Climbs NE and swings into the High Falls Creek valley near 600 m/2000 ft. Ignore the spur to the left which is encountered after the initial switchback and continue straight ahead up the hill. The northern branch crosses High Falls Creek at an elevation of 760 m/2500 ft and continues northward along the west fork of High Falls Creek to 1190 m/3900 ft. A rough trail continues to ''Seagram Lakes.'' This is a good approach to the Tricouni area, and was in two-wheel drive condition in summer of 1985, although it is steep in parts. The southern branch (graded in 1984) climbs to 730 m/2400 ft on the northwest slopes of Cloudburst. Branch 220 splits near 370 m/1200 ft and climbs N along the side of the Squamish River valley for several kilometres to about 920 m/3000 ft.

4. Turbid Creek road (53.1 km/33 mi): Ascends the north side of Turbid Creek to a fork about 1.6 km from the Squamish main line. The right fork, probably impassable, climbs to 730 m/2400 ft on the south side of Mt. Cayley. The left fork rises to 490 m/1600 ft in an area which is currently being logged.

5. Elaho logging road systems (59.5 km/37 mi): See D below.

6. Branch S-200 (66.6 km/41.4 mi): This old road ascends eastward to about 1340 m/4400 ft. It might be used to gain **POWDER MOUNTAIN** area (the promotional name for snow domes N of Mt. Cayley) to the E. At the top, the road's left fork goes to 1340 m/4400 ft, although it is probably impassable. The right fork was worked on in 1984 and is in four-wheel drive condition to 1390 m/4400 ft.

7. Dipper Creek road (69.2 km/43 mi): The road crosses Squamish River and goes up the northeast side of Dipper Creek ("Headman Creek"). The road ends at the junction of Dipper Creek and "Carnival Creek," its main northern tributary. Provides access to the Blanca Lake area and gentle Exodus Peak.

8. Branch S-500 (69.5 km/43.2 mi): Runs to 1430 m/4700 ft in the valley of "Randall Creek," which drains from the northern boundary of the icefield N of Mt. Cayley. This road has been used to gain the Squamish-Cheakamus divide W of Callaghan Lake, and as an alternative approach to Mt. Callaghan. Four-wheel drive to 1430 m/4700 ft.

9. Branch S-900 (75.6 km/47 mi): Ascends the "Gestetner Creek" drainage to a point immediately S of "Little Ring Peak," and provides the quickest access to the Squamish Glacier.

D. FROM ELAHO LOGGING ROADS

The Elaho River system runs up the east side of the river to 86.9 km/54 mi (past Sims Creek). Future plans call for roads to be pushed further W towards Clendenning Creek, and for a bridge to be put across the Elaho which will give access up Sims Creek. At present, reaching the peaks on the west side of the Elaho River, such as Mt. Tinniswood and Mt. George Edwards, involves a yachting expedition. There are three branch roads.

1. Branch E-100: Just beyond the main bridge across the Squamish River, this road branches N and runs to several spurs which climb to about 600 m/2000 ft on the west side of the upper Squamish River.

2. Branch E-300: This branch begins just past the 66 km/41 mi mark, and gives four-wheel access up the east side of "Maude Frickett Creek," which drains Blanca Lake. In 1984, logging companies pushed this road system further N. Blanca Lake and nearby lakes are a 6 hour pack through mostly pleasant bush.

3. "Gazette Creek" road: Just past the 75.6 km/47 mi mark a branch road gives access up both sides of Gazette Creek (GR 592692 on 92 J/4). The bridge to the south side of the Elaho (just before 61.2 km/38 mi above the confluence with the Squamish River) has been washed out; Weldwood has no plans for replacing it in the near future. A boat crossing should be possible. The roads on the opposite side of the river lead a short distance up "Carol Creek" and "Shadow Creek."

E. FROM LILLOOET RIVER

From Pemberton, a road runs up the southwest side of Lillooet River past Pemberton

Meadows and carries on to well beyond South Creek. However, this road is washed out just before South Creek about 57 km/35.4 mi from Pemberton. Distances are measured from Pemberton.

1. Miller Creek road (5.5 km/3.4 mi): Immediately after the Miller Creek bridge, turn left (along dyke). Follow this road (possibly gated) for 1.5 km to a bridge (generally gated) that crosses the creek. Park here; cross the bridge and continue up the road on the south side of the creek. The road continues to 790 m/2600 ft, where it crosses the south fork. A cattle trail follows the ridge between the two forks to a ford at the lower end of the meadow in the north fork (about 1250 m/4100 ft). There is a dilapidated cabin (belonging to ranchers) at the beginning of the second set of meadows. The cattle track continues up to 1830 m/6000 ft on the ridge N of the meadows.

2. Ryan River roads (17.9 km/11.1 mi): Much logging is currently taking place here, and roads extend up the valley some 30 km (to 1000 m/3300 ft on the south side of the river). This may be a good access route to the Pemberton Icefield. For permission to use the road, ask at the homestead located at this road's junction with Lillooet River main line.

3. Meager Creek roads (60 km/37.3 mi): At 24 km/14.9 mi NW of Pemberton, cross Lillooet River and follow the main logging road (left at all forks) up the Lillooet valley to the Meager Creek turnoff 36 km/22.3 mi beyond the bridge. Stay left at forks in Meager Creek valley until the road crosses to the south side of the creek, then go right to the old hotsprings. Two roads continue up both sides of Meager Creek beyond hotsprings but both are gated and keys are generally unavailable. Some day, for fire fighting purposes, a road may join this valley to the Elaho. These roads took a tremendous beating in October 1984, and floods destroyed much of the roadbed. The Meager Creek bridge and the main road have since been rebuilt.

3a. The VOC has recently built an 8-person hut at 1720 m/5650 ft, SW of Overseer Mountain. Park at hot springs and then continue 1 km up the road. After crossing a bridge located among a group of trees, continue on until you exit from the logging slash. Here, take a spur road left, then, from a clearing further up this spur road, follow a road heading due E uphill into timber. From the end of this road, ascend bush, keeping just S of the ridge between "Pika Creek" (which drains the glacier S of Pika Peak) and "Madhorse Creek" (which is the next creek to the SW); climb to about 1280 m/4200 ft. Contour SE along the bench beside Madhorse Creek for about 1 km, crossing the north fork on logs about 1/4 km above the junction with the south fork. Generally follow the south fork to the cabin. About 1/2 km from the glacier snout, turn sharply to NE and climb lateral moraine to the hut (GR 695965 on 92 J/11). There is a fair climb after one emerges from the trees. Alternatively, a broad, timbered ridge S of Madhorse Creek may be used. From spur roads that climb to 920 m/3000 ft, open timber leads to a subalpine bench that can be followed SE to cabin. This route is faster, but means gaining extra elevation.

Routes

CLOUDBURST MOUNTAIN 1870 m/6136 ft
A pleasant, gentle dome at the south end of the Squamish-Cheakamus divide.
Southwest slopes: The usual approach is via branch 100 of the Squamish River road

(*C2*). When you reach the microwave installation at 915 m/3000 ft, park and hike up through open forests and easy rockslide. Do not contour to the right, but continue to the shoulder at 1620 m/5300 ft, which overlooks the attractive tarns S of the summit. You can either continue up the southwest ridge to the peak, or you can drop to the tarns, swing to the right side of these, and climb the easy talus draw beyond to the upper southwest ridge. NTD; 3 hours up from road.

From the south: From the microwave station, continue on the rough road to the highest spur beyond Cloudburst Creek. Pick up a rough trail here. It runs to the tarns mentioned above, but is broken at two points by rockslides. At the first, make a contour traverse, and at the second, head for the upper righthand corner. Takes 5–6 hours up from the Squamish River road.

SQUAMISH-CHEAKAMUS DIVIDE

In recent years climbing and hiking in this area have increased markedly, which is not surprising when you consider how close it is to Vancouver, and how much good ski touring is available. Much of the rock is volcanic, and some spectacular features have been carved out in the Fee-Cayley area. The divide is one of the few in the Vancouver area which provides a continuous and aesthetic alpine hiking route. The trek from Callaghan Lake (*A4*) to Mt. Brew (*A2*) or Tricouni trail (*A1*) takes a leisurely 3 days. There is now a 12-person (VOC) cabin located at 1620 m/5300 ft on the ridge SSE of Mt. Brew.

TRICOUNI PEAK 2130 m/7000 ft
Highest of the summits between Roe and High Falls creeks.
FA: J. Cherry, A. Fraser, T. Fyles, H. Wynne-Edwards—1931.

From the south: You can easily ascend this summit from the divide to the S, which can be reached by climbing through meadows from the end of the Roe Creek trail (*A1*), or by ascending from the end of the road in High Falls Creek (*C3*). If you are following the main divide N from the Roe Creek trail, or climbing to **CYPRESS PEAK** (2070 m/6800 ft) located to the N, pass around the west side of Tricouni (and sub-peak) on exposed ledges. From the tarns at the head of High Falls Creek the main summit of Tricouni is Class 3–4 on the west side. Another enjoyable way to approach this group is from Mt. Brew (*A2*) or (*A3*). Tricouni is 3–4 hour return trip from where the ridge to Brew diverges from the main divide. There are a number of lesser peaks to climb in this area as well.

East ridge: Approach via the Roe Creek trail (*A1*). The ridge is the righthand skyline as seen from Tricouni meadows. Class 3 except for one short Class 4 lead just below the summit.

North ridge: *FA: F. Baumann and party—1970s.* An exposed, thin ridge-climb of Class 4 to low Class 5 difficulty. The ridge may be gained from High Falls Creek (*C3*) by contouring from the gap between Peak 6575 and Tricouni.

MT. BREW 1740 m/5700 ft
An alpine plateau S of Brandywine Creek and NW of Daisy Lake.
The Mt. Brew trail (*A2*) leads to Brew Lake, the largest of the alpine ponds here at 1430 m/4700 ft. The VOC hut is at 1620 m/5300 ft on the ridge N of the lake. There are several summits around the lake; the highest is the westernmost of the three

peaks, although the name is placed on the middle one on most maps. The whole area is pleasant for hiking, and the Squamish-Cheakamus divide is easily reached. The upper part of the trail is somewhat bushy after spring snow leaves. Mt. Brew has a dramatic exposure on the north side. The area can also be approached via Roe Creek (*A1*), which is longer but safer in winter, or via Brandywine Creek (*A3*), which is less safe in winter but more popular.

The twin towers of Mt. Fee from the west   Bruce Fairley

MT. FEE 2130 m/7000 ft
Two abrupt rock blades located on the Squamish-Cheakamus divide at the head of Brandywine Creek. The south peak is the higher.

When traversing along the divide, Fee is bypassed on the W. To approach from the W, use Turbid Creek logging roads (*C4, right fork*). Climb to a narrow ridge on the Turbid-Shovelnose divide, and ascend an old trail to about 1070 m/3500 ft on the divide. Fee may be approached directly from here. Pack to the turn in the Turbid-Shovelnose ridge at 1520 m/5000 ft, then drop E to camp near the head of Shovelnose Creek just W of Mt. Fee.

A better approach now would be either to ascend directly from the forks in Brandywine Creek (*A3*), or (more enjoyably) to traverse along the divide from Mt. Brew. From the Brandywine Creek road, descend to the bridge (as for Mt. Brew access) and climb 1/2 km beyond to the first switchback. Take the right branch straight ahead here and follow it westward into the valley. Shortly after crossing a bridge the road switches back to the right. Ignore this switchback and continue straight ahead through bush and mature timber to intersect a major stream gully which drops down from the ridge to the N. Cross the gully (do not ascend it!) and climb the low knob (GR 848457) beyond into the wide valley to the W. Smooth sailing from here to the main divide beyond.

South tower: *FA: P. Thompson, M. Wisnicki, R. Woodsworth—1963. FWA: B. Fairley, H. Redekop—December 28, 1985.* A technically difficult climb on rock which tends to break off in large slabs. The first ascent party used spring snow on the west face to help gain the south arête behind the prominent gendarme. One short pitch on loose, dangerous rock gains the arête, which is very narrow, but fairly solid. Two ropes make rappelling much easier. So far as is known, this peak has had only two ascents.

North tower (2070 m/6800 ft): *FA: R. Chambers, H. Rode—1958.* The west-northwest face of this peak is not particularly steep but is rotten and dangerous. Four leads with poor protection. Class 3–4; 2 hours up. Spring snow helps by covering rock.

BRANDYWINE MOUNTAIN 2229 m/7314 ft

Located N of head of Brandywine Creek and E of the main divide.

The Brandywine Creek road (*A3*) has now been pushed to within half an hour of Brandywine meadows. This peak, popular both on skis and on foot, can be ascended without difficulty from the E. **METAL DOME** (2010 m/6600 ft) is the shoulder directly E of Brandywine. Brandywine can be climbed directly from Metal Dome by heading N on the ridge around the head of the basin, or by contouring into a basin SW of the peak, ascending to its west side, and then crossing a small glacier to the summit. Metal Dome itself is climbed via logging roads on its south side, usually on skis (*A3*).

MT. CAYLEY 2380 m/7800 ft

The most prominent summit on the Squamish-Cheakamus divide, located E of the Squamish-Elaho junction.

FA: E. Brooks, T. Fyles, W. Wheatley—1928.

FWA: K. Barnard, E. Butler—January 1985.

A spur leaves the Squamish River road at about 58 km/36 mi, about 2 km before the Elaho road junction. From the end of this spur, climb a 150 m/500 ft bluff on the south side of a small canyon, then follow the ridge crest into the bowl 3 km due W of Cayley. Good travelling in open timber. You then follow a broad ridge E to Cayley. At one time, parties may have gained this ridge via old roads to the N. Parties have also approached via the Turbid Creek (*C4*) Shovelnose Creek divide and the high valley SE of Cayley—a much longer alternative.

South side: Climb glacier to the col dividing Cayley from "Pyroclastic Peak" to the S. Col rim leads to a gully which can be scrambled on rotten rock (snow in spring). Just beyond the head of the gully, a 10 m/30 ft Class 4 gendarme to the N is the summit. The southern arête of Cayley, which parallels the gully, is a pleasant Class 4–5 climb on fairly firm rock. A spire on this arête provides an entertaining climb involving a counterclockwise ascent from the uphill gap through a series of airy clefts; Class 5.

Mt. Cayley, "Pyroclastic Peak" and the "Vulcan's Thumb"   Peter Jordan

North ridge: In spring, this ridge is Class 4 on both rock and snow. Fairly pleasant, nay, almost classic.

"PYROCLASTIC PEAK" 2350 m/7700 ft
A steep, rotten peak immediately S of Mt. Cayley.
FA: R. Chicoine, F. Douglas, R. Wyborn—1971.
FWA: R. Milward, P. O'Reilly, P. Rowat, G. Shannon—1982.
From col between Pyroclastic and Cayley (see entry above), drop W down steep snow, then ascend a steep Class 4 snow couloir for 4 leads up Pyroclastic's N face to the W shoulder. One Class 3 rock pitch leads to the summit. Spring snow is probably useful.

"VULCAN'S THUMB" 2290 m/7500 ft
This spectacular, rotten spire at the end of the ridge S of Mt. Cayley and Pyroclastic dominates the view from the Squamish valley. It is the only peak in this guidebook unclimbed because of difficulty. It is defended by large (and unhealthy) walls on all sides except the N ridge, where it has an estimated 75 m/250 ft of relief above a knife-edge ridge which connects with a spur of Pyroclastic Peak. To reach that spur

from the logging complex N of Turbid Creek (*C4*), climb scrubby, bluffy hillside to E and walk around the crater rim at the top. A steep section below timberline may be bypassed on the right and a gendarme above timberline on the left. Gullies in face beyond gendarme lead (Class 3) to spur overlooking ridge to Thumb.

Lots of luck!

MT. CALLAGHAN 2410 m/7900 ft

Located at the head of Callaghan Creek.

FA: J. Booth, A. Dellow, T. Fallowfield, L. Harrison, E. Henderson—1945. The summit is easily ascended from most sides. It is usually reached by going W up the valley from Callaghan Lake (*A4*); this route takes 3 hours to reach the divide S of Callaghan, and another 3 to reach the summit. The easy summit SW of Callaghan is **RING MOUNTAIN** (2195 m/7200 ft; *FA: J. Clarke—1968*). It is a volcanic crater and while NTD from most angles, the northeast ridge provides Class 3 rock and snow. **PEAK 7400** (2260 m/7400 ft), located 6.4 km/4 mi NW of Callaghan and 2.5 km SE of Squamish Glacier snout, is known as **"LITTLE RING PEAK"**. It has been reached in a day on spring snow from roads on the upper Squamish River (*C9*) and ascended from the southeast side (*FA: J. Clarke—1969*). A 2195 m/7200 ft summit 4.5 km NE of Callaghan was climbed without difficulty by L. Harrison and F. Arundel, who also made early explorations of the area farther N. For other ascents betwen Callaghan and Mt. Fee see *VOCJ* 1970, p. 103.

The traverse from Callaghan Lake to Brew Lake is known as the Powdercap Traverse. Both traverses give access to many glaciated summits ranging from 2100 m/7000 ft to 2450 m/8000 ft in height, most of which are unnamed. Because the area is of limited mountaineering interest, only the named or significant peaks are dealt with in this guide. Most summits are climbed on skis in the spring or winter. The area is well described by both ski guides. See also *BCM* August/September 1969, *CAJ* 1970, and *CAJ* 1983 (includes a sketch map).

MT. SPROATT 1844 m/6051 ft

Sproatt can be easily ascended from 1430 m/4700 ft on its northeast shoulder. Gain this from the Rainbow Lake trail (*A5*). It is also climbed on old roads from the SE to reach basins E of the summit.

From the west: From Tonic Lake (*A5*) ascend to the easy and attractive divide W of Sproatt. **"TONIC PEAK"** to the E can easily be climbed on its west flank from here, and Sproatt itself is a pleasant ramble. You can also gain this area easily by heading E from the Northair Mine (*A4*).

From Alta Lake: From Alta Lake road ascend the Sproatt Creek valley on old logging roads. From the highest road head into the basin E of Sproatt. The peak is easily climbed from here.

RAINBOW MOUNTAIN 2328 m/7639 ft

A pleasant and popular summit at the head of Twentyone Mile Creek (*A5*). From Rainbow Lake (*A5*), hike up the gully to the south shoulder of Rainbow Mountain and follow the open ridge and snowfield back over minor peaks. This takes 6 hours up from cars and is NTD; overnight parties usually camp at the lake. Some parties approach via the Northair Mine by skiing N along the ridge to **"GIN PEAK"** and dropping down north facing gullies to Rainbow Lake (*A4*).

More unusual approaches to Rainbow Mountain include coming along the divide from the SE, gained either from spur roads in Nineteen Mile Creek or from above the pass at the head of Sixteen Mile Creek. It is not uncommon for ski parties to go up the Rainbow Lake trail (*A5*) and then ascend a prominent chute (facing due S) to reach the ridge crest between the east and central peaks. Contour N and W to gain the higher western summit. Some avalanche danger. The routes vary somewhat in winter and skiers should check one of the ski guides for a detailed description.

RHODODENDRON MOUNTAIN 2530 m/8300 ft
Located between the forks of Miller Creek.
FA: A. Black, M. Feller, K. McNaughton—1971.
North side: From the cattle trail on Miller Creek (*E1*), follow meadows along the creek to a lake at 1520 m/5000 ft at the snout of the glacier which feeds Miller Creek. Ascend Rhododendron's north side to gain the upper west ridge. Bergschrund and crevasses on this broad ridge may cause problems. A pleasant weekend mountaineering trip.
East ridge: *FA: P. Jordan, F. Kornelsen, F. Thiessen—1971.* From the 1280 m/4200 ft level of Miller Creek trail (*E1*), ascend to the east ridge and follow this to summit, avoiding gendarmes on glacier to N. Class 3.
East face: *FA: E. Hinze, P. Jordan—1974.* Climb an icefall to gain steep snow. Take a few ice screws in late season. (Ref. *VOCJ* 1974.)

SUGARLOAF MOUNTAIN ("THE STRUNK") 2440 m/8000 ft
Highest summit N of the Miller Creek meadows.
From the top of the cattle trail N of the Miller Creek meadows (*E1*), follow easy east ridge to summit. This is a favourite hike of Pemberton valley residents, also popular with the local ruminants.

SOO BLUFFS
Located N of the mouth of Soo River.
Soo River bluffs rise across the valley to the left (W) of Highway 99 about 85 km/53 mi from Squamish. Cross Soo River on the railway bridge near where the highway to Pemberton first hits the Soo River valley. The bluffs are a 1 hour hike from the bridge. Avoid the swamp by circling right on higher ground. The new Soo River logging road also provides access (*A6*), which would be quicker although a creek hop would be necessary. As a rock climbing area the bluffs are seldom visited now, but the 240 m/800 ft central rib (M. Belford, C. Oloman, R. Pasker) proved to be Class 5 and is recommended. The two visible water streaks are popular, easy ice climbs. They are often the closest frozen falls to the Vancouver area.

IPSOOT MOUNTAIN 2590 m/8500 ft
A sprawling, glaciated summit 12.9 km/8 mi W of Pemberton.
FA: J. Booth, W. Cadillac, A. Dellow, T. Fallowfield, L. Harrison, R. Pilkington.
One approach is to climb from the Rutherford Creek road (*A7*) directly to the ridge E of Ipsoot. The ascent is without difficulty from there. The climb, which is most popular as a ski trip when snow hides bush, can be made more straighforwardly on skis from the south fork of Miller Creek (*E1*) by ascending the Ipsoot Glacier. Two fairly full days.

PEMBERTON ICEFIELD

The large glacial complex between Lillooet River and the head of the Squamish River has seldom been visited on foot. The area is best suited to ski mountaineering. The first activity in the region was a BCMC spring ski expedition (*J. Bryceland, J. Davies, M. Lustenberger, A. Purdey, J. Reiss, R. Thompson—1969*) which travelled down the entire divide along the western part of the icefield and climbed most of the important summits en route (13 in all). They flew by helicopter to the head of South Creek and exited via Dipper Creek, descending the ridge between its forks, and then traversing on the south slopes of the lower valley. This exit route is not a recommended approach except perhaps for gentle **EXODUS PEAK** (2440 m/8000 ft) on the south end of the icefield.

Since then, the traverse has been done several times. Now that the roads have been pushed far up Meager Creek, the most popular version of this traverse is to use the approach to Overseer, up "Madhorse Creek" (*E3a*) and to exit at Callaghan Lake. The original exit is still feasible, and a possible variation on it might be to ski S of Exodus Peak and Blanca Lakes and exit either onto logging roads on the west flank of the Squamish River (*D1*) or onto those in Maude Frickett Creek.

The Overseer group   John Clarke

The quickest approach to the main Squamish Glacier is directly from roads on the upper Squamish River. Other possible approaches to the traverse could be from Rutherford Creek (*A2*), Miller Creek meadows (*E1*), or Ryan River (*E2*).

OVERSEER MOUNTAIN 2745 m/9000 ft
Highest summit of the icefield, located at head of South Creek.

This summit was gained without difficulty both from the pass to the SE and from the col separating it from **SPIDERY PEAK** (2650 m/8700 ft) to the N. Spidery was also climbed with ease from the col. Various other 2450 m–2600 m summits S and SW of Overseer are quite gentle and offer no problems. **PIKA PEAK** (2530 m/8300 ft), to the NW of Spidery Peak and S of the Lillooet-Meager junction, was reached from that junction in 1932 by A. Dalgleish and T. Fyles. Pika is now more easily reached from the Overseer area and is not difficult.

For Pika and Spidery, a 2 or 3 day trip from the end of the road on the southwest side of Lillooet River seems feasible (*E*). For Overseer, an approach from the vicinity of the Harrison Hut (*E3a*) is also used. All of these summits are easily climbed by ascending the broad ridge N of Madhorse Creek.

West face: *FA: R. Driscoll, A. Ourom—July 10–11, 1985.*
Approach from the Harrison Hut or via the east fork of Madhorse Creek (*E3a*). The bottom third of the face is a triangular wall bounded by two couloirs. Climb the couloir on the right to its end (30°) then move left onto the broad central buttress. Scramble to the base of the headwall. Take a clean 5.7 crack directly below the summit, then continue for three additional full pitches on excellent cracks to 5.9. There is some loose rock on ledges, and many possible variations exist. The route ends literally at the summit cairn.

South Ridge: *FA: B. Baker—July 10–11, 1985.*
The complete ridge is a blocky Class 3 climb on enjoyable rock.

LONGSPUR PEAK 2560 m/8400 ft
Highest summit in the eastern part of Pemberton Icefield.

The recorded ascent was up easy snowslopes on the S to the upper southeast ridge. The 2440 m/8000 ft rock horn 3.2 km to the SW was climbed without difficulty from the same glacier, as was its 2440 m/8000 ft neighbour on the W.

"RIDE IN PEAK" 2500 m/8200 ft
FA: R. Brusse, G. McCormack, E. Woodd—July 1984.
Located 4 km NE of Longspur Peak.

Approach via the Ryan River roads (*E2*) and "Sneak Out Creek," which flows NNW into the Ryan at GR 815882 on 92 J/6. The east ridge is a scramble. The first ascent party also climbed **PEAK 8100** (2470 m/8100 ft), 2 km to the N, via the south ridge, **PEAK 7800** (2380 m/7800 ft) and **PEAK 8200** (2500 m/8200 ft), both 2 km to the NW. All were scrambles, as was **PEAK 7982** (2433 m/7982 ft) 1.8 km to S, which they climbed via the long NW ridge. The rock in this area is granitic.

PEAK 7700 2350 m/7700 ft
Located at the head of the Soo River about 7.5 km SSE of Longspur Peak.
FA: G. Woodsworth—1974. The summit is easily approached and climbed from the NW.

West face of Overseer Mountain   Rob Driscoll

BLANCA PEAKS 2130 m/7000 ft

Located N of Blanca Lake and the Squamish-Elaho junction, S of Exodus Peak. The gentle and attractive peaks and lakes in this area may be gained by ascending through steepish forest from the logging spurs on the west flank of the Squamish River valley (*D1*) and trekking NW along a broad ridge. Alternatively, Blanca Lake can be approached through gentle, open timber on Maude Frickett Creek (*D2*). **"BLANCA PEAK"** (2130 m/7000 ft) may be ascended easily from the S. Exodus Peak, located further N, may be reached easily from here. It is also possible to reach Exodus from roads which end at the junction of Dipper and Carnival creeks (*C7*).

ASHLU-SQUAMISH AND ASHLU-ELAHO DIVIDES

This region features summits which are rather icy for hiking and rather bland for mountaineering. With improved access, however, it has become more popular, especially as a ski-touring area. Extension of the logging roads up the creeks feeding Ashlu Creek has made access quite simple. However, currently the bridge across the mouth of the Elaho River is out, so unless a boat is used, access is not possible from the roads running on the south side of the Elaho River or the west side of the Squamish River.

VOC parties initiated serious mountaineering in this area, with most peaks between Mt. Wood and Mt. Crerar being climbed by J. Denton and companions in

1962 and 1963. In 1972, J. Clarke traversed the divide from Mt. Pearkes (see Clendenning Creek chapter) above Jervis Inlet to the Elaho-Squamish junction, climbing pretty well all northern summits en route. The main obstacle was a steep and deep gap down to 1370 m/4500 ft at the head of Deserted River. Most of the summits on the southern part of this traverse were bypassed to N on glaciers (*CAJ* 1973, p. 59).

Another traverse in the area is the Ashlu-Elaho traverse. The route runs from the Squamish-Elaho junction to the Squamish-Ashlu junction or vice versa. From Amicus Mountain, traverse W of Icecap Peak and exit via either the Mt. Wood group or Pykett Peak. This traverse has been made somewhat more difficult with the loss of the Elaho River bridge.

"MT. WOOD" GROUP

This massif forms the southern extremity of the Squamish-Ashlu divide and stands out prominently when you look up the Squamish River valley. The name appeared on early nautical charts and the summit was reached as early as 1919 by A. Maude, F. Perry, and companion. It consists of a series of summits between 2000 m/6500 ft and 2300 m/7500 ft in elevation. The higher, northwestern ones are glaciated. Some parties have referred to the first peak on the ridge as **"BUCK MOUNTAIN"** (1980 m/6500 ft) and the next as **"ZIG-ZAG PEAK"** (2100 m/6900 ft). The 2290 m/7500 ft peak NW of Zig-Zag is called **"MT. STOREY"**, but is actually the highest peak of Mt. Wood.

From the highest eastward running spur of branch A-700 of the Squamish River road (*B4*), ascend N through forest to gain the alpine area E of Buck Mountain. This is bushy in part; it is best to keep on the south side of the crest. The lower summits do not involve glacier travel and are a moderate 1 day return trip. The highest summit is ice-clad and a longish day. Approach from roads in Pykett Creek (*B4*) is also feasible.

"AMICUS MOUNTAIN" 2530 m/8300 ft
A glaciated ridge SW of the Squamish-Elaho junction.
FA: J. Clarke—1968.
This gentle summit is easily climbed over snowslopes from the NE. Access, however, is more complex. Currently, the only feasible line of approach is likely via Pykett Creek (*B4 or B5*) making Amicus a long-weekend objective. **PEAK 8273** (2522 m/8273 ft), located 1.5 km W of Amicus, is reached directly from that peak without difficulty (*FA: J. Clarke—1968*).

PEAK 7800 2380 m7800 ft
Located 3 km E of Ashlu Mountain.
FA: J. Clarke—1969.
There are four high points on the massif. All were ascended without difficulty, as was the 7600 ft (2320 m) peak to the NE and a needle on the intervening ridge.

ICECAP PEAK 2470 m/8100 ft
Located SE of Amicus Mountain at the bend in the Squamish-Ashlu divide.
FRA: P. Bowers, J. Coope, C. Gardiner, A. Macdonald—1964.
This summit was usually approached from glacier basin to the N which was reached from logging roads. It is an easy snow climb from this direction. With the Elaho

bridge washed out, it may be easier to approach from Pykett Peak (*B4 or B5*) via easy divide.

PYKETT PEAK 2470 m/8100 ft
FA: J. Denton, T. Widdowson—1962.
The next snow dome to the S of Icecap Peak. Done most often on skis. From Pykett Creek (*B5*), climb to gain upper cut block at 1220 m/4000 ft. Easy, open timber leads to alpine ridge S of Charlie-Charlie. Farther N, Pykett Peak is easily climbed.

"MT. CHARLIE-CHARLIE" 2410 m/7900 ft
FA: J. Denton, T. Widdowson—1962.
Located just to SE of Pykett Peak. It is likely that the names Pykett Peak and "Charlie-Charlie" were first applied to minor summits just S of Icecap Peak.

ASHLU MOUNTAIN 2590 m/8500 ft
This prominent pyramid is the highest peak on the Squamish-Ashlu divide. Easily seen from Whistler Mountain on a clear day.
FA: J. Denton, J. Pringle—1963.
Approach via Ashlu and Shortcut creeks to Rugged Lake (*B*). If you wish to avoid fording Shortcut Creek, cross it at the road and bushwhack to Rugged Lake on its west side; however, the east bank is less bushy and the fords are manageable.
East ridge: The route is gained from the glacier to the SE by scrambling up a gully and then following the crest to summit; Class 2–3.
From the northwest: *FA: J. Clarke—1972.* From the col NW of Ashlu, ascend steep snow gully and scramble up rock above. In 1972 Clarke also climbed the two 2440 m/8000 ft summits on the main divide NW of Ashlu. The farther one proved easy via its northwest ridge, but the closer one was more difficult. From the col NW of Ashlu, climb steep snow to the ridge SW of Ashlu. Cross a lower summit and a tricky gap beyond, then climb short Class 3–4 rock wall via a Class 5 traverse into an obvious gully to gain the highest peak.
South face: *FA: D. McNab, D. Serl—1983.* Gain the southwest ridge directly from Rugged Lake and ascend this until able to drop right onto snow and glacier which provides access to the south face. Route climbs the left side of the broad buttress on the right side of the face for 6 pitches, then angles left 2 pitches into the headwall of the gully in the centre. Much 5.8, some 5.9. On the whole, the rock is "rough and nubbly;" however, there are some loose blocks. The upper south ridge can also be regained from the glacier below the south face by climbing a very loose gully at the left. Blocky scrambling from notch to summit.

PORTERHOUSE PEAK 2380 m/7800 ft
Located S of Ashlu Mountain.
FA: J. Denton, J. Pringle—1963.
From Shortcut Creek: Ascend the bowl SW of the peak and gain the crest of the south ridge. Contour along the east flank of the peak to reach a scree slope on the northeast side, then ascend to a gully and head for the notch below the summit. Not difficult. (Ref: *VOCJ* 1963, p. 44.)
South face: This route may be ascended by gully in south face (one Class 4 pitch). Summits E of this and Ashlu have also been reached without difficulty.
North of Ashlu Mountain on the divide are several more summits climbed by J.

Clarke in 1972. **"DESERTED PEAK"** (2160– m/7100 ft) is a narrow peak with steep walls on the E and W located 1 km W of the large lake feeding the Deserted River. Directly N of this peak is another 2160 m/7100 ft peak with a rounded summit. All summits between here and Ashlu Mountain were climbed by Clarke in 1972.

Chapter 5
The Tantalus Range

BOUNDARIES:
North: Ashlu Creek
East: Squamish River
South: Mill Creek
West: Clowhom River

FOREST SERVICE OFFICE:
Squamish Forest District
P.O. Box 1970
Squamish, B.C. V0N 3G0
898-9671

LOGGING COMPANIES:

Weldwood
Empire Logging Division
3150 Cleveland Street
Squamish, B.C. V0N 3G0
683-3535
(Ashlu Creek)

Weldwood
P.O. Box 9
Sechelt, B.C. V0N 3A0
685-4727
(Clowhom Lake, Mill Creek)

MAPS:
Federal:
92 G/14 Cheakamus River
Provincial:
92 G/NW

Introduction and History

According to the pioneer Vancouver climber Neal Carter, the Tantalus Range got its name because early climbers in the Garibaldi area were ''tantalized'' by the sight of the ice-crusted peaks of the range thrusting skyward across the Squamish valley. Certainly the Tantalus group has long been considered an area of outstanding quality, offering challenging rock and snow climbs in a setting which feels more remote than other areas in which logging operations extend to timberline.

A number of routes are considered classic. One is the standard route on Tantalus itself, a three or four day excursion on rock, glacier and steep snow; another route is the east ridge of Alpha, a Class 4 climb first put up in the 1960s. To these we may add the routes of the two earliest climbs made on Mt. Dione, which are still considered outstanding. There is some very good rock in the Tantalus Range, notably on the north side of Alpha, but some ornate volcanic debris poised here and there on peaks such as Serratus offers a special kind of alpine challenge that earlier climbers didn't seem to mind.

Lake Lovelywater is one of the loveliest picture postcard lakes in southwestern B.C., and although a fairly gruelling hike of three to four hours and a crossing of the Squamish River are required to reach it, the view on arrival is worth the effort. Peaks shoot upward from the lake on all sides. Some of them are very steep, making the area difficult for hiking and quite hazardous in the winter, since most of the slopes are subject to avalanches.

A climber of any level should find routes to interest him in the Tantalus Range, for there are few spots in southwestern B.C. which pack so many mixed snow and ice climbs into such a compact area. An added bonus is that the Tantalus looks much the same today as it did when the first pioneers entered it, over eighty years ago; it is only when you gaze far into the distance that you see the slash left behind by logging operations. But around Lake Lovelywater, and in the many alpine basins, the scene is just as nature created it, unscarred by industrial progress.

Both Basil Darling and Tom Fyles, two climbers who figured prominently in the early days of mountaineering in the province, showed a keen interest in the Tantalus Range. It was mainly as a result of their efforts that all the major peaks here were climbed before the end of World War I. Darling organized the first four major climbing expeditions into the area. During at least one of these trips, the party crossed the Squamish River, several hundred feet wide in places, on a large fallen log! It is also of note that Tom Fyles once attempted a winter ascent of Tantalus, but was stopped by bad weather.

The BCMC spent a lot of time in the area in the 1960s, with people like the Kafers, Dick Culbert, Alice Purdey, Jack Bryan, Bob Cuthbert and Jim Craig climbing many new routes. However, interest faded out in the 1970s, as the better climbers increasingly turned to rock routes in their search for new, technical climbs. But the story of the earlier ascents still remains impressive. An excellent historical source is Neal Carter, "Early Climbs in the Tantalus Range," *CAJ* 1964, p. 73.

Approaches

A. FROM LAKE LOVELYWATER
One of the drawbacks to climbing in the Tantalus Range is that you must somehow get across the Squamish River without a bridge. (On the other hand this difficulty helps to keep the numbers down.) Take the Squamish Highway to the Cheekye turn-off at Alice Lake. At Cheekye (3.9 km) there is a bridge over the Cheakamus River. Cross it and bear left on a gravel road for 2.3 km, where an obscure dirt track leads to the left. This track crosses several clearings and leads to a cable car crossing on the Squamish River. The last 200 m/660 ft of this track are not driveable. The cable car is always locked, so a canoe or car top boat must be launched. It is best to do this 200 or 300 m upstream of the cable car. When crossing rivers in a canoe, point the bow **upstream** and incline it slightly towards the opposite shore; the current will then push you across. Point the bow downstream and you are likely to end up in Squamish! The Squamish River is dangerous, and canoeists have lost their lives in it in the past. Parts of it are often choked with logjams which create dangerous undercurrents. Always wear a lifejacket when you cross.

The trail begins on the far bank about 100 m/330 ft upstream from the western cable car terminal. It heads N along the river for a short distance, then follows "Lovelywater Creek" up to Lake Lovelywater and a locked cabin at 1160 m/3800 ft, where you will find spots to camp. If you plan to use the cabin, contact the ACC, Vancouver Section; they own and maintain it. The section may be contacted by calling the Federation of Mountain Clubs, 687-3333.

1. North side: A sketchy trail, bushy in spots, leads around the north side of Lake Lovelywater to Lambda Lake. It is best to traverse the first two sets of bluffs at lake level, then strike up into the trees and traverse the steep slopes. A couple of minor streams must be crossed.

1a. Alpha-Serratus col: To reach this col, climb to the shoulder SW of Lambda Lake and weave SW through bluffs. Easiest in spring, when snow covers the bush.

1b. Alpha's east ridge and north side: The easiest way to get to these routes is to start at the lake's outlet and head straight up, through native timber, until you reach the east shoulder of Alpha. The north side is easily gained by crossing the shoulder and traversing glaciers.

1c. Serratus-Ionia basin: Cross the lake to its northwest corner by boat or on spring ice. There you will find a large basin and enough room to camp the Russian army. If you don't have a boat, traverse below the south face of Serratus at about the 1400 m/4600 ft level to gain the basin. There are large hanging glaciers around the west and southwest rim of the basin; if it is cloudy they may not be noticed.

1d. Dione-Serratus saddle: To reach the Dione-Serratus saddle from this basin, climb N over snow or loose rock, up the northwesternmost gully, until you are able to traverse W to the snowslope under Serratus. Ascend this snowslope to cross the Ionia-Serratus col just S of Serratus, then either traverse under the west side of Serratus (a route which may be icy in summer) or descend about 100 m to the basin and work N to the saddle.

2. South side: A trail, recently brushed and flagged, runs from the outlet of Lake Lovelywater along the south shore to a creek; follow it up into the basin between Niobe and Omega. Starting from about the 1520 m/5000 ft level, a fairly easy traverse across the north flank of Mt. Niobe will bring you to the wide Niobe-Lydia col. The Crescent Glacier NE of Lydia is reached either by traversing snow from just below this col or by crossing Lake Lovelywater and climbing up a long, narrow gully which begins at the westernmost tip of the lake. Another way to reach the glacier is directly from the Ionia-Serratus basin (Class 3), but beware of falling ice.

B. FROM MT. SEDGWICK
Several parties have followed a cross-country route from Sedgwick, along Mt. Conybeare, into the Lake Lovelywater area. See the Sechelt-Gibson chapter for approaches to Sedgwick.

C. FROM ZENITH LAKE
A rough trail used to lead from the Squamish River to Zenith Lake, but it has now almost disappeared; only a few aluminum markers remain. The trail was gained by taking a spur left from the Squamish River road, 15.3 km/9.5 mi N of the Cheakamus River bridge at Cheekye.

D. FROM SIGURD CREEK OR POKOSHA CREEK

Starting 35.4 km/22 mi along the Ashlu Creek road (see Squamish chapter, *B*), bush-whack up into the Sigurd Creek valley. At about 1070 m/3500 ft, turn S into a glaciated valley near some small lakes. Pelion and Ossa Mountains are accessible from this spot. This approach is easiest when spring snow is still around. These lakes are more readily approached on skis via Pokosha Creek valley (see Squamish chapter) by traversing from its head southward along slopes to the SE of Sigura Lake.

E. FROM CLOWHOM LAKE AND RIVER

See the Sechelt-Gibsons chapter (*D*) for details on the western approaches to the Tantalus Range.

Routes

MT. THYESTES 1680 m/5500 ft

A minor summit 3.2 km SE of Omega Mountain.
FA: R. McLellan, H. Parliament, F. Roots—September 1942.
An isolated, unrewarding peak easily reached by climbing its northwest slope from "Clytie Lake." Reach Clytie Lake (situated at 1010 m/3300 ft in the basin north of Mt. Thyestes) by descending from the Omega-Iota saddle or by following the Lake Lovelywater trail until somewhat before it comes to Lovelywater Creek.

OMEGA MOUNTAIN 1860 m/6100 ft

This peak stands above the Squamish valley at the southwest end of the Lovelywater cirque.
FA: J. Fyles, T. Fyles—1916. FWA: P. Neilsen, R. Slough—February 22–23, 1964.
North side: The north ridge and north face are Class 3 rock. They may be reached either by ascending the forested ridge directly from Lake Lovelywater's outlet (*A*) or by traversing from part way up the Omega-Niobe basin (*A2*).
West Ridge: Ascend beyond the Omega-Niobe basin to the divide W of Omega. The west ridge is a medium Class 3 climb. Other lines are available on the adjacent face to the S. There are 3 gullies here; the farthest right is the easiest, but it is not a good route for descending Omega as it terminates well below the divide. Takes 4 hours from the lake.

MT. PELOPS 1980 m/6500 ft

Two summits stand immediately S of Lake Lovelywater. Mt. Pelops is the southeastern one.
FA: J. Fyles, T. Fyles—1916.
Southeast ridge: From the Omega-Niobe basin (*A2*), climb scree, rock, and snow to the col between Pelops and minor Iota Mountain to the E. Both are scrambles from here. Class 2–3. Takes 3 1/2 hours from the lake.
East face: *FA: J. Bryan, B. Moss—1962.* Start at the very lowest point on the east face, just to the right of the major gully. Ascend to 60 m/200 ft below the summit; the route then angles left into the gully, and the gully is followed to the peak. Class 4. Takes 4 hours from the basin.

North and west sides: The peak is an easy scramble from either the Omega-Niobe basin or the Lydia-Niobe col.

IOTA MOUNTAIN 1830 m/6000 ft
FA: E. Kingsford Smith, G. Warren—1910. A spur of Pelops; NTD from all directions.

Mts. Niobe and Pelops   Dick Culbert

MT. NIOBE 2010 m/6600 ft
Highest of the summits immediately S of Lake Lovelywater.
FA: E. Kingsford-Smith, G. Warren—1910.
From the south: Niobe is a short scramble from its col with Pelops. Reach the col by traversing Pelops or from the Omega-Niobe basin. The climb takes 3 1/2 hours from the lake.
West ridge: From the Niobe-Lydia saddle *(A2)*, ascend directly up the Class 3 west ridge or swing S to easier ground. Takes 1 1/2 hours from the saddle.
North rib: *FA: R. Chambers, E. Kafer, M. Kafer, M. Lasserre, R. Woodsworth—1963.* This rib runs up the centre of the north face. Reach it as you would the northeast ridge. It is of similar length and difficulty.
Northeast ridge: *FA: J. Bryan, J. Craig, E. Kafer, M. Kafer—1960.* From the

Omega-Niobe basin (*A2*), climb to the right under buttresses which terminate Niobe's northeast ridge. Climb snow to the right of buttresses, then gain the ridge, which is followed to the summit. Class 3. Takes 3 hours from the basin.

LYDIA MOUNTAIN 2040 m/6700 ft
A rock ridge forming the southwest portion of the Lovelywater cirque.
FA: B. Darling, A. Morkill—1914.
FWA: V. Kutscherra, K. Winter—February 22–23, 1964.
Southeast ridge: From the Niobe-Lydia col (*A2*), climb Lydia's southeast divide. This is bushy in the lower part with some small bluffs, including one Class 4 move. Takes 4 hours from the col.

The remaining routes start at Crescent Glacier and run up Lydia's northeastern walls. Two steep buttresses descend from near the summit. The east buttress route takes the northern. Routes are described from N to S.
East buttress: *FA: J. Bryan, F. Critchard—1962.* Follow the buttress along fairly good rock, then, just before reaching a prominent gendarme halfway up, drop into a gully to the left for 30 m/100 ft Class 4–5 climbing. It takes 6 hours from base.
East face: *FA: G. Kozel, D. Williams—1966.* Ascend ledges to right of the gully between buttresses. On the upper part, traverse right over slabs to complete the climb under the main peak. Class 4; 8 pitches.
The Potter's Buttress: *FA: R. Cuthbert, G. Kozel—1968.* Looking from the wall's base you will see 3 summits; this line takes you to the one farthest left. Start on the right of the grassy gully with the overhang at the bottom. Ascend to the grassy ledge; then go 18 m/60 ft left; climb up to your right to avoid overhangs. Go back to the left and ascend the chimney; you will reach a green-stained gully which is climbed to the summit. Class 4–5. Takes 3 1/2 hours from the base.

THE RED TUSK 2100 m/6900 ft
A rotten, reddish horn. The highest peak W of Lake Lovelywater.
FA: B. Darling, A. Morkill—1914.
From the south: The high shoulder E of the summit tusk can be reached by crossing steep snow from the top of Crescent Glacier (*A2*). Alternatively, starting in the gap NE of Lydia Mountain, climb the gully on the south side of the divide. This gap in turn is reached by crossing the moat from Crescent Glacier or by climbing or rappelling down from Lydia's summit. From shoulder, cross the intervening notch and climb to the summit in one Class 4 lead on foul rock. A moderately strenuous weekend.
North ridge: *FA: R. Culbert, A. Purdey—1969.* Cross over the pass between Ionia and Pandareus (see Mt. Pandareus, below), then traverse S along the west side of the divide over scree and snow. Climb S out of the basin here and scramble to divide up loose, Class 3 ribs. Traverse the divide to the base of the summit tower. The tower is 1 1/2 leads on surprisingly firm rock. A stiff Class 4, but likely the best way up the Tusk. Takes 3 hours from the notch, and 1 day return from the lake.

MT. PANDAREUS 2070 m/6800 ft
Located 0.8 km N of Red Tusk, and W of Lake Lovelywater.
FA: H. Genschorek, I. Kay—1949.
Southwest ridge: From the glacier S of Serratus Mountain (*A1c*), traverse upwards S

over snow until you reach the gap between Pandareus and Ionia. Cross this and swing around the west side of Pandareus. Climb loose rock to the southwest ridge and continue to the summit. Class 3. Takes 1 day return from the lake.

West ridge: *FA: J. Bryan, J. Craig, E. Kafer, M. Kafer—1961.* From the Pandareus-Ionia notch, climb easy rock to the gap in the west ridge. Rappel into the notch here and then traverse to the right over the slab below overhang. From here, ascend directly to crest. Class 4. Continue on Class 3 rock to the summit. Takes 1 1/2 hours from the base.

East face: From the glacier S of Serratus (*A1c*), traverse E under the north face, then cross the northeast ridge above the highest gendarme. Traverse under the east face until you can surmount the bergschrund. Angle up the face on good rock, keeping parallel with the northeast ridge. Takes 1 day return from the lake.

IONIA MOUNTAIN 2070 m/6800 ft

A rock ridge S of Serratus Mountain.
FA: H. Genschorek, I. Kay—1949.

From the south: From the notch between Ionia and Pandareus follow the lower, slabby part of the south corner or bypass the corner by climbing S. Continue over loose rock to summit. Class 3–4. Takes 1 hour up from notch.

North side: *FA: J. Bryan, J. Craig, E. Kafer, M. Kafer—1961.* From the glacier S of Serratus Mountain, the northeast rib is clearly visible as the lowest rock descending from the main north divide of Ionia. Follow the crest of this rib from its toe until you reach a gendarme. After 90 m/300 ft of easier rock, traverse the wide ledge on the rib's east face. The crest can be regained in 1 lead up a Class 4 wall. Climb the last gendarme on the ridge, go over slabs and blocks, then climb the west face. Continue up the north divide of Ionia on fairly good rock. Climbing is Class 3 and 4. Takes 4 hours from the base.

West buttress: *FA: R. Culbert, A. Purdey—1969.* This buttress is easily reached from the Dione-Serratus saddle (*A1d*) or the Serratus-Ionia basin (*A1c*) by dropping somewhat and traversing the major ramp southward along the west side of the divide. The ridge is 5 leads of Class 4 climbing, mainly pleasant. Takes 2 1/2 hours up. A tower on this buttress provides a lead of Class 4 from uphill notch.

SERRATUS MOUNTAIN 2326 m/7632 ft

A high, rugged ridge NW of Lake Lovelywater and S of the Tantalus massif.
FA: B. Darling, S. Davies, A. Morkill—1911.
FWA: R. Driscoll, W. Durtler—December 1985.

From the West: The glacial bench to the W of the summit is crossed en route to the Dione-Serratus saddle (*A1d*). From the Ionia-Serratus col, swing under Serratus' southwest nose—crampons are advised late in season. Various Class 3–4 lines go up from the bench, either directly to the peak or to the upper north rib. The climb takes 2 hours from snowline. Poor rock. A full weekend objective.

South ridge: The direct ridge from the Ionia-Serratus col is steep in part and entails substantial Class 4 climbing. There are easier variations farther E. The major gully here is a snow route in spring, and lines between the ridge and gully need not exceed Class 3. Takes 2 1/2 hours from base.

South face: *FA: H. Mather, M. Schliessler—1982.* From the west end of Lake Lovelywater, ascend into the basin S of Serratus and gain the easternmost buttress on

Serratus Mountain from the west   Bill Durtler

the face. Climb it directly to the summit. Reasonable rock; Class 5.6.

East ridge: *FA: T. Fyles, J. Fyles—1916.* From the saddle between Serratus and Alpha (*A1a*), follow the east ridge to the first subsidiary peak or traverse the north side to bypass it, then ascend a gully. The gap beyond may be reached by a rappel or by downclimbing on either side. Traverse back to the ridge crest and continue to summit. Class 3–4. Takes 4 hours from saddle.

North face: *FA: R. Driscoll, B. Fairley, R. Stair—June 1982.* The face was gained from the Alpha-Serratus col (*A1a*) by descending and traversing beneath a large icefall. Snow to 45° with a couple of bergschrunds. It is possible to finish the climb via Class 4 rock. Likely the easiest way up and down Serratus.

ALPHA MOUNTAIN 2305 m/7562 ft
A striking pyramid above Squamish Valley N of Lake Lovelywater.
FA: B. Darling, A. Morkill—1914.

From the southwest: From Lambda Lake (*A*), ascend N up scree and snowslope; then up easy slabs to the prominent shoulder which stands above the Alpha-Serratus saddle and SW of the summit. Follow this ridge to the peak. Not difficult. Takes 3 hours from Lambda Lake.

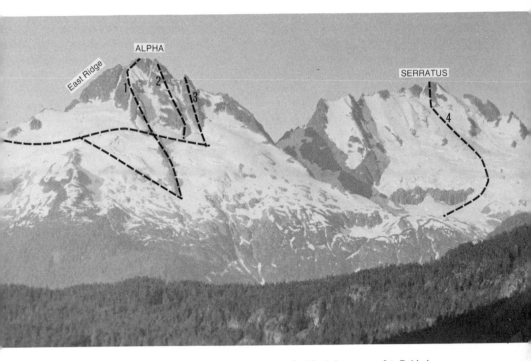

Alpha and Serratus mountains   1.) Northeast ridge   2.) North buttress   3.) Guide buttress
4.) North face
                                                                                    Bruce Fairley

South face: *FA: G. Kozel, C. Oloman—1966.* Several variations have been done on this face. The ridge between the prominent "V" formed by gullies here may be reached on Class 3 ledges, working in from the left. Avoid initial overhang to the right and continue on Class 3–4 rock. Takes 4 hours from base. Easier variations exist. You can also traverse onto this face from the overhang on the east ridge.

East ridge: *FA: J. Bryan, J. Craig, M. Kafer—1961.* From the outlet of Lake Lovelywater, climb N through steep bush to open slopes, then ascend to an obvious notch below 4 minor bumps on the divide. Traverse or bypass these bumps and continue up Alpha's east ridge on good rock. Mainly a Class 3 climb, except for one small overhang passed by a short Class 5 jamcrack on the left. Takes 5–6 hours from the lake. A pleasant and popular climb.

Northeast ridge: *FA: R. Cuthbert, A. Purdey—1968.* This and the next two routes are approached via the east shoulder of Alpha *(A1b)*. The first 10 leads are the hardest: you have to climb up a rib dividing two glaciers—extensive Class 5—and traverse a series of small towers. This lower portion is an aesthetic climb; it can be bypassed by starting to climb at the head of the glaciers. From there, several lines are available. One is to go up the avalanche cone and then climb for 6 leads to the right of the ridge, and follow this with 3 more leads on the sharp snow crest. It should be done early in the season. Mainly a Class 4 climb. (Ref: *CAJ* 1969, p. 76.)

North buttress: *FA: B. Fairley, D. Serl—August 23, 1981.* This is the central of the three climbs on the north side of Alpha. Begin immediately to the right of a major gully/chimney on the east side of the buttress. Five pitches on fine rock in mid-

5th range (which get progressively easier) lead to snow and a finish via Class 3 rock.

Guide Buttress: *FA: H. Bleuer, C. Cairns, M. Down, J. Simpson—June 27, 1978.* Ascend the prominent buttress which rises directly to the sharp gendarme on the northwest ridge. About 6 leads of steep rock ranging to 5.7.

Northwest ridge: *FA: F. Douglas, P. Starr—1969.* Reach the toe of this ridge by dropping from the Alpha-Serratus col (*A1c*), or by traversing the northern snowslopes from the east ridge. The northwest ridge provides 460 m/1500 ft of mixed Class 3–4 rock and is recommended. The prominent gendarme on this ridge may be avoided or traversed (Class 5). A fairly full day on good rock. (Ref. *BCM* 1969.)

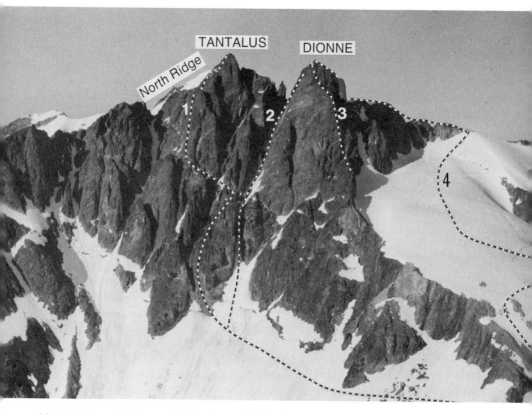

Mts. Tantalus and Dione   1.) West face   2.) Northwest flank   3.) West buttress
4.) Southeast ridge

Dick Culbert

MT. DIONE 2590 m/8500 ft
The southern companion to Mt. Tantalus.
FA: J. Fyles, T. Fyles—1916.
FWA: R. Driscoll, W. Durtler—December 1985.
Southeast ridge: *FA: J. Fyles, T. Fyles—1916.* From the Dione-Serratus saddle (*A1d*), traverse snow on the west side of Dione's long southeast ridge; swing back on snow ramp before coming to the west buttress of Dione; then climb to the southeast

ridge. The major couloir immediately S of the summit may also be used, but it is somewhat more difficult. The original ascent party used the couloir. The summit tusk of Dione is a Class 3 rock climb from the southeast divide. Takes 3 1/2 hours up from the old Red Tit hut. The full southeast divide, if followed from the saddle, provides a lengthy and enjoyable Class 3 and 4 ascent, and was first climbed by J. Owen and P. Neilsen in 1959.

West buttress: *FA: R. Cuthbert, G. Kozel, A. Purdey—1968.* From Dione Glacier, SW of summit, climb 30 m/100 ft up snow couloir; this leads to immediately S of the summit block. Here, make an ascending traverse up and to the left until you reach the face's central gully. Ascend rock on left flank to the gap behind the pinnacle. Climb face upwards and to the right, keeping in the righthand crack all the way to the summit. Class 4. Takes 4 hours from the base. (Ref: *BCM* 1968; *CAJ* 1969, p. 76.)

Northwest flank: *FA: W. Robinson, M. Weitzel—August 1977.* Approach as for the west face of Tantalus, and then climb straight up the couloir between Tantalus and Dione until about 60 m/200 ft from the top. Once there, follow broken ground to the west ridge. Two pitches of beautifully exposed climbing lead to the top.

"THE WITCH'S TOOTH" 2560 m/8400 ft

A sharp pinnacle which sits in the gap between Dione and Tantalus.

FA: G. Coots, A. Gruft, L. Hewitt—June 1965. The first ascent party approached via the southeast ridge on Dione, traversing the northeast side of the peak below the summit to gain its north ridge. Here they followed a rickety Class 4 ridge which leads to the Dione-Tooth gap. They climbed up and around on ledges to gain the northeast side of the Tooth and followed a chimney system, bypassing the chockstone which lies to the right. Traversing and face climbing then led to the summit. Class 5. (Ref: *CAJ* 1966, p. 141.)

MT. TANTALUS 2603 m/8540 ft

Highest summit of the Tantalus Range; viewed to advantage from the Squamish valley and Whistler Highway.

FA: B. Darling, J. Davies, A. Morkill—1911.

From Mt. Dione: *FA: A. Parke, K. Winter—1962.* To bypass the summit tusk of Dione (see Mt. Dione), make a slightly descending traverse on the ledge system, starting from the southeast divide and moving around the east face. Gain the base of a large gendarme ("The Witch's Tooth") on the divide N of Dione by a narrow horizontal crack, then traverse across the east face of the Tooth; alternatively use a longer but easier route through gullies somewhat lower on that side. Continue N, using a gully (right fork) on the southeast face of Tantalus to gain ledges on the east side of the divide, which lead to the final peak. You can also climb to the ridge crest immediately beyond The Witch's Tooth (Class 5). Ascend the ridge crest by a variety of crack and ledge combinations on the southeast, east, or even northeast sides; climbs here need not exceed a stiff Class 3. Tantalus is a 3 day trip. The original ascent was made from the glacier to the E, up to the gap N of The Witch's Tooth—nobody knows if this is still possible. (Ref: *CAJ* 1912, p. 141.)

Northeast side: *FA: N. Carter, E. Nunn, C. Townsend.* Traverse snowslopes from above Zenith Lake on east side of Tantalus' northern divide until you reach a prominent nunatak. Here, climb up the major glacial couloir to the north ridge just below the final summit. This was once the easiest route on Tantalus, but recently a series of bergschrunds have developed across the couloir. The northeast ridge to the left of the couloir is also direct and easy (Class 3–4), but it is sometimes difficult to approach from the glacier. Early season recommended. The nunatak, incidentally, is a 12 m/40 ft Class 3 climb from its uphill side.

North ridge: *FA: V. Brink, N. Carter, A. Cooper, R. McLellan, R. Rolick, L. von Zuben, R. von Zuben—1944.* From Zenith Lake (*C*), ascend over snow until you gain the main divide (about 1920 m/6300 ft). The ridge crest is a longish climb, mainly Class 3, on rock and snow. Bypass sub-peaks. Avoid much of this crest by walking snowslopes on the west side of the divide and regaining the crest before its main northern spur. Bypass to the E a false summit just before the main peak. The full divide traverse is a fairly lengthy day trip return from Zenith Lake.

West face: *FA: R. Cuthbert, G. Kozel, A. Purdey—1968.* From the Dione-Serratus saddle (*A1a*), traverse snowslopes to N, then drop to saddle in the ridge extending from the west buttress of Dione. Drop N down steep snow into the basin under the west face; then traverse to the toe of the ridge which descends from The Witch's Tooth. Climb this about 240 m/800 ft to a minor peak. Climb down to bypass the next pinnacle on the right, then regain the rib crest beyond. Cross the couloir on the left to a major ledge and follow this to its end. Climb the wall here to a ridge, which is followed to the summit of a major tower. Rappel off this and go 20 m/75 ft up and to the right to climb a poor crack (5.7 and loose). Continue up and to the right from the top, then follow the ridge to the summit. Takes 15 hours up. (Ref: *BCM* 1968; *CAJ* 1969, p. 76.) In August 1978 a party of four (*R. Barr, B. Blann, C. Blann, and J. Howe*) climbed the direct west face to within 80 m/260 ft of the summit.

ZENITH MOUNTAIN 1981 m/6500 ft
A minor summit immediately W of Zenith Lake.
FA: V. Brink, H. Parliament, F. Roots—May 1944.
Southwest ridge: From a camp on the shoulder SW of Zenith the summit is an easy walk with a good view. Also a short hike from Zenith Lake.
Northeast face: *FA: F. Douglas, N. Humphrey—1973.* From Zenith Lake (*C*), start directly under the northeast face, and climb up an obvious ramp which ascends to the right. At the ramp's top, traverse left and then climb to the summit ridge. Four leads of Class 4 and moderately aesthetic.

PELION MOUNTAIN 2290 m/7500 ft
The eastern and higher of the two major summits in the northern Tantalus Range.
FA: V. Brink, R. McLellan—1944.
Southwest ridge: Cross the col SW of Zenith Mountain and follow the divide NW to Pelion. Ascend its southwest ridge via the west flank to about 1860 m/6100 ft, then traverse into the snow basin which lies between Ossa and Pelion. Scramble up the southwest slopes of Pelion. Class 2–3. Takes 5 hours from Zenith. The Ossa-Pelion col may also be reached directly from Sigurd Creek (*D*). These peaks are two-day outings from Sigurd Creek and three-day outings from Zenith Lake.
North ridge: *FA: J. Clarke, M. Lustenberger, M. Putz, G. Walter—1968.* From the head of Sigurd Creek (*D*), climb to the glacier NW of Pelion, then climb up its Class 3 north ridge on fairly good rock. The peak can also be climbed on skis from this direction.
Northeast ridge: *FA: J. Clarke—1969.* From the major waterfall at about 760

m/2500 ft on Mawby Creek, climb to N through bluffs and bush until you reach open country at 1520 m/5000 ft. Climb Pelion's northeast spur, which joins the north ridge at 1890 m/6200 ft. This route is not recommended because of the bushy approach.

OSSA MOUNTAIN 2260 m/7400 ft
A double summit located W of Pelion.
FA: J. Bryan, R. Chambers, H. Rode—July, 1960.
From the north: *FA: M. Putz, G. Walter—1968.* Sigurd Creek (*D*) is the logical approach. From the col between Ossa and Pelion, traverse snow under the north side of Ossa's east peak. Climb a Class 3 gully to the main ridge of the summit. A gap just before the peak is Class 3–4. The ridge between the two summits can also be approached directly over glaciers from Sigurd Creek. From the ridge, the lower east peak is a Class 3 rock climb.
West ridge: *FA: J. Clarke, T. Rollerson—1967.* From the head of Sigurd Creek (*D*), ascend the divide NW of Ossa, and then follow the west ridge to the summit. Drop to the S to avoid a gap just before the summit. Class 3.

Chapter 6

Howe Sound-West Side

BOUNDARIES:
North: Mill Creek, Red Tusk Creek, Monmouth Creek
East: Howe Sound
South: Georgia Strait
West: Sechelt Inlet, Salmon Inlet, Clowhom Lake

FOREST SERVICE OFFICE:
Sechelt Forest District P.O. Box 4000
Sechelt, B.C. V0N 3A0
885-5174

LOGGING COMPANIES:

Canadian Forest Products
Mainland Logging Division
2800-1055 Dunsmuir Street
P.O. Box 4942
Bentall Postal Station
Vancouver, B.C. V7X 1B5
(McNab, McNair, Sechelt creeks)
661-5380, 884-5264 (local)

Weldwood of Canada
Clowhom Operations
Sechelt, B.C. V0N 3A0
(Clowhom Lake)
685-4727

MAPS:
Federal:
92 G/11 Squamish
92 G/13 Jervis Inlet
Provincial:
92 G/NW

92 G/12 Sechelt Inlet
92 G/14 Cheakamus River

Introduction

Most Vancouver mountaineers know this region only because of the popular climb of Mount Sedgwick, which shows up frequently on club schedules. The climb requires a ferry ride to the pulp mill operation at Woodfibre, on the west shore of Howe Sound. A road runs west from the town to Henriette Lake, and from there a good trail winds past several attractive alpine lakes to follow the broad south ridge to the summit. The great east face of Sedgewick has long enticed skiers, for it is a commanding sight from the Squamish Highway, offering as it does an unimpeded ski descent of some 1000 metres. Unfortunately for the ecstatic skier, the run terminates in the bushy headwaters of Mill Creek, so the complete descent of the face has not proven popular, although a few skiers have descended part of it.

Other summits in this area receive little attention; they are reserved for a hardy band of eccentrics who can tolerate greater exposure to coastal bush than most of us. For the mountain bike user this is a good area, for logging roads in varying conditions run up most of the creek drainages.

Approaches

You can easily reach the southern part of the Sechelt-Gibsons area by catching one of the regularly scheduled government ferries running from Horseshoe Bay to Langdale. The highway continues NW from Langdale to the town of Sechelt and beyond. A second road goes right from Langdale to Port Mellon, a milltown at the mouth of the Rainy River.

A. FROM PORT MELLON ROAD

1. McNair Creek road: This road (currently driveable) leaves the Port Mellon road 1 km before Port Mellon. It follows the northeast side of McNair creek for 6 km, switchbacks, and ends at 730 m/ 2400 ft, due SE of Panther Peak.

2. Rainy River road: From Port Mellon, a disused road (four-wheel drive at best) follows the east side of Rainy River for 6 km/3.7 mi to a bridge. A spur road climbs NE from here to 910 m/3000 ft (SW of Mt. Varley); the main road continues on the west side of the river for 3 km, then recrosses again to the east side. After 5 more km, the road ends NE of Tetrahedron Peak, near a lake at 1040 m/3400 ft.

B. FROM HOWE SOUND

1. McNab Creek roads: The logging camp 1 km W of the mouth of this creek can be reached by boat, floatplane, or by walking powerlines from Port Mellon. Roads ascend the west side of the creek to its head, and join the Sechelt Creek roads (*E1*). Major spurs ascend the north side of Box Canyon Creek to 910 m/3000 ft and the south side of the next western tributary, heading N and up to 700 m/2300 ft.

2. Potlatch Creek roads: The McNab Creek road forks 3 km from the logging camp. The right fork crosses the creek and climbs SE to 460 m/1500 ft. It then contours around the south and southeast sides of Mt. Wrottesley into Potlatch Creek. Spur roads climb to 760 m/2500 ft on the south side and to 820 m/2700 ft on the southeast side of this mountain. The main road goes several kilometres up each side of the creek. There are currently plans for further extension.

3. Foulger Creek spur road: An old spur ascends the north side of the south branch of this creek to 730 m/2400 ft.

C. FROM WOODFIBRE

The town of Woodfibre is reached by a regularly scheduled free ferry from Darrell Bay, 4 km S of Squamish on Highway 99. The mills at Woodfibre and Port Mellon often cast nauseating palls over Howe Sound.

1. Woodfibre Creek road: From the town, a locked road climbs the north side of this creek to 640 m/2100 ft, just E of Henriette Lake. Recent hydro construction has developed spur roads which reach the ridge crest to the south, just E of Brennan Lakes. A trail also ascends this ridge crest, meeting an old woodstave pipeline which runs out of Brennan Lake. There is a cabin at the mouth of the lower Brennan Lake which is often unlocked—check with the engineering office if you want to use it.

2. *Mill Creek road:* A road climbs the northeast side of this creek for about 2 km.

D. FROM CLOWHOM LAKE AND RIVER

A logging road begins at the head of Salmon Inlet. It follows the northwest side of Clowhom Lake to its head, and after a further 2 km, it crosses to the east side of Clowhom River.

1. *Red Tusk Creek road:* After crossing to the east side of Clowhom River, continue for 1 km. Take the second turn to the right, which ascends the northeast side of Red Tusk Creek to 850 m/2800 ft. You will arrive less than 2 km SW of the Red Tusk.

2. *Taquat Creek road:* The first right fork in the main road after the Clowhom River bridge runs S for 2.5 km and forks. The left fork climbs the north side of Taquat Creek to 670 m/2200 ft, then crosses and runs back on the south side for 1 km.

3. *Dempster Creek road:* The right fork of the Taquat Creek road continues S to reach Dempster Creek at 460 m/1500 ft.

E. FROM SALMON INLET

These roads are accessible only by boat or plane.

1. *Sechelt Creek roads:* The major complex of logging roads in this valley is fairly accurately depicted on 92 G/11 and 92 G/12. Note the spurs which ascend the west side of Slippery Creek to near Slippery Lake. Also note the main (north-side) road, which approaches Sechelt Lake, and the upper south-side roads, which connect to the McNab Creek system and also climb the upper south fork to near its end.

2. *Thornhill Creek roads:* Logging roads on both sides of this creek (as shown on 92 G/12) ascend to about 910 m/3000 ft, ending NW of Tetrahedron Peak.

Routes

LEADING PEAK 754 m/2475 ft
The summit of Anvil Island in Howe Sound.

Travel by boat to the mouth of Champside Creek on the south side of the island. Ascend to E of the creek, then follow the broad south ridge to the summit. NTD, but there are dangerous bluffs E of the route.

PANTHER PEAK 1691 m/5548 ft
Located W of Rainy River and visible from much of Vancouver.

FRA: ACC party—1933.

South ridge: Just after the first Rainy River bridge (*A2*), a short spur ascends W into the creek valley S of Panther Peak. Follow the south side of the creek to the south ridge, and continue along the ridge to the summit. Easiest in spring, when snow helps to cover bush in the valley. A 1 day return trip from the road. Access from McNair creek (*A1*) may also be possible.

Southeast face: *FA: R. Culbert, R. Cuthbert—1968.* This is the dark wall visible from Vancouver and Howe Sound. Approach from the creek to the S. Only the central "V" between the two prominent gullies is not bush-choked. The route runs just to the right of centre on this portion, past a prominent cave. Rock is poor and protection cracks scarce. Takes 5 hours from base. Class 5. Probably best left alone.

Northwest ridge: *FA: K. Hunt and party—1955.* At 2 km past the first bridge on the Rainy River road (*A2*), a bushy side road heads left into the valley between Tetrahedron and Panther. From the road's end, continue up the valley N of Panther until a prominent snow gully gives access to the open country NW of the summit. Hike up the final peak's ridge. Takes 1 day return from cars.

TETRAHEDRON PEAK 1737 m/5699 ft

Highest summit at the head of Rainy River. Visible from much of Vancouver.
FRA: ACC party of 16—May 21, 1939.
Approach as you would for the northwest ridge of Panther Peak. At the end of the bushy side road, in the valley SE of Tetrahedron, you should find an overgrown trail. In any case, the route goes up the valley until it reaches the second of three major creeks running down from the Tetrahedron massif. Ascend this creek, taking the right fork, then make an ascending traverse under the bluffs until open timber gives access to the Tetrahedron-Rainy col. Scramble W to the summit. NTD but bushy in parts. Takes 4 hours from road. Reach the more gentle **"RAINY MOUNTAIN"** (1650 m/5400 ft) immediately E of Tetrahedron from the above-mentioned col. Both Tetrahedron and Rainy can probably be reached from where the Rainy River road (*A2*) ends at 1070 m/3500 ft, to the NE, or from the Thornhill Creek roads (*E2*) to the NW.
West buttress: *FA: G. Woodsworth—1974.* From the Panther-Tetrahedron col (see Panther, northwest ridge) hike N over subsidiary bumps to the base of the final tower's west buttress. Low Class 5 for about 150 m to the summit.

MT. VARLEY ("McNAB LIONS") 1639 m/5378 ft

Highest summit between Rainy River and McNab Creek.
FRA: R. Fraser, E. Fuller—1923.
From the end of the eastern spur of the Rainy River logging roads (*A2*) SW of Mt. Varley, ascend NE until you reach the southwest ridge, just below timberline. Follow this ridge to the summit. Takes 2 hours from the road. NTD. It may also be possible to approach along the westward running logging spurs which begin in McNab Creek (*B1*) and end SE of Mt. Varley. The term "McNab Lions" originally applied to two summits farther N. They have not been visited much because of the longer approach, but reports say that their ascent is not difficult.

MT. WROTTESLEY 1625 m/5330 ft

A broad, open dome which dominates the western rim of Howe Sound.
FRA: BCMC party, led by E. Fuller—1925.
FRWA: B. Bylsma, J. Gardner, H. Haberl, R. Tomich—January 1980.
From Camp Potlatch, a summer camp at the mouth of Potlatch Creek (*B2*), ascend N for 2 km on a trail which runs parallel to the creek. Turn W, cross the logging road coming from McNab Creek, and continue along the trail on the N side of the creek. You will end up SE of Mt. Wrottesley's east ridge which veers S to the summit. The climb is NTD. An easy day return and a pleasant summit. The extensive logging planned for the Potlatch Creek drainage will likely change the approach. Wrottesley is also occasionally climbed from the McNab Creek road (*B1*).

MT. ELLESMERE 1402 m/4600 ft

A creek drains the south side of this peak. From Camp Potlatch (*B2*), ascend the creek's west side to Ellesmere's south ridge; the summit is then easily reached. An easy 1 day return trip.

"SECHELT RIDGE" 1620 m/5300 ft
Located SE of Sechelt Lake.
From Henriette Lake (*C1*), ascend to Sylvia Lake at 1280 m/4200 ft. Pass around the north side to gain Sechelt Ridge's east ridge. Ascend this, passing the initial bluffs on the north side. Alternatively, contour around the north side of Henriette Lake and ascend to the col at 1160 m/3800 ft by way of the valley to the W. The ridge to the N is then easily climbed. The climb takes 5 hours from Woodfibre. The northwest summit of this ridge is known as **"NOOTKA PEAK"** (1625 m/5333 ft).

MT. SEDGWICK 2077 m/6815 ft
A prominent, barren summit located W of Woodfibre and clearly visible from Britannia Beach.
FA: H. Dowler—1908.
A marked trail, beginning at the north shore of Henriette Lake (*C1*), climbs the ridge to the NW. It leads to the nearest summit of minor **MT. RODERICK** (1460 m/4800 ft), about 3 hours hike from the road. Another 3 hour ramble along the divide brings you to the summit of Sedgwick. The mountain is well suited to skiing, but approaching on skis is a long haul. Steve Grant skied most of the east face of Sedgwick a few years ago. Possible alternative approaches are from Red Tusk Creek (*D1*) to N, and from Taquat Creek (*D2*) to W. Getting lost when descending Sedgwick is a common problem if visibility is poor. Make sure you are on Roderick's southwest, rather than southeast ridge, when descending to Henriette Lake.
West ridge: An easy climb from the col with Mt. Conybeare, made by parties traversing from the Tantalus Range.

MT. DONALDSON 1520 m/5000 ft
An open summit N of upper Sechelt Creek.
Easily approached from the SW via the Sechelt Creek system of roads (*E1*).

"THE TOUCH-AND-GO TOWERS"
A group of seldom visited, rotten volcanic towers located on the west side of the mouth of the Squamish River. They are situated in heavy forest and bush between about 200 m/700 ft and 500 m/1700 ft. A boat is required for access.

"THE CASTLE"
Most conspicuous of the towers.
FA: J. Archer, J. Owen, E. Pigou—1958. Approach from the west (uphill) side, via an overgrown logging road. The north ridge is Class 4 on rotten rock. The east face is a long Class 5 climb on poor and bushy rock (*H. Crabtree, L. MacDonald*).

"TEAPOT TOWER"
The most difficult of the towers.

FA: R. Culbert, J. Owen—1958.
A totally overgrown road leading W from tidewater at the mouth of the Squamish
River passes below Teapot Tower, which appears as a reddish brown cliff N of, and
above, The Castle. Route goes up the north edge for 2 1/2 leads with poor protection. The first lead is wild. Take 60 m of rope to rappel the west face.

"MEMORIAL TOWER"
FA: R. Culbert, G. Headley, A. Shives, G. Woodsworth—1961. Hidden in the forest 1 km NNE of the Teapot. Reach it by hiking uphill from where overgrown road
passes under powerline. From the uphill notch, make a short rope throw, then climb
Class 4 chimney.

"CHOCKSTONE TOWER"
Stands on the south rim of a bottleneck canyon that flows into Monmouth Creek
about 1/2 km west of tidewater.
Walk up the canyon until waterfalls and cliffs impede progress, then climb steep timber to the canyon rim near the tower. *FA: J. Baldwin, R. Culbert, J. Owen—1959,*
via the Class 5 east ridge. The west ridge is equally difficult *(FA: F. de Bruyn, A.
Ellis, A. Shives, G. Woodsworth—1961). The* **"FANG"** and **"FORTRESS"** are
two towers on the canyon rim, above the Chockstone. Both are easy from the rim.
The east face of the Fortress was climbed by J. Owen and E. Pigou—a lengthy Class
5 route.

Chapter 7

Narrows and Sechelt Inlets

BOUNDARIES:
North: Deserted River, Ashlu Creek
East: Pokosha Creek, Clowhom River, Clowhom Lake
South: Salmon Inlet, Sechelt Inlet
West: Jervis Inlet

FOREST SERVICE OFFICE:
Ministry of Forests
P.O. Box 4000
Sechelt, B.C. V0N 3A0
885-5174

MAPS:
Federal:

92 G/12 Sechelt Inlet	92 G/13 Jervis Inlet
92 G/14 Cheakamus River	92 J/4 Princess Louisa Inlet

Provincial:

92 G/NW	92 K
92 J west half	

Introduction

This section contains some fairly high but remote peaks, particularly in its western half. Access to much of the area requires the use of boat, floatplane or helicopter. There are possibilities for technical climbing, but the area is perhaps better suited to alpine rambling and ski touring.

Approaches

To reach many parts of Narrows Inlet, you need to use a boat, floatplane or helicopter. Several high lakes, especially Phantom Lake, appear suitable for floatplane landings. Boats and planes are available in Squamish and Sechelt.

A. FROM CLOWHOM LAKE AND RIVER

1. Clowhom road: A logging road begins at the head of Salmon Inlet. It traverses the northwest side of Clowhom Lake, and 2 km above the head of the lake crosses to the east side of Clowhom River. It runs along this side to 640 m/2100 ft, 1 km E of Phantom Lake.

2. Clowhom spurs: Three important spur roads branch from the Clowhom road. The first leaves the road at its halfway point beside Clowhom Lake, and climbs the creek which drains the south side of Tzoonie Mountain. When the creek forks, the road branches, and both branches can be followed to 640 m/2100 ft. The second spur begins near Clowhom Lake's head, and climbs both sides of the creek S of Phantom Mountain to an elevation of 1000 m/3300 ft. A final spur climbs to 910 m/3000 ft along the south-draining tributary which forms a watershed with Pokosha Creek.

B. FROM SALMON INLET

1. Misery Creek roads: Roads run through most of the Misery Creek valley. The most interesting is the main line, which climbs the east side of the creek to just S of a lake 2 km S of Misery Lake.

2. Western roads: A system of roads crosses the western end of the divide between Salmon and Narrows inlets. This area appears to be of little mountaineering interest.

C. FROM NARROWS INLET

1. Tzoonie River road: From the head of Narrows Inlet, a road follows the west side of Tzoonie River, crossing Chickwat Creek after 6 km/3.7 mi. After 2 km more it forks. The right fork continues along the river, crossing to the east side and ending 1 km from a lake NW of Tzoonie Mountain.

2. Chickwat Creek road: The left fork of the Tzoonie Creek road makes a hook into the Chickwat Creek valley, and follows Chickwat Creek on alternate sides almost to its head. A spur leaves the road 1 km after it crosses the creek, climbs W toward the pass dividing the Earle Range, and ends at 1070 m/3500 ft.

3. Tzoonie River road's left fork and spurs: The first major fork of the Tzoonie River road is 3 km from the head of Salmon Inlet. The left fork climbs SW. Spurs run to 1070 m/3500 ft, E of Mt. Sumner, and to 980 m/3200 ft on both sides of the creek SE of Mt. Draw.

D. FROM SKOOKUMCHUCK NARROWS

From Egmont, just E of Earl's Cove on Highway 101, cross the spectacular tidal rapids of Skookumchuck Narrows to a road beginning at the mouth of Earle Creek. (It is shown on 92 G/12 and 92 G/13.) It climbs along the creek, and then up to 1400 m/4600 ft, S of Mt. Sumner. Its right fork switchbacks to 1190 m/3900 ft, SE of Mt. Drew, and the left fork to the same height SW of Mt. Louie.

E. FROM JERVIS INLET

1. Treat Creek road: A road climbs the south side of Treat Creek, crossing to the north side at 550 m/1800 ft and ending at about 1100 m/3600 ft. A branch also takes in much of the upper north side of the valley.

2. Perketts Creek roads: A road from Treat Creek climbs the east side of Jervis Inlet into Perketts Creek, which is reached at 610 m/2000 ft. Roads continue up both sides of the creek to about 1160 m/3800 ft.

3. Vancouver River roads: From Vancouver Bay, a disused former railroad grade follows the south side of the river to 240 m/800 ft. The north-side road (also an old railroad grade and in poor shape) follows both of the major upper forks to 550 m/1800 ft.

4. High Creek road: A branch of the Vancouver River system goes N into High Creek valley, which it follows to 790 m/2600 ft, E of Mt. Spencer.

5. *Glacial Creek roads:* The road on the east side of this creek reaches 1100 m/3600 ft, NW of Mt. Spencer. A branch reaches 910 m/3000 ft in the unnamed north fork. A separate road attains a similar height in the next creek E, ending W of a 1982 m/6503 ft survey point.

6. *Stakawus Creek roads:* One road climbs to 700 m/2300 ft on the east side of the creek, and another to 550 m/1800 ft in the creek's eastern fork.

7. *Tsuahdi Creek roads:* A road climbs NE from the Stakawus Creek system to reach Tsuahdi Creek, a southern tributary of the Deserted River system, at 460 m/1500 ft. It follows the southwest fork to a tiny lake at 1280 m/4200 ft, and follows the main branch to 850 m/2800 ft.

F. FROM ASHLU CREEK

Access to the northeastern part of the Narrow's Inlet area from Ashlu Creek is described under the Squamish section. Such access is referred to here by geographic name. Spurs from the Ashlu south-side road ascend into Pokosha and Marten creeks drainages, while a branch off the Ashlu main line crosses to the south side into Falk Creek. The main line continues to near timberline ESE of Mt. Crerar.

Routes

PHANTOM MOUNTAIN 1884 m/6181 ft
Located N of the head of Clowhom Lake.
FRA: E. McMynn survey party—1952.
Ascend this peak without difficulty from Phantom Lake, which can be reached by floatplane or from the Clowhom River road (*A1*). Alternatively, climb spurs which start at the head of Clowhom Lake (*A2*). These ascend into the valley S of Phantom Mountain, which should be easily approached from this point.

TZOONIE MOUNTAIN 2100 m/6900 ft
A double summit at the head of Clowhom River. Incorrectly marked on Map sheet 92 G/13.
FA: J. Fyles, T. Fyles—1940.
The 1939 party bushwhacked SE from a point 3 km S of the head of Narrows Inlet to the divide; they climbed minor **PEAK 6501** (1982 m/6501 ft) and camped on its southwest side. They then followed the divide N and E to Tzoonie. Though they are credited with the first ascent of Tzoonie, they actually climbed the 2100 m/6900 ft peak 3 km SW of the Tzoonie Mountain marked on 92 G/13. Their route was up steep snow to the base of a rock below two summit horns, then up a loose chimney to the final ridge; 14 hours return from camp. The best modern approach to this mountain appears to be from the Tzoonie River roads to the NW (*C1*) or by floatplane to any of a number of lakes in the vicinity. Tzoonie Lake has been used as a landing site for climbing the easy 1980 m/6500 ft summit to the NE. (Ref: *CAJ* 1940, p. 149.)

TZOONIE AREA PEAKS
In 1974, John Clarke traversed from Phantom Lake to the Ashlu River; he climbed

the easy group of 2070 m/6800 ft peaks 5 km SW of Phantom Lake, all the summits on the ridge NW of the north end of the same lake, the 2070 m/6800 ft peak mapped as Tzoonie on 92 G/13 (via the southeast ridge), and the 1980 m/6500 ft peaks 2 km SE of the head of Falk Lake. This last is a beautiful horn with a glacier in the basin to the north which terminates in a tiny turquoise lake. Clarke traversed the ridge NE of this peak to the 6600 ft peak at the end, before descending to Ashlu Creek via the steep, busy north side of Falk Creek. He described this region as very attractive alpine country. (Ref: *CAJ* 1975, p. 2.)

MT. DREW 1860 m/6100 ft
This mountain, like Mt. Louie and Mt. Sumner, appears approachable from the Earle Creek roads (*D*). Roads in Treat (*E1*) or Perketts (*E2*) creeks provide access to the 1925 m/6314 ft peak at their head.

MT. CHURCHILL 1980 m/6500 ft
A striking tusk located above Jervis Inlet N of the mouth of Vancouver River.
FRA: F. Baumann, P. Macek, R. Price—1972.
Take the old road up the west fork of High Creek (*E4*), then cross the creek and climb N until you reach the lake W of Mt. Churchill. Churchill's west face is 2 1/2 leads of up to Class 5.4. Rumours persist of a previous ascent of this peak, and a wooden cross has been on the summit for some time, but so has a considerable amount of other junk which has obviously been left by helicopter parties. Churchill's northern companion, **MT. SPENCER** (1860 m/6100 ft), also appears to offer climbing challenges; you might be able to approach it from Glacial Creek (*E5*).

MT. CRERAR 2225 m/7300 ft
Located at the head of Ashlu Creek.
FA: J. Clarke, B. Handfork—1969.
This party approached via the south side of Deserted River (old trail), then up the northwest ridge. Tsuahdi Creek roads (*E7*) now provide good access to the E. The first and lower northwest summit is Class 3 rock via its northwest ridge; the second summit is Class 4 via the west face, which is reached by skirting on the south side of the divide. Takes 3 days return from Jervis Inlet. A lower southeast peak was climbed by J. Denton and J. Pringle in 1963 via the southeast ridge (Ref: *VOCJ* 1963, p. 45).

"CHIMAI MOUNTAIN" 2301 m/7551 ft
A glaciated summit between Ashlu and Falk creeks.
FRA: J. Clarke, M. Ruelle—1969.
At present, the best access to this peak is via the roads which cross to the south side of Ashlu Creek at Tatlow Creek (*F*). From here ascend to the forested east ridge to the timberline and thence to the summit. Extension of Falk Creek road might make approach from S feasible.

MT. JIMMY JIMMY 2204 m/7231 ft
A gentle, glaciated massif above Ashlu Creek and NW of the Tantalus Range.
FA: E. McMynn survey party—1952.
Via Pokosha Creek: Take the highest road on the west side of Pokosha Creek (*F*)

and ascend the slopes to a lake at the base of Jimmy Jimmy's east shoulder. Hike up the shoulder and the snowslopes to the easy summit beyond. Another route was put up from the head of Pokosha Creek by G. Walter and party by ascending the glacier on its east side to gain the southeast ridge. Traverse W to reach the summit.

Via Coin Creek: Drive to Coin Creek (*F*) on the SE side of Ashlu Creek, and then ascend the obvious ridge between Coin and Marten creeks to gain the glacier at 1830 m/6000 ft. The summit is the highest peak on the divide to the W. A 1 day return trip.

Southwest ridge: *FA: H. Mather, M. Schliessler—1982.* From Phantom Lake, ascend N through bush on the east side of the creek past two lakes to timberline. Continue N from here up the valley until you reach the glacier on the divide (1740 m/5700 ft). Descend W to a flat area in the headwaters of Clowhom River at 1370 m/4500 ft. Climb N to the southwest ridge and from there, climb to the summit. The final section involves some dangerously loose, low Class 5 rock. A full 1 day return trip from Phantom Lake.

"BOGUS MOUNTAIN" Reportedly quite high.

Located roughly N of the Reality River.

North face: *FA: R. Culbert, G. Woodsworth—1960s.* Begin with a stiff lead of Class 4 up overhanging grooves and bottoming cracks, then transfer right to follow faint ribs for several more leads of Class 4–5 climbing. Finish via indescribably rotten rock, avoiding waterfalls on the left. Take a minimal rack and probably kletterschues. Some prospecting experience desirable.

East ridge: *FA: D. Serl and ACC party of at least 17.* Take enjoyable cracks and slabs, musing all the while on Castaneda. Best when iced up or half-covered with rotten snow. Several difficult bits occur here and there on this line, which is easily worth the poke.

Southeast ridge: *FA: J. Baldwin, J. Clarke—1980s.* Approach via the Homathko Icefield. Several river crossings are necessary. Ridge is NTD, so you should have time to climb several other peaks the same day. Sir Norman Watson attempted the route in the 1930s and wrote a voluminous book on the epic.

West glacier: *FA: K. Ricker, W. Tupper—1970s.* Approach via kame terraces and glacial till. The start of the route is marked by a large erratic. Outflank arcuate morainal furrows to gain glaciers on the lefthand side (looking up) which are followed to summit. Route is well cairned; not suitable for small children or dogs. The next party is asked to retrieve a theodolite inadvertently left on a glacial boulder pedestal. A round of readings would be appreciated before bringing it back.

Northwest rib: *FA: C.S. Bungi, Friend McNeil.* The route is obvious. Quite suitable for dogs and small children.

South-southwest ridge: *FA (although they deny it): M. Feller, R. Wyborn.* The approach is incredibly bushy and dismal. Only those of very tough mettle should even consider it.

Chapter 8
Powell-Jervis

BOUNDARIES:
North: Little Toba River, Toba River, Toba Inlet
East: Skwakwa River, Jervis Inlet
South: Georgia Strait
West: Homfray Channel

FOREST SERVICE OFFICES:

Sechelt Forest District
P.O. Box 4000
Sechelt, B.C. V0N 3A0
885-5174

Powell River Forest District
7077 Duncan Street
Powell River, B.C. V8A 1W1
485-9831

LOGGING COMPANIES:

MacMillan Bloedel
Weldwood of Canada Ltd.
Stillwater Logging Division
4400 Marine Avenue
Powell River, B.C. V8A 2K1
485-4214
487-9144

Goat Lake Operations
Wolfson Creek, R.R. #3
Powell River, B.C. V8A 5C1

MAPS:
Federal:
92 F/16 Haslam Lake
92 J/4 Princess Louisa Inlet
92 K/2 Toba Inlet
92 K/8 Little Toba River

92 G/13 Jervis Inlet
92 K/1 Powell Lake
92 K/7 Redonda Island

Provincial:
92 F/NE
92 J

92 G/NW
92 K

Introduction

This vast area encompasses all the country between Jervis Inlet and Toba Inlet, and includes the drainage of the Powell and Daniels rivers. It is a huge area, little known to mountaineers, but a glance at the map sheets will tell you that there is mile after mile of alpine ridge and basin country to explore, particularly between Skwakwa, Little Toba, and Powell rivers. Large numbers of peaks in the region remain unclimbed, but most do not appear to be difficult. Many of the northern peaks are difficult to approach without using a boat, floatplane or helicopter. The peaks on the east side of Powell Lake can often be reached by road.

The most recent descriptions of the area have been supplied by the Vancouver mountaineer John Clarke, who made a solo traverse down the divide north of the Daniels River, and followed the divide south down the east side of Powell River. He reported huge granite walls ringing the upper Daniels River, with great, clean slabs sweeping straight down to the valley floor. He also found the alpine character of the high ridges extremely pleasant, affording easy travel and continuously fine views. The Powell-Jervis country is a little far off for weekend trips from Vancouver, but backpackers who have more time to spend could easily spend several weeks above tree line here, exploring alpine lakes and summits which have never been visited.

Approaches

Take the regularly scheduled B.C Ferry from Horseshoe Bay to Langdale. Follow Highway 101 past Sechelt to Earls Cove. A second ferry goes from here to Saltery Bay. The highway then continues on through Powell River to its end at Lund.

A. FROM THE MACMILLAN BLOEDEL (STILLWATER) MAIN LINE
MacMillan Bloedel has built a major network of roads N of Lois Lake. Current maps are available from MacMillan Bloedel in Powell River. The main line begins about 11.3 km/7 mi W of Saltery Bay, just before the highway crosses Lois River. It follows the west side of Lois Lake for 13 km/8 mi, then forks. The right fork continues on for another 27.5 km/17 mi to Freda Lake.
1. Freda Lake spur roads: Spurs beginning 40.2 km/25 mi from the highway climb the north tributary to 980 m/3200 ft. The main road (overgrown) continues E from Freda Lake to near "Jenna Lake", giving access to the north face of Mt. Freda.
2. McVey Lake road: At 29 km/18 mi, a right fork leads along the north side of a creek to Murphy and then McVey Lake; washed out at the present time.
3. East branch: This forks right at 25.7 km/16 mi, and forks again 4 km later. Branch "E-100" goes N, then E along a creek valley to Alpha and Beta lakes, providing excellent access to the west and north sides of the "Big Knucklehead." The east branch itself continues E to the moribund Powell River Ski Club area, cutting directly below the southwest side of Diadem Mountain. Of interest to rock climbers is "Third Lake Slab" at 37 km/23 mi, a steep 245 m/800 ft slab of granodiorite. The east branch provides good access to the south and west sides of "The Knuckleheads."
4. Third Lake branch: This road branches from the M&B main line at 20 km/12.5 mi. Just beyond the locked gate at 35 km/21.8 mi, the road splits. The west fork extends to 40 km/25 mi on the west side of the valley; the east fork continues along Lois Lake, and reaches the north end of Khartoum Lake at 46.5 km/29 mi from the highway.
5. "J" branch: This cuts E at approximately 33 km/20.5 mi on the M&B main road (just past Phelan Lake) and gives access to McVey Lake drainage and the south face of Mt. Freda.

B. FROM THE WELDWOOD (GOAT LAKE) MAIN LINE
This road leaves the highway 2 km W of Lois River, about 14 km/9 mi from Saltery

Bay. It is roughly parallel to the MacMillan Bloedel main line for its first 11.2 km/7 mi, and the two roads connect at three points. The road continues past Horseshoe, Dodd, and Windsor lakes to the east side of Goat Lake. At 48.3 km/30 mi from the highway, the road reaches the head of Goat Lake. There is a gate at the head of Goat Lake; contact Weldwood Logging Company for the key.

1. Eldred River road: The road continues from Goat Lake along the east side of Eldred River to major forks at 120 m/400 ft, about 7 km/4.5 mi from the head of Goat Lake (B branch). The road then crosses the east fork and continues along the east side of the river to further forks at 270 m/900 ft (another 8 km/5 mi). The left branch then climbs to 750 m/2500 ft in the valley 3.5 km W of an unnamed lake mapped at 3918 ft. The right branch ascends the valley S of Peak 6103 (1860 m/6103 ft) for about 4 km (D branch, *B8*).

2. Tin Hat Mountain: At 19.3 km/12 mi along the Weldwood main line, a left fork leads to "Spring Lake." From here, a trail ascends N to Tin Hat Mountain (1220 m/4000 ft), which provides good views of Powell Lake and the surrounding area.

3. Branch GL-1: At 33 km/20.5 mi, a series of roads branch from the Weldwood main line and follow an unnamed creek ESE toward the cirque of peaks to the W of Freda Lake. GL-1 crosses the creek at 640 m/2100 ft and heads N and E, dropping into the next valley and gaining the west shoulder of Peak 5026 (1532 m/5026 ft). Roads on both sides of the unnamed creek advance almost to the unnamed lake mapped at 1036 m/3400 ft, 1 km SW of Peak 5802 (1768 m/5802 ft), and there are spurs which go even higher.

4. Branch GL-2: This branch heads E at 35 km/21.8 mi and climbs to the end of the valley NW of Skwim Lake at 1000 m/3300 ft. It gives excellent access to the southern portion of the Powell divide.

5. Beartooth Mountain, "A" branch: At 1.5 km past the head of Goat Lake, "A" branch crosses the Eldred River. It follows the west side for 2 km both N and S. About 2 km N of the bridge, an overgrown spur climbs W to 920 m/3000 ft in the valley due E of Beartooth Mountain, while just opposite the Eldred River crossing an overgrown spur climbs W up into the steep cirque below the sharp peaks S of Beartooth.

6. "B" branch: At 54 km/34.6 mi, there is a major fork. "B" branch ascends in an easterly direction towards a series of unnamed lakes S and W of Peak 5793 (1766 m/5793 ft). Roads on either side of the creek currently reach to about the 760 m/2500 ft level, and there are spurs to 920 m/3000 ft. The main branch, along the south side of the creek, ascends from the unnamed lake mapped at 550 m/1800 ft to 920 m/3000 ft in the bowl N of the large lake mapped at 1344 m/4410 ft. This road system offers promising access to the Mt. Alice area.

7. West main branch: This branch crosses the Eldred River at 56 km/35 mi (bridge passable to foot traffic only) and ascends into the long valley which runs SW to the lakes E of "Mt. Baldy."

8. "D" branch: At 60 km/37 mi, another major series of roads heads E into the large valley W of Mt. Alfred. Roads ascend both sides of the creek; those on the north bank climb to 760 m/2500 ft, only about 4 km W of Mt. Alfred.

9. "G" branch: At 65 km/40.5 mi, the main line crosses the Eldred River. At this point a branch heads SW for 4 km along the unnamed creek draining the north side of the "Slide Mountain" area (2090 m/6858 ft).

C. FROM POWELL LAKE

A number of road systems begin from Powell Lake. Boat or floatplane is necessary to reach them; these are available at Powell Lake Marina (483-3313), and Powell Air (485-4262), at the mouth of the lake.

1. Beartooth Creek approach: An old road ascends the north side of the creek from its mouth. A trail then leads to its major northeast fork. This is crossed and a draw ascended SE to reach the west ridge of Beartooth Mountain at 1370 m/4500 ft.

2. Jim Brown Creek road: an old road follows this creek to 460 m/1500 ft.

3. Powell River road: This road follows the Powell River from the head of Powell Lake. The upper east fork now reaches tree line 2 km NW of an unnamed lake mapped at 1436 m/4710 ft. The south branch of this fork extends to within 1 km of Peak 5941 (1811 m/5941 ft), while the upper north fork extends to 370 m/1200 ft.

    3a. West branch: The west branch of the Powell River road follows this gradual valley to about 340 m/1100 ft.

4. Olsen Creek road: A road follows the north side of this creek, eventually joining roads in the Theodosia Creek watershed.

D. FROM TOBA INLET

Again, you need to use a boat or floatplane to reach this area.

1. Theodosia River road: A road climbs quite far up this river from the head of Theodosia Inlet, connecting with the Olsen Creek road en route. High spurs run up both of the river's upper eastern tributaries. There are long-term plans to extend this road along the east side of Theodosia and Okeover inlets, and connect it with the highway.

2. Forbes Creek road: An old road ascends into the south fork of this creek to about 660 m/2170 ft.

3. Homfray Creek roads: Old logging roads climb to about 580 m/1900 ft on both sides of Homfray Creek. From their end, a trail leads N to a lake at timberline. This is a B.C. Forest Service Recreation area.

4. Snout Point road: A road ascends the creek draining the northeast side of Mt. Grazebrooke to 800 m/2620 ft, E of that mountain.

5. "Nor Creek" valley: Currently, there are plans for logging in this watershed, the first major one E of Hat Mountain.

6. Chusan Creek road: A new road leads to almost 760 m/2500 ft; this valley will be logged over the next decade.

E. FROM LITTLE TOBA RIVER

The Toba River road is itself of no relevance to access in this area, as it follows the north side of the river. However, it crosses to the south side just past the Little Toba River.

1. Main road: There is much current and projected logging activity in the Little Toba valley. Currently the main road follows the east side of the Little Toba River to a major east-northeast tributary (Lunar Creek but called "Lightning Creek" by locals). The road currently crosses this and continues to about 550 m/1800 ft. A branch is planned to cross the river into the southern tributary which forms a watershed with Skwakwa River.

2. Southwest-side road: Just before Lunar Creek there is a bridge to the southwest side. A road follows the river SE for 4 km.

F. FROM SKWAKWA RIVER
This river drains into the head of Jervis Inlet. A road follows the east side of the river for 5 km, where it crosses to the W and continues just past Pilldolla Creek.
1. Barkshack Creek road: A road ascends the south side of this creek to 370 m/1200 ft; it then crosses the creek and contours N towards Pilldolla Creek.
2. Pilldolla Creek road: A road runs up the north side to 370 m/1200 ft.

G. FROM JERVIS INLET
1. Lausmann Creek road: An old road climbs to 460 m/1500 ft in the Lausmann Creek valley.
2. Slane Creek road: A road reaches 460 m/1500 ft on the northwest side; it crosses to the southeast side and switchbacks to 790 m/2600 ft.
3. Smanit Creek road: This road ascends the west side to forks in the creek at 430 m/1400 ft.
4. Crabapple Creek road: This road ascends the northwest side of the creek to 790 m/2600 ft, NW of Mt. Frederick William.
5. Osgood Creek road: A short road reaches 670 m/2200 ft on the northeast side of this creek.
6. Seshal Creek roads: Roads here rise to 520 m/1700 ft on the northeast side of the creek, and to 610 m/2000 ft on the southwest side.
7. Brittain River track: A disused track begins where this river empties into Princess Royal Reach of Jervis Inlet. It follows the river to a triple fork at 210 m/700 ft and then climbs the east fork to 670 m/2200 ft.

Routes

MT. ALFRED 2380 m/7810 ft
Located W of the head of Jervis Inlet.
FA: A. Dalton, P. Easthope—1929.
Take the old road *(G1)* up Lausmann Creek and spur road up the east flank of Mt. Alfred. Climb to timberline, then W to (unmapped) glacier, which is followed to Alfred's northeast shoulder and then to the névé beyond. The final summit is a scramble from the N. A good approach from the W is via "D" branch *(B8)*.

MT. ALICE 1794 m/5886 ft
Stands SW of the head of Jervis Inlet.
A logging road runs from the inlet *(G1)* for some distance up the shoulder NE of Mt. Alice. From there, follow the divide back, which is mainly easy travel through open forest. Roads in Slane Creek *(G2)* might also prove a feasible approach to the southeast side. Perhaps the best way currently, however, is via "B" branch *(B6)*.

MT. WELLINGTON 1684 m/5525 ft
Located across Jervis Inlet from Malibu.
FRA: A. Dalton, P. Easthope—1941.
A very old road climbs from the inlet to 1070 m/3500 ft on the slope N of McCannel Lake. From there, swing to the W, going over or around easy **MT. ARTHUR**

(1609 m/5280 ft), to scramble up Wellington from the S. The Smanit Creek road (*G3*) is a possible alternative approach to NW.

MT. FREDERICK WILLIAM 1740 m/5700 ft
Overlooks the final bend of Jervis Inlet.
This mountain forms a horseshoe around Crabapple Creek and is ascended from a short road (*G4*) in that vicinity. The ridge is an enjoyable and scenic traverse. The highest (unnamed) summit to WSW is shown at 1818 m/5965 ft.

MT. CAMBRIDGE 1510 m/4955 ft
Located to E of Brittain River. Old roads (*G7*) in the Brittain River valley or more recent roads (*G6*) in Seshal Creek appear to offer access.

DIADEM MOUNTAIN 1740 m/5700 ft
Located 6 km/3.6 mi E of Freda Lake.
This summit might be most easily reached by climbing NE from Freda Lake (*B*) to the ridge leading SE to peak. "Third Lake branch" (*A4*) cuts directly below the southwest face. Peaks along the Parker Range were ascended by the W.R. Bacon geological party in 1950 and 1951.

"MT. FREDA" 1890 m/6200 ft
Located S of Freda Lake.
FRA: P. Lockie, T. Pickles—1950.
From Freda Lake: From the southwest end of Freda Lake (*A*), take the spur road around the lake's southeast side, and from the end of this go S up a small valley to timberline NW of Mt. Freda. Continue over heather, etc. to summit. Pleasant and NTD.

MT. CALDER 1465 m/4806 ft
Located opposite Vancouver Bay. *FRA: W.R. Bacon survey party—1950 or 1951.* NTD.

"THE KNUCKLEHEADS" 1680 m/5500 ft
FRA: G. Stanley—1932.
Drive up the east complex (*A3*) of the Freda Creek logging system, keeping on the low road until past the spur leading to the old ski lodge. Continue E to the spur N of Branch E-5000, and from there go up the obvious draw. Some scrambling on summit. An easy, 1 day trip. The southwest face is also a scramble (*M. Conway-Brown, R. Richards—1980*).

BEARTOOTH MOUNTAIN 1770 m/5800 ft
A sharp summit located E of Powell Lake and NW of Goat Lake.
FA: P. Lockie, R. Simmonds—1935.
This peak has traditionally been reached via Powell Lake and Beartooth Creek (*D1*). Just before the end of the draw leading to the west ridge, cut left and scramble up ridge to 20 m/65 ft dip, then traverse to left around a minor bump to the face of final peak beyond. Ascend this by a steep gully to the northwest ridge, and follow the ridge to the summit. Class 3–4; 8 hours up and a rather full day return. Beartooth and

adjoining peaks are now more easily reached from logging spurs ascending W from near the mouth of Eldred River (*B5*). This side also seems to offer some worthwhile climbing challenges.

"RAINBOW PEAKS" 1846 m/6056 ft
A group of rocky peaks S of Beartooth Mountain.
FRA: P. Lockie, R. Simmonds—1935.
One approach is by boat to the mouth of the creek which drains these peaks' southwest sides. Bushwhack up the north side of the creek to bluffs at 1070 m/3500 ft, then switch to south side and climb to the 1340 m/4400 ft col. A ridge involving some scrambling then leads NE to the summit. A branch of the Eldred River road system (*B1*) can also be followed S along the west side of Goat Lake until it is possible to bushwhack into the saddle N of Rainbow Peaks. The walls on the northeast side of the Rainbows are big.

"MT. BALDY" 2017 m/6618 ft
Located 3 km NW of Beartooth Mountain.
FRA: A. Adams, R. Simmonds, O. Stevenson—1939.
Approach via the west main branch (*B7*) or Beartooth Mountain (*B5*). A steep, obvious draw drops to Powell Lake from just S of the summit. Ascend this to the 610 m/2000 ft level, then take a side-draw to the left. This leads to plateau WNW of Baldy. Continue over open and pleasant terrain. Not difficult.

"SLIDE MOUNTAIN" 2090m/6858 ft
Located at the head of McMillan Creek.
FA: I. Kay—1942.
From Powell Lake, ascend by the main (northeast) fork of McMillan Creek to camp at the lake at 1128 m/3702 ft, SW of Slide Mountain. The summit is gained by scrambling up the ridge from near the northwest end of the lake. The ridge is sharp near the top. Slide Mountain has also been climbed as a 3 day return trip from the spur road which branches from the Jim Brown Creek road (*C2*), 5 km up from Powell Lake. A better choice now is from the west main branch road (*B7*).

"LOCKIE'S TABLE" 1855 m/6085 ft
A gentle summit rising E of the head of Powell Lake.
FRA: P. Lockie, B. Stenberg—1952.
The ascent is not difficult from the head of Powell Lake. The northern summit may be reached in about 8 hours by following ridges from about 3 km up Powell River.

"OZZIE'S TIT" 1910 m/6267 ft
Located between the Powell and Daniels rivers at GR 054748.
FA: G. McCahon and party—1970s.
The peak was approached from the valley to the W and climbed via the north ridge without difficulty.

PEAK 6245 1900 m/6245 ft
A broad and isolated massif surrounded on three sides by the Powell River at GR 116743.

FA: J. Clarke—October 1985.
From roads to the E of the peak in the upper Powell River (*C3*), cross the river and ascend W through pleasant wooded country. Emerge into a wet, meadowy valley. Gain the gentle ridge to the S at this point. From here the east ridge can be attained, which is (despite maps) Class 4. Descend via the west ridge, dropping SE through scrubby bluffs and then traverse the south side of the peak on grassy benches.

Peaks around the head of the Daniels River   John Clarke

POWELL DIVIDE TRAVERSE

In September 1984, J. Clarke (Ref: *CAJ* 1985) made a 3-week solo traverse down the divide W of the Little Toba and Skwawka rivers. The whole area is a rugged arctic-alpine wilderness of granitic ridges clothed in heather and grasses. It is strewn with dozens of alpine lakes which are tucked into deep, shady pockets. Most of these have granitic slabs shooting straight into the water. The area has a very remote character despite being not far from Vancouver. Clarke began from Toba Inlet on roads in Chusan Creek (*D6*), using the ridge W of that creek to gain the divide crest mapped as a boundary on 92 K/1 and 92 K/8. The climbing began at **PEAKS 5987** (1825 m/5987 ft) and **5823** (1775 m/5823 ft) N of the upper Daniels River and ended (with discovery of an air-drop devoured by hungry wolverines) at **PEAK 6249** (1900 m/6249 ft), 4.5 km W of Mt. Alfred. All peaks on the divide itself were climbed and the following side trips made: **PEAK 6328** (1929 m/6328 ft); **PEAK 6734** (2052 m/6734 ft); **PEAK 7100** (2160 m/7100 ft) NE of **PEAK 7206** (2200 m/7206 ft); **PEAK 6542** (1994 m/6542 ft); **PEAK 6400** (1950 m/6400 ft) 1 km SW of **PEAK 6453** (1967 m/6453 ft); the group of peaks N and NE of the lake mapped at 3490 ft (1064 m) in the upper Skwawka River; **PEAK 6460** (1970 m/6460 ft) SW of the same lake. **PEAK 5924** (1805 m/5924 ft) yielded colossal views down toward Jervis Inlet. Clarke exited into the branch of the Eldred River W of the lake mapped at 1194 m/3918 ft (*Bl*). Roads come to 750 m/2500 ft in this valley. The one tricky part of the trip (apart from long storms) was the descent from **PEAK 6520** (1990 m/6520 ft) at GR 148724 on 92 K/8, where it was necessary to drop down the southeast ridge to gain a diagonal ledge leading down to the basin to the S. Peak 6520 was first occupied by a helicopter survey party. Most other ascents are presumed to be first ascents by Clarke, except for the three peaks below.

PEAK 6372 1942 m/6372 ft
Located S of the head of Chusan Creek. Cairn found, but no record.

PEAK 6526 1989 m/6526 ft
Located at GR 123837, E of the lake mapped at 4072 ft (1241 m) at the head of "Well Creek." *FA: P. Scheiber, T. Scheiber.* Party approached via a 9 day bushwhack from Powell Lake. What more can one say?

PEAK 6460 1970 m/6460 ft
Located N of the head of Pilldolla Creek. Cairn found, but no record.

"TRIPLE PEAKS" 1966 m/6449 ft
A ridge of summits located 5 km E of Goat Lake.
Parties have approached this group by floatplane to "Emma Lake," the large lake mapped at 4410 ft (1344 m), and thence down the divide to the south. A tricky gap at 1615 m/5300 ft just N of the peaks is descended using a gully to the S, giving access to a glacial basin on the northwest side of **PEAK 6353** (1936 m/6353 ft). The peaks are easy ascents from here.

"SKWIM MOUNTAIN" 1615 m/5300 ft
Located 0.5 km NW of Skwim Lake.
A steep tower, Skwim has been climbed via the loose Class 3 south ridge. The north ridge is steep, but easy.

PEAK 5802 1768 m/5802 ft
Located 3 km NW of Freda Lake. This stately peak is easily approached from most directions.

MT. CRAWSHAY 1540 m/5380 ft
Located W of Theodosia River, in the Unwin Range. On Map 92 K/2 the name is positioned about 1 km SE of the correct location.
FRA: J. Christianson, F. Dawe—1952.

The first recorded ascent party approached from the Forbes Creek road (*D2*), but logging operations on Theodosia River (*D1*) have reached the base of this summit and better routes will likely be found from that side.

THEODOSIA MOUNTAIN 1829 m/6002 ft
Located S of the large lake at the head of Bradburn Creek.
FRA: P. Lockie, D. Lyon, B. McKnight, C. Schiel, A. Smith—1959.
The original ascent involved a bushwhack from Powell Lake to easy southwest ridge. The more obvious approach is now from Theodosia River (*D1*).

MT. DENMAN 1960 m/6430 ft
A sharp rock summit located N of Forbes Creek near Homfray Channel.
FA: J. Dudra—1955.
Route of original ascent is unknown. The summit was reached in 1966 (*E. Culos, A. Francescutti, A. Riley*) from Forbes Creek (*D2*) by ascending bushy slopes between the two creeks W of Mt. Denman. Ascend a narrow ridge here and cross on ledge to under peak. Climb the west ridge on steep but firm rock.

MT. AIKEN 1800 m/5900 ft
A minor summit W of Mt. Denman. The road beginning at Foster Point to W of Aiken goes to 1000 m/3280 ft. It appears easy to ascend from here to summit, and then along an open ridge to Mt. Denman.

MT. WHIELDON 1800 m/5900 ft
Located above the mouth of Toba Inlet. The Snout Point road (*D4*) seems to offer access to the east side of the ridge connecting this peak and **MT. GRAZEBROOKE** (1680 m/5510 ft). Contours indicate little difficulty.

JULIAN PEAK 2130 m/6987 ft
A high summit SE of the head of Toba Inlet. Roads in Chusan Creek (*D6*) probably give decent access to the southwest side. **PEAK 5790** (1765 m/5790 ft), about 2.5 km NW of Julian, is likely the summit ascended in 1933 by N. Carter and H. Dalgleish.

MT. ADDENBROKE 1620 m/5140 ft
The highest point on East Redonda Island. From Pendrell Sound, climb overgrown logging roads to 950 m/3000 ft. Ascend the valley here through timber, skirting the base of cliffs to the col about 1 km NE of Addenbroke. From the col scramble up the ridge to the pleasant summit plateau. Picnic lunch recommended.

Chapter 9

Clendenning and Sims Creeks

by Robert Driscoll

BOUNDARIES:
North: Toba River
East: Skwawka and Little Toba rivers
South: Deserted River
West: Elaho River

FOREST SERVICE OFFICES:

Squamish Forest District
P.O. Box 1970
Squamish, B.C. V0N 3G0
(Elaho River roads)
898-9671

Sechelt Forest District
P.O. Box 4000
Sechelt, B.C. V0N 3A0
(Jervis Inlet access)
885-5174

Powell River Forest District
7077 Duncan Street
Powell River, B.C. V8A 1A1
(Toba River roads)
485-9831

LOGGING COMPANIES:

Empire Logging Division
Weldwood of Canada Ltd.
P.O. Box 280, 3150 Cleveland Street
Squamish, B.C. V0N 3G0
892-5244

Goat Lake Operations
Weldwood of Canada Ltd.
P.O. Box 16, Wolfson Creek, R.R. #3
Powell River, B.C. V8A 5C1
487-9144

MAPS:
Federal:
92 J/4 Princess Louisa Inlet
92 J/12 Mount Dalgleish
92 K/9 Mount Argyle

92 J/5 Clendenning Creek
92 K/8 Little Toba River

Provincial:
92 J
92 K

Introduction and History

The Clendenning Creek area is the most remote in the guidebook. It is not serviced by any road driveable from the Vancouver area, although it can be approached using roads from Jervis Inlet or the Toba River. Neither of these approaches, however, comes close to penetrating the heart of this rugged wilderness.

The remoteness of Clendenning Creek is, of course, a large part of its attraction. Any party climbing here can be almost guaranteed that they will have the field to themselves and, although most peaks have now had first ascents, there are still scores of new routes to be climbed. Reports say the rock is sound and that there is an extensive network of glaciers which provides quick approaches at high elevation, including the ten kilometre Clendenning Glacier, which drains into the lake feeding Clendenning Creek.

The major logging company active in the area is Weldwood; their future plans call for roads to be pushed further up the Elaho River. Very likely, one day a bridge will cross the Elaho and new roads flung through the area. The thought of logging trucks invading this sheltered retreat is not too comforting, but easier access will certainly mean new opportunities for many climbers.

There have been few visitors to the Clendenning Creek area, and their visits have been separated by years of inactivity. First to explore this area was the redoubtable Stanley Smith, whose exploits were described in the Historical Introduction. Although we cannot be sure of the route he took to reach Chilko Lake, recent research has confirmed that on his way he passed through the Clendenning Creek area.

The first real climbing in the area began in the southern region. Between 1929 and 1941, A. Dalton and P. Easthope made several ascents in the Queens Reach group, taking boats up Jervis Inlet and using existing logging roads and creeks to get closer to the peaks.

Later, in 1950, the B.C. Electric Company carefully surveyed the area to find out if it would be practical to divert the Elaho River into Princess Louisa Inlet as part of a power generation scheme. These surveyors made a number of first ascents in the course of their operations.

After that, the area was deserted until the 1970s, when the Vancouver mountaineer and explorer John Clarke made two separate traverses through the region, ending them at logging operations on the Toba River. A large ACC camp was held in the area around Doolittle Creek and the Clendenning Glacier in 1979. John Clarke then cleaned up most of the unclimbed peaks in the region with his third visit in 1984.

For maps showing the locations of many of the features mentioned in this chapter, see *CAJ* 1980, pp. 55–56 and pp. 74–79; and *CAJ* 1983, pp. 21–23.

Approaches

A. FROM THE EAST
Drive up the Elaho River road (see Squamish-Pemberton Icefield chapter). Cross the river by boat and work up Clendenning or Sims creeks. Not very feasible at present as avalanche alder is overpowering.

B. FROM JERVIS INLET (SOUTH)

1. Mt. Pearkes roads: Old roads, now choked with brush, run to 1220 m/4000 ft up an unnamed creek south of Mt. Pearkes and north of the Deserted River.

2. Potato Creek road: A 4.8 km/3 mi road runs up Potato Creek from Jervis Inlet, but travel in this valley is grim because of thick bush.

3. Hunaechin Creek road: Once beyond the 8 km/5 mi road which leads you to the 610 m/2000 ft level southeast of Mt. Alexander, travel in this valley is even grimmer than on the Potato Creek route. Horribly overgrown roads run up the south side to a creek which drains the west side of Mt. Albert.

4. Skwawka River roads: Logging roads are being extended up Skwawka River from the head of Jervis Inlet. At present, they reach into its western tributary, Pilldolla Creek. On the east side they extend to opposite Barkshack Creek at 300 m/1000 ft.

C. FROM PRINCESS LOUISA INLET

The spectacularly beautiful Princess Louisa Inlet is separated from Jervis Inlet by minor tidal rapids. The Malibu camp here is a private resort for Biblically-inclined recreationists.

1. Loquilts Creek trail: From the head of this inlet (Princess Louisa Park), reach the high divide west by taking the trail up the east side of the creek (past falls) to the 1400 m/4600 ft ridge S of the lake at the head of Loquilts Creek. Head E under cliffs, hike up the granite ramp, then drop to the lake and head N beyond to the open, easy divide.

D. FROM THE NORTH

From the mouth of the Toba River, a road runs for 29 km/18 mi along the south side of the river to the logging camp (watch out for bears near the garbage dump). The logging camp also has a landing strip for wheeled aircraft which was destroyed in the summer of 1985 but will likely be rebuilt. There are regularly scheduled flights in and out of this camp when the strip is open. Contact Weldwood for details.

1. Little Toba River roads: Logging roads are being extended right to the back of the drainage (12 km/7.5 mi), but unfortunately the roads end at less than 610 m/2000 ft.

2. Racoon Creek roads: Logging roads climb both sides of Racoon Creek (about 5 km), ending low in the valley. J. Clarke used these roads to exit from one of his traverses. The descent directly down Racoon Creek into the Toba River logging system is impossible without long rappels at the 200 m/650 ft headwall just W of "Racoon Pass." Descent is possible further N from the Jimmie Creek area. (Ref: *CAJ* 1980, p. 74.)

3. Jimmie Creek roads: Roads push 6 km/3.7 mi up the north and south sides of Jimmie Creek as shown on the federal maps. J. Clarke used one of these roads to exit from this area on his 1972 ski traverse. The drainage is known as "Boulder Creek" by Weldwood and its employees. Jimmie Creek is shown in a different location on provincial maps.

4. Upper Toba River roads: A logging road follows the east side of the Toba River until the river forks sharply to the SE. Then the road crosses to Toba's northwest side and goes out of the guidebook range. On the northeast side of the southeast fork, the main line continues to the 1000 m/3300 ft level and ends at an obvious forked creek. Plans are being made to log right to the head of the Toba River, so watch for roads to be extended (possibly on both sides of the river).

Routes

MT. PEARKES 2130 m/7000 ft
FRA: Underhill survey party—1956.
Located above Jervis Inlet 3.2 km N of Deserted River.
Roads from Jackson's logging camp 3.2 km NW of Deserted Bay lead to 1220 m/4000 ft on the southwest side of Mt. Pearkes. Swing onto the south shoulder and hike to the summit. NTD. To reach the ridge beyond, go around the peak which lies to the SE. The two 2130 m/7000 ft peaks which stand above the Elaho River at the northeast end of the ridge can also be reached in this way. In 1972, J. Clarke traversed from Mt. Pearkes to the Elaho-Squamish junction. The main obstacle was a steep, deep gap down to 1370 m/4500 ft at the head of the Deserted River (see Squamish-Pemberton Icefield chapter).

MT. ALEXANDER 2332 m/7650 ft; MT. VICTORIA 2042 m/6700 ft
Two summits located on the Hunaechin-Skwawka divide.
FA: A. Dalton, P. Easthope—1931.
The first ascent party climbed Alexander after a long, unpleasant pack up Hunaechin Creek (*B3*) and gained Mt. Victoria by traversing back from Mt. Alexander at about the 1830 m/6000 ft level. They encountered difficulties on the final rock face. Approach from the Skwawka River (*B4*) would be more advisable now. This party almost certainly also climbed **"PILAETUS PEAK"** (2044 m/6705 ft) on **BLASTUS RIDGE** on the return traverse. (Ref: *CAJ* 1941, p. 18.)

"SUN PEAK" 2290 m/7500 ft
Located E of the lake at the head of Loquilts Creek.
FA: Seattle Mountaineers party—1940.
From the top of the ramp on the approach to Loquilts Lake (*C1*), climb E up gullies to Sun Peak's easy southwest ridge. A pleasant 1 day return hike from Princess Louisa Inlet.

MT. ALBERT 2532 m/8308 ft
Located between Hunaechin Creek and Princess Louisa Inlet.
FA: P. Dalton, P. Easthope—1929.
From near Hamilton Island in Princess Louisa Inlet, a road angles W to 610 m/2000 ft, and from there a crude trail is marked to the col behind Mt. Helena. This point is now more quickly reached by traversing easy **MT. HELENA** (1661 m/5451 ft; *FRA: P. Dalton, P. Easthope—1929*) itself, from roads which climb to over 1070 m/3500 ft from Jervis Inlet 4.8 km NW of Malibu (*C*). The 2290 m/7500 ft ridge south of Albert is next ascended, its first summit avoided by ascending to the right. Cross N between the summits of this ridge to névé and continue to Mt. Albert. NTD. A moderate weekend trip from Malibu. (Ref: *CAJ* 1930, p. 155.)

Mt. Alexander

Mt. Tinniswood   John Clarke

MT. TINNISWOOD 2590 m/8500 ft
A prominent summit 12.9 km/8 mi N of Princess Louisa Inlet.
FA: A. Dalton, P. Easthope—1941.
Southeast Ridge: Continue through ugly bush from the end of the Hunaechin Creek
road (*B3*) to its major east fork. Go up this fork 0.4 km until below a large falls,
where a log allows crossing. Ascend steep, messy, timbered ridge onto **MT.
GEORGE EDWARDS** (2260 m/7400 ft), the summit of which was traversed by
the original ascent party to reach Tinniswood's loose, Class 3 southeast ridge. Not
recommended. (Ref: *CAJ* 1941, p. 14.)
From Princess Louisa Inlet: *FA: D. Bjerke, L. Bjerke, D. Boudnot, R.
Jones—1973.* The main divide north of Princess Louisa Inlet may be reached by the
Loquilts Creek trail (*C1*) or by following ridges NE from the Mt. Helena area (see
Mt. Albert). Follow divide NW, swinging around the east side of Mt. Casement.
Pitch camp in this area, then ascend to the southeast ridge of Tinniswood which is
climbed on snow to summit. Not very difficult. A 3–4 day return trip.

MT. CASEMENT 2290 m/7500 ft
Located 3 km S of Mt. Tinniswood.
FA: C. Jennings, J. Nairne, H. Smythe—1966.
The pass SE of this peak can be reached from Princess Louisa Inlet as for Mt. Tinniswood, and Mt. Casement can then be reached by climbing over snow and broken rock. A 3 day trip.
   In August 1977, J. Clarke traversed from Blastus Ridge, just N of Mt. Alexander, to the Toba River. He considered this to have been the most scenic of his many high alpine traverses.

PEAK 7609 2320 m/7609 ft
Located 2.5 km NW of Mt. Alexander.
FA: J. Clarke—August 1977. Via east face to southeast ridge. NTD.

"HUNAECHIN PEAK" 2318 m/7605 ft
Located 4 km NNW of Mt. Alexander.
FA: J. Clarke—August 1977.
Via the east ridge. Clarke also climbed a 2260 m/7400 ft peak W of Hunaechin Peak via its east ridge. NTD.

PEAK 7300 2230 m/7300 ft
Located E of the head of Hunaechin Creek. Climbed via the easy north ridge.

BLÜMLISALP MOUNTAIN 2141 m/7025 ft
Located at the head of the Clendenning Glacier.
FA: J. Clarke—August 1977. Via south slopes.

"BEACH GROUP"
The name given to the group of peaks about 8 km/5 mi NW of the snout of Clendenning Glacier. Named for the unusual ridge-top sand dunes on Beach Mountain. No concession stand reported yet.

BLACKFIN PEAK 2525 m/8285 ft
Located S of Racoon Creek. This high and isolated peak commands excellent views of the Clendenning Glacier area.
FA: J. Clarke—1977.
North ridge: *FA: J. Clarke—1979.* Ascend from Wave Glacier. NTD.
Limpet Ridge: *FA: P. Durnford, J. Lixvar—1979.* Limpet Ridge runs N–S from Blackfin Peak to Breaker Peak.

BEACH MOUNTAIN 2541 m/8040 ft
Located about 7 km/4.3 mi NW of the toe of Clendenning Glacier.
FA: J. Clarke—1977. Via the south ridge.
North ridge: *FA: Large ACC party—1979.* NTD.
Surf Glacier icefall: *FA: G. Barford, P. Durnford, K. Martin—1979.* A Class 3 route.
Southwest slopes: The tourist and descent route. NTD.

BREAKER PEAK 2290 m/7500 ft
Located 2.5 km SW of Beach Mountain.
FA: J. Clarke—1977. Via the northwest slopes. Gentle.
Northeast arête: *FA: R. Sauser, E. Zenger—1979.* Three leads of up to Class 5.6 on granitic rock.

COMBER PEAK 2225 m/7300 ft
Located immediately NE of Breaker Peak.
FA: J. Clarke—1977.
NTD. Breaker and Comber give excellent views of the spectacular 1220 m/4000 ft Terrific Glacier icefall.

"LITTLE TOBA PEAK" 2471 m/8107 ft
Located S of upper Little Toba River.
FA: J. Clarke—1977. The east ridge is NTD. A 2230 m/7300 ft peak E of Little Toba Peak was ascended by the west ridge.

On map sheet 92 K/8, NW of the Little Toba River, **PEAK** 6913 (2107 m), **PEAK 7412** (2259 m), and **PEAK 6134** (1870 m) appear to be untouched, as do the subsidiary peaks of Blackfin Peak (see entry this chapter). The seven summits surrounding the glacier 4 km W of Blackfin were all climbed by J. Clarke in August 1984. He approached from logging roads along the Little Toba River. All were easy. **PEAK 7722** (2354 m) had precipitous north and west faces and was ascended via the south ridge. The other six peaks were named by an ACC group who explored the area extensively in 1979 (Ref: *CAJ* 1980, p. 57–74).

BALLPEEN MOUNTAIN 2358 m/7738 ft
FA: P. Durnford, N. Lambert, K. Martin—1979. Via SE slopes; NTD.

BELINDA MOUNTAIN 2397 m/7865 ft
FA: J. Lixvar, K. Martin, P. Martin—1979. Route ascends south slope; NTD.

BERM PEAK 2380 m/7800 ft
FA: Possibly by S. Smith and Doolittle—1893; otherwise by J. Clarke. Can be climbed on a traverse from Ball Peen Peak to **ALBINO DOME** (2396 m/7860 ft).

"JUBALAY MOUNTAIN" 2350 m/7700 ft
FA: B. Allen, D. Feuchuk—1979. Via easy slopes from Belinda Lake.

JOINTED MOUNTAIN 1878 m/6162 ft
FA: G. Barford, J. Lixvar—1979. Via easy slopes from Belinda Lake.

SWEDE SAW MOUNTAIN 2350 m/7700 ft
Located just W of Ballpeen Mountain. Unclimbed.

"STAIRCASE SUMMIT" 2292 m/7519 ft
FA: G. Barford, N. Lambert—1979. Traverse over north and south ridges; NTD.

WINDIGER MOUNTAIN 2435 m/7990 ft
East face and ridge: *FA: R. Sauser, E. Zenger—1979.*
From the Clendenning Glacier climb conspicuous snow fan and gully on the right side of the face to the waterfall. This gives access to slabs. Cross slabs to small icefield. Three pitches of 5.5 climbing link the two icefields. Climbing is generally in chimneys and an open book. Some Class 5 on sound rock beyond second icefield.

TEETER PEAK 2440 m/8000 ft
This and the following two peaks are located above Wave Creek on the southwest edge of the Elaho Plateau icefield (see *CAJ* 1980, p. 77).
FA: J. Clarke—1972.
Northwest ridge: *FA: J. Bussell, P. Bussell, I. Kay, J. Kay—1979.* NTD.

TOTTER PEAK 2500 m/8200 ft
FA: J. Clarke—1972. Via N slopes; NTD.

RACOON MOUNTAIN 2468 m/8097 ft
Located E of Racoon Lakes.
FA: J. Clarke—1972. Via SE ridge.
Southwest slopes: *FA: K. Hunt, A. Parke—1979.* NTD.
Northwest ridge: *FA: Large ACC party—1979.* NTD.
Southwest face of the west peak: *FA: R. Babicki, K. Balik, R. Sauser, E. Zenger—1979.* Route starts almost directly below the summit on the southwest side and heads left initially (5.2) before traversing up and back to the centre of the face (5.4). Route again heads left before finishing directly below the summit. The 5.7 crux is just below the summit. The difficulty increases as the climb progresses. Class 5.7; 3 hours; 300 m/1000 ft (Ref: *CAJ* 1980, p. 77 and sketch map).

MITTLEBERG MOUNTAIN 2706 m/8878 ft
Located about 6 km/3.7 mi W of the head of Toba River. *FA: J. Clarke—1972.* Clarke also climbed the 2620 m/8600 ft peak to the SE.

"ELAHO RANGE PINNACLES" 2440 m/8000 ft (GR 418994)
J. Clarke climbed these four pinnacles in 1972. They were named by a large BCMC party which climbed them in 1979. The four needles rise sharply above the head of the Toba River and are located 3 km E and slightly N of Mittleberg Mountain.

ELAHO MOUNTAIN 2822 m/9260 ft
The highest summit in the region, at the head of Elaho Glacier. This elegant peak has presently seen only four ascents.
FA: J. Clarke—1972. Via the W ridge.
North-northwest ridge: *FA: BCMC party—1979.* Gained via glacier to the N. Class 3.

MT. DOOLITTLE 2659 m/8725 ft
Named for Stanley Smith's unheralded partner. Located 3 km W of lower Clendenning Glacier. *FA: J. Clarke—1972.*

MT. CLENDENNING 2530 m/8300 ft

Located W of Clendenning Glacier, about 1.5 km SSW of Mt. Doolittle.
FA: J. Clarke—1972.
J. Clarke also climbed the 2530 m/8300 ft peak W of Mt. Clendenning. Mts. Doolittle and Clendenning crown the mighty Terrific Glacier icefall. Note that the traverse around Clendenning Lake (which you have to make to gain the Clendenning Glacier) involves crossing dangerous, stagnating ice.

BOTTIGER PEAK 2505 m/8220 ft

This pyramid-shaped peak rising above the Schlusseloch Glacier appears to offer many routes.
FA: J. Clarke—1972.
This summit rises over 5500 ft from the Little Toba River. Clarke also made the first ascent of the 2440 m/8000 ft peak directly to the W.

FRONTLINE MOUNTAIN 2272 m/7455 ft

Located E of the Clendenning Glacier snout. Unclimbed.

MT. BOARDMAN 2650 m/8695 ft

FA: J. Clarke—1972. Via the north ridge.
Via the Military Glacier: *FA: Large ACC party—1979.*
Via Assault Glacier and short north arête. Ascend Military Glacier on its attractive north lateral moraine to reach base of Mt. Boardman.

HOWITZER PEAK 2530 m/8300 ft

Located 2 km SE of Mt. Boardman. *FA: J. Clarke—1972.* Bumplets.

CORPORAL MOUNTAIN 2498 m/8195 ft

The northwesternmost summit on **ROSS RIDGE**. NTD. This and the following three peaks were traversed from S to N by J. Clarke in 1972.
North ridge: *FA: K. Balik, K. Ricker—1979.* NTD.
West ridge: *FA: R. Sauser, E. Zenger—1979.* Climb is 200 m of Class 4 slabs, followed by 4 pitches of low Class 5 on good rock.

SERGEANT MOUNTAIN 2559 m/8395 ft

NTD via southeast side. Alternatively, from Corporal Mountain, ascend steep northwest snowslopes avoiding obvious bergschrund. Class 3. (*K. Balik, K. Ricker—1979.*)

MT. WHITING 2592 m/8505 ft

This heavily glaciated peak is the crest of Ross Ridge. NTD. **PEAK 8197** (2498 m/8197 ft) and **PEAK 8300** (2530 m/8400 ft) at the west end of Ross Ridge were also climbed by J. Clarke in 1972. NTD.

J. Clarke made the following easy first ascents of peaks E of Ross Ridge. (They are named after military casualties.)

MT. RALPH 2519 m/8266 ft
The easternmost peak in the area. It rises steeply above the junction of Clendenning Creek and the Elaho River.

PEAK 7900 2410 m/7900 ft
Located 1.5 km NW of Mt. Ralph.

MT. POLLOCK 2493 m/8180 ft
This double summit is 2.5 km W of Mt. Ralph.

MT. OSWALD 2530 m/8300 ft
J. Clarke also climbed the 2367 m/7765 ft peak 2 km N of Oswald's double summit.

MT. VANSTONE 2320 m/7620 ft
Climbed via the north ridge.

MT. PERKINS 2605 m/8540 ft
Spectacular icefalls shape this high summit. Climbed via the south ridge.

South of Mt. Ralph between Sims and Clendenning creeks, **PEAK 7405** (2257 m/7405 ft), **PEAK 7150** (2179 m/7150 ft), and **PEAK 7527** (2294 m/7527 ft) await recorded ascents, although some were probably climbed by the survey parties of the 1950s.

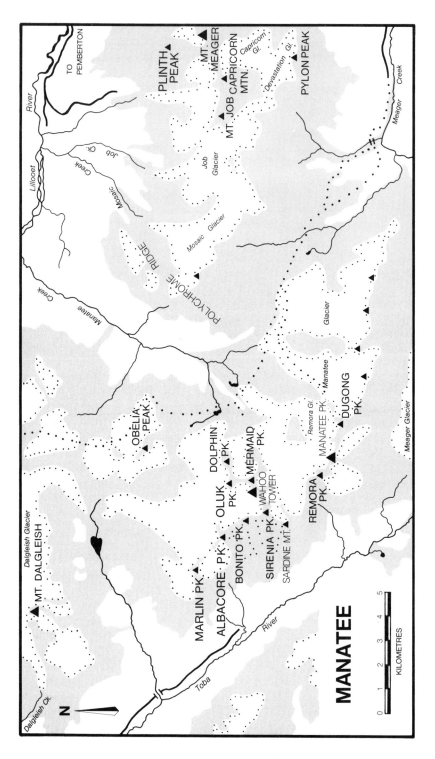

MANATEE

N

KILOMETRES

0 1 2 3 4 5

Chapter 10

Manatee and Meager Groups

by Robert Driscoll

BOUNDARIES:
North: Lillooet River and Icecap
East: Lillooet River
South: Meager Creek
West: Toba River

FOREST SERVICE OFFICE:
Squamish Forest District
P.O. Box 1970
Squamish, B.C. V0N 3G0
898-9671

LOGGING COMPANIES:

C.R.B. Logging
P.O. Box 381
Squamish, B.C. V0N 3G0
(Meager Creek)
892-3501

Squamish Mills
4427 Pemberton Avenue
Squamish, B.C. V0N 3G0
(upper Lillooet River)
892-3577

MAPS:
Federal:
92 J/11 North Creek

92 J/12 Mount Dalgleish

Provincial:
92 J (west half)

92 K

Introduction

This region was not covered in Dick Culbert's *Alpine Guide* of 1974, but new roads up Meager Creek since that time have made the area popular among skiers and climbers. There have been several club-sponsored trips held in the Manatee Glacier area, and its potential for alpine mountaineering and technical climbing is now well known among Vancouver mountaineers. Although they are easier to reach on foot, the Meager Mountain group of peaks is not too attractive to climbers, because the rock quality of many of the summits is poor. Some of the alpine benchland around these peaks makes for pleasant camping, however, and the weird pinnacles and the variety of rock colours in the area are fascinating in themselves.

The Manatee area can be recommended as a good "mixed" alpine climbing centre; you can climb a moderate line one day, go for a scramble the next afternoon, then tackle a technical rock climb on a third day. The hike into the area at present takes about two days, and once above Meager Creek, the walking is exceptionally pleasant. The meadows here have not been hiked much yet, but when they become better known, this situation is likely to change.

Approaches

A. FROM THE LILLOOET RIVER ROAD

From Pemberton a road runs up the southwest side of the Lillooet River past Pemberton Meadows. Drive 22 km/13.6 mi NW of Pemberton, then cross the Lillooet River and follow the main road (left at all forks) for another 36 km/22.3 mi to the Meager Creek turnoff. The Lillooet River main line is a B.C. Forest Service road.

1. Plinth Mountain spur road: Beyond the Meager Creek turnoff, the main Lillooet River road formerly crossed to the southwest side of the river and continued on, finally curving S around the northwest flank of Plinth Peak, and nearly reaching the glacier N of Job and Capricorn. This crucial bridge washed out in October 1985; it is not known if there are plans to replace it.

2. Pylon Peak spur road: On the Meager Creek road (left fork) the first right branch is a spur road that switchbacks high onto the flanks of Pylon Peak, which can be easily ascended in a day from the road. The peaks beyond are easily gained over glaciers. In 1931 the Carter party ascended the ridge opposite "Pika Creek" and placed their camp at GR 654044 (approximate); this approach is still feasible.

3. Meager Creek main line: This road continues to a major fork. The left fork drops down past logging camps, crosses the creek, then continues along the right side to Meager Creek hotsprings (less than 1 km from the fork), now closed after being flooded in the fall of 1984. The right fork climbs up and shortly comes to a gate which may be locked. Park well off the road. It is 6 km/3.7 mi beyond the gate to the end of the logging road. With the Hydro camp up the road now dismantled, it is probably possible to drive the road to its end. From there, drop straight down to the north bank of Meager Creek, avoiding thick bush at the end of the road. Continue along the bank for 0.5 km (one very steep and tricky traverse) to the junction of Meager Creek and Devastator Creek, a large creek which drains the Meager group's south side. Cross Devastator Creek on a logjam just upstream from the confluence and continue N across a flood plain for 1.5 km. (This area was the site of a landslide in 1975.) NOTE: This creek crossing is very problematic. If the logjam has opened up, the creek cannot usually be forded and there is **no** practical alternative access. Try to determine before you go if Devastator Creek can be crossed. Gain the ridge above by climbing NW up any one of several gullies (easiest with spring snow), or by climbing the steep, treed slopes through which the gullies run. Neither alternative is attractive. Once on the ridge, travel over open meadows and gentle glaciers. From a camp in the heart of the Manatee group, it is 1 long day or 2 very short days out to cars. An excellent, meadowed camp spot is on the strip of moraine about 2 km E of Dolphin Mountain, between two unnamed lakes.

Flying in and then skiing or hiking out has become a popular method of visiting this area, but see the potential problem with creek crossings noted above. Currently, no road or trail runs up Manatee Creek, but eventually it will be reached by the logging road which is steadily chewing up the Lillooet valley. The logging roads in this area are currently active and closed to the public at the bridge crossing the Lillooet River (22 km/13.6 mi past Pemberton) from 6:00 a.m. to 6:00 p.m. on weekdays. Be careful to park out of the way of logging trucks, and don't obstruct gates.

Routes

MEAGER GROUP
A group of sharp, rotten, volcanic peaks.

PLINTH PEAK 2680 m/8790 ft
Highest summit of the region, located above Lillooet River at the group's northeast corner.
FA: N. Carter, A. Dalgleish, T. Fyles—1932.
Ascent from SE is NTD. In 1977, B. Gall, J. Gudaitis and M. Mosely traversed the north flank of Mt. Meager, then climbed a rotten gully to gain Plinth Peak.

MT. MEAGER 2650 m/8680 ft
Located just SE of Plinth Peak.
FA: N. Carter, A. Dalgleish, T. Fyles, M. Winram—1931.
South ridge: Climb Meager's south ridge beginning near a very prominent gendarme (Perkin's Pillar). Circle the first summit on the right to gain the notch beyond, then continue up the south arête to the main summit. Rotten but NTD.
North side: *FA: D. Hughes, G. Mumford, J. Weller—1982.* Steep snow and some mixed climbing. Exposed at top of gully.

"PERKIN'S PILLAR" 2500 m/8200 ft
A huge tower mounted to the W of Mt. Meager and easily gained from the three-way pass between Meager, Plinth and Capricorn. Named for an outfitter who supplied Meager's first ascent party. Unclimbed.

PYLON PEAK 2470 m/8112 ft
Located above Meager Creek and S of Devastation Glacier.
FA: N. Carter, A. Dalgleish, T. Fyles, M. Winram—1931.
Cross a schrund and climb steep snow on the north face to gain the east ridge at a conspicuous notch. The summit ridge is loose but not difficult.

DEVASTATOR PEAK 2490 m/7600 ft
An outrider 1 km SW of Pylon Peak.
FA: N. Carter, A. Dalgleish, T. Fyles, M. Winram—1931.
It appears to be easily climbed from the N or NE.

CAPRICORN MOUNTAIN 2570 m/8429 ft
Located 3 km N of Pylon Peak and 3 km SW of Plinth Peak.
FA: N. Carter, A. Dalgleish, T. Fyles, M. Winram—1931.
From the south: Ascend easy snowslopes from S or SE.
South ridge: *FA: B. Gall, J. Gudaitis, M. Mosely—1977.* Class 3.

MT. JOB 2490 m/8180 ft

The main summit of this peak is currently unclimbed. A possible route would be via the ridge connecting Job with Capricorn Mountain. To climb the west peak (2440 m/8000 ft), approach the west side of the mountain via glaciers to the N. The west face is broken, with the last pitch loose Class 5.6. *(FA: S. Heiberg, H. Rode—October 1984.)* The connecting ridge with the main summit appears difficult and unstable.

MANATEE GROUP

This group sports a half dozen major peaks and a wide variety of alpine terrain and scenery. All alpine travellers will find a visit to this pristine area worthwhile. The rock is variable, but Wahoo Tower, Sirenia Mountain and their outliers offer superb lines on solid rock. Manatee itself is quite loose. Rather incongruously, the peaks of this group are named after a variety of maritime creatures, particularly tropical marine sport fish and mammals. Unfortunately, most names have escaped the topographic maps despite their official recognition quite some years ago.

OBELIA PEAK 2740 m/8990 ft

The isolated northern peak of this group.
FA: J. Horgan, A. Menninga, P. Plummer—1967.
Southeast ridge: This long ridge can be gained in many places from the N and S. Some exposed Class 3–4.
Northwest ridge: *FA: G. Barford, P. Jordan, G. McCormack, A. Pearson—1984.* Reach the base of the ridge by ascending the Dolphin Glacier. The ridge is mainly Class 3; the 1 pitch of low Class 5 on the last tower before the summit could probably be bypassed. Nice blocky rock. The east peak is NTD from the S *(FA: J. Cicero, M. Thompson—1984).*

MARLIN PEAK 2627 m/8620 ft

Westernmost peak of this group.
FA: All members of a BCMC expedition—1967. NTD from most, if not all directions.

ALBACORE PEAK 2620 m/8600 ft

A nondescript peak 2 km NW of Wahoo Tower.
FA: J. Clarke, J. Horgan, E. Kafer, P. Plummer—1967. NTD via southeast ridge.

BONITO PEAK 2772 m/9097 ft

Located 1 km W of Wahoo Tower.
FA: E. Kafer, H. Munger, P. Munger, P. Plummer—1967. Class 4 via the southeast ridge.

SIRENIA MOUNTAIN 2853 m/9359 ft

Located S of the head of Sirenia Glacier.
FA: All members of a BCMC expedition—1967.
East ridge: Ascend the glacier and a steep gully to the Sirenia-Wahoo Tower col.

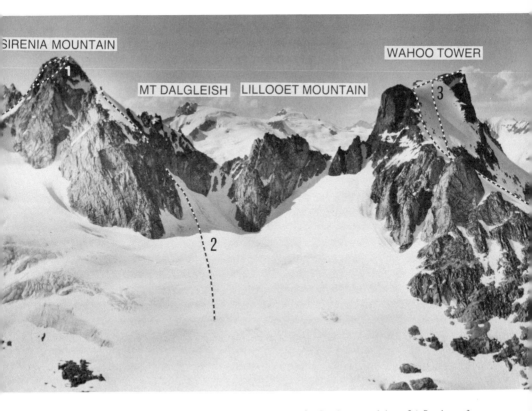

Sirenia Mountain and Wahoo Tower   1.) South face   2.) Southeast couloir   3.) Southeast face

Peter Jordan

From here, the ridge (rotten at first) leads past a gendarme to a snowy section. The summit tower is pleasant Class 3.

Southeast couloir: *FA: M. Bitz, G. Maurer—1984.* Ascend from the Remora Glacier between Sirenia and Wahoo Tower to the base of this prominent couloir. It is 150 m/500 ft high, and steepens to 50° before intersecting the east ridge 2 pitches below the top.

South face: *FA: N. Abrahams, J. Gudaitis—1979.* Reportedly a fine rock route, but details are lacking. Let us know the story if you climb it!

South buttress: *FA: P. Jordan, G. McCormack—1984.* After 1 pitch up from west ridge, traverse the south face on a Class 3 ledge to the buttress below the summit, which is climbed directly for 2 leads to low Class 5.

West ridge: *FA: G. Maurer, M. Thompson—1984.* Snowslopes lead from the S to the col between Sirenia and the first pinnacle to its W. Follow the ridge (good rock) for 1 pitch, then make an ascending traverse on its south side for 2 pitches to reach easy ground W of the summit. Class 5.8; A1. The harder second pitch can be avoided by traversing to the south face (see south buttress route above).

"SARDINE MOUNTAIN" 2650 m/8700 ft
An outlier 1 km SW of Sirenia.
FA: BCMC party—1979. NTD from NE.

WAHOO TOWER 2850 m/9350 ft
A stunning black tower when viewed from the N.
FA: All members of a BCMC expedition (via two routes)—1967.
Southeast face: *FA: J. Clarke, A. Menninga, P. Plummer—1967.* Now the standard route. Ascend snowslopes on the SE from the Remora Glacier. In good conditions the final steep slopes lead directly to the col between the south and main peaks. Otherwise, climb the rib to the left (looking up) which is somewhat rubbly Class 3 and follow the skyline ridge N to the summit, which is a spacious plateau.
Northwest arête: *FA: J. Horgan, B. Howard, E. Kafer, H. Munger, P. Munger—1967.* This is solid Class 4 climbing with 2 pitches of low Class 5.
The Articling Blues Buttress: *FA: R. Driscoll, W. Durtler, B. Fairley, K. Legg—September 14–15, 1985.* An outstanding line, easily visible from many points in the Coast Mountains to the N. The route essentially follows the line of the north buttress. Gain the toe of the buttress via crack systems to the left, wherever the moat permits. Climb to the first of many large ledges and follow cracks and grooves up a further two pitches from the west end of this ledge. Climb a steep face beside the huge chimney cleaving the buttress to gain a spacious ledge with much loose rock. Broken ground, a steep wall and nice cracks and dihedrals lead in 2–3 pitches to a snow ledge. Above, lieback to the right and continue up tough finger cracks (5.10). Traverse left to gain a gully, followed by a loose corner system. An easy pitch over blocks, more clean dihedrals, and some fine face and crack climbing gain the summit. About 12 hours up, and hardhats are mandatory. There is some 5.10, but most of the climbing is in the 5.7 to 5.9 range. Many route variations are possible, and a Smoke Bluffs free rack should do for protection. A few shorter pitches may help cut rope drag. Descending the east face in running shoes is tricky, and parties should carry ice-axes in anticipation. A great mountaineering workout.

MERMAID PEAK 2704 m/8870 ft
Located just E of Wahoo Tower.
FA: J. Clarke, A. Menninga, P. Plummer—1967.
NTD from the S, although some pleasant rock climbs from the glacier under Wahoo Tower look possible.
Southeast ridge: *FA: J. Cicero, M. Thompson—1984.* The complete southeast ridge is Class 3 on blocky granite.

OLUK PEAK 2700 m/8860 ft
Located 1 km N of Wahoo Tower.
FA: J. Clarke, J. Horgan—1967. Climbed via south ridge, which is straightforward.

"TEREDO PINNACLE" about 2600 m/8530 ft
A tower on the north ridge of Oluk.

North buttress of Wahoo Tower   Bruce Fairley

FA: B. Howard, A. Menninga—1967.
From the notch, the exposed west face is 1 1/2 leads to mid Class 5 on good rock.

DOLPHIN PEAK 2530 m/8300 ft
The E shoulder of Oluk.
FA: J. Clarke, J. Horgan—1967. NTD via the west ridge.

REMORA PEAK 2710 m/8900 ft
The northwest peak of Manatee; notable for a prominent white tower (metamorphosed limestone) on its north side.
FA: J. Clarke, B. Howard, E. Kafer, H. Munger, P. Munger—1967. Climb to the Manatee-Remora col; the east ridge is NTD.
North buttress: *FA: P. Jordan, G. McCormack—1984.* This elegant rock and snow buttress leads directly to the summit. Gain the buttress via a snow ramp on the east side. Two leads on loose Class 4 rock are followed by 2 leads on mixed snow and rock, then 4 on snow to 50°.

MANATEE PEAK 2859 m/9380 ft
Highest peak in this group.
FA: J. Clarke, B. Howard, E. Kafer, H. Munger, P. Munger—1967.
Southwest face: Traverse from the Remora-Manatee col. Class 3 snow leads to the top.
Northwest ridge: *FA: BCMC party—1979.* An easy route on poor rock, starting at the Manatee Remora col. Class 3.
East ridge: *FA: BCMC party—1979.* A loose ridge beginning at the Manatee-Dugong col.
Southeast face: *FA: BCMC party—1979.* Traverse onto this ice face from the base of the east ridge.

DUGONG PEAK 2775 m/9100 ft
A double summit at the head of the west branch of the Manatee Glacier.
FA: J. Horgan, A. Menninga—1967.
Easy snowslopes lead to the summit block, which is Class 4 on loose rock by a north-side chimney.
West ridge: *FA: J. Gudaitis—1979.* NTD.
South ridge: *FA: BCMC party—1979.* Much scree walking, with some loose Class 4–5 near the top.

POLYCHROME RIDGE 2506 m/8221 ft
A broad, gentle ridge on the southeast side of Manatee Creek. Excellent views of the Meager and Manatee groups. The four minor summits on the south rim of the Manatee Glacier are easily climbed from the N; those on the south side of the Meager Glacier (**"BELUGA PEAK"**) are likewise NTD. The Alpine Club camp of 1976 was located near here (Ref: *CAJ* 1977, p. 61).

Chapter 11

North Creek and Vicinity

by Kevin Haberl

BOUNDARIES:
North: Bridge River
East: Railroad Creek-Hurley River Road
South: Lillooet River
West: Bridge Glacier, Drainage E of Bridge Peak

FOREST SERVICE OFFICE:
Squamish Forest District
P.O. Box 1970
Squamish, B.C. V0N 3G0
898-9671

LOGGING COMPANY:
Squamish Mills
4427 Pemberton Avenue
Squamish, B.C. V0N 3G0
892-3577

MAPS:
Federal:
92 J/11 North Creek   92 J/12 Mount Dalgleish
92 J/13 Stanley Smith Glacier   92 J/14 Dickson Range
92 J/15 Bralorne

Provincial:
92 J   92 K

Introduction and History

This area is likely to become more popular over the next few years. The building of the Hurley River road through Railroad Pass to the town of Gold Bridge, and the extension of logging roads along the Lillooet River, have opened up valleys to the weekend mountaineer which were considered expeditionary destinations only a few years ago. An ascent of Mt. Samson used to be something of an event; the climb is still a fine adventure, but now a determined party can easily do it in a weekend. Although many parties, particularly from the BCMC, have knocked around the peaks to the west of Railroad Pass over the past ten years, the opportunities for good scrambling, alpine climbing, and ski touring have not yet caught fire with the general mountaineering community. The building of a private cabin by the BCMC in 1986 in

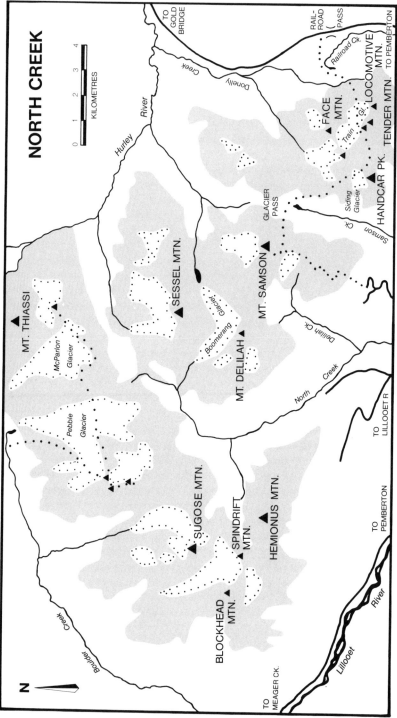

NORTH CREEK

KILOMETRES
0 1 2 3 4

the North Creek may stimulate more interest in this area.

The northern half of the North Creek area is still largely considered expeditionary country. Only a few parties have passed through this region of small icefields and rocky summits, but there have been some enthusiastic reports of the wonderful climbing to be had on peaks such as Mt. Thiassi. Many of the valleys here are reasonable approaches in spring, but become horrendous thrashes once the snow has melted, so anyone planning an extended venture into the mysterious country around Mt. Vayu or The Frost Fiend should think about going early in the season and taking skis.

Undoubtedly, some great deeds wait to be done by the venturesome around the headwaters of the many creeks draining this extensive alpine area. Parties inclined to strike out on their own should consider a trip here before the inevitable pollution of logging debris and industrial exploitation scar this corner of the province which is still left to the nomad and wanderer. For a good article and map describing the area, see *CAJ* 1977, p. 18.

Approaches

A. FROM THE LILLOOET RIVER ROAD

The Lillooet River road is in good condition and runs NW from Pemberton up the southwest side of the Lillooet River to Pemberton Meadows and beyond. About 22 km/13.6 mi from Pemberton, a fork to the right leads to a bridge across the Lillooet River. After another 1.5 km this road forks, with the lower branch continuing up the river. This road follows the north side of the river to a few km beyond Salal Creek, at which point it crosses back to the south side of the Lillooet and climbs above tree line (see Manatee-Meager chapter). Just after Boulder Creek (called by its old name, "Pebble Creek," on most maps), the road roughens to four-wheel drive.

1. The North Creek roads: The roads on both sides of North Creek give the best access to timberline from the Lillooet River road. About 1 km before crossing North Creek, a spur road climbs up the south side of Mt. Samson to around the 1220 m/4000 ft mark. Drive and walk this to its end, then ascend through reasonable bush onto the divide S of Samson; alternatively, swing NW into the basin at the head of Delilah Creek.

Another road branches up from the Lillooet about 0.5 km after it crosses North Creek. This road also branches. The lower fork ends at about 1000 m/3300 ft in the North Creek drainage (this fork has been used for a ski-touring approach, although there is some avalanche danger), and the upper fork climbs to over 1220 m/4000 ft on the slopes S of Hemionus (W of North Creek).

1a. North Creek route: From logging roads on the west side of the creek, the BCMC has recently flagged a route which makes a descending traverse to reach tall, open timber on the valley floor. The route will marginally improve summer access but is avalanche prone in winter.

2. Boulder Creek spur road: A short spur road climbs up the north side of Boulder Creek (formerly "Pebble Creek") onto the south ridge of Mt. Athelstan. This gives fairly quick access to the alpine country W of Boulder Creek. The Boulder Creek valley is very steep and not recommended for travel.

3. Salal Creek approach: After the Lillooet River road crosses Boulder Creek, it climbs to over 760 m/2500 ft on the southwest side of Mt. Athelstan, then ascends again to cross Salal Creek near its confluence with the Lillooet River. Some hikers have climbed Salal Creek from here, but this is not recommended. Currently, the best approach is to continue along the Lillooet River road until you reach its high point a few km E of Salal Creek, and then to traverse the west side of Athelstan between 910 m/3000 ft and 1070 m/3500 ft. This approach, like many in the area, may be bushy after the spring snow leaves. Travel is good above the fork in Salal Creek, however.

B. FROM THE HURLEY RIVER ROAD (RAILROAD PASS ROAD)

Take a fork to the right from the Lillooet River road about 10 km/6 mi after crossing the Lillooet River bridge (*A*). This road's upper branch climbs up the east flank of Railroad Creek to Railroad Pass (1400 m/4600 ft), crosses the pass, and descends along Donelly Creek to the Hurley River. It follows the east side of the Hurley until 5 km below Lone Goat Creek, where it crosses the Hurley River bridge to the west side and continues to Gold Bridge (48 km/29.8 mi from the Lillooet River road). Gold Bridge has a good all-weather road connecting it to Lillooet. At the Hurley River bridge, a spur follows the east side of the river to Bralorne, and an old road follows the west side of the Hurley (upstream from the bridge) giving access to Lone Goat Creek.

1. Green Mountain spur road: This spur road begins 38.5 km/23.9 mi from the Lillooet River road turnoff, and 9.3 km/5.8 mi from the bridge at Gold Bridge. From the bridge across the Bridge River at Gold Bridge, proceed S towards Downton Lake and the Lajoie Dam, turning left after 1 km onto the Hurley River road. At 6.8 km/4.2 mi, a spur road climbs to a landing on the right; this may be signposted "BR 9." Go through the landing and along a rough track for 0.5 km. Here an old road begins which climbs Green Mountain to a lookout cabin at 2010 m/6600 ft. The cabin sleeps four and is currently open to the public.

2. Lone Goat Creek approach: Approach the creek using the old road running upstream on the west side of the Hurley River, immediately after the Hurley River bridge. The 1965 party used this route to reach Thiassi, The Frost Fiend, and the surrounding summits. However, it should be noted that this party travelled up the valley on spring snow; once the snow melts, this approach is an ugly thrash.

3. Railroad Pass: Take the Hurley River road to Railroad Pass, and ascend the upper reaches of Railroad Creek to the small alpine lakes at the head of Donelly Creek. From here Face Mountain and adjacent summits are easily approached. A long, westward traverse just S of Face Mountain on the Train Glacier provides weekend access to Mt. Samson. A spur leaves the Hurley River road at about 670 m/2200 ft. It crosses Railroad Creek and leads N to logging slash at about 1160 m/3800 ft on the shoulder SE of Locomotive, Tender and Caboose mountains. Easy forest leads to timberline. This approach gives access when the Hurley River road is closed by snow.

Routes

MT. SLOAN 2723 m/8940 ft
A wonderful summit 19 km/12 mi W of Bralorne.
FA: C. Fenner, B. Hardie, T. Pollard, G. Tanner, T. Waldon—1949.

South gully: From the end of the Green Mountain spur (*B1*), follow the divide S until it is possible to drop down one of the snow/scree slopes into Ault Creek. Cross the creek and gain the glacial cirque SE of Mt. Sloan. Ascend the glacier to the headwall. A large, hidden gully, which is unmistakable, runs into this cirque providing a straightforward Class 3 route to Sloan's summit. Variations on the south ridge are possible.

Southeast buttress: *FA: D. Anderson, S. Coombes, R. Fabiche, P. Jordan—September 30, 1984.* Begin to the left of "Dragon couloir," a prominent gully on the east face which runs to the summit area and is clearly visible from Ault Lake. The route is Class 3–4 with 1 half-pitch of mid Class 5 about halfway up. A few medium to large nuts may be useful.

Northeast ridge: *FA: P. Kubik, E. Zenger—1976.* This striking ridge may be gained from Ault Creek. Drop into the creek and descend through slides and bush until it is possible to follow a dirty gully up onto the ridge. If you avoid the difficulties to the left by occasionally traversing out onto the face, the climb is Class 4. Class 5 will be encountered if you stick to the ridge crest. An exhilarating and dramatic route.

North face: *FA: B. Fairley—July 1983.* Ascend the northeast ridge (see above) to the first steep gendarme, then drop down a Class 3 gully to the north flank. Make an ascending traverse to the centre of the face. Cross bergschrund in the centre of the face and ascend steep snow gullies and Class 4 rock, emerging 1 pitch to the E of the summit. Good exposure. Takes 11 hours return from Green Mountain. (Ref: *CAJ* 1984, p. 76.)

PEAK 8380 2554 m/8380 ft
A dark rock tower 2 km S of Mt. Sloan.

From the North: The peak has probably been climbed via the large snow basin to the N, finishing on the west ridge. An extremely steep gap on the east ridge stopped a recent attempt on this ridge, but a route of Class 5 difficulty undoubtedly exists here. There is no information on the group of peaks to the W, which appear attractive and not difficult.

THE FROST FIEND 2620 m/8500 ft
Central and highest of three summits E of Surfusion Glacier.
FA: R. Culbert, A. Purdey—1965.
This peak is reached from the head of Lone Goat Creek (*B2*) (winter/spring only), either by crossing first to Surfusion Glacier or by traversing over two cirques on the east side of the intervening divide. Summit is Class 3 on rock from the S.

MT. VAYU 2774 m/9100 ft
Located 3 km WNW of The Frost Fiend.
FA: R. Culbert, A. Purdey—1965.
Surfusion Glacier may be reached by crossing the high col from Lone Goat Creek (*B2*) (winter/spring only). From the glacier snout, traverse into basin SE of Mt. Vayu and ascend to the col on its east ridge. This may be corniced but is not difficult. The two 2590 m/8500 ft rock summits N of Surfusion's western lobe are both Class 2–3 rock scrambles from the divide with the Thiassi Glacier.

"LONE GOAT SUMMIT" 2590 m/8500 ft
FA: R. Culbert, A. Purdey—1965.
The highest summit around the head of Lone Goat Creek (*B2*), above Surfusion Glacier. Its east ridge is not difficult and the other peaks farther S are climbed from the divide here.

Looking north to Mt. Thiassi   John Clarke

MT. THIASSI 2740 m/9000 ft
The highest summit between the heads of Hurley River and McParlon Creek.
FA: R. Culbert, A. Purdey—1965. No established approaches.
From the east: Ascend Thiassi Glacier from the E to the col between the main southeastern summits. Both may be climbed from here; the highest peak involves a sharp Class 4 ridge with a tricky gap.
Northwest face and west ridge: *FA: P. Jordan, C. McNeil—July 1977.* From the glacier on the northwest side of Thiassi, ascend steep, loose gullies to the ridge crest. Climb major gendarme (Class 5), and from there climb the Class 4 ridge to the summit. Good granitic rock on roped pitches. (Ref: *CAJ* 1978, p. 82.)

PEAK 8540 2603 m/8540 ft
Located 1.6 km S of Mt. Thiassi, at the head of the McParton Glacier.

FA: J. Clarke—1972.
The peak is a straightforward ascent via the south ridge; its southeastern neighbour is easily ascended from the SW.

PEAK 7330 2240 m/7330 ft
Located between the toe of the McParlon Glacier to the E and the toe of the Pebble Glacier to the W.
FA: BCMC party—July 1982. NTD from the S. Great views of Thiassi.

PEAK 8600 2620 m/8600 ft
A group of summits 7 km/4.4 mi SW of Mt. Thiassi, and immediately W of the Pebble Glacier.
FA: J. Clarke—1972.
Approach via North Creek (*A1*). There are three peaks in this group. The highest one, farthest NE, is Class 4 via its eastern rock ridge, but snow on the north side appears easier. The other two are lower (2620 m/8600 ft) and are not difficult from the col between.

SESSEL MOUNTAIN 2710 m/8900 ft
Located 4 km NW of Mt. Samson.
FA: J. Clarke—1974.
Ascend directly to the summit from the Boomerang Glacier, using North Creek (*A1*) or Railroad Pass (*B3*) approaches. J. Clarke climbed the other summits on this massif from Sessel as far E as **PEAK 8133** (2480 m/8133 ft).
North face: *FA: BCMC party—July 1982.* Ascend the glacier directly from the small lake 3 km N of Sessel. The BCMC had a camp at this lake in 1982. A topping alpine outing—recommended!

PEAK 8519 2597 m/8519 ft
Located 1 km NW of Sessel Mountain.
FA: J. Clarke—1974. NTD via the ridge from Sessel.
North ridge: *FA: BCMC party—July 1982.* A pleasant Class 3 from the attractive lake 2 km to the N.

MT. DELILAH 2604 m/8545 ft
Situated 3 km W of Mt. Samson.
FA: J. Clarke—1974.
You can easily ascend the east ridge from the Samson-Delilah col (*A1*). From Delilah, the summits 1.5 km S and 2 km NW can also be climbed (*J. Clarke—1974*).
From the southwest: Approach from North Creek basin to the southwest slopes and adjacent ridge. NTD.

MT. SAMSON 2800 m/9200 ft
Highest of the summits S of head of Hurley River.
FA: J. Ronayne, R. Ronayne, P. Tait—1935.
Approach either from the roads in North Creek (*A1*) or from Railroad Pass (*B3*).
From the south: Gain the glacier S of Samson, then climb up ridge to summit. NTD. Moderate snow routes have also been done on the southwest face.

Northeast ridge: *FA: P. de Visser, C. Oloman, B. Thompson, B. Wood—1975.* This long, corniced ridge is reached via buttresses on the east side about halfway up the ridge. Mostly Class 3, but up to low Class 5.

East face: *FA: M. Wyborn, R. Wyborn—1975.* Ascend buttress which reaches northeast ridge about 100 m/330 ft below the summit. Mostly Class 3 with some Class 4 near the top. A mixed rock and snow climb.

FACE MOUNTAIN 2470 m/8100 ft

Located 3.5 km W of Railroad Pass.

This and the surrounding summits offer nice hiking, and can be approached easily from Railroad Pass (*B3*). See accompanying map for peak names in this area. The Semaphore Lake area (GR 974050) is a popular base for wandering over and among this gentle group of peaks.

HEMIONUS MOUNTAIN 2260 m/7400 ft

Highest summit between the west fork of North Creek and Lillooet River.

FA: D. Lyon, A. Parke, K. Ricker—1976.

Approach via North Creek (*A1*); climb to the ridge SE of the peak. Bypass rock pinnacles on their east sides, then scramble up the easy Class 3 south buttress.

SPINDRIFT MOUNTAIN 2380 m/7800 ft

Located WNW of Hemionus at GR 787082. *FA: ACC-BCMC party—1976.* Using North Creek (*A1*) approach, climb the steep southwest arête to the west summit, then traverse to the higher east peak.

BLOCKHEAD MOUNTAIN 2410 m/7900 ft

Located 1.5 km NW of Spindrift. *FA: ACC-BCMC party—1976.* From glacier SW of Spindrift, ascend to col with Spindrift, then up the southeast ridge. NTD.

SUGUS MOUNTAIN 2470 m/8100 ft

Located 2 km N of Spindrift.

FA: G. Woodsworth—1974.

South ridge: Approach by North Creek (*A1*) route; the minor summits NW from Sugus along the divide can also be ascended.

Southeast slopes: *FA: E. Zenger and party—1976.* A good place to give your telemark skis a workout.

MT. ATHELSTAN 2770 m/9100 ft

Highest summit between Boulder and Salal creeks.

From Boulder Creek: *FA: J. Clarke—1972.* Approach using Boulder Creek (*A2*), then ascend the broad south ridge from the end of the logging road. **PEAK 8120** (2474 m/8120 ft) SSE of Athelstan also be traversed during the approach. Both the south and west ridges of Athelstan have been described as enjoyable Class 3 climbs. (Ref: *VOCJ* 1983, p. 40.)

From the Lillooet River road: From this road (*A*), ascend directly through open forest and up the west side of avalanche paths on the southwest face to timberline. Cross the southwest spur ridge and descend onto the southwest glacier; from here, gain the upper stretch of the west ridge. Class 3.

PEAK 8355 2547 m/8355 ft
On the divide 3 km NNE of Athelstan. *FA: J. Clarke—1972*. This and other summits on the divide have been easily traversed, using the Boulder Creek (*A2*) and Salal Creek (*A3*) approaches.

MT. GUTHRUM 2703 m/8867 ft
Rises 3 km S of Athelney Pass.
FA: H. Kellerhals, R. Kellerhals—1964.
Approach via Salal Creek (*A3*), and then climb the north ridge from Athelney Pass to a subsidiary peak, avoiding the gendarmes by ascending gullies. From here, a narrow, easy ridge leads to the summit. Alternatively, from its col with Icemaker Mountain, the peak is a slack ski ascent in the spring.

ICEMAKER MOUNTAIN 2710 m/8900 ft
Located 1 km E of Mt. Guthrum.
FA: H. Kellerhals, R. Kellerhals—1964.
Easily ascended using the Salal Creek (*A3*) approach. Gain the Guthrum-Icemaker col and ascend the west slopes for a million dollar view.

PEAK 8500 2590 m/8500 ft; **PEAK 8600** 2620 m/8600 ft
On the divide, 1 km S of Ethelweard. *FA: J. Clarke—1972*. Easy scrambles.

MT. ETHELWEARD 2770 m/9100 ft
Located 3 km E of Athelney Pass. The federal topographic sheet locates it incorrectly 3 km to the ENE of the true location.
FA: J. Clarke—1972.
Climb this mountain from the divide to the S. The highest summit is the most northwesterly. Traverse the entire summit range for an enjoyable day on good rock. Avoid a step in the southeast ridge of the main peak by using south-facing gullies.

FASP MOUNTAIN 2486 m/8156 ft
Located 5 km E of Icemaker at GR 810211 on map 92 J/11.
FA: First Aid Ski Patrol party—1975.
Gain the easy south ridge via the glacier on the W, then climb snow to summit. The summits on the divide between Fasp and Icemaker were traversed from W–E by J. Clarke in 1972.

OCHRE MOUNTAIN 2541 m/8336 ft
Located 2 km N of Athelney Pass.
FRA: H. Kellerhals, R. Kellerhals—1964.
Approach via Salal Creek (*A3*). Scramble up easy southwest slopes. A small mining cabin sits just below Athelney Pass on the SW side. Lots of prospecting has been done in this area.

"SALAL PEAK" 2530 m/8300 ft
Located 2.5 km W of Athelney Pass.
FA: By prospectors.
A huge, sprawling summit housing a large glacier on its north side. From Athelney

Mt. Ethelweard Peter Jordan

Pass ascend easy southeast slopes to gain the icefield which leads to the summit. Not difficult.

WHITE CROSS MOUNTAIN 2440 m/8000 ft

Highest summit between Salal Creek and Bridge Glacier.
FA: H. Kellerhals, R. Kellerhals—1964. Easily ascended from W or NE, using Salal Creek (*A3*) approach.

Chapter 12

Southern Chilcotin Ranges

BOUNDARIES:
North: Relay Creek, Lizard Creek, Warner Pass
East: Fraser River
South: Bridge River, Downton Lake, Carpenter Lake, Seton Lake
West: Nichols Creek, Griswold Creek

FOREST SERVICE OFFICE:
Lillooet Forest District
Box 10, 1210 Main Street
Lillooet, B.C. V0K 1V0
256-7531

LOGGING COMPANY:
Evans Forest Products
Box 880
Lillooet, B.C. V0K 1V0
256-4266

MAPS:
Federal:
92 J/14 Dickson Range   92 J/15 Bralorne
92 J/16 Bridge River   92 O/2 Tyaughton Creek
92 O/3 Warner Pass

Provincial:
92 J/NE   92 K
92 I/NW   92 O

Introduction

This region is drier than the more westerly areas covered in this guide, and the long ridges, gentle summits, and pleasant valley systems make the area excellent for alpine rambles, extended backpacking and ski touring. Early in this century, prospectors swarmed over the area; the trails they left are still the best approach routes in the region today, and many of the cabins they built are still standing. Some of these cabins are private, and the public's right to use them should not be taken for granted. However, a number are left unlocked and are available for casual use by hikers.

The southern Chilcotin is the most parklike area in this guidebook. It is an area that closely resembles the Cariboo country to the east. Huge tracts of open grassland stretch away from the heads of Tyaughton and Lizard creeks; stately groves of aspen line the Gun Creek trail and other important routes into the region's interior. Valley bottoms are high by Coast Mountains standards, but bush can still be just as thick as on the coast. Thick lodgepole pine and spruce make travel slow in valleys where trails have not been built.

All peaks in this area have at least one route that is an easy hike or scramble from base to summit, and most peaks are easy from all sides. Anyone planning an extended backpacking holiday in a wild, beautiful, uncrowded setting should definitely consider this region; it offers a refreshing change of pace from the more rugged parts of the Coast Mountains to the south and west.

Recent articles on this region include *VOCJ* 1976, p. 29, and 1978, p. 9; and *CAJ* 1978, p. 82 (includes map).

Approaches

A. FROM THE LILLOOET-GOLD BRIDGE ROAD

A good all-weather road follows the north side of Carpenter Lake and connects the towns of Lillooet and Gold Bridge. Most access roads start here.

1. Slok Creek forest road: Cross the bridge across the Bridge River about 7 km/4.25 mi from Lillooet. Turn right immediately onto the Slok Creek road, which runs along the west side of the Fraser River. A road to the left branches off after 40 km/25 mi and leads into McKay Creek, providing access to the area around Slok Hill (1920 m/6300 ft). At 50 km/31 mi the Leon Creek road branches W and climbs Leon Creek to an elevation of more than 1525 m/5000 ft. It was mainly two-wheel drive in 1984. The Slok Creek road continus N in rough condition, eventually reaching Big Bar on the Fraser River.

2. Yalakom River road: Leaves the Carpenter Lake road 30.5 km/19 mi from Lillooet and climbs beyond the head of the Yalakom River. This is the best access for the Camelsfoot and Shulaps ranges. Cross the first bridge at 9.5 km/6 mi, then continue along the road for 1 km. Here, the road doubles back along the west side of the river, and continues for another 1 km to a switchback, where a trail leading to timberline begins. The Yalakom road continues NW in deteriorating condition, eventually linking with roads running in from Marshall Lake in the Poison Mountain area. Other roads link from the E and eventually run to Big Bar on the Fraser River. These last may be undriveable. There is no longer a good road in Ore Creek.

3. Marshall Lake road: Begins 64 km/39.8 mi from Lillooet and climbs in two-wheel drive condition to well beyond Marshall Lake. Rough roads extend up Relay Creek and a new track has been pushed up toward Quartz Mountain. The Marshall Lake road merges with the Tyaughton Lake road shortly before reaching Taylor Creek (*A4a*).

3a. Jim Creek road: This old, steep mining road, condition unknown, runs from Marshall Lake up the west side of Jim Creek to over 2130 m/7000 ft on the spur ridge S of East Liza Creek. A branch road runs up the southeast fork of Jim Creek to an alpine meadow at 1980 m/6500 ft.

4. Tyaughton Lake road: Leaves the Lillooet-Gold Bridge road about 13 km/8 mi before Gold Bridge (85 km/53 mi from Lillooet); it is well signposted. The road passes the east shore of Mowson Pond, climbs to the south end of Tyaughton Lake, down the west shore, then up Relay Creek. The Gun Creek road branches to the left about 4 km from the Lillooet-Gold Bridge road.

4a. Relay Creek and Tyaughton Creek trails: Continue straight up the main road to where Tyaughton Creek flows into Relay Creek; from here, good horse trails continue up both Relay Creek and Tyaughton Creek to alpine country. A short trail branches from the Tyaughton Creek trail and follows the creek to Spruce Lake; it is a good way to connect with the Gun Creek system. A trail up Bonanza Creek leads to Taylor Basin, condition unknown. From upper Tyaughton Creek, a trail climbs to "Deer Pass," 4 km northwest of Mt. Sheba, and descends to Trigger Lake. Another trail (incorrectly located on map 92 O/3) heads up Lizard Creek. Also, a new fire-access road in four-wheel drive condition has been pushed up Mud Creek.

4b. Taylor Creek road: About 4 km N of Tyaughton Lake, the road descends steeply to the north fork of Cinnabar Creek. Immediately after the creek crossing, a track leads uphill to the left. This is the start of the old Taylor basin road, which climbs some 12 km/7.5 mi to old cabins in Taylor basin at the head of Taylor Creek. Much of this road is in rough four-wheel drive condition. It is popular among hunters. It is also a good ski-touring route in winter. From Taylor basin, a trail also leads W into Eldorado basin (see below).

4c. "Cinnabar Basin" trail: Immediately before reaching Tyaughton Lake, there is a steep, righthand curve in the road. About 200 m/650 ft beyond, a spur road to the left enters large clear-cut logging blocks. Proceed straight ahead, then bear right, go up a slight hill, take the left fork, then the next right fork (obscure), which puts you onto an important road climbing to 2130 m/7000 ft in four-wheel drive condition. Before reaching "Cinnabar Ridge," about 6 km/3.7 mi from the logging blocks (about 1800 m/5900 ft), a good horse trail to the left leads westward into Cinnabar Basin (head of Pearson Creek). You can follow trails W and N into the Eldorado Creek drainage and beyond to the Spruce Lake area—some route finding is necessary. When you drop down to Spruce Lake, it is critical to follow the southernmost creek: GR 049496 on map 92 J/15. An exceptionally fine high route.

5. *Gun Creek road:* About 13 km/8 mi before reaching Gold Bridge, a road heads N past Mowson Pond and Tyaughton Lake to Relay Creek. About 4 km up this road, a spur heads W into the Gun Creek valley. This road soon deteriorates into a good horse trail, which continues up Gun Creek past Trigger Lake (at this point it grows faint but can still be followed) to the alpine country beyond. The main track forks 1 km after Trigger Lake. The right fork climbs to "Deer Pass" (*A4a*) and the left fork continues up Warner Creek, over Warner Pass, and down into the Taseko drainage. The road was bulldozer graded to Roxey Creek in 1983.

5a. Roxey Creek road: An old mining road climbs Roxey Creek to about 1800 m/6000 ft between Dickson and Penrose. There is a small, unlocked cabin at the head of this road. The bridge at Roxey Creek provides the only access across Gun Creek.

5b. Slim Creek: Thick spruce and pine make travel slow in Slim Creek. A few old blazes mark spots on an old game trail criss-crossed by blowdowns. It is a 2–3 day pack from Gun Creek to alpine terrain at 1830 m/6000 ft. A canyon near Leckie Creek must be avoided in thick bush. An approach from the trail in upper Gun Creek offers a more pleasant alternative.

5c. Leckie Creek horse trail: An old horse trail which offers reasonable travel is rumoured to go up Leckie Creek. However, Gun Creek must be forded, which is possible only with low water in late summer and autumn.

6. *Penrose Creek track:* From Gold Bridge, drive SW past Lajoie Dam and up and

around the north side of Lajoie Lake ("Little Gun Lake"). A track continues to the 1130 m/3700 ft level of Penrose Creek, from which a steep upward climb leads to the Penrose group. To reach it, drive past Little Gun Lake, take the first spur to the right as it climbs uphill, then go straight ahead at the next fork. The old road swings to the N, then heads NW up the flank of Penrose to follow the southeast ridge. Flagging is in place.

B. FROM DOWNTON LAKE
It is possible to cross Downton Lake by boat and then climb directly up into the Dickson Range. This offers quick but strenuous access to the more westerly peaks. An old trail from the end of the lake runs up the north bank of the Bridge River past Nichols Creek and into the north fork of the Bridge. (Ref: *CAJ* 1956, p. 51.)

Routes

"GLACIER VIEW PEAK" 2324 m/7626 ft
Located W of Nichols Creek. *FRA: F. Dawe, N. Phillips, N. Wilson—1935.* This bald dome is an easy ascent from the west side of the Nichols Creek-Bridge River junction.

PEAK 8180 2493 m/8180 ft
The west portal of Griswold Pass.
FRA: S. Golling, P. Jordan, C. McNeill, T. O'Connor—July 1977.
Easily scrambled from Griswold Pass. **PEAK 8179** (2493 m/8179 ft) E of the pass is of similar difficulty. The 2489 m/8167 ft peak S of Peak 8180 is known as **LEPTON MOUNTAIN** (*FRA: J. Baldwin, J. Heineman—1982*).

"MUON MOUNTAIN" 2520 m/8266 ft
Located 3 km ESE of Griswold Pass. A muon is an atomic particle.
FRA: I. Kay, A. Melville, H. Winstone—1955.
This party also climbed **PEAK 8200** (2500 m/8200 ft) 2 km to the SE and the cluster of summits 4 km SW. All are easy. (Ref: *CAJ* 1956, p. 51 and map.)

MT. WARNER 2833 m/9296 ft
Located 1 km NE of Warner Pass.
This mountain and nearby Wilson Ridge are easy, pleasant climbs from the Warner Pass area and the Denain Creek basin. A traverse along the ridge from Warner to Lizard Lake is also pleasant and is recommended.

MT. SHEBA ("SHEBA'S BREASTS") 2650 m/8700 ft
A double summit on the Gun-Tyaughton Creek divide.
The ascent is not difficult from Hummingbird Lake, while the east ridge is a rock scramble.

RELAY MOUNTAIN 2702 m/8866 ft
This peak, along with nearby **CARDTABLE MOUNTAIN** (2523 m/8277 ft) and **CASTLE PEAK** (2490 m/8169 ft), form the group between the Relay Creek and

Tyaughton Creek valleys. Good trails lead through this area and across the head-waters of Paradise Creek.

ELDORADO MOUNTAIN 2447 m/8029 ft
The highest summit between Gun Creek and Tyaughton Creek E of Spruce Lake. Probably best reached via Taylor Creek (*A4b*) or Bonanza Creek (*A4a*).

LECKIE RANGE
This group, sandwiched between Slim and Leckie creeks, has been seldom visited, although summits rise to heights of 2610 m/8560 ft. Little is known of their potential.

DICKSON RANGE
Exploration in the western half of this range has been almost exclusively carried out by John Baldwin and Jean Heineman, occasionally accompanied by others. The small icefields, broad valleys, and many summits make the area excellent for ski touring, and almost every summit and glacier has been climbed. The area between the head of Slim Creek and Griswold Pass features vast meadows and offers wonderful hiking in season. Once above tree line you can easily reach the knot of summits surrounding **SCHERLE PEAK** (2650 m/8700 ft), and few are more difficult than Class 2. (Scherle was a surveyor killed in a helicopter crash in the 1970s.) Technical climbs have only been made on the extreme eastern portion of the range, probably because the access to that area is much more reasonable.

DICKSON PEAK 2809 m/9217 ft
Located 7 km/4.4 mi W of Gun Lake.
FA: Probably by survey party.
South face: From Roxey Creek road (*A2a*), climb to glacier at the head of the valley, then climb up Dickson's easy south slopes. An ice-axe may be needed to gain the toe of the glacier.
North ridge: *FA: B. Fairley, H. Redekop—May 18, 1981.* This ridge was gained at the 2440 m/8000 ft level. Moderate snow and some exposure. Three rock steps offer short difficulties in the low Class 5 range; these can be avoided to the left. About 12 hours return from Roxey Creek. Pleasant.

PEAK 8000 2440 m/8000 ft
Located 1 km N of Mt. Penrose. A scramble from the col with the north peak of Mt. Penrose.

MT. PENROSE 2627 m/8616 ft
Located 3 km SE of Dickson Peak.
FA: Probably by W. Manson and Senator Penrose.
Southeast ridge: You can easily reach the southeast ridge from Penrose Creek (*A6*); some loose scrambling is involved near the top. The corpulent American senator after whom the peak is named ascended most of the route on an equally corpulent horse; it is reported that the horse never quite recovered from the experience.
North peak, east buttress: *FA: B. Fairley, H. Redekop—June 1981.* This short

route begins from the col between the north peak of Penrose and the 2440 m/8000 ft peak to the NE. There are 5 pitches of climbing to 5.4, followed by some scrambling. Nearby **"MISTAKEN MOUNTAIN"** (2600 m/8540 ft) appears to have some nice climbing potential.

SHULAPS RANGE

SHULAPS PEAK 2775 m/9105 ft
This is the namesake of the Shulaps Range, a group of high but mostly gentle summits running NE of Carpenter Lake and Tyaughton Creek. Shulaps Peak is a stiff Class 2 over snow and loose rock from the southeast fork of Jim Creek (*A3a*). Although a long walk, Shulaps Peak is less steep from the Brett Creek trail to the S. This good trail climbs from Marshall Lake road (*A3*) up the northwest side of Brett Creek, then traverses E to cross the divide north of gentle **REX PEAK** (2684 m/8807 ft) before descending along the north side of Shulaps Creek to Yalakom River valley (*A2*). Its connections on this side are presently obscured by logging. To climb Shulaps Peak, continue up Brett valley to the very last meadow, hike up scree northward toward a break in the headwall, then continue to Shulaps Peak's easy east ridge.

BIG DOG MOUNTAIN 2862 m/9391 ft
Located at the north end of Shulaps Range, W of upper Yalakom River.
This region has some fine meadow and hiking terrain. A road from the Yalakom River road (*A2*) climbs up near Blue Creek to a mining camp at 2010 m/6600 ft. A spur climbs to a lake at 2290 m/7500 ft, SE of Big Dog. The summit from there is an easy trek, as are several other of the high ridges in the friendly but rubbly northern Shulaps Range. All of these are NTD except for a more abrupt tusk of elevation 2640 m/8650 ft above the south fork of Blue Creek just SE of Peak 9085 (2770 m/9085 ft) (*FA: N. Purssell, R. Purssell, D. Salo—1969*), which is climbed via a gully on the north side. (Ref: *CAJ* 1971, p. 66.) A trail from the mining camp crosses a 2380 m/7800 ft pass to the SW and descends to Liza Lake.

CAMELSFOOT RANGE
This gentle set of open ridges NE of Yalakom River is largely cattle range and hence widely laced by trails. At 21 km/13 mi from Lillooet, the road to Bralorne crosses Applespring Creek, and a trail up the west fork of this is in good condition, leading to open country on the south end of the range. Another major cattle track climbs from a short distance up the Yalakom River road (*A2*), along Fred Creek, and then up **MT. DUNCAN** (2186 m/7172 ft). There are some problems with private property at the beginning of this trail. Summits further N, including **MT. BIRCH** (2230 m/7312 ft) appear to be more easily reached from Leon Creek (*A1*). This entire area is pleasant meadow country.

MISSION RIDGE 2404 m/7886 ft
Located N of Seton Lake.
A microwave station road in reasonable condition climbs from Mission Pass to 1950 m/6400 ft on the west end of Mission Ridge. Summits on the west end of the ridge

are easily gained from there and provide a good viewpoint. You can get to the higher peaks farther E by following the divide or swinging around the north side on an old trail. (See also Mt. McLean, Lillooet chapter.)

Chapter 13

Cadwallader Range and Tenquille Lake

by Anders Ourom

BOUNDARIES:
North: Cadwallader, Standard, and McGillivray creeks
East: Gates and Birkenhead rivers
South: Lillooet River
West: Railroad and Donelly creeks, Hurley River

FOREST SERVICE OFFICES:

Ministry of Forests
P.O. Box 1970
Squamish, B.C. V0N 3G0
898-9671

Lillooet Forest District
P.O. Box 10
Lillooet, B.C. V0K 1V0
256-7033

MAPS:
Federal:
92 J/7 Pemberton
92 J/11 North Creek

92 J/10 Birkenhead Lake

Provincial:
92 J/SE

92 J/NE

Introduction

This area of interconnecting alpine ridges lies north of Pemberton. Only the peaks on its fringes are accessible to the weekend mountaineer which has led to concentrated activity in places like Tenquille Lake and McGillivray Pass. As both areas usually get large dumps of snow which persists well into spring, these spots are popular destinations for ski-touring parties. There are many possibilities for long alpine traverses here, and a great chance to get out and feel like an explorer. There are no trails at all running through the interior of the range, but much of the country is pleasant tarn and basin land. The rock is quite good, and if the area were less remote more climbing would probably have been done here, particularly given the region's relatively dry climate.

The approach to the McGillivray Pass side of the range may take you through the old mining town of Bralorne, once the site of booming goldfields. Houses and sheds from the 1930s still stand—deserted now—and an old concentrator bears picturesque testimony to the former economic importance of this area. From the concentrator, a pleasant 15 km trip on foot or ski takes you to McGillivray Pass, where moose are still occasionally seen traversing the marshy uplands. The approach from the south into the pass is made from the B.C. Rail main line and, for variety, you can always

CADWALLADER RANGE AND TENQUILLE LAKE — 165

begin a journey to McGillivray by hopping the train in North Vancouver.

The Tenquille Lake area, farther to the west, has plenty of open alpine country. Recently, parties have struck out to the north from this area to visit the fine meadows around Mt. Noel and its subsidiary peaks. This is a good area to head for when you seek the solitude of infrequently visited back country.

There have been a number of recent additions and corrections to the names in the Cadwallader Range (*CAJ* 1979, p. 74; and provincial map 92 J/NE). A number of names from the tales of J.R.R. Tolkien have been given to peaks in the area, although he apparently disapproved of such unauthorized transfers from his imaginary world to the real one (see *The Letters of J.R.R. Tolkien*, London, George Allen and Unwin, 1981, pp. 300, 349, and 371).

An early trip to the area is described in *CAJ* 1939, p. 64. A traverse from McGillivray Pass to Tenquille Lake is described in *BCM* 1982, p. 46.

Approaches

A. FROM CADWALLADER CREEK

At present, there are no logging roads on this side of the Cadwallader Range, although plans call for a road up Noel Creek by 1989. Noel Creek is bad travelling at present. Parties have skied to the head of Cadwallader Creek in spring, but it is bushy in summer. Access to McGillivray Pass is detailed in the Bendor Range chapter.

B. FROM BIRKENHEAD RIVER

From Pemberton, drive E on Highway 99 for 7 km/4.3 mi to Mt. Currie. From here, the road continues N along the Birkenhead River, eventually turning NE along the Gates River and ending at D'Arcy, at the head of Anderson Lake.

1. Owl Creek approach: A road branches to the left from the D'Arcy road 5 km/3.1 mi N of Mt. Currie, just past Owl Creek. It climbs to 1100 m/3600 ft on the north side of the creek, although it is not driveable this far. A trail begins at its end and leads to the unnamed first lake. It continues (less distinctly) to Owl Lake at 1190 m/3900 ft. There is also a side trail which leads to the four lakes in Owl Creek's east fork. Formerly, Owl Lake could be reached directly from the Lillooet River by trail, but the washout of the Wilson Road bridge has made access more difficult. There is also a rough road climbing SW from the highway to a microwave station at 1705 m/5600 ft, S of the lakes in Owl Creek's east fork.

2. Birkenhead River road: at 17 km/10.5 mi from Mt. Currie, on the D'Arcy road, a road branches left and leads to Birkenhead Provincial Park. It is driveable to the outlet of Birkenhead Lake (about 9 km/5.6 mi). The road continues along the northwest side of the lake, although currently blocked by a rockslide, and eventually joins the road in Blackwater Creek (see below).

2a. Tenquille Creek road: Just before Birkenhead Lake, a road branches to the left. After following 1.5 km along the east side of Birkenhead River, it crosses to the west side of the river. This road is at present washed out. A second road which begins just inside the park also leads to this point. The road then follows the west side of the river to its junction with Tenquille Creek. The right branch crosses to the north side of Birkenhead River and soon ends. The left fork follows the south side of

Tenquille Creek for 3 km, ending at 1250 m/4100 ft. There is an old prospector's cabin at GR 087957 above the valley floor to the SW of Tenquille Lake.

3. Blackwater Creek road: About 34 km/20.6 mi from Mt. Currie, a road branches left. It follows the north side of Blackwater Creek to join the Birkenhead Lake road. There is a gate just after it enters the park.

3a. Birkenhead Peak Road: 1 km after the Blackwater Creek road leaves the highway, a branch heads left. It zigzags to a microwave station at 1920 m/6300 ft on the northeast side of Birkenhead Peak.

C. FROM LILLOOET RIVER AND HURLEY RIVER

From Pemberton, the Lillooet River road runs NW along the floodplain of the Lillooet River. After about 22 km/13.6 mi, it crosses to the northeast side of the river and continues for some way.

1. Tenquille Lake trail: A trail branches to the right from the Lillooet River road, just after it crosses to the northeast side of the Lillooet River. The trail climbs steeply, ascending the Wolverine Creek valley into Tenquille Pass just W of Tenquille Lake at 1645 m/5400 ft. This trail originally began downstream at Gingerbread Creek. The old and new trails merge at the 915 m/3000 ft elevation. There is a public cabin at Tenquille Lake, built by Pemberton residents in the 1940s.

2. Railroad Pass road (Hurley River road): About 10 km/6.2 mi after crossing the Lillooet River, a signposted road branches to the right. It was recently graded, and climbs to Railroad Pass (1400 m/4600 ft). It then descends into the Hurley River valley and eventually leads to Gold Bridge and Bralorne (some rough parts, good clearance needed). At about 915 m/3000 ft, the last of several spurs forks to the right. From its end, a trail traverses SE, gradually gaining height and intersecting the Tenquille Lake trail at 1495 m/4900 ft in Wolverine Creek. It is likely that this new trail will supersede the old Tenquille Lake trail. It is heavily used by snowmobiles in winter and spring.

3. Hurley River road, southeast fork: At the point 2 km before the Hurley River forks, a road branches to the right and traverses into the southeast fork of the Hurley River valley. It ends at 1310 m/4300 ft to the E of Grouty Peak (incorrectly marked Chipmunk Mountain on the federal map sheet). Noel Creek is usually gained from this vicinity.

Routes

MT. RONAYNE 2255 m/7400 ft

A broad summit N of Pemberton. At present, it appears that the Owl Lake road and trail *(B1)* on the south side is the best approach. Ascend to the southeast ridge from the junction of the main and east branches of Owl Creek, and climb NW over an intervening peak to the summit.

SUN GOD MOUNTAIN 2410 m/7900 ft

Incorrectly marked on 92 J/10. Located 6 km/3.7 mi W of the south end of Birkenhead Lake and correctly positioned on provincial map 92 J/NE.

FA: J. Ronayne, P. Tait—1931.

The loss of the Birkenhead River bridge W of the Birkenhead Lake will complicate the approach. From the Tenquille Creek road (*B2a*), ascend S along the creek which drains the north side of the peak. At timberline, veer SW towards the west ridge's saddle, which leads to the summit (NTD). The northeast arête, reached by veering E anytime above timberline on the approach, is Class 3-4 if you bypass the gendarme on the E. Cerulean Lake to the W is a good campsite, and **SEVEN O'CLOCK MOUNTAIN** (2315 m/7600 ft) to the S is NTD (*FRA: S. Fall, K. Ricker, N. Purssell—1971*).

BIRKENHEAD PEAK 2523 m/8278 ft
A large, glaciated massif E of Birkenhead Lake. From the microwave station (*B3a*), climb SE, then NW over a 2285 m/7500 ft summit to a col, then ascend the north ridge. Good views.

STANDARD RIDGE 2135 m/7000 ft
An easy ridge SW of McGillivray Pass (*A*), best noted for good skiing and for the remains of a telegraph line running along its crest.

PROSPECTOR PEAKS 2500 m/8200 ft
Located NW of forks of McGillivray Creek.
FRA: N. Carter and party—1930s.
Easily reached by following ridges S from McGillivray Pass (*A*). The first summit is traversed to reach the higher southeastern one. A low Class 3 climb.

MT. TAILLEFER 2410 m/7900 ft
Located between the heads of Phelix Creek and Cadwallader Creek.
FA: J. Fyles, T. Fyles, P. Long, N. Maude—1919.
From N of Prospector Peaks, follow the divide W and ascend the east ridge (NTD) or north side (Class 3). The 2255 m/7400 ft peak 1.5 km S is easily reached by the connecting ridge.

MT. WEINHOLD 2255 m/7400 ft
Three km N of Mt. Taillefer; named after a couple killed in a skiing accident in McGillivray Pass.
FA: P. Jordan, F. Thiessen, E. White—1972.
This peak can be reached by following ridges N from Mt. Taillefer or by sidehilling from the S. The connecting ridge with Mt. Taillefer has one Class 4-5 discontinuity.

MT. SHADOWFAX 2285 m/7500 ft
Located 2.5 km W of Mt. Taillefer.
FA: F. Thiessen, E. White—1972.
Reached via ridges leading S, then W from McGillivray Pass (*A*). The northwest ridge is Class 3-4. Other sides appear to be easier.

MT. ARAGORN 2470 m/8100 ft
Located 2 km W of Mt. Shadowfax.
FA: P. Jordan, F. Thiessen, E. White—1972.
This peak is easy from most directions, although the northeast face appears difficult. Avoid belligerent Nazguls at all costs, especially the big, black hairy ones.

Mt. Taillefer   Peter Jordan

MT. GANDALF 2375 m/7800 ft
Located 1 km S of Mt. Aragorn.
FA: P. Jordan, F. Thiessen, E. White—1972.
Reached via the easy ridge connecting it to Mt. Aragorn, with some entertaining summit pinnacles. The provincial map 92 J/NE has erroneously interchanged the positions of Shadowfax and Gandalf.

PEAK 8200 2500 m/8200 ft
An impressive granitic horn, located at GR 124058. *FA: L. Soet—1975.* An easy scramble from the SW.

"VALPOLICELLA PEAK" 2350 m/7700 ft
Located at GR 129087 on 92 J/10. *FRA: K. Foess, M. Lawler, R. Schewing, F. Sheppard, R. Walker—August 1979.* NTD via the west ridge.

PEAK 8200 2500 m/8200 ft
A long peak E of the headwaters of Noel Creek at GR 118112.
FA: P. Jordan, J. Matthewson, J. Sibley—1983.
The main peak is Class 4 by its southeast ridge; the southeast peak is Class 3 via the northwest ridge. Nice granitic rock.

SUNSHINE MOUNTAIN 2315 m/7600 ft
Located due S of Pioneer Mine. From the long-defunct Bralorne ski hill, an old trail leads S to timberline and then to the summit. You can then travel SE over some interesting summits to Mt. Aragorn. There is also a long-disused trail running part way up Chism Creek from Cadwallader Creek (*A*).

NOEL MOUNTAIN 2530 m/8300 ft
A remote summit which has been reached by open ridges leading N from Tenquille Lake (*C2*) and by a direct approach from Hurley River road (*C3*).

GOAT PEAK 2470 m/8100 ft; TENQUILLE MOUNTAIN 2400 m/7900 ft
Located NW of Tenquille Lake (*C2*). A gully leads N from Tenquille Pass to the divide, which is easily followed W and E to either summit. Alternatively, ascend N from Tenquille Lake into the basin E of Tenquille Mountain and traverse W to the summits. Goat Peak may be climbed directly from the new Tenquille Lake trail (*C2*) as it traverses the peak's southern side. Other summits in the vicinity include **MT. McLEOD** (2165 m/7100 ft), **MT. BARBOUR** (2285 m/7500 ft) S of Tenquille Lake, and **COPPER MOUND** (2165 m/7100 ft) SW of the lake. None of these are difficult. Finally, there is a trail heading NE from the lake to Grizzly Pass.

CHIPMUNK MOUNTAIN 2375 m/7800 ft
The highest peak (GR 048029) of the incorrectly marked (on 92 J/10) "Sun God" massif. From Grizzly Pass, traverse NE to the pass S of Chipmunk. This pass can also be reached from the new Tenquille Lake trail (*C2*) by ascending an unnamed creek to the pass 2.7 km NNW of Goat Peak; from here, traverse E. Ascend N to divide, then E to peak. NTD.

GROUTY PEAK 2330 m/7644 ft
Incorrectly marked "Chipmunk Mountain" on 92 J/10. This peak is easily reached from several points on the Hurley River road (*C3*). The most pleasant route is to take easy bush from Railroad Pass to the ridge crest, and then ramble N for about 5 km to the summit; a very scenic hike.

Chapter 14

Bendor Range

BOUNDARIES:
North: Bridge River, Carpenter Lake
East: Mission Pass road, Anderson Lake
South: McGillivray Creek, Cadwallader Creek
West: Hurley River

FOREST SERVICE OFFICE:
Lillooet Forest District
P.O. Box 10
Lillooet, B.C. V0K 1V0
256-7033

LOGGING COMPANY:
Evans Forest Products
P.O. Box 880
Lillooet, B.C. V0K 1V0
256-4266

MAPS:
Federal:
92 J/9 Shalalth   92 J/10 Birkenhead Lake
92 J/15 Bralorne   92 J/16 Bridge River

Provincial:
92 J/NE

Introduction

This is a region of high but dry alpine ridges and only a few small glaciers. Although access tends to be lengthy, the area has some good rock and extensive open ridges well suited to lengthy traverses. The only such traverse recorded to date was in 1980 when Miriam Doroghy and Len Soet ascended Fergusson Creek, climbed Mt. Truax, and continued SE to McGillivray Pass. Many of the peaks in the central part of the range have no recorded ascents. However, prospectors have been very active in the region for many years, and it is probable that many of the peaks received the attention of these incidental mountaineers.

Approaches

A. FROM GOLD BRIDGE HIGHWAY AND MISSION PASS ROAD

From Lillooet, reached by either the Duffey Lake road through Pemberton or by the Fraser Canyon, an all-season gravel road leads W along the north side of the Bridge River and Carpenter Lake to the towns of Gold Bridge and Bralorne. Carpenter Lake is impounded at its eastern end by the Terzaghi Dam. From Gold Bridge, you can cross the dam and climb a steep, narrow road over Mission Pass (10.5 km/6.5 mi) to the towns of Shalalth and Seton Portage between Seton and Anderson lakes. The powerline road from D'Arcy also gives access to Seton Portage, but it is steep and sometimes very rough.

1. Whitecap Creek/powerline road: Currently the best approach to the road in upper Whitecap Creek on the east side of the range. At an abrupt switchback on the Mission Ridge road (9.5 km/5.9 mi from Terzaghi Dam turnoff) turn right. Follow the powerline road for 6.5 km/4 mi to Whitecap Creek. Bear right and follow the main road to 1220 m/4000 ft near the head of the creek. Rough two-wheel drive.

2. Whitecap Creek main line: From Seton Portage, the main road goes W to Anderson Lake. Immediately after crossing Whitecap Creek bridge, you can (at low water), double back and ford the creek (four-wheel drive). This road joins the powerline road (*A1*) higher up. Locals in Seton Portage may know of other access lines; the provincial map indicates the main line can be gained without fording the creek.

B. VIA ANDERSON LAKE ROAD

A road follows the northwest shore of Anderson Lake from Seton Portage to D'Arcy; it was graded in 1983. There are several steep, rough, narrow hills. Information on its current status is available from B.C. Hydro, Seton Portage, 256-7044.

1. McGillivray Creek trail: Drive N from D'Arcy on the powerline road for about 9 km. A road goes left 0.5 km before McGillivray Creek. Follow this and take the right fork shortly after, cross the creek, and continue along the road (possibly four-wheel drive) to its end, at about 975 m/3200 ft, 5.1 km/3.2 mi from the powerline. Just before the road ends in slash, a spur heads left. The trail begins at the road's end and drops to join the old horse trail leading to McGillivray Pass. It was cleared and marked in 1981. A full day to the pass.

Alternatively, take the B.C. Railway to McGillivray Falls. Just S of the station a horse trail leads up to the powerline, S of McGillivray Creek. Active logging may recently have disrupted the start of this trail.

C. VIA GOLD BRIDGE

The town of Gold Bridge can be reached via the Gold Bridge Highway from Lillooet (*A*), or from Pemberton via the Hurley River forest road.

1. Truax Creek road: From Gold Bridge, the road passes the Gold Bridge Hotel and continues along the south side of Bridge River and Carpenter Lake for about 12 km/7.5 mi. This road eventually climbs S into Truax Creek (four-wheel drive), ending at some old mine workings at 1950 m/6400 ft. A new logging spur ascends the first major creek entering from the W, providing access to the ridges NW of Mt. Truax. The lower parts of the road have seen recent logging activity and are two-wheel drive.

2. *Lindsey Creek road:* A road climbs to McDonald Lake. From its N end, an old mining trail ascends Lindsey Creek to timberline.

3. *Fergusson Creek trail:* Begin at the old gas station at Brexton, 4 km S of Gold Bridge on the road to Bralorne. The old road is driveable for a short distance, and then deteriorates into a track ascending Fergusson Creek past a cabin at 1770 m/5800 ft. The track eventually reaches old mine workings at 2500 m/8200 ft—higher than many peaks in the Coast Mountains.

D. VIA CADWALLADER CREEK

A good road leads S from Gold Bridge to Bralorne. The maintained section of this road ends at the old Pioneer concentrator on Cadwallader Creek, 3 km SW of Bralorne. A very rough road then follows the N side of the creek past Hawthorn and Piebiter creeks, eventually entering the Standard Creek valley. The road becomes a trail which climbs into McGillivray Pass and then descends McGillivray Creek to Anderson Lake (*B1*). The trail is swampy but easy to follow; it was upgraded in 1983. There are several cabins in McGillivray Pass, which provides access to the southeastern Bendor Range.

1. *Piebiter Creek road:* Beginning 13 km/8 mi from Pioneer concentrator/Cadwallader Creek bridge, an old mining road runs up Piebiter Creek from the Cadwallader Creek road to 1585 m/5200 ft. It is four-wheel drive. There is a small cabin which sleeps four at this point. The valley beyond is brushy and swampy in part but it can be used as ready access to the interior of the Bendor Range.

Routes

MT. TRUAX 2880 m/9450 ft

The highest peak of the northwestern Bendor Range, NE of Bralorne. The ascent is not difficult from either the Fergusson Creek trail (*C3*) or Truax Creek road (*C1*).

MT. FERGUSSON 2595 m/8510 ft

From the Fergusson Creek cabin (*C3*), climb SW to timberline and Mt. Fergusson's long, easy NW ridge.

MT. WILLIAMS 2790 m/9150 ft

This summit is probably best approached from the Truax Creek road (*C1*).

MT. BOBB 2845 m/9330 ft

This peak, in the centre of the range, is difficult to approach but easy to climb from the SW. Probably an overland approach from Fergusson Creek (*C3*) or Truax Creek (*C1*) is the most feasible one. A sketchy old trail is reported to be in Hawthorn Creek to the S, starting off Cadwallader Creek road (*D*). **PEAK 8530** (2600 m/8530 ft) and **PEAK 8720** (2658 m/8720 ft) to the SW of Mt. Bobb feature fine granitic exposures on their N sides.

McGILLIVRAY PASS AREA
This is a high, but fairly gentle area, featuring good meadows but poor rock. Ski touring is excellent here, as is avalanche potential.

ROYAL PEAK 2345 m/7700 ft
FA: Likely by prospectors.
A nondescript knob NW of McGillivray Pass. Ascend to col SE of summit from the pass (*D*), then scramble to top. A good ski ascent.

MT. McGILLIVRAY 2590 m/8500 ft
FA: Likely by prospectors.
A major peak of dark, loose rock overlooking McGillivray Pass (*D*). From the pass, ascend to saddle SE of summit, then climb SE ridge. Class 2. The north ridge is Class 3 and exposed.

MT. PIEBITER 2560 m/8400 ft
The northeastern neighbour of McGillivray. Probably easiest reached by dropping from col SE of McGillivray into head of Connel Creek, and climbing Piebiter's S slopes.
Northwest ridge: *FA: M. Condor, B. Fairley—August 1983.* Reached via Piebiter Creek (*D1*). Near the head of the valley, you should swing to the S to gain the base of the rock, avoiding bluffs at the head of the valley. A Class 3 spine-like, exposed ridge. Decent rock. Descent is via gentle glaciers to the S.

WHITECAP MOUNTAIN 2925 m/9595 ft
A high, glaciated summit. From saddle SE of Mt. McGillivray, drop into Connel Creek and follow it down to where it turns SE. Ascend NE over meadows and scree to summit. A long day return from McGillivray Pass and an outstanding ski-tour featuring 1250 m/4100 ft of descent on smooth slopes. An approach from Whitecap Creek (*A1*) might also be possible.

NOSEBAG MOUNTAIN 2242 m/7356 ft
Located 11 km/6.8 mi due W of Mission Pass and N of Whitecap Creek. You could probably approach it most easily by heading W from Mission Pass over high, upland ridges, or by heading straight up from Whitecap Creek.

Chapter 15

Duffey Lake Road Peaks

BOUNDARIES:
North: Seton Lake, Anderson Lake
East: Phair Creek watershed divide
South: Stein River watershed north divide
West: Birkenhead River, Van Horlick Creek

DEPARTMENT OF HIGHWAYS:
Squamish, B.C.
(Duffey Lake Road)
898-5613, 898-3132

FOREST SERVICE OFFICES:

Lillooet Forest District
P.O. Box 10, 1210 Main Street
Lillooet, B.C. V0K 1V0
256-7531

Squamish Forest District
P.O. Box 1970
Squamish, B.C. V0N 3G0
898-9671

LOGGING COMPANIES:

Evans Forest Products
P.O. Box 1970
Squamish, B.C. V0N 3G0
265-4266

Weldwood of Canada
3150 Cleveland Street
Squamish, B.C. V0N 3G0
892-5244

MAPS:
Federal:
92 J/7 Pemberton
92 J/9 Shalalth

92 J/8 Duffey Lake
92 I/12 Lillooet

Provincial:
92 J/NE
92 I/NW

92 J/SE

Introduction

It is convenient to group all those summits together that are most easily reached from the Duffey Lake road, which runs between the towns of Mount Currie and Lillooet. The region has not been an area of concentrated mountaineering activity in the past. Like the south Chilcotin, it is characterized by high ridge systems and valleys which are more gentle than those farther south. It is an area ready-made for the imaginative backpacker, who can put together almost any number of scenic traverses if he or she knows how to read a map carefully.

Access into many of the creek drainages in this area has improved greatly since Dick Culbert published his *Alpine Guide* in 1974, but there are still some sections, particularly in the Cayoosh Range itself, which rarely see any traffic. One added attraction is the abundance of wildlife in the area; sightings of deer, porcupine, marmot, and even goat are not uncommon. Weather tends to be drier here than in the ranges to the south and west, and this is true also in winter, so that many pleasant ski-touring trips up the various road systems here have been made in the last couple of years. In short, this is not an area characterized by "big routes," but is ideally suited to exploration with map, compass, camera and good companions. The area, like the Lillooet chapter, has been given a wilderness treatment, so as to leave some room for the exploratory spirit. Those desiring further detail are referred to *Exploring the Stein River Valley* (Freeman and Thompson).

Approaches

A. VIA THE DUFFEY LAKE ROAD

This signposted road leaves the town of Mt. Currie (0 km) E of Pemberton, follows the Birkenhead River for 9.5 km/6 mi to the head of Lillooet Lake, then turns NE to climb Joffre Creek before crossing Cayoosh Pass N of the Joffre area (23 km/14.5 mi). From here it descends Cayoosh Creek, passes Duffey Lake, and ends at the town of Lillooet—92 km/58 mi in total. The road is sometimes kept open during the winter; check with the Highways Department. For access from the Duffey Lake road to the Joffre area (Joffre trail, Cerise Creek, Casper Creek, Van Horlick Creek) see Joffre chapter.

1. North Joffre Creek road (17 km/10.6 mi from Mt. Currie; 75 km/47.4 mi from Lillooet—estimated):
A spur road here leads to North Joffre Creek. This is the usual winter access to the Place Glacier area.

2. Cayoosh Pass road (24 km/15 mi from Mt. Currie; 68 km/43 mi from Lillooet):
This road ascends upper Cayoosh valley immediately E of Cayoosh Pass, W of Mt. Rohr. After the Duffey Lake road crosses the bridge over Cayoosh Creek (GR 377814 on 92 J/8), climb for a short distance, then turn N and follow an old road for 2 km, taking the left branch at the fork. After parking, follow this branch to its end, cross the creek at about 1400 m/4600 ft, and then follow the west side of the creek to a pleasant lake at 1740 m/5700 ft, which makes a fine campsite. In winter, it is easiest to park further up the road in a plowed parking area and ski straight N until you intersect the road.

2a. Cayoosh Mountain spur: This road contours around the east flank of Cayoosh Mountain on the west side of Cayoosh Creek for a distance of about 3 km.

3. Van Horlick Creek road (36.5 km/23 mi from Mt. Currie; 55.5 km/35 mi from Lillooet): See Joffre chapter.

4. Blowdown Creek road (46.5 km/29 mi from Mt Currie; 45.5 km/29 mi from Lillooet): This road begins across from an unmistakable, steep clear-cut which ascends the hill on the north side of Cayoosh Creek. The road leaves the Duffey Lake road steeply to the S and follows the east bank of Blowdown Creek to about 1525 m/5000 ft where a private mine road begins (*A4a*). Branch roads at 5 km and 8 km/5 mi give access to the west side of the creek.

4a. Silver Queen Mine road-Cottonwood Creek trail: A private mine road (not gated; two-wheel drive condition) climbs out of Blowdown Creek (*A4*), crosses the 2160 m/7100 ft pass to the E of the drainage above "Kidney Lakes," and descends the south fork of Cottonwood Creek to the Silver Queen mine. The road sticks to the north side of the creek, crossing to the S at about the 1460 m/4800 ft level (lower mine portal), then switchbacking up to the upper mine at 1980 m/6500 ft. A rough trail continues down Cottonwood Creek for several km; condition unknown.

5. Hurley silver mine road (47 km/30 mi from Mt. Currie; 45 km/28 mi from Lillooet): A bridge here crosses to the west side of Cayoosh Creek. The old road led up the south side of an unnamed creek to 1620 m/5300 ft, but it is best to take the newer logging road which climbs a horrendous clear-cut via steep switchbacks to about the same elevation on the north side of the creek. From here, hike a wooded ridge onto the divide E of Haylmore Creek.

6. Gott Creek roads (59.5 km/37 mi from Mt. Currie; 32.5 km/21 mi from Lillooet): Road building got underway again in this drainage in 1984, and in the future roads will extend a considerable distance up the drainage. Present terminal elevation is over 1220 m/4000 ft.

7. "Boulder Creek" road (63.5 km/40.3 mi from Mt. Currie; 28.5 km/17.7 mi from Lillooet: Boulder Creek is the major drainage between Phair and Gott creeks. An excellent (two-wheel drive) road ascends this creek almost to tree line. The road enters to the W of the creek, ascends through a steep slide, crosses to the east side, then climbs high along the east flank. This road gives wonderful access to scenic alpine country to the E, S, and W, but logging in this area is active and proceeding rapidly; when it ceases the road will quickly wash out.

8. Downton Creek (70.7 km/44.7 mi from Mt. Currie; 21.4 km/13.3 mi from Lillooet): Present plans call for roads to be built in this drainage within two years.

9. "Seton Ridge" road (75 km/47.4 mi from Mt. Currie; 17 km/10.6 mi from Lillooet): Here a bridge crosses Cayoosh Creek, and a good road ascends to 1400 m/4600 ft on the east end of Seton Ridge at the eastern end of the Cayoosh Range. The road crosses the ridge, then descends a considerable distance towards Seton Lake. From the high point of the road, where it crosses the ridge, an excellent trail leads westward following the divide N of Copper Creek into the alpine country between Downton Creek and Lost Valley Creek.

10. Enterprise Creek road (84.5 km/52.5 mi from Mt. Currie; 7.5 km/4.7 mi from Lillooet): This two-wheel drive road drops down from the Duffey Lake road, crosses Cayoosh Creek, and ascends the north side of the Brew massif to about 1370 m/4500 ft. Not likely to give good access to anything; all routes on Brew Mountain are best gained from Brew Mountain trail (Lillooet chapter, *C1*).

B. VIA BIRKENHEAD RIVER ROAD

This road goes N from the town of Mt. Currie to the south end of Anderson Lake, where a rough four-wheel drive road leads to Seton Portage. B.C. Hydro maintains the roads along Anderson Lake. Better roads carry on from here to Lillooet. All distances are from Mt. Currie Townsite.

1. Spetch Creek road and trail (12.3 km/7.6 mi): Cross Spetch Creek on the bridge at 13.5 km/8.3 mi, then double back immediately on the old road to the river. This road (not driveable) climbs the east side of Spetch Creek for 3 km, then crosses to the west side and ascends in a series of switchbacks. An old trail climbs into the basin W of Cassiope, and though much of this can no longer be followed, the country is pleasant travel. Takes 4–5 hours to basin. Stay on the west side of the creek once the crossing has been made.

2. Place Creek (21.5 km/13.4 mi): This was once a flagged route leading up to the snout of the Place Glacier; now only a few tapes remain. Bush is fairly open. A small glaciology cabin is located on the glacier.

3. Eight Mile Creek road (26 km/16 mi): Weldwood Logging Company is now logging this area. A two-wheel drive road leads to 1100 m/3500 ft as marked on 92 J/7. Before driving up, call Weldwood to check whether the road is gated.

4. Haylmore Creek (34 km/21 mi): Turn right into Devine to gain this system. Roads are as marked on 92 J/9 and 92 J/8. The spur road on the south side of the creek is closed, but a four-wheel drive road runs up the north side to about 800 m/2600 ft where it is washed out. Starting to brush in. A horse trail ascends the east fork to tree line as shown on map 92 J/8. There is an abandoned alpine settlement on the road in northeast fork.

Routes

SAXIFRAGE MOUNTAIN 2500 m/8200 ft
Located between the headwaters of Spetch Creek and North Joffre Creek.
FRA: B. Erikson, N. Kerby, M. Jordan, P. Jordan—1970.
Reach this friendly group of summits from the end of the Spetch Creek trail (*B1*) by travelling E over open country to their easy southeastern slopes. Saxifrage is NTD by its southwest ridge, but the minor **"CASSIOPE MOUNTAIN"** (2290 m/7500 ft), located on the same ridge at GR 288786, is most easily reached from the S, as its southwest ridge is a Class 2–3 scramble. This area can also be reached from Place Glacier (*B2*) or from Joffre Creek (*A1*). (Ref: *VOCJ* 1982, p. 135 [map].)

MT. OLDS 2530 m/8300 ft
Located 4 km N of Saxifrage, at the head of Place Gacier.
The first ascent of this and other peaks surrounding Place Glacier was by R. Gilbert and glaciology surveys in the late 1960s.
An easy scramble by the rocky west ridge from the saddle between Mt. Olds and Mt. Oleg.

"MT. OLEG" 2590 m/8500 ft
Highest summit in the Place Glacier area, located W of the glacier. From Place Glacier (*B2*) hike up snowslopes toward saddle between Oleg and Mt. Olds to the E. Continue on gentle slopes to summit.

MT. GARDINER 2380 m/7800 ft
A rock peak rising SW of the snout of Place Glacier.
Reach the summit easily by climbing to the col SE of Mt. Gardiner, then scrambling up the south ridge. The northeast ridge, reached directly from the Place Glacier cabin (*B2*), is Class 3.

GATES PEAK 2380 m/7800 ft
Stands above and to NE of the Place Glacier cabin.
Ascend E from cabin (*B2*) up goat trail and scree to ridge S of peak, then follow divide to summit. Not difficult.

CIRQUE PEAK 2500 m/8200 ft
The main summit E of Place Glacier.
From Place Glacier (*B2*), ascend to the prominent basin on the north side of Cirque Peak, and then climb to its north ridge. This ridge is Class 3 rock. From Place Glacier, reach the two 2440 m/8000 ft summits SE of Cirque Peak by climbing to the divide with Joffre Glacier and ascending to the E.

CAYOOSH MOUNTAIN 2590 m/8500 ft
Located W of the head of Cayoosh Creek and N of Cayoosh Pass (GR 340832).
From Cayoosh Pass: Take the Cayoosh Mountain spur (*A2a*) and contour around the east side of Cayoosh Mountain, ascending into an open alpine basin SE of the peak. Contour around the east ridge (to the N of you) and gain the glacier which drains the east side of the peak. Ascend to the col which divides the northeast glacier from the east glacier, then scramble the south ridge to the summit. This trip usually takes 7–8 hours return on skis.
From North Joffre Creek: *FA: H. Rode and party—July 1978.* Ascend the southwest slopes of the peak from the spur road in North Joffre Creek (*A1*) until you reach a basin with a small tarn, shown on maps. From here the southwest ridge is easily gained and followed without difficulty to the summit.
South slopes: Either of the above routes may be gained by ascending the south slopes of the peak directly from the Duffey Lake road from a point above the Joffre Lakes parking lot (see Joffre chapter).

MT. ROHR 2440 m/8000 ft
Located W of Duffey Lake.
From Cayoosh Pass: Take the road which runs up the east side of upper Cayoosh Creek (*A2*), until you reach the end of the spur. You should be near the creek which drains the large lake WNW of Mt. Rohr. It is a 2 hour hike to this lake at 1830 m/6000 ft, and 2 more hours over pleasant, easy terrain to the summit of Rohr. A popular ski trip.
Southwest slopes: From the Duffey Lake road ascend southwest slopes to **PEAK 8000** (2440 m/8000 ft), about 2 km W of the peak. Follow the west ridge of Rohr to the summit. Those who attempt a direct assault on the summit from the road will regret it.

PEAK 7900 2410 m/7900 ft
Located 1 km S of the lake at the head of the west branch of Spruce Creek (GR 373878).
FRA: P. Jordan—September 1, 1974.
From the end of the logging roads in upper Cayoosh Creek (*A1*), hike to the lake at 1735 m/5700 ft. Peak 7900 rising above the lake and its 2315 m/7600 ft neighbour to the SE are easily climbed from here.

MT. MARRIOTT ("ASPEN PEAK") 2750 m/9015 ft

Located 9 km/5.5 mi S of Devine.

From the south: This summit is now most commonly reached from upper Cayoosh valley (*A2*). Open country, pleasant for hiking, separates the road and the peak. The southwest ridge of Marriott is a long, picket-like formation, involving several gendarmes and much scrambling; Class 3–4.

From the north: From the road on the east side of Eight Mile Creek (*B3*), take a track which swings into the next valley to the E ending at about 1060 m/3500 ft. Hike up this valley until you are under the summit. If you swing to the S of the final peak you can avoid the Class 5 gap in the north ridge.

NEQUATQUE MOUNTAIN 2650 m/8700 ft

Located 1 km NNW of Mt. Marriott.

FRA: P. Kubik, E. Zenger—1975.

About 1 km W of Devine on the Birkenhead Road (*B*), a logging road climbs a short distance up the hillside through private property. Bash straight up the bushy slopes to Nequatque Lake (1800 m/5900 ft); 5 hours. The central buttress on the north face involves a few Class 5 pitches and a point of aid. Descend to S, then back over the east ridge to lake. On the same outing P. Crean ascended the two 2500 m/8200 ft peaks SSE of the lake on the east ridge of Nequatque; NTD.

"SILVER QUEEN MOUNTAIN" 2165 m/7100 ft

Located 8 km/5 mi ESE of "Blowdown Pass" at GR 680760. The Silver Queen Mine Road (*A4a*) terminates in a cirque N of this summit. From here the northeast ridge is NTD.

PEAK 8400 2560 m/8400 ft

Located at the head of Van Horlick Creek at Gr 507686.

FA: N. Purssell and party—September 1978.

From the upper east fork of Van Horlick Creek (*A3*) ascend the glacier on the north flank of Peak 8500. The southeast ridge of Peak 8400 can be easily climbed from the col between it and Peak 8500. This latter peak has also probably been climbed from this point.

GOTT PEAK 2530 m/8300 ft (on 92 J/8)

Located at the head of Gott Creek.

This name has been applied to more than a few of the summits in this area, including the 2440 m/8000 ft summit 4 km S of Gott, and the 2805 m/9200 ft mountain 7.5 km/4.7 mi to the NE. Most of these summits can be easily and directly approached via the pass at the head of Blowdown Creek road (*A4*). The high, gentle divide gives the whole region a great potential for hiking and ski touring, and interest in the area is gaining momentum. In 1969 J. Clarke visited the range W of Gott Creek. He approached along roads that ascend to almost 1525 m/5000 ft on the slope across Cayoosh Creek from the Hurley silver mine road and climbed all the peaks on the divide between the 2650 m/8700 ft one at the north end, and Gott Peak at the south end. All NTD.

"GOTCHA PEAK" 2440 m/8000 ft

Located 1 km S of "Blowdown Pass" and S of "Kidney Lakes" (GR 603782). A scenic ramble.

"NOTGOTT PEAK" 2440 m/8000 ft

Located 4 km S of Gott Peak. This peak is marked as Gott on provincial maps. NTD. The peaks 3 km W of Notgott have been explored by BCMC ski parties, and a horseshoe traverse of all peaks at the head of Blowdown Creek has also been made.

BOULDER CREEK SUMMITS

The alpine country surrounding "Boulder Creek" (*A7*) is exceptionally pleasant scrambling terrain. Reach the ridge of peaks to the E of the creek directly from a number of points along the Boulder Creek road. All appear to have been climbed.

"MOUNT RUSSELL" 2500 m/8200 ft

Located on a four-way divide at the head of Boulder Creek. Easy from most directions.

"WONDER MOUNTAIN" 2745 m/9000 ft; PEAK 8500 2590 m/8500 ft

Located W of the head of "Boulder Creek," (GR 661906 and 665890)
FRA: R. Brusse, G. McCormack—1983.
Both peaks are easy scrambles from Boulder Creek (*A7*). It seems likely that all peaks in the Boulder and Gott drainages were climbed by prospectors or outfitters either in the late 1800s or early 1900s.

PEAK 9000 2745 m/9000 ft

Most northerly 9000 ft peak on the divide between Gott Creek and "Boulder Creek." *FRA: C. Adam, J. Barnes—1970.* NTD from NW.

"ELUSIVE PEAK" 2800 m/9200 ft

Located E of upper Gott Creek and 7.5 km NNE of Gott Peak (GR 626869). Also once referred to as Gott Peak. *FRA: F. Baumann, K. McKenzie, R. Price—1983.* Easy via west ridge. This party also climbed the 8700 ft peak to the N.

Chapter 16

Joffre Group

by Kevin Haberl

BOUNDARIES:
North: Joffre Creek, Cayoosh Creek
East: Van Horlick Creek
South: Twin One Creek
West: Lillooet Lake, Joffre Creek

FOREST SERVICE OFFICE:
Squamish Forest District
P.O. Box 880
Squamish, B.C. V0N 3G0
898-6791

LOGGING COMPANIES:
Evans Forest Products
P.O. Box 1970
Squamish, B.C. V0N 3G0
265-4266

MAPS:
Federal:
92 J/7 Pemberton   92 J/8 Duffey Lake

Provincial:
92 J/SE

Introduction

Joffre is one area mountaineers head for when they wish to teach novice climbers something about the joys of climbing. This concentrated little area of peaks has everything a student of the mountains could wish for. There are ice faces, rock faces, glaciers and couloirs, icefalls, alpine lakes and ridges galore. The approach via the Joffre Lakes trail is one of the most pleasant imaginable, involving a hike through virgin coastal forest along a well-marked trail, and ending at an inviting alpine lake spread beneath rock walls and snow faces.

Probably almost any peak in the Joffre area could be climbed in a day by an ambitious party, but this is one area where it is nice to linger and take in some of the scenery as well. Even if you are not a climber it is well worth making the hike into Upper Joffre Lake to view the great icefall of the Matier Glacier which tumbles down from the steep slopes of Mount Matier.

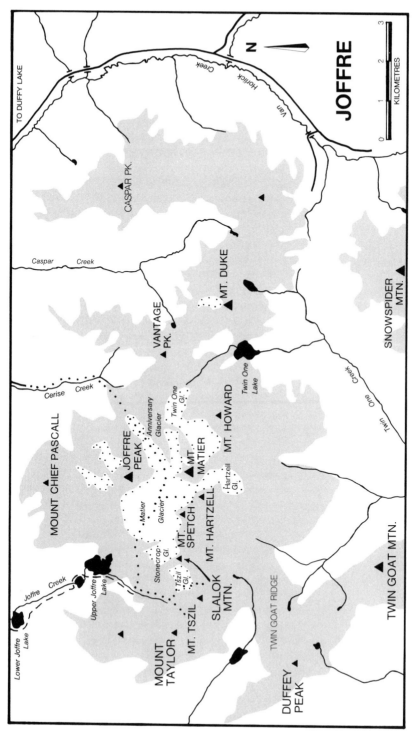

JOFFRE

N

KILOMETRES

TO DUFFY LAKE

Horlick Creek

Van

CASPAR PK.

Caspar Creek

MT. DUKE

SNOWSPIDER MTN.

VANTAGE PK.

Cerise Creek

MOUNT CHIEF PASCALL

Anniversary Glacier

Twin One Gl.

JOFFRE PEAK

MT. MATIER

MT. HOWARD

Twin One Lake

Twin One Creek

Matier Glacier

Hartzell Gl.

Stonecrop Gl.

MT. SPETCH

MT. HARTZELL

Tszil Gl.

SLALOK MTN.

Joffre Creek

Upper Joffre Lake

MOUNT TAYLOR

MT. TSZIL

TWIN GOAT RIDGE

TWIN GOAT MTN.

Lower Joffre Lake

DUFFEY PEAK

Mountaineers who are new to the sport will probably come to know the Joffre area quickly; it is a popular destination on organized climbing club schedules. Some of these peaks have never been climbed in winter, but now that the Duffey Lake road to Lillooet is being kept open all year round, winter treks into this area will be easier.

If you have questions concerning mountain names in this area, consult *CAJ* 1979, p. 75; *CAJ* 1980, p. 84; and an excellent article including maps in the *Avalanche Echoes*, May 1980 by Karl Ricker.

Approaches

A. FROM THE DUFFEY LAKE ROAD (JOFFRE CREEK)
This good two-wheel drive road starts at the town of Mt. Currie, ascends from the W along Joffre Creek, climbs up through Cayoosh Pass, and ends in Lillooet. It gives easy access to the Joffre group for most of the year and is sometimes open in winter (to check phone the Ministry of Highways). All distances are measured from the turnoff in the town of Mt. Currie. Distances from Lillooet are from the bridge at the mouth of Cayoosh Creek.

1. The "Joffre Lakes" trail (23.6 km/14.7 mi): Pull off into the major parking area on the south side of the road. The well-marked Joffre Lakes trail begins here. Climb it past two lakes to a third lake at the head of the valley and continue on the west side of this lake into "Tszil Creek," where you will find good but limited campsites among the trees; 3 hours from road. From camp, climb up the moraine, then, using either the western or eastern edges of the icefall, climb onto the Matier Glacier which lies below Mt. Matier and Joffre Peak. Be careful of avalanching ice if traversing under the icefall to gain the eastern edge.

2. The Cerise Creek road (41 km/25.5 mi): An important approach route for the northeast side of Joffre, and for the Matier Glacier. This road (four-wheel drive condition) branches off the Duffey Lake road and traverses W, ascends to the S, climbing to about 1520 m/5000 ft. A new bridge now crosses Cerise Creek, giving access to the west side, but it is best to stay on the east side if you are heading for Joffre or for the Anniversary Glacier. Takes 1 1/2 hours to reach timberline. The glacier which leads from Cerise Creek to the Joffre-Matier Col is the Anniversary Glacier.

3. The Caspar Creek road (36.4 km/22.6 mi): Leaves the Duffey Lake road at this point and ascends to 1550 m/5100 ft. If tree planting continues, the road will be kept in good two-wheel drive condition for another year. Take the major left branch after the turnoff heading S into the Caspar Creek valley. "Caspar" is incorrectly spelled "Casper" on map 92 J/8.

4. Van Horlick Creek roads (44.1 km/27.4 mi): This lengthy road climbs the E side of Van Horlick Creek for 15 km/9.5 mi almost to the valley head. The entire drainage has been or will shortly be logged; the roads are probably in good (two-wheel drive) condition. At this point, the road up the main creek ends at about 1500 m/4600 ft level. A bridge crosses from S to N at about 1360 m/4450 ft (12 km/7.5 mi from the Duffey Lake road), giving access to Caspar Peak and the Mt. Duke area. There is a major fork at 9 km/5.5 mi where a road ascends the east fork of Van Horlick Creek to almost 1585 m/5300 ft. When you follow this fork, stay on the east side of the creek; this gives the best access to the upper Stein basin to the S via the 1890 m/6200 ft pass at the head of the creek.

B. FROM TWIN ONE CREEK
Shortly after crossing the bridge at the upper (northern) end of Lillooet Lake, the Duffey Lake road cuts off left up the hill. Stay to the right at this fork and follow the road on the east shore of Lillooet Lake for about 11.3 km/7 mi, until you reach the first major valley to the left. Twin One Creek roads currently lead about halfway up this valley, and an old trail climbs from here to the lake below Mts. Howard and Duke. Plans to log more of this area in the near future mean logging spurs will run almost to the valley head, undoubtedly making this valley the best approach route to the eastern summits of the Joffre group.

Routes

DUFFEY PEAK 2233 m/7325 ft
Located 3 km northwest of Twin Goat Mountain.
FA: Likely by topographic survey party.
Connected to Tszil Mountain and Twin Goat Mountain by **TWO GOAT RIDGE**. The col between Duffey Peak and Twin Goat Mountain can be reached directly from Lillooet Lake by climbing the prominent gully, keeping left at all forks except the last. This col may also be gained by a high traverse from Tszil.

TWIN GOAT MOUNTAIN 2130 m/7000 ft
Located above Lillooet Lake, 3.2 km N of Twin One Creek's mouth (*B*).
FRA: T. Anderson, J. Juri, G. Richardson, B. Thornton—1963.
Ascend Twin Goat Mountain's east ridge from 6.4 km/4 mi up Twin One Creek trail or climb to the southwest ridge from 3.2 km up the creek. NTD; takes 6 hours to summit.

MT. TAYLOR 2320 m/7600 ft
Located 1 km NW of Tszil Mountain. Easy ascent from the Tszil-Taylor col.

TSZIL MOUNTAIN 2380 m/7800 ft
Located about 1 km W of Slalok Mountain.
FA: Likely by the Alpine Crafts climbing school or C. Adam.
Reach Tszil Mountain by ascending the Tszil Creek valley running SW from the lake at the head of Joffre Creek (*A1*). Gain the summit either by scrambling up the west side or by climbing snowslopes on the north side. You can also climb a 240 m/800 ft prominent couloir on the north side which provides 45–50° snow and ice (steeper at the top in early summer).

SLALOK MOUNTAIN ("REX'S PILLAR") 2650 m/8700 ft
A prominent peak located about 2 km W of Matier and visible from Pemberton.
FA: C. Adam, T. Anderson, G. Richardson—1963.
North side: From the lake at the head of Joffre Creek (*A1*), climb to the right of the prominent glacier tongue until you reach Stonecrop Glacier on the north side of

Slalok. Continue up the right side of glacier directly to summit. Takes 4 1/2 hours up from lake.

North face: This hanging glacier provides 5 pitches of ice and snow to 50°. An easy day from the road.

West ridge: From the lake at the head of Joffre Creek (*A1*), head up the Tszil Creek valley to the SW, then ascend to the divide at the head of "Tszil Glacier," W of Slalok. The west ridge is an hour's climb from here. Class 3–4.

East side: From a short way up the main part of Matier Glacier, ascend Slalok's northeast snowslopes to the north ridge and follow this to summit. From farther S on the glacier, the east face is a more direct ascent on 45° snow (ice in late summer). Takes 4 hours up from lake.

MT. CHIEF PASCALL 2190 m/7200 ft
Located 2 km N of Joffre Peak. Likely NTD from the end of the Cerise Creek road (*A2*).

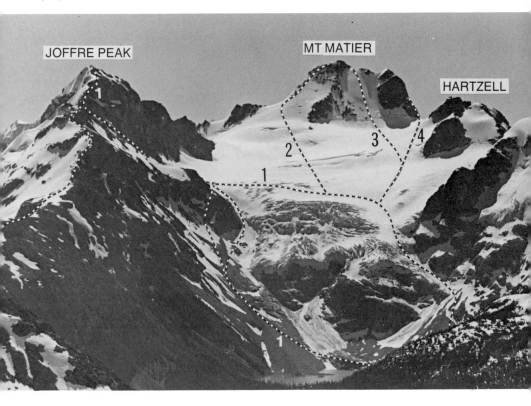

Joffre Peak and Mt. Matier   1.) Northwest ridge   2.) Northeast ridge   3.) Northwest face
4.) West buttress   Peter Jordan

JOFFRE PEAK 2710 m/8900 ft
Located N of Mt. Matier at head of Joffre Creek.
FA: R. Chambers, P. Sherman—1957. Via the southeast face, which is now sometimes used for descent.

FWA: D. Fox, B. Kay, R. Tomich—January 1984.

Northwest ridge: From the Matier Glacier at the head of Joffre Creek *(A1)*, climb an obvious gully to the low point in Joffre's northwest ridge. This ridge is largely a Class 3 rock climb. Keep to the left of crest where necessary. There is one tricky Class 4 notch which is easiest with spring snow. The entire northwest ridge when climbed from the Duffey Lake road is apparently an excellent outing *(S. Fuller, D. Serl—1985)*. The north ridge is the usual descent for all routes.

Northeast pillar: *FA: J. Buszowski, W. Robinson—1980.* Climb the face of the vertical pillar on the right side of Joffre's face. Some large, loose blocks. Avoid final yellow overhangs by traversing left into the grotty gully dividing the pillar from the northeast face route. Descend via north ridge and northeast flank. Eight pitches to 5.8 on pillar plus a few aid moves. Takes 12 hours from bivy.

The west face of Joffre Peak   1.) West face   2.) Southwest rib   3.) Southwest gully   Don Serl

Northeast face: *FA: S. Flavelle, D. Lane—1979.* Approach from Cerise Creek *(A2)* logging roads. Follow huge ramp between the impressive vertical buttress on the right and the dangerous couloir on the left (see above). Route begins almost inside the couloir and climbs a left-facing corner-chimney. The second pitch is the crux; it is a wide crack on the steep wall (visible from below). Four more pitches lead to the snowpatch; 3 more mixed pitches lead up gully to the summit. Descend steep snowslopes and icefalls on the same face but further N. Class 5.8. Takes 11 hours from cars to summit.

Northeast couloir: *FA: F. Douglas, N. Eggers, M. Feller, N. Humphrey, M. Starr, M. Wyborn, R. Wyborn—1973.* There are several interesting routes on this side. The one recorded here climbs the obvious snow couloir to just S of the summit. This involves 610 m/2000 ft of steep snow followed by Class 4 rock at head. Approach from Cerise Creek (*A2*).

East ridge: *FA: D. Serl and a large ACC party—1980.* Route consists of 150 m/500 ft of easy rock, 150 m of easy snow, and 150 m of Class 3 and 4 rock. Takes 3 hours. Descend via southeast face.

Southeast face: Follow snow slopes right, then back left and up to the right of the south ridge.

South ridge: *FA: R. Griffiths, E. Silva-Whyte, D. Steel—1974.* Gain the col between Joffre and Matier from either Joffre or Cerise creeks (*A1 or A2*). Scramble up ridge to prominent buttress, then descend to the right on snow. Climb ledges to the right of buttress (Class 5), then follow on left of ridge crest until forced through a gap onto the crest again. Continue up ridge, bypassing exposed gap on ledges. Takes 3 hours from col.

Southwest gully: *This route was soloed by an anonymous Aussie in 1971.* It is most feasible in early season when the route is steep snow. Under these conditions, it is the easiest route on the mountain.

Southwest rib: *FA: S. Flavelle, D. Mitten—1975.* Follow rib to the left of southwest gully. Rock is not outstanding; mid-5th Class in difficulty.

West face: *FA: P. Stange, E. Zenger—1973.* A gully runs to the summit ridge of Joffre from the Matier Glacier (*A1*). Start from snow tongue well left of the gully, scrambling up and right to chimney (Class 5.2). Ascend, and when you reach the rock above the gully, continue onto shoulder. Route ascends on and to the left of this rib. Climbing is to Class 5.4; recorded time was 2 hours up from glacier. Good rock.

West face: *FA: C. Doyle, M. Simpson—1979.* Somewhere to right of above route. Described as steep, loose, and unpleasant.

MT. SPETCH 2590 m/8500 ft
Located 1 km E of Slalok Mountain.

From the south: From the Spetch-Slalok col, ascend via 40–45° snowslopes on south side.

North arete: *FA: J. Oswald, G. Walter—1971.* Class 4 on poorish rock.

East ridge: From Hartzell-Spetch col; Class 3 on poor rock.

MT. HARTZELL 2590 m/8500 ft
Immediately W of Matier, and southeast of Spetch.

From Matier Glacier: Ascend to col between Hartzell and Matier, then ascend snowslopes to easy Class 3 rock of the summit ridge.

West face: From Hartzell-Spetch col; class 3 on poor rock.

North ridge: From the Hartzell-Spetch col the ridge is a short Class 3–4 rock climb.

MT. MATIER 2770 m/9100 ft
Highest summit in the area between Lillooet and Duffey lakes.
FA: R. Chambers, R. Mason, C. Scott, P. Sherman—1957.

Northeast ridge: The Joffre-Matier col is reached directly from the Matier Glacier (*A1*) or from the Anniversary Glacier (*A2*). The ridge is a Class 3 climb over snow and rock. The summit may be done in 1 day from cars, but many parties prefer to camp beside the upper lake in Joffre Creek (*A1*). Ski parties make this a 1 day trip by skiing up Cerise Creek (*A2*) to its head and ascending steep Anniversary Glacier to the col.

Northeast face: *FA: R. Griffiths, J. Howard, H. Short, R. van Doorninck—1972.* From the Joffre-Matier col, there are two possible routes, both fairly steep. On the first you climb up on left side to avoid bergschrund, then traverse across top of schrund to the east ridge which is followed (Class 3) to summit. On the second route you climb up the centre of the face to rock buttress; ice is 60° in places. Both take 5 hours up.

Complete northeast face: *FA: K. Cover, B. Gavin—June 1985.* From Caspar or Cerise Creek (*A2, A3*), reach the snout of the glacier dropping NE between Matier and Mt. Howard. Hike up the glacier until able to gain a steep upper glacier to the N. Ascend upper glacier, generally staying just N of the northeast ridge. Ice to 60°; 7 hours up.

Southeast ridge: *FA: J. Howard and party—1970s.* From the head of Cerise Creek (*A2*), climb to the pass W of Vantage Peak. Ascend glacier at the head of Twin One Creek until you reach the col separating Matier from Mt. Howard to the SE. Matier's southeast ridge is a Class 3 climb. Use snow on east flank to bypass a gendarme.

West buttress: *FA: M. Scremin, D. Serl—June 1983.* From Matier-Hartzell col, climb loose gully to the right about 100 m/330 ft, then ascend the right wall onto open face. Two rope-lengths take you onto shoulder, then you climb right and up on superb rock for 4 more lengths to ridge crest above, and from there climb to summit. Class 5.6. Takes 2 1/2 hours.

Northwest face: The obvious and attractive face at the head of the Matier glacier (*A1*). It provides a direct line on steep snow and alpine ice leading straight to the summit. Carry a few screws.

MT. HOWARD 2530 m/8300 ft
Located 1.5 km SE of Matier.
FA: J. Hutton, R. Mason, S. Scott—1957.
The summit ridge may be reached by climbing a fairly easy chimney on the northwest side, gained from the Twin One Glacier.

VANTAGE PEAK 2230 m/7300 ft
At the head of Cerise Creek (*A2*), 2.5 km NE of Mt. Howard.
FA: J. Hutton, R. Mason, S. Scott, P. Sherman—1957.
Ascent is easy from Howard-Vantage col via west slopes. Alternatively, ascend to just W of summit via steepish north snowslopes.

MT. DUKE 2380 m/7800 ft
Located between heads of Caspar and Twin One creeks.
FRA: T. Anderson, M. Juri—1966.
The summit has formerly been approached via the Twin One trail but is now more directly accessible from roads on Caspar Creek (*A3*) and Cerise Creek (*A2*). The south ridge is known to be easy and other routes will doubtless be found.

CASPAR PEAK 2410 m/7900 ft

The highest summit E of Caspar Creek at GR 468767; probably unclimbed. There is some nomenclature confusion in this area: "Caspar" has incorrectly been used for the 2320 m/7600 ft summit about 2.5 km ESE of Mt. Duke, and possibly also for the 2260 m/7400 ft peak about 1.7 km SE of Mt. Duke. The area appears to offer an excellent traverse route into the Joffre group from roads on the west side of Van Horlick Creek (*A4*).

Chapter 17

Lizzie Lake

by Anders Ourom and Karl Ricker

BOUNDARIES:
North: North fork of Lizzie Creek; west fork of north Stein River
East: Southwest branch of Rutledge Creek
South: Upper Mehatl River, Rogers Creek
West: Lillooet River, Lillooet Lake

FOREST SERVICE OFFICE:
Squamish Forest District
P.O. Box 1970
Squamish, B.C. V0N 3G0
898-9671

LOGGING COMPANY:
B.C. Forest Products
Maple Ridge Division
11641 224th Street
Maple Ridge, B.C. V2X 6A1
(Rogers and Gowan creeks)
467-1511

MAPS:
Federal:
92 J/1 Stein Lake
Provincial:
92 J/SE

Introduction and History

Access to this area has improved in recent years due to logging in Lizzie and Rogers creeks. Its popularity has also increased, particularly with hikers, alpine ramblers, and ski tourers. The area offers open alpine ridges, meadows, and lakes, as well as access to the Stein divide and the pristine upper Stein valley. There are a few small glaciers and many possibilities for pleasant, non-technical mountaineering. The area has long been popular with residents of Pemberton. Several built a small cabin in the headwaters of Lizzie Creek in 1968 (*CAJ* 1982, p. 62). This is maintained and used by the Richardsons and Nickersons, two of the four builders now living on Lillooet Lake, but is open to the public. In about 1965 Tom Anderson traversed most of the Lizzie basin ridge crest from Lizzie Lake north. In 1972 a VOC party traversed the Stein divide, beginning at Lizzie Lake and ending at Kwoiek Creek (*VOCJ* 1972, p. 45).

There are many new names in this area which have not yet appeared on maps. Most of these are listed in *CAJ* 1982, p. 72. A good map of the area east of Lizzie Lake is found on p. 112 of *Exploring the Stein River Valley*, which also contains other useful information.

Approaches

The Lizzie Lake area is usually reached via logging roads rising from the Lillooet Lake road. From Pemberton, drive E to Mount Currie, then turn right on the Duffey Lake road. After 9 km/5.6 mi the road crosses a river at the head of Lillooet Lake, and in another 1.5 km it forks. The left fork climbs to Duffey Lake, while the right branch continues along the east side of Lillooet Lake. Distances are measured from this junction. The eastern part of this section might also be reached by floatplane to Elton or Tundra lakes.

A. LIZZIE CREEK

About 33 km/20.5 mi from the junction the road crosses Lizzie Creek. A logging road branches left soon after. In 0.5 km it crosses to the east side and forks.

1. North fork: The left fork climbs the north branch of Lizzie Creek to about 1065 m/3500 ft, north of Meadow Dome.

2. Lizzie Lake: The right fork follows the east side of the main creek. Its left branch reaches 1490 m/4900 ft in the east fork of the creek near timberline. The right branch eventually approaches Lizzie Lake where there is a B.C. Forest Service campsite. From here a trail ascends the east side of the lake, passing through a small canyon to reach a log cabin in a hanging valley at 1615 m/5300 ft. These roads are driveable at the present.

3. Southwest fork: Fairly low down, an old road crosses to the west side of the creek. It climbs to 1280 m/4200 ft in the southwest fork, north of Cloudraker Mountain.

B. ROGERS CREEK

This creek is currently being logged. Continue down the east side of Lillooet Lake and River to about 37 km/23 mi from Lizzie Creek (70 km/43.5 mi from the junction). A good road leads up the east side of the creek to 550 m/1800 ft, where it crosses to the northwest side and continues to 700 m/2300 ft SE of Cloudraker Mountain. The usual onslaught of spurs in the upper valley will no doubt follow.

C. GOWAN CREEK

About 12 km/7.5 mi further S down the east side of Lillooet lake, roads ascend Gowan Creek to an elevation of 1280 m/4200 ft. The road begins on the east side of the creek, but switches to the west side after several kilometres. At the last major forks in Gowan Creek the road branches; the left fork continues up the valley almost to tree line. Although no outstanding summits can be reached from this road, it does give access to the seldom-visited Nahatlatch-Lillooet Divide. It is currently in four-wheel drive condition.

Routes

The first ascents of most peaks in this area were by Tom Anderson and friends, in the mid-to-late 1960s.

LONG PEAK 2285 m/7500 ft

A long ridge 3 km SE of the Lizzie Creek cabin.
FRA: T. Anderson, E. Clifton, R. Corbett.
Go E then S via a trail from the cabin (*A2*) to the mouth of Long Lake; go around this, then ascend the creek S to the divide. From here the peak is a scramble by its southwest ridge. **DIVERSION PEAK** (2285 m/7500 ft) 2 km to the SW is easily reached by the connecting ridge.

ARROWHEAD MOUNTAIN 2165 m/7100 ft

An innocuous open ridge 2 km E of the cabin. It can be easily climbed from most directions and would be an ideal objective for a family outing.

TYNEMOUTH MOUNTAIN 2195 m/7200 ft

Another pleasant, open summit on the ridge between Long Peak and Arrowhead Mountain. Easily climbed by ascending valley ENE from Long Lake to Moraine Pass.

ANEMONE PEAK 2255 m/7400 ft

FRA: T. Adam, T. Anderson—1967.
This peak can be climbed by ascending NE directly from the cabin or, more pleasantly, by following a trail ENE for 2 km to a pass north of Arrowhead Mountain. From the pass ascend NW to 2135 m/7000 ft col between Anemone and **TABLETOP MOUNTAIN** (2225 m/7300 ft) to the E. Either summit is Class 2 from here. Tabletop can also be climbed directly from the SE or NE. **WHISKY PEAK** (2000 m/6600 ft) and **WHITE LUPINE RIDGE** are located immediately NW and N of the cabin and are an easy hike.

CLOUDRAKER MOUNTAIN 2375 m/7800 ft

A glacier-hung peak SE of the mouth of Lillooet Lake.
FRA: T. Anderson, M. Juri, G. Richardson—1967.
This peak is usually reached by the rolling ridge leading SW to it from Long Lake, crossing **SHIELDS PEAK** (2100 m/6900 ft) en route. From Lizzie Creek cabin (*A2*) it is a long day return, with some Class 3 snow near the top. The first ascent party climbed it directly from Lillooet Lake, while Rogers Creek roads (*B*) might now offer access to the southeast side. A good spring ski objective.

WILD ONION RIDGE

The collective name for a group of minor summits NW of Cloudraker Mountain. First ascended by G. Richardson and party from the forks of Lizzie Creek.

TUNDRA PEAK 2440 m/8000 ft

Reach the 1890 m/6200 ft Cherry Pip Pass WSW of the peak either by following a cairned route from Lizzie Creek cabin (*A2*) or from the end of the east branch road (*A2*). From the pass, traverse around the south side of a 2375 m/7800 ft summit, then ascend N to main peak (minor Class 3). One can also climb from the small lake S of Tundra Peak to its southeast ridge and the top. This mountain offers good views of Tundra Lake to the SE, a popular hiking destination at the head of the Stein River.

CALTHA PEAK 2375 m/7800 ft
Located 2 km SE of Tundra Peak, this peak is easy from the SW and offers some scrambling from the W and NW.

PRIORY PEAKS 2315 m/7600 ft
A prominent peak just S of Meadow Dome.
FRA: T. Anderson, G. Richardson, B. Thornton—1967.
The first ascent party ascended NE from Lizzie Creek logging roads (*A2*) to timberline, then circled around to climb peak from the E. **MEADOW DOME** (2251 m/7386 ft) to the N and **BELLAVISTA RIDGE** to the E are also pleasant and easy objectives. Logging roads to the N (*A1*) or SE (*A2*) are other feasible approaches to this group.

STEIN-LIZZIE DIVIDE
This is a series of high summits on the divide between Stein River and Lizzie Creek. Going N from Tundra Peak, these are **AURORA PEAK** (2440 m/8000 ft), **LINDISFARNE MOUNTAIN** (2530 m/8300 ft), **MEDITATION MOUNTAIN** (2560 m/8400 ft), **PHACELIA PEAK** (2400 m/7900 ft), **BRIMSTONE MOUNTAIN** (2250 m/7400 ft) and **STORM PEAK** (2500 m/8200 ft). The last four were climbed during a 1967 traverse by T. Anderson.

TWIN TWO PEAK 2315 m/7600 ft
Located S of Twin Two Creek at GR 427656. No details on climbs of this peak are available.

MT. SKOOK JIM 2620 m/8600 ft
The highest summit SE of Stein Lake.
FA: C. Adam, T. Anderson—1967.
From Caltha Mountain traverse SE along ridge to easy **VANGUARD PEAK** (2225 m/7300 ft). Turn E and ascend glacier to col N of Mt. Skook Jim. Both Skook Jim and **"MT. CLINE"** (2530 m/8300 ft) to N are Class 3 from here, while the summit (**"SNOWBLOOD"**), 1 km SSW of Skook Jim is NTD.

MOUNT KLACKARPUN 2620 m/8600 ft
Located S of Elton Lake.
This peak might be reached from Elton Lake (floatplane required), but the easiest current approach is probably over the glacier SE of Mt. Skook Jim. Neither Klackarpun nor the intervening rotten **CREVASSE CRAG** (2500 m/8200 ft) are difficult. The 1972 VOC party travelled along the divide E from here; none of the summits are difficult.

Chapter 18

Lillooet-Nahatlatch-Stein

BOUNDARIES:
North: Cayoosh Creek, Seton River
East: Fraser River
South: Nahatlatch River
West: High divide from Phair Creek to the Stein River headwaters

FOREST SERVICE OFFICES:

Lillooet Forest District
P.O. Box 10, 1210 Main Street
Lillooet, B.C. V0K 1V0
256-7531

Chilliwack Forest District
P.O. Box 159
9850 South McGrath Road
Rosedale, B.C. V0X 1X0
794-3361

LOGGING COMPANIES:

Evans Forest Products
P.O. Box 880
Lillooet, B.C. V0K 1V0
(all drainages north of Stein River)

256-4266

B.C. Forest Products
P.O. Box 100
Boston Bar, B.C. V0K 1C0
(Stein River and all drainages south
to the Nahatlatch)
876-9214

MAPS:
Federal:
92 G/16 Glacier Lake
92 I/4 Lytton
92 I/12 Lillooet
92 J/8 Duffey Lake

92 H/13 Scuzzy Mountain
92 I/5 Stein River
92 J/1 Stein Lake
92 J/9 Shalalth

Provincial:
92 G/NE
92 I/SW
92 J/SE

92 H/NW
92 I/NW

Introduction

In the mountains south of Lillooet, the backpacker will find many miles of open and interconnected ridges to explore, some of which have hardly been travelled since the heyday of the 1920s and 30s, when packers and prospectors moved back and forth across the region in search of game and gold. For the skier, logging operations in the last ten years have opened up some broad valleys reaching deep into the heart of the upper Stein River country, and the ski tourer will find that these wide, sweeping valleys have drier snow than on the Coast (see, for example, *VOCJ* 1984, p. 3).

The mountaineer will find fine, challenging climbing on peaks which are among the highest in southwestern B.C., and some difficult alpine climbs on these major summits may still await discovery.

It often comes as a surprise to Vancouver climbers to learn that this area contains glaciation. The Rutledge Glacier system at the head of Kwoeik Creek is framed by a series of granitic peaks, and great walls shoot up from the glacier to the summits above. There are also many deserted alpine meadows in the upper Kwoiek and Stein basins, and Boulder and Texas creeks are both easy approaches to the enormous, high ridge systems radiating from Mt. Brew. An enjoyable way to spend a weekend is to ramble back and forth among these ridges and basins where wildlife is still plentiful, and the clouds, even if threatening, rarely bring prolonged downpours. Since trails in the Lillooet region are not often destroyed by spring run-offs, they tend to stay in good shape.

For those who enjoy scrambling, new roads which run up the north fork of Kwoiek Creek have made Skihist Mountain more approachable recently. However, even the standard route on the peak involves some careful route finding, and parties are advised to carry a rope. Petlushkwohap, Stein and Brew are all higher than 2750 m/9000 ft, and none are diffucult to climb, although the ascents require at least a weekend. Since 1974, when Dick Culbert described the Lillooet region as one of the least explored areas for mountaineering in southwestern B.C., much more interest has been shown in the area. But there is still lots of room for the adventurous off-trail explorer to make new traverses and discover surprising new climbs.

In this chapter, an attempt has been made to preserve more of a wilderness flavour by minimizing the information about the peaks, thus leaving more scope for the exploratory spirit. Large stretches of alpine country have been left undescribed, either because no information is available or because technical description seems unnecessary. Those who desire fuller description will find it in *Exploring the Stein River Valley* (Freeman and Thompson).

Approaches

A. FROM THE BOSTON BAR FERRY

1. Nahatlatch River road: The Nahatlatch River is a major drainage 15 km/9.3 mi from the new bridge that crosses the Fraser River from Boston Bar to North Bend. Proceed N on a reasonable gravel road (the west-side road) following a powerline down the west side of the Fraser River. This road receives a yearly face lift but there are rough spots; most sturdy two-wheel drive vehicles should have no trouble. Bear right at a fork a couple of kilometres before the Nahatlatch River. The road drops steeply to the river and climbs steeply up the other side. The road leading W up the Nahatlatch basically follows the north side of the river to Mehatl Creek, past Frances, Hannah and Nahatlatch lakes. The bridge at Tachewana Creek is washed out, so it is no longer possible to proceed to Mehatl Creek.

1a. Log Creek main line: Begins 10 km/6.2 mi from the Nahatlatch River bridge and extends up Log Creek (an important tributary of the Nahatlatch) to close to the head of the valley. At 8.9 km/5.5 mi, a branch road ascends the north fork to 1370 m/4500 ft into the basin E of Kwoiek Needle, and B.C. Forest Products plans to push another 150 m/500 ft higher. This development would extend the road almost to tree line. The Log Creek main line currently runs to 1280 m/4200 ft on the north side of the river and to 1370 m/4500 ft on the south side. All roads are presently two-wheel drive.

1b. Squakum Creek roads: Abandoned, undriveable roads 20 km/12.5 mi from the Nahatlatch River bridge climb Squakum Creek on its north side to 1235 m/4050 ft.

2. Kwoiek Creek roads: A bridge crosses the mouth of Kwoiek Creek to reach these roads 28.5 km/17.7 mi from the bridge at Boston Bar. They are in largely two-wheel drive condition at present and are being actively logged. The main road basically follows the north side of the creek 10.5 km/6.5 mi to a junction with North Kwoiek Creek *(A2a)*. It then continues past Kwoiek Lake and Kokwashay Lake, before crossing the creek to the S again just before John George Lake, a further 10 km/6.2 mi from the junction with North Kwoiek Creek. The road ends at a clearing 27 km/16.8 mi from the west side road (GR 770535).

To gain the Rutledge Glacier area from this point, proceed up the fork of the creek running in from the W and follow it through open timber as it turns S into a swampy valley flooded by beaver dams. Some thick, unpleasant bush must be travelled to gain the narrow basin N of the Rutledge. At least one party has proceeded to Kwoiek Peak by climbing to Stukolait Lake and traversing steep slopes to the W of the lake, but this route is very bushy and unappealing.

2a. North Kwoiek Creek road: This road was in fine two-wheel drive condition in the summer of 1985. It runs up the creek, switching sides several times for 10.5 km/6.5 mi. From this point, the hike to the head of the valley is fairly straightforward, although a couple of stretches of bad slide alder must be crossed. Takes 2 1/2 hours to "Skihist Lake" on the east side of Skihist Mountain. This route is now the logical approach to Skihist Mountain.

2b. Antimony Lake trail (Eagle Ridge trail): This trail used to run from a point about 100 m/330 ft W of the bridge over North Kwoiek Creek, but logging and burns have made the initial sections difficult to follow. The best approach now is to park at a logging spur 21 km/13 mi NE of Kwoiek Creek's mouth, ascend the spur past two switchbacks, and after about 2 km take the short spur which cuts sharply left. From the top of this spur, head up through open bush to the W of a creek, cross the creek after about 1 km, and intersect the Antimony Lake trail at about 1980 m/6500 ft on the east shoulder of Eagle Ridge. The trail follows the divide SW, then it traverses to Antimony Lake, E of Antimony Mountain.

2c. Kokwaskey Lake spur: Begins 21 km/13 mi from the mouth of Kwoiek Creek. Ascend the spur to the left which climbs a short distance towards Kokwaskey Lake. The bushwhack southward up Chochiwa Creek is extremely bad—dense, dense slide alder on steep, steep hillside. The approach to Haynon Lake via roads in Log Creek makes more sense.

B. FROM THE LYTTON FERRY

At Lytton take the turnoff to Lillooet, cross the Thompson River, then take the first left to the Lytton ferry, which can accommodate three small cars. All distances are from the Lytton ferry.

1. Stryen Creek route (1.6 km): Take the Lytten ferry, then turn N for Stryen Creek and the Stein River; proceed 1.6 km to Earlscourt Farm. Enter the farm road and follow the orange markers to a visitors' registration board which is in front of the main farmhouse. All vehicles should register here—the land is private, and parking privileges are granted by permission of the farm owners. Proceed N to the parking area. From there, a marked route leads to the Stryen Creek trail (maintained by the Forest Service) which may be picked up above the cattle pastures at the mouth of Stryen Creek. The trail begins from the top of a private road at about 550 m/1800 ft; it heads up the east flank of Stryen Creek, and leads up the east fork to about 1580 m/5200 ft and up the west fork to about 1460 m/4800 ft. One old cabin sits at ''The Forks,'' and another one sits further up on the harder-to-follow, somewhat bushy west fork.

2. *Stein River route (1.6 km):* If you plan an extensive trek through the Stein drainage, you should consult *Exploring the Stein River Valley*.

Take the Lytton ferry and turn N for the Stein River along the road on the west side of the Fraser (the west-side road). Use the Earlscourt Farm parking area as for the Stryen Creek trail *(A1)*. From the marked route, instead of heading W to Stryen Creek, cross an irrigation ditch and follow a fence N, then W through fields and drop down into the Stein River to gain the south-side trail. The trail is in good condition for the first 24 km/15 mi, where it passes through an old homestead near Ponderosa Creek. About 2.5 km after Earl Creek, cross from the south to the north side of the river by means of a deteriorating cable car. Be very cautious using it. From the crossing, the trail is rougher, more overgrown, and washed out in parts. There is a small, roofed shelter at Ponderosa Creek, and the trail beyond that point is sketchy to nonexistent.

2a. *Cottonwood Creek:* For routes in this drainage, see the Duffey Lake chapter.

2b. *North-side trail:* The west-side road crosses the Stein River 6 km/3.7 mi from the Lytton ferry, and a trail along the north bank of the Stein begins about 1 km further on, just before the main road swings N again. Turn sharply left onto an overgrown track under the B.C. Hydro powerline. The trail follows the north bank for a few kilometres.

3. *Siwhe Creek trail (26.2 km/16.3 mi):* A cattle trail in good condition begins 41.8 km/26 mi from Lillooet. It ascends Siwhe Creek to Devils Lake at 1710 m/5600 ft. Pick up the trail behind the farmhouse at the top of the first switchback. An excellent area for hiking. About 6 1/2 hours to the lake.

C. FROM LILLOOET VIA THE WEST-SIDE ROAD

Head S from Lillooet past Evans Forest Products mill, cross Cayoosh Creek, take the right fork at the Shell station immediately past it, and turn left 100 m/330 ft later onto Texas Creek road (the west-side road), which is signposted. Distances are from the Lillooet train station.

1. *Riley Creek road and Brew Mountain trail (13.7 km/8.5 mi):* Just before the Fraser River road (the west-side road) drops sharply into Riley Creek, a spur branches right and leads past a white-gated entrance to a private home. Follow the road as it turns right, left, then makes a sharp right again, ending at a gate on private property. You should ask for permission to park and to proceed up the trail. The Brew Mountain trail begins behind the barn on this residence. It follows an old road grade then cuts across a bushy gully into mature forest. It is brushed out each year and in good condition. It leads to the cirque at 2010 m/6600 ft, E of Mt. Brew. The two resident dogs, by the way, are named Leif (Elkhound) and Freckles (Springer Spaniel) and they are friendly if spoken to in suitable tones.

2. *Texas Creek road (19.3 km/12 mi):* The Forest Service maintains the lower sections of this road. The road threads through a canyon for 9.7 km/6 mi (watch for falling rocks) then forks, with the Texas Creek fork (south fork) climbing to 1370 m/4500 ft. Normally in four-wheel drive condition from shortly after this fork, but currently in two-wheel drive condition almost to the valley head. Some logging is currently taking place in the south fork.

2a. *Skimath Creek road:* At 4.8 km/3 mi from the fork with Molybdenite Creek, an old four-wheel drive road ascends this drainage. The Forest Service was planning to build a trail here in 1985.

2b. *Molybdenite Creek road:* This road begins 9.7 km/6 mi from the mouth of Texas Creek. Normally, it is in two-wheel drive condition for only about 1 km past the fork. It climbs to about 2130 m/7000 ft, switchbacking onto the ridge to the N from meadows at the head of the north fork. Excellent access to the Brew divide. At 7.6 km/4.7 mi, a branch to the left up the south fork (four-wheel drive) leads to beautiful "Molybdenite Lake."

3. *Della Creek roads:* Old logging roads used to climb the slopes N of this creek; however, they have been abandoned for years and presently nothing is known of their condition.

Routes

NAHATLATCH NEEDLE 1890 m/6200 ft
An inaccessible appearing summit located 4 km N of the Nahatlatch River between Tachewana and Squakum creeks. No one has admitted to climbing it.

PYRAMID MOUNTAIN 2201 m/7221 ft
Located between Kwoiek and Log creeks. Best approach now is from the new road in the north fork of Log Creek (*A1a*).

KWOIEK NEEDLE 2620 m/8600 ft
FA: Probably by prospectors around 1890.
FRA: J. Betts, W. Henderson, F. Smith—1929. (See CAJ 1930, p. 39.)
This summit has traditionally been approached via the long southeast divide, which could be gained from the north fork of Log Creek (*A1a*). There is one Class 4 discontinuity on this route. You can also approach via roads on the main line of Log Creek and scramble up the south face. BCMC parties have also approached the peak from Kwoiek Creek; the ascent is not difficult. Yet another route is to ramble up the southwest ridge from the Chochiwa Glacier.

TACHEWANA PEAK 2470 m/8100 ft
Located along the southern rim of Chochiwa Glacier at the head of Tachewana Creek. *FRA: R. Chambers, R. Culbert, R. Hutchinson, R. Mason—1958.* This and nearby peaks are easy ascents from the Chochiwa Glacier.

PEAK 8400 2560 m/8400 ft; PEAK 8600 2620 m/8600 ft
Located between Tachewana and Kumkan peaks. *FA: L. Churchill, P. Kubik, C.*

Levin, H. Scotney, P. Waddington—August 1971. Ascend from the Chochiwa Glacier.

KUMKAN PEAK 2710 m/8900 ft
Located 3 km SE of Kwoiek Peak.
FA: R. Culbert, A. Dellow, R. Hutchinson, R. Mason—1958.
Traverse loose rock across the west face and scramble up the couloir to between Kum kan's summits. Class 3. The northwest ridge and east buttress have also been easily climbed.

HAYNON PEAK 2500 m/8200 ft
Located immediately N of Haynon Lake. You can easily reach this summit from a camp at Haynon Lake. One approach is to gain the col SW of Haynon, and scramble up from there.

KWOIEK PEAK 2734 m/8969 ft
A heavily glaciated summit, easy to climb from most directions.
FA: Topographic survey party.
South ridge: A scramble. Gain the south ridge easily from either the Kwoiek or Rut-ledge glaciers *(A2)*. A complete S–N traverse of the Kwoiek Peak horseshoe is Class 4 and requires a rope and a few slings. A snow slog from the SE is also available.
North glacier: *FA: A. Jones, J. Peepre—August 26, 1984.* Approach via Stukolait Lake. Gain the glacier by climbing vertical bush and rockslides, and then traverse along ledges. The glacier itself is straightforward. A full day.

TIARA TOWER 2590 m/8500 ft
An impressive group of three rock towers mounted on the ridge SE of Mehatl Peak.
FA: B. Butler, P. Kubik, G. Mumford—1971.
From the vicinity of Kwoiek Peak (see above), descend into the valley of North Mehatl Creek, and camp below the walls of Tiara Tower. Scramble to the base of its east ridge and climb snowslopes on its south side. Several leads of Class 3 and 4 rock on the ridge complete the climb. A fairly long day, and one of the biggest routes in this region.

MEHATL PEAK 2650 m/8700 ft
An attractive, glaciated rock summit on the south edge of Rutledge Glacier, definitely lower than Kwoiek Peak.
FA: R. Culbert, A. Dellow, R. Hutchinson, R. Mason—1958.
East ridge: A Class 3 scramble.
North face: *FRA: Very large BCMC party led by R. Wyborn—July 1982.* Snow and the possibility of ice to 50° in late season.
West ridge: *FA: J. Byers, S. Golling, T. O'Conner—July 1972.* Class 3.

"THE WOODPILE" 2560 m/8400 ft
A blocky summit located directly N of the Rutledge Glacier.
FA: B. Fairley, E. Woodd—July 12, 1982.
Gain the southeast ridge from the col between it and the long northwest ridge of

Kwoiek Peak. Traverse two minor bumps before reaching the final 180 m/600 ft of the climb (these may be bypassed). Mainly Class 3, with minor Class 4–5 on the final arête. A few slings provide sufficient protection. Descend via the northwest ridge and snowfields along the north flank of the mountain. Other routes are possible on the peak, and the rock is good.

"CRESTLINE MOUNTAIN" 2440 m/8000 ft
A tent-shaped peak located 2.4 km W of the toe of Rutledge Glacier.
FA: B. Fairley, E. Woodd—July 13, 1982.
Traverse easy snowslopes gained from the toe of Rutledge Glacier into a snow bowl E of the summit. The final southeast arête is Class 3 with minor Class 4 on good rock.

THE NAHATLATCH-LILLOOET DIVIDE
This is a vast stretch of alpine country, but there are no records of climbing or exploration in it. Many summit names which appear on map 92 G/16 commemorate servicemen who died in World War II. The divide could be approached from Gowan Creek (see Lizzie Lake chapter) or from spurs that run up into the basin E of Whiskey Lake. This region is a mystery area—write if you have details!

MT. NIELSEN 2650 m/8700 ft
Located 3 km SW of Doss Peak. Named for an active Vancouver climber and rescue team member, killed in an avalanche on Mt. Baker in 1966. *FA: P. Nielsen, G. Walker—1960.* The east ridge is a scramble.

DOSS PEAK 2590 m/8500 ft
FA: Probably by prospectors.
A 4.8 km trail connects Antimony Lake ("Blue Lake") (*A2b*) with a small lake 1.6 km SE of Doss Peak. An easy ascent from here. The other logical approach is from the North Kwoiek Creek road (*A2a*).

ANTIMONY MOUNTAIN 2650 m/8700 ft
South face and southeast ridge: Approach from Antimony Lake (*A2b*). A scramble.
North ridge: An old trail traverses scree slopes E of Antimony Lake. Use it to gain the Skihist-Antimony col and the north ridge, which is NTD. You can also approach the north ridge from Skihist basin (*A2a*).

SKIHIST MOUNTAIN 2970 m/9750 ft
The highest summit in this guidebook. A long N-S trending ridge located at the head of North Kwoiek Creek.
FA: By prospectors.
South slopes and the south ridge: These may be approached from Antimony Lake via the pass N of Antimony Mountain (*A2a or A2b*). An old trail crosses scree slopes E of the lake to this col. Class 3.
Southeast ridge: From Antimony Lake, ascend headwall directly NW to **CLAIMPOST PEAK** (2650 m/8700 ft) on the divide SE of Skihist. Descend its loose north ridge for around 1.5 km—a long Class 3–4 traverse along the narrow

divide, much up and down and considerable exposure. An airy gap at mid-point will likely require a rope. Takes 5 hours from lake to summit; Class 3–4.

East glacier: *FA: H. Habgood, J. Sibley—July 2, 1984.* From the lake E of Skihist, traverse north slopes of **PEAK 7700** (2350 m/7700 ft) and then follow connecting ridge toward Skihist. Where the ridge steepens at 2440 m/8000 ft, descend to the glacier and ascend snowslopes to false summit. Finish via the southeast ridge.

PEAK 9100 2775 m/9100 ft

Located 2.5 km NE of Skihist Mountain. *FRA: D. Adshead, S. Oates—October 1984.* Via east-southeast ridge. A scramble with one exposed Class 4 gap.

"WINTER PEAK" 2680 m/8800 ft

Located 2 km S of Petlushkwohap Mountain. *FRA: K. Barnard—December 1983.* Via Class 3 west ridge. There is some exposure. (Ref: *VOCJ* 1983, p. 64.)

PETLUSHKWOHAP MOUNTAIN 2960 m/9700 ft

FRA: Topographic survey party—1935.

Via Stryen Creek: Gain the divide W of Stryen Creek (*B1*) and contour around the head of Earl Creek. The climb via the east or south slopes is not difficult.

Via North Kwoiek Creek: Petlushkwohap has been approached by ascending to the col W of Winter Peak and traversing the west face of Winter Peak to the col S of Petlushkwohap. Class 3; ice-axe required early in season.

AKASIK MOUNTAIN 2470 m/8100 ft

Located at the north end of the divide between Stryen and Earl creeks. A scramble via Stryen Creek (*B1*).

MT. ROACH 2643 m/8672 ft

FA: By prospectors.

Comprises the divide between the east and west forks of Stryen Creek; a popular climb. The southwest ridge is scrub and scree. The southeast slopes are also slack.

NIKAIA MOUNTAIN 2560 m/8400 ft

Located at the head of the east fork of Stryen Creek.

FRA: W.H. Mathews, C. Ney—1941.

West ridge: It is a 5–6 hour pack to a camp spot at the head of the southeast fork of Stryen Creek (*B1*). From here, climb S into skyline col on the ridge W of Nikaia and follow this to summit. There are a few thin spots near the summit; 8 hours return from camp.

North face: *FRA: G. Barford, J. Harrison, G. McCormack—June 1973.* Snow to 45° up the prominent north face couloir.

KLOWA MOUNTAIN 2470 m/8100 ft

A peak with a steep north face, located at the head of Nikaia Creek. Its recent mountaineering history is unknown, although the first ascent was made as early as 1890 by the geology team of G.M. Dawson and M. McEvoy.

STEIN MOUNTAIN 2746 m/9010 ft
The immensely long southeast ridge of Stein was climbed to a height of 2350 m/7700 ft in October 1977 by S. Bell and D. Kasian. From there, they descended into the basin S of Stein and finished the climb via the easy south slopes. The north peak, apparently higher, is Class 3–4 from the south peak.

PEAK 8900 2715 m/8900 ft
Located 1.6 km W of Stein Mountain. *FRA: S. Bell, D. Kasian—October 22, 1979*. Via the east ridge. An easy day for a lady.

SIWHE MOUNTAIN 2855 m/9366 ft
Little is know about this remote summit. Some lengthy ridge climbs are most likely available from Siwhe Creek (*B3*) or the Stein River (*B2*).

ASKOM MOUNTAIN 2560 m/8400 ft
A scree ridge located W of the Fraser River, 24 km/15 mi S of Lillooet.
FA: G.M. Dawson, M. McEvoy—1890.
Drive S down the west side of the Fraser River from Lillooet, and then up a logging road N of Della Creek (*C3*). Take the left fork to its end. Ascend W to Askom's east ridge and follow the horse trail to a camp at 1710 m/5600 ft. Continue up the east ridge above Intlpam Creek over grass and scree. NTD but no water above 1710 m/5600 ft.

MT. BREW 2890 m/9470 ft
A massive summit located S of Lillooet.
FA: By packers or prospectors.
FWA: B. Fairley, H. Redekop—March 1983.
Approach via the Riley Creek road and the Brew Mountain trail (*C1*).
East ridge: Ascend the north flank of this ridge on snow or in gullies and take a long walk to the summit.
Northeast face: *FA: S. Golling, P. Jordan—June 1973*. Steep spring snow to 50°.

"CAYOOSH WALL"
A large bluff at the mouth of Cayoosh Creek, just SW of Lillooet. Its scruffy appearance has kept many climbers away. To reach the face, cross the dam just W of the bridge over Cayoosh Creek and follow the road and floodwash to the base.
The Weremouse: *FA: A. Clayton, R. Cuthbert—June 1972*. Begin at a large, white slab below a yellow overhang, turn to the right, then head straight up in several pitches to the first tree ledge. It is also possible to swing further right and gain the lefthand buttress of a broad gully which is followed to the same tree ledge. From here, several pitches of scrambling lead to the summit. Lots of potential for variation; somewhat scrubby. Many pitches to 5.5. (Ref: *CAJ* 1973, p. 62.)
On Black Lassie's Trail: *FA: P. Kendrick, G. Maurer, R. Tomich—May 2–3, 1981*. Begin to the right of the Weremouse route, and follow a faint buttress to the right of a wide gully area, which leads in 5 pitches to a prominent gendarme. Several more pitches lead to a gravel ramp. Climb a chimney and face in a corner which leads upward from here, gaining a tree ledge. About 90 m/300 ft of Class 4 complete the climb. (Ref: *CAJ* 1982, p. 63.)

Descent Note: The descent is time consuming. Follow a goat trail N down the skyline, then traverse E to the last large scree gully. A rappel or two may be necessary.

MT. McLEAN 2435 m/7988 ft
Located NW of Lillooet.
From roads above Main Street in Lillooet, find the gravel road that leads S around a shoulder overlooking the village and into Town Creek. This road climbs Town Creek, passes over the divide onto the south flank of McLean, and leads along a water pipeline for about 1 km. A flagged trail in good condition heads off to the left, leading to McLean's summit on the east end of Mission Ridge. Nice meadows. The summit is unfortunately spoiled by transmitter towers and attendant garbage.

Mission Ridge can also be reached from roads in Camoo Creek. From the turnoff in Lillooet to Gold Bridge and Bralorne it is about 24 km/15 mi to the side road leading downhill to a bridge across the Bridge River. Once across the bridge, there is a junction at 4 km. Take the right branch which switchbacks up to a powerline cutting across the north side of Mission Ridge. The road formerly continued to Mission Pass (see Bendor chapter), but is now impassable. The lower section was two-wheel drive in 1984.

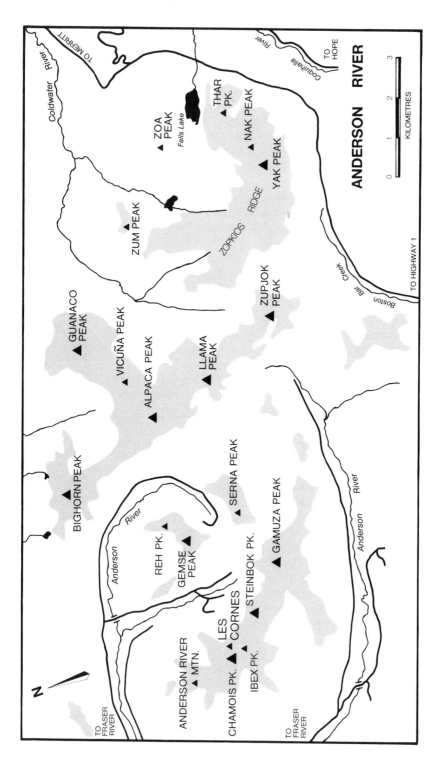

ANDERSON RIVER

KILOMETRES

0   1   2   3

Chapter 19

Anderson River-Coquihalla

by Bruce Fairley and Karl Ricker

BOUNDARIES:
North: Anderson River, Uztlius Creek
East: Vuich Creek, Tulameen River, Britton Creek, Coldwater River
South: Highway 3, Eighteen Mile Creek
West: Fraser River

FOREST SERVICE OFFICES:

Chilliwack Forest District
P.O. Box 159
9850 South McGrath Road
Rosedale, B.C. V0X 1X0
794-3361

Merritt Forest District
P.O. Box 609
Merritt, B.C. V0K 2B0
378-6171

LOGGING COMPANIES:

Pretty's Timber Co.
P.O. Box 37
Harrison Hot Springs, B.C. V0M 1K0
(Coquihalla)
796-2539

Weyerhauser Ltd.
Houston Avenue
Merritt, B.C. V0K 2B0
(Spius Creek)
378-5166

Cattermole Timber
R.R. #1 (Vancouver)
Sardis, B.C. V0X 1Y0
(Anderson River) (Chilliwack)
294-9891, 823-6525

Balco Industries Ltd.
Voight Street
Merritt, B.C. V0K 2B0
(upper Coldwater)
378-2224

MAPS:
Federal:
92 H/6 Hope
92 H/14 Boston Bar

92 H/11 Spuzzum
92 I/3 Prospect Creek

Provincial:
92 H/SW
92 H/NE

92 H/NW
92 I/SW

Introduction and History

This large region can be divided into two distinct areas of very different character. The southern half, which is composed mainly of widely-spaced forested summits, is usually beset with access problems and of little mountaineering interest. The contrasting northern section is a concentrated group of granitic summits with good access, some excellent lines, and increasing appeal to the climbing public. The northern section, the so-called ''Anderson River Group,'' is the main subject of this chapter.

The first exploration oriented to climbing in this area was undertaken in 1961, when the first ascents of major peaks in the western cluster were made. This was followed by a lull of a dozen years before parties looking for more technical lines returned to the area. Since that time, the popularity of this group has positively boomed, and many difficult and exciting routes have been climbed.

Many of the first technical lines in the Anderson River group were put up by Phil Kubik and Ed Zenger; the north buttress of Chamois remains the most popular of the climbs established in this period. In 1979, Scott Flavelle and John Howe climbed the northeast buttress of Steinbok, an exceptional technical endeavour on what is likely the cleanest and most imposing line in the Anderson River drainage. Their climb had a stimulating effect and other technical ascents followed, with Robin Barley figuring prominently in this trend.

Early and continuing exploration of the eastern half of the area has followed a different course; most of the recorded ascents have been accomplished on club trips led by Karl Ricker, who has visited the Boston Bar Creek side of the range each autumn for the past ten years. The Coquihalla, in fact, is particularly suited to autumn trips, when cooler weather, absence of bugs, and fall colours accentuate the many varied climbing and scrambling challenges available.

Approaches

A. FROM THE COQUIHALLA HIGHWAY
This is a major new four-lane highway which runs from Hope to Merritt via the Coquihalla River, Boston Bar Creek, and the Coldwater River. Because this book went to press before the highway was completed, all distances are estimated. All distances are measured from the major bridge crossing the Coquihalla river and leaving the Hope-Princeton Highway 5 km E of Hope. The old Coquihalla road is reached by following signs to Kawkawa Lake/Kawkawa Lake Park. It rejoins the new highway after about 8.5 km/5 mi.

1. Peers Creek road (5 km): An old logging road leads up this drainage; however, it is now completely washed out and travel in the upper stretches of the drainage is tough going. See the Manning Park chapter for a fuller description of this historic access into the Brigade Trail area.

2. Sowaqua Creek road (14.5 km/9.5 mi): A bridge formerly crossed the Coquihalla River from the west to the east bank at this point. It is not known if this bridge will survive highway construction. A road led S from the bridge for 0.5 km to Sowaqua Creek. The road up this creek is also totally washed out.

3. Dewdney Creek road (17.5 km/11 mi): This road follows Dewdney Creek SE to Tulameen Mountain.

4. Carolin mine road (18 km/11.5 mi): This road is found on the west bank of the Coquihalla River, immediately after the highway crosses from E to W. Stern ''No trespassing'' signs are posted. It leads up slopes to the W of Ladner Creek to 1095 m/3600 ft and gives access to easily-ascended Spider Peak.

5. *The old Coquihalla canyon road (25 km/15 mi):* The old Coquihalla road crossed a bridge to the right at this point, headed S, swung around the S end of a broad ridge and then proceeded NE to the Coldwater River. The road might still give useful access to Needle Peak.

5a. *Hidden Creek:* The open ridge on the S side of the creek gives good access to Coquihalla Mountain and the Bedded Range.

6. *Fallslake Creek road (45 km/28 mi):* This is the most important access route leading from the highway. A paved road to the W (encountered about 1 km S of a bridge crossing a huge dry gulch) climbs about 0.5 km to a compressor station and large parking area. From here Zopkios Ridge is easily gained by climbing W into the basin between Thar and Nak peaks. You can also reach Falls Lake by ascending Fallslake Creek, which is located a short distance farther N. The Forest Service has a campground at the lake, and there are plans for trail construction in and around the basin here, including a trail to "Little Douglas Lake," between Zoa and Zum peaks. The Fallslake Creek road continues northerly to link up with the Coldwater River road system described below, which in turn rejoins the new highway N of the Coquihalla Lakes area.

7. *Tulameen road (52 km/32.5 mi):* A good two-wheel drive road ran from the old Coquihalla road to Tulameen at this point. It is not known how new construction will affect it, however.

8. *The upper Coldwater River road (53 km/33 mi):* You can easily locate this important road system; it leaves the main highway to the W at the Highways yard just before the highway passes under a major bridge. Take the road for 3.5 km where a fork to the left leads to Fallslake Creek, as described in *A6*, above. At 7 km/4.2 mi the upper Coldwater road descends and crosses a creek. A trail on the east side of this creek runs to "Little Douglas Lake" between Zoa and Zum peaks. The road then continues into the basin E of Alpaca Peak and provides excellent access to the summits in that area.

9. *July Mountain road (57 km/35.5 mi):* A road leads W up the broad valley to the S of July Mountain, in an area which is being actively logged at present. Another branch of this road, not shown on maps, leads into the basin NE of the peak.

10. *Juliet Creek road (63.5 km/39.5 mi):* A road goes W up Juliet Creek, through a broad valley N of July Mountain, eventually reaching around to the W side of the peak.

11. *Coldwater River road (81 km/50.5 mi):* Leads N to Merritt and S to Brookmere, Tulameen, and eventually Princeton. It is a well-maintained gravel road, and is paved north of Kingsvale. From just beyond the town of Brookmere at a T junction a road to the right climbs towards Mt. Thynne (pronounced "thin"), an area which has been heavily logged in recent years.

B. FROM FRASER RIVER

1. *Qualark Creek road:* Immediately after crossing the Coquihalla River (*A*), go left on Union Bar Road and continue N on the east side of the Fraser River for about 16 km/10 mi. This is four-wheel drive from shortly beyond Kawkawa Lake. After 21.6 km/13.2 mi, this road climbs due E to 1160 m/3800 ft in Qualark Creek, S of Spider Peak. Spur roads along the way give access to Ogilvie and Jorgenson peaks.

1a. *Suka Creek:* An old road up this creek beginning at 18.3 km/11.4 mi is presently impassable to vehicles, but may offer a decent approach to the high country N of Squeah Mountain.

2. Anderson River road: Logging roads head S from the east side of the Alexandra Bridge (40 km/25 mi N of Hope). Go left at forks at 5.8 km/3.6 mi and 11.7 km/7.3 mi and follow the road up over 820 m/2700 ft ridge (locked gate) before descending to Anderson River near the forks. Roads up the S fork (E Main) are in good condition now, but the more important roads up the N fork are in rough shape. The bridge crossing Anderson River to N-600, 610 and 611 is currently out, greatly lengthening the approaches to the popular Chamois/Steinbok area; this will be reopened eventually, but not too soon. The north and south main lines are still driveable. This system of roads is usually gated.

2a. Siwash Creek: Go right at fork at 11.7 km/7.3 mi. The road climbs to over 1010 m/3300 ft in the north fork, and is still being extended.

C. VIA THE COLDWATER RIVER ROAD/HIGHWAY 8

This region is not really mountainous country, but there is potential for ski touring. The best sources of road information are the logging companies in Merritt.

1. Spius Creek: About 2 km W of Canford on Highway 8 a road (Petit Creek road) begins which ascends the W side of Spius Creek and continues on eventually to Boston Bar. At 13 km/8 mi a branch to the right goes S and then W up Prospect Creek, and can be used to gain Stoyoma Mountain to the S and Mt. Hewitt Bostock to the SW. Upper Spius Creek can also be reached from roads in Maka Creek (*C3*).

2. Midday Creek: 16.5 km/10.25 mi S of the Highway 5/Coldwater River road junction. A road from this point signposted Patchett Road leads W up the NE side of Midday Creek to a major junction with the Spius Creek road systems. Roads branching N to the Coutlee Plateau are very rough travel at this time.

3. Maka Creek: From Kingsvale (25 km/14.5 mi S of Merritt on the Coldwater River road) a gravel road leads W to "Gillis Lake" then swings NW down Maka Creek. At 10 km/6 mi there is a fork, with the left branch heading S up Maka Creek with one important spur (2 km to the S) going over the Cascades into Uztlius Creek, eventually reaching Boston Bar on a lower Anderson River road. At 20 km/12.5 mi an important switchback heads S up Spius Creek, just beyond where Maka and Spius creeks converge. A second branch road crosses Maka Creek just beyond and the first right after this crossing leads toward Stoyoma Mountain.

D. MOWHOKAM-MICOAMEN ROAD

About 16 km/10.4 mi E of Lytton a road leaves the Trans Canada Highway at the Thompson rail siding. It ascends to a high pass on the southeast side of Mt. Lytton, descending more gradually thereafter to the Trans Canada Highway about 17 km/11 mi N of Boston Bar at Inkitsaph.

Routes

Most of the mountains in the western and central Anderson River group are gained by easy bushwhacks from the Anderson River roads (*B2*). Those to the E are reached via upper Coldwater Creek road (*A10*). See the area map for more detail.

ANDERSON RIVER MOUNTAIN 1977 m/6485 ft

The most northwesterly summit in the group, located between the north and south forks of the Anderson River.

FA: Survey party.

Ascended by climbing SE from Anderson River forks. Could be more easily scrambled up from the ''gorge'' between this massif and Chamois Peak.

CHAMOIS PEAK 2010 m/6600 ft

The first mountain SE of Anderson River Mountain.

FA: A. Bentzen, H. Mutch, G. Woodsworth, R. Woodsworth—August 31, 1962.

West side: From the Class 3 ''rotten gorge'' between Chamois and Anderson River Mountain, scramble up the west side and ridge to the top. The gorge is reached by ascending along the base of the northeast ridge of the peak.

North buttress: *FA: P. Stange, E. Zenger—July 26, 1975.* From the toe of the buttress on a smooth slab, climb to a treed ledge, keeping left of an open book. Climb up right through a chimney and a gully to a long, exposed, sloping grass ledge with a few trees. From the end of this ledge, step left onto a sloping platform from which a small, vertical step (5.4) leads into a gully. Climb this until about 10 m below a prominent roof; then go left on slabs (5.4, much harder when wet) to a belay ledge. Go around bulge, then right for 15 m/50 ft into a 5.4 crack which leads up to another slab, again crossed to the left. Gain the exposed crest and follow it to the summit. Class 5.4, 4–6 hours. It is difficult to retreat from this route. Descend via the Chamois-Anderson Mountain col and glacier to the S. Mainly Class 3–4 with 4 pitches of Class 5. (Ref: *CAJ* 1983, p. 70.)

Northeast face: *FA: J. Bates, E. Zenger—1975.* Climb the face between the northeast ridge and Chamois' north buttress.

Northeast ridge: *FA: B. Casselman, R. Culbert, N. Humphrey—1975.* ''A dirty unrewarding climb . . . good for Tarzan.'' Class 3–4, not as impressive as it looks.

East face: *FA: B. Berntsen, W. Woodhouse—June 1978.* Climbs the centre of the face on the other side of the northeast ridge from the northeast face. Ascend a ramp (Class 4) to mid height on the face, then climb straight up 6 leads to Class 5.7.

''LES CORNES'' 1980 m/6500 ft

These are the rocky ramparts on the east side of Chamois Peak. They have yielded some long, high-quality rock climbs.

Springbok Arête (southeast buttress): *FA: R. Barley, D. Cheesmond, G. Lacey, C. Lomax—September 1981.* Begin 150 m/500 ft up the side of buttress at an obvious left-leaning ramp, leading to a prominent orange rockfall scar; this first pitch is a decomposing gully. Step right and climb hollow flakes to bushes on left. Ascend a 40 m/120 ft crack trending left into ramp, then continue up the arête for 120 m/400 ft where a thin 5.9 crack curves back right to a tree below the orange scar. The eighth pitch diagonals left up an awkward off-width to the edge of the buttress, then takes a route through tottering blocks and twin cracks to a cramped belay stance. Follow a 5.10 crack and continue up left to a heathery bay, then hand traverse left to a tree ledge. Four pitches of cracks, liebacks, grooves, and chimneys lead to the summit; 14 pitches, Class 5.10, 10 hours up—probably fast. To descend, continue over minor summit, au cheval down ridge, and drop W via rappel into the gully leading S. One further rappel at mid-height is needed. (Ref: *CAJ* 1982, p. 60.) Recommended.

Lumberjack Wall: *FA: R. Barley, J. Howe, P. Shackleton—July 1982.* This route climbs the southeast face to the right of the Springbok Arête. Start just right of the toe of the buttress in a snowy recess and climb 6–8 rope-lengths up the obvious bushy diagonal break, keeping left where possible, to an area of decomposed red rock overlooking the ramp of Springbok Arête. Climb up right over loose blocks, up a chimney in the left side of a detached flake, and up steep layback cracks to a large, treed ledge below the headwall (bivy). From here, climb left up overlap, right up ramps and corners, left up face cracks to a dead tree, then left again along heathery ramp. Climb a steep layback, then tension left and up to a steep crack system; climb this to exfoliating chimneys. Aid up chimney and climb over the perched blocks above to an overhanging crack (off route pin above). Go left along an exposed ramp to the Springbok arête route, which is followed to the summit. 19 pitches, Class 5.9, A2. (Ref: *CAJ* 1983, p. 70.)

IBEX PEAK 2010 m/6600 ft
Located 1.5 km SE of Anderson River Mountain; formerly called North Anderson River Peak. It is the highest summit in this western cluster.
FA: A. Bentzen, H. Mutch, G. Woodsworth, R. Woodsworth—August 31, 1962.
North ridge: From the Chamois-Ibex col, climb the north ridge, a stiff Class 3. The slabby rock just right of the north ridge is recommended, also Class 3.
Southeast ridge: *FA: R. Barley, P. Shackleton—July 1981.* Reported to be pleasant climbing to 5.8, about 6 pitches. Variations to 5.9 are also possible.
East ridge/face: *FA: K. Flavelle, S. Flavelle—July 13, 1982.* The ridge can be followed in its entirety, though the climbing doesn't really start until on the steeper face. After the notch in the ridge, the route is mostly bushy grooves, bushy cracks, and slabs. A shoulder stand was used to overcome a steep little wall just above the last of the worst bush. Eventually the route had to go right to gain the north ridge below the summit. 600 m/2000 ft; Class 5.10.

STEINBOK PEAK 1980 m/6500 ft
Located 0.5 km SE of Ibex, with a huge northeast buttress. Formerly called "South Anderson River Peak."
FA: R. Culbert—1961.
West ridge: From Ibex-Steinbok col, the west ridge and southwest side offer little of technical interest.
South ridge: *FA: J. Bates, E. Zenger—September 1975.* Mainly Class 2–3 with three Class 5 leads (to 5.6). These can be bypassed to the W. Rock is crumbly in some places.
Northeast buttress: *FA: S. Flavelle, J. Howe—July 1979.* This buttress is perhaps the most striking feature in the area, sweeping 700 m/2300 ft directly to the summit. Scramble up left side of buttress to grassy ledges as slab steepens. Climb right on slab to a bush pullup over the overhang. Leave the bush as soon as feasible, slab climbing between ledges (5.9) to gain a ledge on the crest below a steep, smooth slab with many cracks. The nailing begins here. Head for the left side of the arching roofs.

The north buttress of Steinbok Peak Scott Flavelle

Once above them, climb up, then right, traversing way around the crest (face climbing 5.7) to a stance on the north face. A small corner, and then face cracks, lead upwards.

After cresting again, the line trends right to gain a long ledge high on the north face. Another face crack heads toward Mosquito Roof. A free move overcomes the roof and two further leads of Class 4–5 gain the top. Most of the aid pitches have some free climbing. The aid is mostly in thin cracks with the free climbing using stoppers and Friends for protection. The first ascent party fixed 4 pitches, then had one bivy half way up. There are several ledges on the route, though none in the middle section. V, 5.9, A3. (Ref: *CAJ* 1980, p. 73.)

GAMUZA PEAK 1920 m/6300 ft
Located 1.5 km SE of Steinbok; the southernmost summit in the western cluster of peaks.
FA: P. Kubik, G. McCormack—June 15, 1976.
West ridge: Climb a prominent gully which slashes through the north face to reach the west ridge crest just before traversing E to the summit. Descend by the easy east ridge to the Serna-Gamuza col.
North ridge: *FA: G. Mumford, E. Zenger—June 16, 1976.* Avoid the smooth slab E of the gully used to reach the west ridge by ascending a short way up this gully to gain the easier right side of this slab. Ascend onto the northwest arête which leads directly to the summit. Class 5.5.

SERNA PEAK 1770 m/5800 ft
A small summit between Gemse and Gamuza. *FRA: E. Zenger—October 16, 1982.* Via gully on the north side. NTD.

GEMSE PEAK 1860 m/6100 ft
Located 3 km E of Chamois Peak.
FA: P. Kubik, E. Zenger—October 11, 1974.
East ridge: Ascend to Gemse-Reh col (2 pitches, Class 3–4) from the northwest side. The east ridge is mainly Class 3–4 with a few short Class 5 steps. The crux is a 7 m/23 ft Class 5.5 slab near the top. The easier sections are a little bushy.
South ridge: Probably the best descent route; there is a short Class 4 section and a nice "airy" ridge. In approaching from the west stay under the open slabs, as all shortcuts through them require a rope.
Northwest buttress: *FA: S. Golling, N. Humphrey, C. McNeil—1975.* This route starts out at Class 4 but gets continuously more difficult. Up to 5.8 with one point of aid. The slabs here may be difficult to protect.

REH PEAK 1770 m/5800 ft
Located just NE of Gemse.
FA: P. Kubik, E. Zenger—October 1974.
Southwest ridge: An easy walk from the Gemse-Reh col.
North ridge: *FA: P. Kubik, E. Zenger—October 1974.* A pleasant climb involving 3 or 4 pitches along a knife edge arête. The west side is vertical while the east side consists of 60° slabs. Good rock, little bush, 5.2.

Southeast side: *FA: T. Clayton, E. Hinze, S. O'Donnell—1975.* A bushy Class 3–4 route leading to the southeast ridge. Not recommended.

GUANACO PEAK 2100 m/6900 ft
Immediately S of the pass between East Anderson River and Coldwater River.
FA: Large BCMC party led by K. Ricker—September 1981.
Approach via upper Coldwater River road (*A8*). An easy climb via short gullies from Guanaco-Vicuña col.

VICUÑA PEAK 2100 m/6900 ft
Located 1.5 km SW of Guanaco.
FA: P. Kubik, E. Zenger—October 13, 1974.
Approach via the upper Coldwater road (*A8*).
Southwest ridge: The climb starts from the left end of a prominent white ledge. The first 3 leads are Class 5 (to 5.6) followed by a pitch of Class 4 and some scrambling.
Northeast ridge: *FA: J. Gudaitis, S. Heiberg—September 1981.* Bushy. Sneak around the left side of the steep wall (rappel on descent) and climb easy cracks and ledges back to the crest; 2 hours return from the Guanaco-Vicuña col. Class 3–4.

ALPACA PEAK 2040 m/6700 ft
Located 1.5 km SW of Vicuña.
FA: P. Kubik, E. Zenger—1974.
Approach all routes from the upper Coldwater road (*A8*) or from Zopkios Ridge (*A6*).
Via northwest ridge: Class 3. It is a nice walk N to **BIGHORN PEAK** (1900 m/6200 ft) from the low point between the two. **LLAMA PEAK** (1900 m/6200 ft) is a bump on the ridge about 2 km S of Alpaca; this ridge can be followed a further 2 km S to **ZUPJOK PEAK** (1830 m/6000 ft).
The Ricker Route: *FA: K. Ricker, A. Meninga—September 1984.* The Alpaca-Vicuña col may be gained from the upper Coldwater road (*A10*) in about an hour by skirting rockslides lower down and gaining slabs leading to the east ridge of Llama Peak. There is extensive route potential along the east-northeast face of this monolith. The recorded route begins 200 m/650 ft S of the col on basal slabs, and gains an obliquely trending gully and ramp system. Class 4; some chock anchors required. There is some minor bush on the upper pitches of this 8-pitch climb. (Ref: *CAJ* 1985, p. 47.)
The Heiberg Route: *FA: S. Bloxsome, S. Heiberg—September 1984.* Begin adjacent to and above the Ricker Route on obvious corners leading to a final deep gully, which yields excellent rock on its right side. About 5 pitches. (Ref: *CAJ* 1985, p. 47.)
Southeast ridge: *FA: BCMC party—1984.* A pleasant hike on interesting slabs.

ZOPKIOS RIDGE 1920 m/6300 ft
Maps have misplaced this feature; it is located between Yak and Zupjok peaks. It can be reached from either of these peaks, via Falls Lake (*A6*), or from "Little Douglas Lake" (*A8*), but the new highway will offer the most direct access via the south or west facing slopes. The two north ribs of the ridge are easily reached from the upper Coldwater road (*A8*).

ZUM PEAK 1860 m/6100 ft

Located at the north end of Zopkios Ridge. It does not appear difficult.

YAK PEAK 2040 m/6700 ft

On Zopkios Ridge, 2.5 km SW of Falls Lake.

From the south: Hike NW from Fallscreek road (*A6*) into basin between Nak and Thar peaks. Continue over Nak or around on the talus of the north side. Yak has a large north face. The short east face has been climbed by at least three different crack systems; it is easily bypassed to reach the summit.

Southwest face: *FA: P. de Visser, L. Soet, M. Wyborn, R. Wyborn—September 1982.* Route takes the obvious open gully up the face, taking right fork, then climbing out on right side. Nine pitches, 4 of which are Class 5. There is a 5.8 crux to get out of the gully. (Ref: *BCM* 1984, p. 24.)

West ridge: *FA: K. Flavelle, S. Flavelle—1980.* Gain the col between Yak and the minor bump to the W. The ridge is low Class 5 with the usual heather, bush and odd bit of slimy rock thrown in for laughs.

Yak Crack: *FA: J. Bennetto, R.Cox—August 23, 1985.* This route climbs the obvious diagonal fault line on the south face of Yak. Begin on the left side of the face and ascend the huge flake to a good ledge, then go right, following the line of weakness across the face. There are several small roofs to overcome. At the top of the obvious crescent, climb over the roof into a groove (5.8) which is followed to a good belay. The next pitch finishes in a chimney, after which a pitch of corner cracks with some loose rock leads to a belay in the mouth of a small cave. Continue right to gain the base of the huge corner which splits the upper south and east faces. Sustained 5.7 climbing in the corner leads to easier ground and the summit. Take large Friends if you've got them and some skinny pegs. Fourteen pitches to 5.8.

Porcelain Chicken: *FA: J. Bennetto, R. Cox—August 25, 1985.* This route takes the longest of several prominent dihedrals which border the south and east faces of Yak. There is much sustained mid Class 5 climbing, both crack and face, with moves to 5.8. The climb ends on the shoulder of loose blocks 7 pitches up because of loose rock bands above on the east face. Two long diagonal rappels gain the trees. A few small pitons may be useful.

NAK PEAK 2010 m/6600 ft

Located on the ridge immediately E of Yak.

The north ridge is an easy scramble from the Nak-Thar basin (see Yak Peak). The east side has seen some short rock climbs to Class 4; the rock is crumbly but bush-free. (*J. Bryan, R. Culbert, P. Kubik, W. Saunders, E. Zenger—1974.*) The provincial map (92 H/NW) has inverted the position of Yak and Nak.

THAR PEAK 1920 m/6300 ft

Located 0.5 km S of Falls Lake (*A6*).

From the east: Via east slopes or from Nak-Thar basin. This peak also has a steep north side, though reportedly loose and mossy. **ZOA PEAK** (1250 m/4100 ft) stands 1.5 km NW of Falls Lake.

Yak Peak and Yak Crack Rick Cox

JULY MOUNTAIN 2125 m/6973 ft

Located 5.5 km/3.4 mi NE of Guanaco Peak.

Approach via July Mountain road (*A9*) or Juliet Creek (*A10*). The summit is an easy hike from E or S, and probably offers good hiking along connecting ridges.

NEEDLE PEAK 2075 m/6800 ft

An abrupt granite summit between Coquihalla River and Boston Bar Creek.
FA: Likely by surveyors.

Southwest ridge: From the old Coquihalla River road (*A5*) climb slopes S of Needle Creek, contouring into valley to cross this creek at 1220 m/4000 ft. Do an ascending traverse along base of slabs (to avoid bad bush) to col SW of Needle Peak. This ridge is narrow in places but not difficult.

East buttress: *FA: F. Douglas, P. Starr—June 1974.* Reportedly a good rock route, with a couple of pitches to 5.7.

North ridge: Traverse snowslopes below northeast face from base of east buttress, and scramble (4th class) up firm rock to top.

SPIDER PEAK 1580 m/5200 ft

Located between Siwash and Qualark creeks.

Approach via Qualark Creek (*B1*) or Carolin Mines road (*A4*). The S slopes are mellow. **"THE MEDICINE MAN"** (**"THE POINTING ROCK"**) is a 25 m/80 ft pinnacle at about 1190 m/3900 ft across the Fraser River from Yale. *FA: A. Milliken—1960* via Class 2–3 south side.

SQUEAH MOUNTAIN 1800 m/5900 ft

Located about 15 km/9.3 mi NNE of Hope. Probably best approached via Suka Creek (*B1a*) and the intervening divide.

JORGENSON PEAK 1830 m/6000 ft

Located 4 km S of Squeah Mountain.

From ill-defined roads on west side (see Ogilvie Peak) hike E to low point in divide, then N to summit. Alternatively, traverse over from summit of Ogilvie.

OGILVIE PEAK 1645 m/5400 ft

This rises immediately northeast of Hope, and is climbed largely by Hope residents.

West ridge: Follow Qualark Creek road (*B1*) until shortly beyond where this descends to cross railway, and climb E on a deteriorating logging road to about 1010 m/3300 ft. Here it splits, with the N branch going to Jorgenson Peak and the S going to about 1220 m/4000 ft on the west ridge of Ogilvie. A pleasant walk from here to summit.

North ridge: It was formerly possible to gain this ridge by hiking south from the north branch of the Qualark Creek road (*B1*). The ridge was a cruise. Deteriorating logging roads have dampened recent enthusiasm for this project, but the possibility of reactivated logging is always present.

From the old Coquihalla road: Take the old Coquihalla road (*A*) about 5 km E to a noisy pumping station, then go left on a rough track which climbs E to antenna on ridge at 550 m/1800 ft, above a bend in the Coquihalla River. The "Goat Bluffs Trail" can be found in timber 50 m NW of the antenna. It may be followed to 1070 m/3500 ft, where it hits the ridge north of Railway Creek. Continue up the ridge to a minor summit and drop beyond to Ogilvie's easy southeast ridge.

MT. JARVIS 1707 m/5600 ft
Located between Peers Creek and Sowaqua Creek.
A cable car climbs from Lear on the Coquihalla River to a micro-wave station atop Jarvis. There is no obvious hiking route, as all approaches appear quite unpleasant.

TULAMEEN MOUNTAIN 2286 m/7499 ft
Located 23 km/14 mi E of Hope at head of Tulameen River.
FA: Likely by prospectors in the early 1900s.
This mountain is fairly easily reached along a pleasant, open divide from the NW. That divide may be gained by driving up Tulameen River from Princeton, then up an old mining road in Vuich Creek. Alternatively, the divide is attained on a trail which leads E from end of Dewdney Creek road (*A3*) on a spur at 1223 m/4000 ft on the east flank of the valley head.

MT. SNIDER 2040 m/6700 ft
Located between Sowaqua and Dewdney creeks. Hike up the northwest side of the mountain from highest spur roads in Dewdney Creek drainage (*A3*).

COQUIHALLA MOUNTAIN 2160 m/7088 ft
A summit of the Bedded Range, about 7 km/4 mi SW of Needle Peak.
FA: Likely by surveyors.
This is a fairly strenuous day trip from the old Coquihalla River road, starting from near where it crosses Hidden Creek (*A5*), and climbing to divide S of this valley. Follow this SE to Coquihalla Mountain by scrambling up its west ridge.

STOYOMA MOUNTAIN 2282 m/7486 ft
Highest of the summits W of Spius Creek.
FRA: E. Machalette—1911.
This area of meadows, lakes and broad cirques is popular with Merritt residents. It used to be reached by roads in upper Spius Creek (*C3*), but newer logging roads swing easterly around the mountain (*C1*) to intercept the old road at Prospect Creek (1700 m/5560 ft). Take old road from here to lake 2 km SSW of the summit where there is an unlocked cabin for public use. The summit is a 1 hour hike from "Cabin Lake." A trail traverses slopes W from the lake, giving access to the 2255 m/7400 ft summit ("Stoyoma's Widow") above a lake 5 km WSW of Stoyoma.

MT. HEWITT BOSTOCK 2150 m/7100 ft
A large, double summit massif SE of Cowhead Pass at the headwaters of Prospect Creek. From the uppermost spurs in the creek basin a prominent cattle trail contours the southeast side of a very broad northeast ridge and subsidiary peak of the north-west summit. It climbs to a pass from where an ascending traverse leads to the col between the two main peaks, from which either summit is easily gained.

JACKASS MOUNTAIN 2008 m/6588 ft; KANAKA MOUNTAIN 1890 m/6200 ft

Cariboo goldrush legends and stories associated with these summits surpass the peaks in colour and quality, but if you really want to climb them, you will no doubt find a way.

MT. LYTTON 2044 m/6706 ft

This peak marks the northernmost point of the Cascade Mountains. From the Nicoamen-Mowhokam road (*D*) at its high point, hike up slope or use logging spurs to gain the main broad ridge crest. An old trail from the Trans Canada Highway 5 km S of Lytton can also be used, but this makes for a much longer trip.

Chapter 20

East Harrison

BOUNDARIES:
North: Rogers Creek, Nahatlatch River
East: Fraser River
South: Fraser River
West: Harrison Lake, Lillooet River

FOREST SERVICE OFFICES:

Chilliwack Forest District
P.O. Box 159
9850 S. McGrath Road
Rosedale, B.C. V0X 1X0
794-3361

Squamish Forest District
P.O. Box 197
Squamish, B.C. V0N 3G0
898-9671

LOGGING COMPANIES:

B.C. Forest Products
Boston Bar Division
P.O. Box 100
Boston Bar, B.C. V0K 1C0
(Nahatlatch River, Kookipi Creek)
876-9214

Maple Ridge Division
11641 224th Street
Maple Ridge, B.C. V2X 6A1
(East side of Harrison Lake)
465-5401

Rennie Logging Ltd.
36555 Trans Canada Highway R.R. #1
Yale, B.C. V0K 2S0
(Spuzzum Creek, Urquhart Creek)
863-2314

Lineham Logging Ltd.
Harrison Lake Division
7050 Rockwell
Harrison Hot Springs, B.C. V0M 1K0
(Big Silver Creek)
796-9166

Pretty's Timber Co.
P.O. Box 37
Harrison Hot Springs, B.C. V0M 1K0
OR: P.O. Box 10116
Vancouver, B.C. V7Y 1C6
(Cogburn Creek)
796-2539

MAPS:

Federal:
92 G/9 Stave River
92 H/5 Harrison Lake
92 H/12 Mount Urquhart
92 J/1 Stein Lake

92 G/16 Glacier Lake
92 H/11 Spuzzum
92 H/13 Scuzzy Mountain

Provincial:
92 G/NE   92 H/NW
92 J/SE

Introduction

This section includes a good deal of infrequently visited country, in part due to highly variable access. Most approaches entail long stretches of logging roads and it takes only one washout to spoil a weekend. You should check with the appropriate logging company before planning a trip here.

The area tends to be characterized by a number of outstanding summits separated by wide stretches of more gentle country. Urquhart is a fine rock peak, The Old Settler offers an interesting traverse, and Breakenridge, a heavily glaciated massif, has some interesting potential on most sides. The last reported trip into the country between Breakenridge and Cairn Needle was by Doug Kasian and Brian Rundle (Ref. *CAJ* 1978, p. 81) who climbed all minor summits on the divide between these two peeks. A number of peaks in this area, possibly including Mt. Fagervik, remain unclimbed, despite reasonable access and intriguing topography.

Approaches

A. FROM HARRISON LAKE
Good roads run up the east side of Harrison Lake, giving access to the peaks in this area. From Harrison Hot Springs a road leads E then N along the lake, past the Rivtow Straits yard to Sasquatch Provincial Park. It continues along the east side of Harrison Lake past a logging camp (Bear Creek) at Cogburn Creek to a second camp (Silver River) at Big Silver Creek where the road turns inland. There is currently much active logging in this area and therefore several gates.

1. Slollicum Creek: Just beyond the entrance to Sasquatch Provincial Park, 7 km/4.2 mi from the Rivtow yard, a road climbs into the Slollicum Creek basin and ends at 1340 m/4400 ft on the south ridge of Lookout Peak. This gives good hiking access to Lookout Peak, Slollicum Lake (1250 m/4100 ft), and Slollicum Peak, although the old trail here has now disappeared.

2. Cogburn Creek: 29.8 km/18.5 mi from the Rivtow yard, the road passes a logging camp (Pretty's) and in another 2 km crosses Cogburn Creek. There is a gate 100 m further on. The road forks here, with the right branch climbing to about 910 m/3000 ft in the main branch of the creek. Presently, it is two-wheel drive for about 18 km farther. Spurs climb to 910 m/3000 ft on the east side of The Old Settler, just NE of a lake at 1130 m/3700 ft.

2a. Settler Creek: Old roads ascend this creek to near the lake at its head, but are washed out. At the present there are plans to rejuvenate the lower part of this road, which branches right off Cogburn Creek road after 6.8 km/4.2 mi.

2b. North tributary: 2 km up Cogburn Creek, roads branch left and climb to 1010 m/3300 ft on the extreme southwest shoulder of the Urquhart massif and to 1220 m/4000 ft on the east side of Peak 5403 (1647 m).

2c. Talc Creek: This road leaves the main road just before it crosses Cogburn

Creek. It follows the northeast side of Talc Creek to near the head of the valley and is reportedly in good condition, providing favourable access to the southwest side of The Old Settler.

3. Big Silver Creek: The camp at the mouth of Big Silver Creek is 39 km/24.5 mi from the Rivtow yard. From here, the road runs along the east side of the creek for about 14.5 km/9 mi past a second camp. It crosses to the west side and continues for about 14 km/8.4 mi to past Butter Creek, E of Cairn Needle. This road is gated near its start; keys may be obtained from Lineham Logging or at their camps.

3a. Hornet Creek: 3 km from Big Silver logging camp the road forks. The right branch follows the south side of Hornet Creek to about 670 m/2200 ft (active and gated at the present), W of Mt. Urquhart. There is also a short, disused side road up Hornet Creek's major south tributary.

3b. Clear Creek: After crossing Hornet Creek, the main road continues along Big Silver Creek for 3 km more, where it forks again. The right branch (four-wheel drive at best) follows the southeast side of the creek to 790 m/2600 ft.

3c. Snowshoe Creek: An old road runs a short way up the north side of this creek, giving access to the northeast side of Breakenridge.

3d. Butter Creek: This valley is being logged at the present by B.C. Forest Products and appears to open up the east side of Cairn Needle.

4. Stokke Creek: Old roads climb this creek from its mouth on Harrison Lake (boat required) to 760 m/2500 ft, W of the Breakenridge massif.

B. FROM LILLOOET RIVER

From Pemberton, a road runs down the northeast side of Lillooet Lake to its mouth. There is a bridge just below here; roads continue on both sides of Lillooet River to the head of Harrison Lake. Those on the west side are currently in good condition, while those on the east side are deteriorating pending renewed logging. There is a second bridge a few km above the head of Harrison Lake. A road follows the west side of the lake from Harrison Mills to its head, but is generally in poor condition.

1. Gowan Creek: An old road climbs the east, then the west side of this valley to 640 m/2100 ft.

2. Rogers Creek: This is being actively logged by B.C. Forest Products at the present, with roads going to about 760 m/2500 ft.

C. FROM FRASER VALLEY

From Hope, Highway 1 follows the east side of the Fraser River past Yale and Spuzzum to a crossing at Alexandra Bridge. It then continues on the east side of the river to Boston Bar and points N. There is an aerial ferry at Boston Bar to the west side and roads in Scuzzy Creek and Nahatlatch River.

1. Emory Creek: From 1 km before Emory Creek Provincial Park, a road branches left. It traverses into the Emory Creek valley and follows it to its headwaters where it joins roads up Garnet and Ruby Creeks.

2. Sawmill Creek: A road climbs N from Yale to cross Yale Creek. It continues N, traversing near powerlines and then into a washed-out bridge at Sawmill Creek. The head of this valley can be reached by rough spurs climbing N 4 km before this washout. The roads turn W and climb to a crossing to the north side at 910 m/3000 ft. Here they meet a road which follows the north side of the valley from the vanished bridge, and which ends at 1190 m/3900 ft.

3. Inkawthia Creek: From the Sawmill Creek washout, the road continues N and eventually turns W into Inkawthia Creek, which it follows almost to the lake at 1340 m/4400 ft. This and the Sawmill Creek road appear to offer decent foot access to the ridges N of Mt. Fagervik and E of Mt. Urquhart.

4. Spuzzum Creek: This major road system leaves the highway 0.5 km before the creek at a "Rennie Logging" sign. Advance arrangements should be made with this company. Good roads follow the north side of this creek to 910 m/3000 ft, near its divide with Clear Creek. There are bridges to the south side on both sides of the major unnamed southwest tributary. The western road (at present washed out) reaches 850 m/2800 ft in the west fork of this tributary, and the eastern (active) 1040 m/3400 ft in the east fork.

4a. Urquhart Creek: There are bridges across Spuzzum Creek on both sides of Urquhart Creek. The western road follows the northwest side of Urquhart Creek to 940 m/3100 ft and the eastern one follows the southeast side to the same height. Side roads follow the west side of the unnamed southern tributary to 820 m/2700 ft and the east side to 1010 m/3300 ft. This road system offers good access to the Mt. Urquhart area.

5. Scuzzy Creek: Probably named after a CPR steamer, the **Scuzzy**, which worked the Fraser Canyon in the 1880s prior to completion of the railway. After crossing the Boston Bar aerial ferry, drive S to Scuzzy Creek. An active logging road follows this valley to a washout at 730 m/2400 ft, SE of Scuzzy Mountain. Plans at the present are to reopen this road past here and extend it to 1220 m/4000 ft S of Mt. Nesbitt. A spur will climb to 1370 m/4500 ft in the valley SW of Scuzzy Mountain.

5a. Southwestern Scuzzy Creek: An active logging road follows the east side of the upper southwest fork to 980 m/3200 ft, with spurs up southeastern tributaries.

5b. Northwestern Scuzzy Creek: A new road follows the major northwest fork of the creek to 1190 m/3900 ft, S of The Nipple. Plans at the present are to extend it to a point E of Mt. McEwen.

6. Nahatlatch River: A road begins N of the Boston Bar aerial ferry and ascends W in this large valley. Currently it is washed out at Tachewana Creek, making access to the south side road (and spurs) after this point impractical. Eventually, the south side will open up, giving access to the little-frequented northern part of this section.

6a. Kookipi Creek: Presently there is a washed-out bridge crossing to the south side of Nahatlatch River just below Frances Lake. From here roads ascend the east side of Kookipi Creek to 880 m/2900 ft. Plans at the present are to construct a road on the south side of the Nahatlatch to connect with this road. After being reopened, the road will be extended to forks W of Mt. McEwen.

Routes

BEAR MOUNTAIN 1040 m/3400 ft

A pleasant walk for good views a couple of km E of Harrison Hot Springs. Turn right on Lillooet Road, just before reaching Harrison Lake. Drive 3.5 km beyond the B.C. Forest Service office (stay left) to a parking spot at the end of an overgrown road. Follow old logging roads to the S, then climb talus and ridges to the open summit.

SLOLLICUM PEAK 1564 m/5131 ft

From the right branch of the Slollicum Creek road (*A1*) you can gain the summit by a bushy scramble for good views of the lake and the mountains to the N. The former trail is pretty well ancient history.

LOOKOUT PEAK 1520 m/5000 ft

Located 12.9 km/8 mi N of Harrison Hot Springs.

From the end of the Slollicum Creek road (*A1*) on the south ridge of Lookout, it is a bushy hike to the summit.

THE OLD SETTLER 2132 m/6994 ft

A large, horseshoe-shaped massif and the dominant summit at the south end of the Fraser-Harrison divide.

Once considered a fairly remote peak, The Old Settler is, in fact, not too difficult to reach and is, for the moment, a feasible weekend objective. The peak is unusual in that a conspicuous geological contact zone splits the south summit from the rest of the massif. The south end of the massif is brownish red gabbro, while the central and northern summits are of serpentinite, schist and quartz diorite. Unusually for the Coast Mountains, the red rock is excellent and the dark rock is questionable! The Old Settler has always been a popular objective of the BCMC and most of the routes on the mountain have been put up during BCMC excursions. The following approaches may be used.

Via Talc Creek: Take the Talc Creek exit (*A2c*) and drive or walk to the highest spur on northeast flank of the valley. This ends near a creek from "Daiphy Lake" at 1430 m/4700 ft below Settler's west face. Cross two small gullies from end to pick up patchy trail which ascends across creek at 1160 m/3800 ft and continues to the lake. This trail begins by following an old road bed and is very overgrown with alder. Look for it where the road levels out into an alder flat, and expect bushwhacking; 3 hours up from the road.

Via Cogburn Creek: It is an easy hike to the lake on the northeast side of mountain, 45 minutes from the highest spurs (*A2*).

Via Emory Creek: From Trans Canada Highway take the road up Emory Creek (*C1*) to beneath Mt. Baird, where the road follows a powerline S over pass to Garnet Creek. To reach camp for The Old Settler, swing to S of Baird (old trail) and camp on divide to W.

Via Settler Creek: The roads in this drainage (*A2a*) were only driveable for a short period; it is unknown if anyone has ever approached the peak via this valley.

All routes given below are climbed from the basin to the W. The summit is actually the northernmost hump.

The traverse from south to north: This is a highly recommended line involving a variety of climbing techniques on pleasant terrain. It is best to begin at the south end of the massif and traverse to the N. You will need a rope as there are 1 or 2 rappels and a couple of rock steps on which some parties may wish to rope up. The rock on the south peak is excellent—rough with all kinds of handholds and cracks—and is mainly Class 3 (one short Class 4 step). There is also a short Class 4 section on the central peak. It is necessary to rappel from this summit. Occasionally you may encounter a bergschrund problem. The final climb to the highest summit is a scramble.

The descent, unfortunately, is not as enjoyable. You should traverse N from the main summit into a loose gully (either by downclimbing or on rappel) which is followed to scree or snow.

South peak—west buttress: *FA: G. Mumford, T. Ryan—September 1977.* From the floor of the basin the reddish rock of this route looks unappealing but it is, in fact, a wonderful climb—an abundance of holds on solid and unusual rock. Class 4. Recommended.

West couloir: *FA: J. Bryceland and party—June 1982.* This is the prominent couloir which splits the south and central peaks. Snow to about 45°. It is sometimes necessary to ascend rock to the left or right in order to avoid crevasses that span the entire width of the couloir.

"The Contact Zone": *FA: BCMC party—1980.* This route follows the zone of contact between the red gabbro of the south summit and the darker rock of the northern peaks. It ascends the wall on the left side of the west couloir beginning near the base of the couloir and traversing easterly across the face to gain the steep upper section of well-broken gabbro. Some hard Class 5 climbing is involved.

Central peak—west buttress: *FA: M. Down, K. Duck—June 20, 1982.* The route begins at the righthand corner of the west face of the central peak at the bottom lefthand edge of the west couloir and ascends the easy-angled and broken lower half of a wide amorphous buttress for about 460 m/1500 ft. Class 3. Beyond this point the climb is consistently Class 5.5 to 5.7. The route follows a series of steeper buttresses through to the top, with one long pitch of 5.8 providing the crux. Although the buttress is large and somewhat intimidating and unappealing when viewed from the bottom, route finding is not difficult. However, protection is thin in places and there are some long lead outs in mid-5th Class and better. Horizontals, knife-blades and helmets recommended. Some loose rock, notably on the first half of the route.

West face: *FA: E. Zenger and companion—1970s.* This route ascends the 270 m/900 ft face just below the highest northern summit on loose, unpleasant rock. Difficulty is to mid-5th, but the line is not recommended.

MT. BAIRD 1832 m/6010 ft
A gentle summit 4 km SE of The Old Settler.
From the Emory Creek road (*C1*) where it passes over the divide into Garnet Creek, Mt. Baird is a 3 1/2 hour ascent through slash and easy bush on the south side to a pleasant summit.

MT. URQUHART 2100 m/6890 ft
An abrupt summit E of central Harrison Lake, visible from Trans Canada Highway near the Yarrow exit. Best approached from Urquhart Creek roads (*C5a*).
FA: Topographic Survey Party.
Southwest ridge: *FRA: K. Dixon, G. Laughlin, H. Redekop—April 1974.* To follow the probable route of the first ascent party, you approach this ridge from the Harrison Lake side. It is NTD. The 1974 party made the ascent as an easy snow climb.
Northwest ridge: The easiest route up the peak. Reach the broad northwest ridge from below Urquhart's north face and follow it to the summit. Alternatively, traverse around the mountain to complete the climb on the west side. Class 3.
North face: *FA: P. Kubik, S. Werner—September 18, 1977.* Begin at about the centre of the face just right of a vertical band of light gray rock. Traverse into this

band and climb it to about half way up the face (Class 3). Climb a Class 4 pitch to a prominent diagonal gully on the left side of the face which is then followed for 2 pitches. There are several more Class 3–4 pitches to the summit. An icefall may block access to this route for much of the season. (Ref: *CAJ* 1981, p. 64.)

Northeast ridge: *FA: P. Kubik, E. Zenger—1976.* This climb of 700 m/2300 ft is easier than it looks. The first two thirds are somewhat bushy, but the upper third of the climb offers 5 leads of enjoyable climbing to Class 5.6. Stay on the ridge crest the entire way. About 7 hours from base to summit. (Ref: *CAJ* 1976, p. 56, photo.)

South face: *FA: D. Herchmer and party—summer 1974.* The original ascent party approached from Urquhart Creek (*C4a*), skirting the northeast ridge and the east face on a pocket glacier and slabs. Ascend the face on Class 4 and low Class 5 rock slabs to summit.

MT. BREAKENRIDGE 2385 m/7825 ft
A heavily glaciated ridge rising E of the top of Harrison Lake.
Approach via Big Silver Creek (*A3*) or Stokke Creek (*A4*). NTD from the S; likely also an easy ascent from the W.

"TRAVERSE PEAK" 2440 m/8000 ft
A 3 km-long ridge running N–S, located 3 km N of Mt. Breakenridge.
FA: D. Kasian, B. Rundle—July 31, 1977.
The first ascent party traversed the various humps of this summit from S–N; they gained the summit via the south slopes. NTD.

"VISTA PEAK" 2190 m/7200 ft, possible higher
A 2 km-long ridge located 3.5 km SSE of Cairn Needle. The summit is a rock tower mounted on the north end of the peak.
FA: D. Kasian, B. Rundle—July 31, 1977.
The first ascent party made the climb via the south ridge on a traverse of the entire massif from S–N. Class 3.

"SURPRISE SUMMIT" 2285 m/7500 ft
Located 1 km SE of Cairn Needle. *FA: D. Kasian, B. Rundle—July 31, 1977.* Class 2 by the south ridge.

CAIRN NEEDLE 2245 m/7700 ft
Located NE of the head of Stokke Creek.
FA: R. Culbert, E. Lance, A. Purdey—1967.
Butter Creek road (*A3d*) appears the best approach at the present, although the recorded ascent was from Stokke Creek (*A4*). The north ridge is Class 2–3. (Ref: *VOCJ* 1967 p. 59.) Peaks to the W and above the forks of Stokke Creek were also climbed by this party.

"CAM'S PEAK" 2070 m/6800 ft
Located 2 km SSW of Scuzzy Mountain. *FRA: C. Dolman, D. Kasian—January 30, 1977.* Approach from Scuzzy Creek road (*C6*) and climb from S. Not difficult.

SCUZZY MOUNTAIN 2217 m/7274 ft
The highest summit between the forks of Scuzzy Creek.
FA: Topographic Survey party.
The northern side appears interesting. This peak has been approached by Scuzzy Creek road (*C6*) and climbed from the easy southwest slopes.

FRASER PEAK 1950 m/6400 ft
A double-summitted horseshoe 3 km W of Scuzzy Mountain.
FRA: D. Kasian—October 15, 1977.
The east ridge is reported to be excellent solid, blocky granite to low Class 5. Scuzzy Creek road (*C6*) and ridge to S of peak provide an approach.

PEAK 6600 2010 m/6600 ft
The high point on the broad ridge connecting Fraser Peak and Mt. Nesbitt. This ridge was traversed from N-S by D. Kasian, who recommended it as "fine open alpine country." NTD. (Ref. *CAJ* 1980, p. 72–73.)

Chapter 21

The Chehalis

by Bruce Fairley and Don Serl

BOUNDARIES:
North: Sloquet Creek and south boundary of Garibaldi Park
East: Harrison Lake
South: Fraser River
West: Stave River and Stave Lake

FOREST SERVICE OFFICE:
Maple Ridge Forest District
22747 Selkirk Avenue
Maple Ridge, B.C. V2X 2X9
467-6971

LOGGING COMPANIES:

Canadian Forest Products Ltd.
Mainland Logging Division
Harrison Camp, Box 11
Harrison Mills, B.C. V0M 1L0
(Statlu, Skwellepil, Eagle creeks,
Chehalis Lake)
796-2757

Pretty's Timber Co. Ltd.
P.O. Box 37
Harrison Hot Springs, B.C. V0M 1K0
796-2539
OR: P.O. Box 10116
Vancouver, B.C. V7Y 1C6
(Twenty Mile Creek, Kirkland Creek)
681-6105

MAPS:
Federal:
92 G/8 Stave Lake
92 H/5 Harrison Lake

92 G/9 Stave River
92 H/12 Mount Urquhart

Provincial:
92 G/NE
92 H/NW

92 G/SE
92 H/SW

Introduction and History

The Chehalis was almost unknown ten years ago, when Dick Culbert published his *Alpine Guide*. Canfor, the main logging company in the area, guarded their road system with excessive vigilance, and only a few isolated sorties into the area had been made by occasional exploratory parties.

Now that Canfor has opened the roads, the Chehalis offers more great alpine rock climbs to mountaineers than any other area in the guidebook. There are climbs here that easily rank with those on Slesse, and on the whole the rock is finer: clean, blocky granodiorite, which gives fine friction and plenty of protection cracks. Most

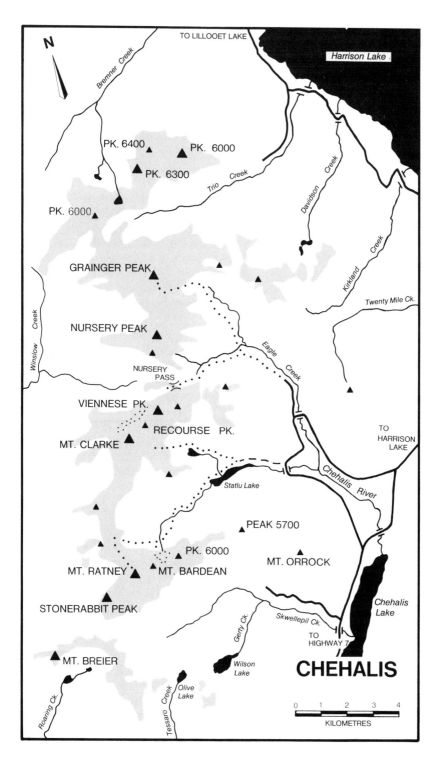

N

TO LILLOOET LAKE

Harrison Lake .

Bremner Creek

PK. 6400   PK. 6000

PK. 6300

Trio Creek

Davidson Creek

Kirkland Creek

PK. 6000

Twenty Mile Ck.

GRAINGER PEAK

Winslow Creek

NURSERY PEAK

Eagle Creek

NURSERY PASS

VIENNESE PK.

RECOURSE PK.

MT. CLARKE

TO HARRISON LAKE

Chehalis River

Statlu Lake

PEAK 5700

PK. 6000

MT. RATNEY   MT. BARDEAN

MT. ORROCK

Chehalis Lake

STONERABBIT PEAK

Skwellepil Ck.

Gerty Ck.

TO HIGHWAY 7

MT. BREIER

Wilson Lake

CHEHALIS

Roaring Ck.

Tessaro Creek

Olive Lake

0	1	2	3	4

KILOMETRES

of these wonderful climbs have only been done once.

The Chehalis range consists of a series of deep valleys with the peaks arranged around them. The Ratney group is the furthest south of the main uplifts. The peaks here are fairly easy climbs from the south, and the summits are open and pleasant. The northern exposures of Mount Bardean, however, contain some of the steepest, cleanest, and most continuous alpine rock climbing in the guidebook area. The north ridge of Mount Ratney is a pleasant route of moderate difficulty, with one sensational lead.

Immediately to the north is the Clarke group, with its well-fractured and solid rock. There are several shorter lines available here, as well as several outstanding routes of greater difficulty. The north ridge of Mount Clarke and the north face of Viennese in particular are two of the great climbs in southwestern B.C. The south face of Viennese gives parties who climb at less exacting standards a chance to get out on a big wall, which, although steep, makes only moderate demands on skill or nerve.

The major summit to the north of the Clarke group is Mount Grainger, which features exceptionally fine rock and several steep, hard climbs, as well as several more alpine routes. Much of the area north of Eagle Creek, comprising the drainage of Trethaway and Tipella creeks, is still virtually unexplored from a mountaineering point of view.

The Clarke massif itself is well suited to traverses, although an ability to climb in the mid Class 5 range is needed. There is little developed hiking in the area, which is unfortunate as Statlu Lake is one of the most attractive alpine lakes in southwestern B.C. Reaching any of the climbs here will require some bushwhacking.

The first major climb in the area was made in the 1930s, when a group of four bushwhacked up from Stave Lake and climbed Mount Grainger, the highest peak in the area. It was 45 years before Grainger was climbed again, when a party from Chilliwack, which included Neil Grainger, for whose brother the peak was named, spent several weekends building an access trail before making the climb. In the 1950s and 60s, Howard Rode of the ACC made first ascents of Mount Clarke and Mount Ratney, accompanied by Ian Kay and John Dudra.

In more recent years, the most persistent climber in the Chehalis has been Don Serl, who has now established more routes in the area than almost everyone else put together. Another climber, the solitary Doug Kasian, has roamed the lower summits of the Chehalis extensively. Although his efforts cannot, in terms of the difficulties faced, compare with those of Serl and his friends, Kasian's winter ascent of Mount Robertson showed determination and originality, and it was one of the better winter climbs made in the last decade.

An excellent article is "The Chehalis Range - A Climbing History" by Don Serl; *CAJ* 1980, p. 11.

Approaches

A. FROM THE CHEHALIS RIVER MAIN LINE

You can use this road to approach almost all of the Chehalis mountains; it gives reasonable access to the major summits around Statlu Lake, as well as to the alpine terrain around the forks of Statlu Creek.

Take the turnoff for Hemlock Valley ski area, just W of where Highway 7 crosses the Harrison River. The first left turn puts you on the Chehalis main line; the Canfor office and yard are here at the turnoff. Canfor publishes a good map of this road system, which you can pick up at their office. The area is closed Monday to Friday, 6:00 a.m. to 6:00 pm. All distances are measured from Highway 7.

1. Statlu Creek roads (16 km/10 mi): Immediately after crossing Statlu Creek, go left to gain access to the upper Statlu drainage. Stay in the valley bottom, crossing Statlu Creek at 1.5 km and again at 4 km.

1a. Statlu Creek, north fork (22 km/13.7 mi): About 2 km beyond the third Statlu crossing, turn right just before the bridge (well marked on map 92 G/8). The first roads on the east side of Statlu's north fork are decrepit, but the west-side road is currently in good shape and gives extremely easy access to the summits on the Statlu-Roaring Creek divide.

1b. Blacklock Creek (22 km/13.7 mi): Continue straight ahead on the Statlu Creek road and cross the creek for a final time, then stay on its right side to reach a bridge 1.5 km further on. It is best to park and walk from here.

1c. Statlu Creek, south fork (23.6 km/14.7 mi): Condition unknown, but likely impassable.

2. Skwellepil Creek roads (31.5 km/19.6 mi): Go right at the main bridge over Statlu Creek at 16 km/10 mi and continue another 15.5 km/9.6 mi to Skwellepil Creek. Presently, you can drive for several kilometres along the roads on the south side of Skwellepil creek. They give easy access to the summits to the S. The north-side roads are in bad repair, but still give hikers access to southern side of the Ratney group. A new road is planned to run from the south fork of Skwellepil Creek up Gerty Creek to Wilson Lake.

3. The Chehalis River and Eagle Creek roads (34 km/21.1 mi): Map 92 G/9 accurately shows road locations in these drainages. The Chehalis main line crosses a bridge over the Chehalis River at 34 km/21.1 mi. Roads form a loop from here up both sides of the river and up both sides of its major northern tributary, Eagle Creek. Cross the Chehalis River bridge and climb a four-wheel drive road along the east side of the river and up the east side of Eagle Creek. At a major fork roughly 4.5 km from the Chehalis River bridge, bear left and downhill. The road crosses Eagle Creek and turns back S on much the same level. Then it turns W above the Chehalis River and descends along a very rough, narrow track. It crosses the Chehalis River again (the bridge is in poor condition) and links up with the south-side road (described below). Park at the top of this last hill or you may not be able to get your vehicle back up again! To reach Statlu Lake, walk down the hill and turn sharply right just before the upper Chehalis River bridge. Follow a very rough road uphill to its end (0.7 km) at a small parking lot. The obvious trail along the north side of Chehalis River to Statlu Lake begins here.

The shortest walk into Statlu Lake, if you don't have a four-wheel drive, is to take the southern road (washed out after 0.3 km) which branches off the Chehalis main line at 33.5 km/20.7 mi, just before it reaches the first Chehalis River bridge. Walk this road about 3.5 km to join the route just beyond the upper Chehalis River bridge.

3a. To reach the Clarke group's north or south side: Follow a trail around the north side of Statlu Lake to where it fades out in a rockslide below a giant gully about a quarter of the way along the north lakeshore. Cross the rockslide, traversing to the W at a gentle upward gradient. Cross wet slabs and bush until you reach a major creek in a deep gully. Ascend steeply E of the creek, then angle left (NW), crossing a deep tributary gully and climbing steeply into forest beyond. Once in open timber, head NW to gain a small upper lake at 1010 m/3300 ft (GR 668861). From here, a huge gravel gully and/or bushy forest to its left lead you up into alpine terrain.

A more pleasant and less bushy approach (which is a bit more time consuming) is to climb the giant gully above Statlu Lake to its head, and then ascend W through about 200 m of bush onto the open ridge crest, which provides easy walking and fine views. Follow this N and then W to just short of the minor 1980 m/6500 ft summit at the east end of the Clarke group. There are good spots for camping here. Angle down W across snowslopes and meadows until it is possible to traverse slabs around the S of this summit, into the basin below Viennese Peak.

You can also descend northwards from just beyond the campsite into Nursery Pass to approach the north-side routes, although the Eagle Creek approach described below is likely preferable. Allow 3 or 4 hours from the rockslide to the campsite, and proportionately more beyond.

3b. To reach the Ratney group's north side: Follow the northern lakeshore to the west end of the lake (bush). From here, there are two alternatives. One is to keep on the north side of the major creek draining into the lake and continue through mature timber, using dry stream beds further up to gain the upper basin. The other is to traverse SW to gain rockslides on the south-side valley flank and traverse these (some bad bush) to where a major gully runs down from the east side of the vertical toe on the northeast ridge of Bardean. Use this gully, and the bush on its west side, to gain a wide ramp leading W to a snowpatch. Broken rock and slabs lead to a second ramp; climb bush or one Class 5 pitch to slabs above, leading W to the snowfields below Bardean. This section may be rappelled on return (look for rappel station near upper creek crossing, just before the creek plunges over the headwall).

3c. To reach the Grainger-Nursery Pass area: After crossing the Chehalis River bridge at 34 km/21 mi, continue on the road up the east side of the river, and again bear left at the major fork about 4.5 km past the bridge. After crossing Eagle Creek, about 1 km farther on, take the next right and continue up the west bank of Eagle Creek to a logging landing where a trail and partly flagged route leads on up the west side of the creek to the basin SE of Grainger Peak. To reach Nursery Pass, follow the north side of the west fork of Eagle Creek, the second major drainage to the left, rather than the main channel.

B. FROM HARRISON LAKE

A rough two-wheel drive road goes up the west side of Harrison Lake and links up with the Lillooet River logging roads. Short sections of this road often slip into four-wheel drive condition, so it may be worth checking ahead with the B.C. Forest Service.

1. Mystery Creek roads: Roads in this drainage head W to connect with the upper Chehalis-Eagle Creek roads described above.

2. Twenty Mile Creek roads: Two-wheel drive roads climb this drainage to 915 m/3000 ft. Gated. Keys available from Pretty's Lumber camp at Twenty Mile.

3. Kirkland Creek Roads: Two-wheel drive roads ascend to 1220 m/4000 ft. Also gated. Key available at Twenty Mile logging camp.

4. Trio Creek roads: Roads in this drainage are totally overgrown.

5. *Bremner Creek road:* An ancient road, overgrown with bush, leads up Bremner Creek valley into some topographically intriguing terrain. From here, it may be possible to find some old tracks into the headwaters of Doctors Creek. Lots of bush thrashing.

6. *Tretheway Creek and Tipella Creek roads:* Logging roads formerly ran up these drainages to the W of Harrison Lake, but they have not been used in over ten years and will be undriveable. Although overgrown in spots, there is no alternative access to this country. These roads are probably most easily travelled on skis in winter.

7. *Kenyon Lake roads:* Drive to Davis Lake Provincial Park on the east side of lower Stave Lake. From here, active logging roads (gated) lead N to Kenyon Lake, nearly joining roads from the north end of Stave Lake. There are major logging road complexes in Lost and Terepocki creeks.

Routes

MT. ST. BENEDICT 1250 m/4100 ft
A hiking objective E of Davis Lake.
Take Sylvester Road (6.5 km/4 mi E of Mission) N to Davis Lake Provincial Park. A trail here runs up the south side of Murdo Creek to gain old logging roads on the west flank of Mt. St. Benedict. Before crossing Murdo Creek, take a right fork and follow a marked trail up to McKay Lake. From here the summit is easily gained.

DEROCHE MOUNTAIN 1370 m/4500 ft
Located between Norrish Creek and the Fraser River.
From the town of Deroche on Highway 7 walk a steep, rough road N up hillside to major forks at 455 m/1500 ft. Take the right fork across Pye Creek and then the spur cutting back onto the ridge to 1065 m/3500 ft. From there it is an easy hike along the ridge to the summit, which has a good view.

NICOMEN MOUNTAIN 1220 m/4000 ft
Located 5 km SW of Deroche Mountain. Easily reached from the end of left fork of the road (see above) via its northeast slopes.

MT. KLAUDT 1370 m/4500 ft; MT. KEENAN 1400 m/4600 ft
Located on either side of the Hemlock Valley ski development, and easy hikes from there.

STATLU CREEK SUMMITS
To say that these summits are seldom visited is an overstatement. Doug Kasian, who make it a project to climb as many of these peaks as possible during the 1970s, was probably the first and last to visit many of them, although Don Crawhurst and Fred Gazeley (who did the first ascent of Mt. Bardean) apparently did considerable earlier unrecorded activity in the area. These summits are all low compared to the groups further north. The climbs are arranged north to south. (Ref: *CAJ* 1978, p. 34.)

MT. BREIER GROUP
Located N of the head of Statlu Creek, 3 km directly N of Blinch Lake. Approach

via North Statlu Creek and Roaring Creek (*Ala*). D. Kasian made a complete traverse (E–W) of the peaks in the Mt. Breier cirque, excluding Breier itself in August 1977. "A fine group of friendly summits," all granitic. **MT. BREIER** (1534 m/5032 ft) appears unclimbed. Located 4 km N of Blinch Lake and probably low Class 5. Described as "a fine blade of a peak."

OLIVE LAKE GROUP
Located around the head of Tesaro Creek.
On October 3, 1977, D. Kasian traversed (E–W) the group of peaks surrounding Olive Lake. He reported that this traverse was less pleasing than the Breier traverse. **PEAK 4700** (1435 m/4700 ft), to the W of Olive Lake, is a summit of clean white granite with possible route potential on its north face.

BLINCH LAKE PEAKS
The approach from Statlu Creek (*Ala*) is steep and bushy. If you have a two-wheel drive, you can approach via Lost Creek and roads along Salsbury Lake and Terepocki Creek, but you need to get a key to the logging gate located 4 km N of Davis Lake. About 0.6 km from the gate, take the left fork, descend to a bridge across Lost Creek, then continue along the west side of the creek. The road then runs N along a bench to the E of Salsbury Lake. When 2 km N of the lake, take the left fork and follow it down to a crossing of Terepocki Creek. The left branch here goes to Kenyon Lake, the right branch to 640 m/2100 ft on the slopes southwest of Blinch Lake. **PEAK 4900** (1490 m/4900 ft), **PEAK 4600** (1400 m/4600 ft), **PEAK 4900** (1490 m/4900 ft), and **PEAK 4500** (1370 m/4500 ft) are grouped (W–E) around Blinch Lake. All are easily scrambled from the S. (*FRA: D. Kasian—1977.*) Reports indicate that Peak 4500, E of the lake, has a good rock face on its western exposure.

MT. FLETCHER 1416 m/4646 ft
A minor bump located 3 km W of Chehalis Lake.
FRA: L. Harrison, Mr. McEwen—September 20, 1941.
Bushy from all approaches. In 1977 D. Kasian visited the minor summit 2.5 km due S of Mt. Fletcher; he reported some nice meadows on the north side. NTD.

PEAK 5100 1554 m/5100 ft
A minor summit 2 km W of Mt. Fletcher.
FA: D. Kasian—September 16, 1977.
The southeast ridge is NTD. Descend via the same route; the companion ridge to the W is bluffy.

MT. JASPER 1400 m/4600 ft
A sprawling massif forming the southern divide between Statlu Creek and Blacklock Lakes.
FRA: P. Berntsen, D. Kasian—December 23, 1976.
Approach from Statlu Creek (*Ala*). NTD by the west gully.

MT. KETTLEY 1394 m/4574 ft
The minor summit at the head of Blacklock Creek.

FRA: D. Kasian—December 28, 1976.
The recorded route from Lost Creek is not recommended. The best routes are either the climb up the north ridge or the traverse from south Statlu Creek (*A1c*). From this drainage you can easily ascend Peak 4600 ft (1400 m), 3 km SE of Kettley. Reportedly a pleasant area.

"RATNEY GROUP"

MT. ORROCK 1557 m/5108 ft
Easternmost summit of the Ratney Group.
FRA: D. Kasian—1977.
The southeast ridge is NTD. The lower 800 m/2625 ft include an old burn, which should be bypassed.

"MT. BARDEAN" 1930 m/6300 ft
A broad, buttressed crest 4 km WSW of Statlu Lake (GR 644821).
FA: D. Crowhurst, F. Gazeley—August 21, 1970.
From the south: Via Skwellepil Creek (*A2*). Large avalanche fans lead out of the creek bed; the upper reaches are pleasant hiking.
All other routes approach from the Chehalis River and Statlu Lake (*A3b*).
Northeast ridge: *FA: J. Halliday, P. Kubik, L. Soet, E. Zenger—August 5, 1978.* This route avoids the vertical toe on the lower third of the route. From well up the prominent (snow) gully to the E of the ridge, traverse face right (exhilarating Class 4) to a point above the snow patch on the ridge, then follow the crest to the summit. Three pitches of mid-5th at the top. A recommended climb.
The Tuning Fork: *FA: M. Down, J. Elzinga, D. Serl—July 2, 1980.* Reach the crest of the lower ridge from the right via a short, difficult pitch just above the ridge's toe. The sustained difficulties begin above a tiny snowpatch at the top of the Class 3 lower ridge. The route tends towards and climbs a prominent left-facing dihedral. The crux is a series of overhangs 6 pitches up, which the original party freed on the left. A pendulum was necessary on the final headwall. Class 5.8, A1; 16 pitches. A full day from the base and highly recommended. (Ref: *CAJ* 1981, p. 40.)
Flavelle-Beckham route: *FA: P. Beckham, S. Flavelle—July 22, 1984.* From the top of the lower ridge, climb Class 3 ramps and ledges to the right of the main left-arching crack systems. Climb a prominent left-facing corner and continue straight up for a pitch, gaining an obvious shallow corner system on the crest of the buttress. Continue near the crest, finishing via 150 m/500 ft of Class 3 scrambling to the right. A couple of pitches include 5.10 climbing. The party downclimbed much of the route, rappelling 5 times to regain the lower ridge.
Northwest buttress: *FA: D. Jones, D. Serl, J. Wittmayer—August 11, 1979.* The lower part of the route is characterized by short walls and heathery ledges. The upper part involves corners and cracks to 5.7. Takes 6 hours up from base.

The Ratney Group   1.) Northeast ridge   2.) The Tuning Fork   3.) Flavelle-Beckham route
4.) Northwest buttress   5.) Raisin Rib   6.) North ridge   Bruce Fairley

STONERABBIT PK.

MT RATNEY

MT BARDEAN

PEAK 5900

6

5

4

3

2

1

Bardean descent routes, north side: Descend by either of two routes. Traverse to Ratney and rappel/downclimb the north ridge (recommended), or downclimb and rappel the very bushy bluffs E of the northeast ridge.

"MT. RATNEY" 1960 m/6434 ft
A pleasant, rounded summit at the three-way divide between Chehalis River, Skwellepil Creek, and the east fork of Winslow Creek (GR 638819).
FA: J. Dudra, H. Rode—September 3, 1950.
North ridge: Class 4 to 5 with a strenuous corner pitch (which may be bypassed to the left) to conclude the climb. Although the original party approached via Stave Lake and Winslow Creek, the approach is now made via Statlu Lake (*A2*). This route is downclimbed and rappelled as the best way of regaining the lake from the Ratney-Bardean group. A strenuous weekend objective, it would be popular if it were more accessible. (Ref: *CAJ* 1952, p. 163.)
Northeast face (Raisin Rib): *FA: B. Fairley, H. Mutch—August 1984.* Take the line of the weakness up the northeast face, using the rib which is furthest E on the wall. Ascend slabby rock and snow to the base of the icefall in the Bardean-Ratney cirque. Traverse beneath the icefall (quickly!) to gain a ledge which leads to a faint rib. Ascend this directly, avoiding a headwall several pitches up by traversing left on ledges. Rock is somewhat slabby and awkward, but no harder than 5.7.
Via southeast slopes: *FA: Large BCMC party led by E. Kafer, M. Kafer—July 1975.* Approach from well up Swellepil Creek (*A2*) using avalanche fans to gain the Bardean-Ratney col. NTD.

STONERABBIT PEAK 1830 m/6000 ft
A blade-like summit 1.3 km W of Mt. Ratney.
FA: Large BCMC party led by E. Kafer, M. Kafer—July 1975.
East ridge: Climbed as a traverse from Ratney. Descend southwest ridge of Ratney until forced to double back S into southwest cirque, which is contoured to the base of the ridge. An exposed Class 3–4. (Ref: *CAJ* 1976, p. 54.)

CLARKE GROUP

PEAK 5900 1770 m/5800 ft
The southernmost peak in the Clarke cirque, located 2 km WNW of Statlu Lake (GR 660851).
FA: B. Fairley, H. Redekop—June 1979. A pleasant walk via the north ridge.

MT. CLARKE 2171 m/7100 ft
A broad mountain which forms the highest crest between Statlu Lake and Winslow Creek. Named for logger Cliff Clarke, who hiked from Harrison Lake to Stave Lake with his wife and two daughters—for recreation!
FA: I. Kay, A. Melville, F. Miles, H. Rode—July 2, 1949.
Northwest ridge: This route was originally gained from Winslow Lake via the long, western ridge systems extending from Clarke. It has since been climbed from Nursery Pass and the north side of the massif (*A3a*). Approach from the S of Clarke may be even more feasible. There is some Class 4 on this route, described by one

Mt. Clarke   1.) Southwest ridge   2.) South face   3.) Southeast ridge   Bruce Fairley

commentator as "beautiful granite." The crux is a chimney containing rock of loose persuasion. (Ref: *CAJ* 1950, p. 145; *CAJ* 1982, p. 60.)

Southwest ridge: *FA: D. Serl, J. Wittmayer—October 18, 1976.* This route involves about 8 enjoyable pitches of up to 5.7. There is some steep climbing in both the first and second steps; the top of the ridge eases off into scrambling.

Southeast ridge: This is the long ridge visible NW from the cirque below the Clarke group. It appears to terminate in a steep buttress. From the cirque, ascend a scrubby, treed area to gain the col between this buttress and Peak 5900 to the S. The complete ridge is not recommended, as it is infested with krumholz. The west-side approach to the upper ridge cannot be recommended either: it is marred by much scree and loose rock, although the south face may be easily climbed directly. The best proposition is to angle up the southeast face and gain the ridge from the E where it steepens towards the summit. Class 3, and the easiest way up Clarke.

East ridge: *FA: B. Fairley, H. Redekop—May 19, 1979.* This route, which rises out of the Clarke-Recourse col, involves about 6 pitches of climbing up to mid-5th difficulty. Crux is a 5.5 jamcrack.

North ridge: *FA: D. Serl, J. Wittmayer—July 15, 1979.* The first ascent party approached via the huge scree gully above Statlu Lake and the ridges leading NW towards Viennese Peak. They then descended to the north cirque at Nursery Pass. It may be easier to reach this pass via the west fork of Eagle Creek (*A3c*), particularly

by late season when the stream bed can be walked. An exceptional route. The climb begins with 200 m/650 ft of steep cracks and corners leading through a prominent white rock scar (now rated 5.10). Above the toe, the climb becomes more moderate, with short, difficult problems interspersed with much climbing in the mid-5th range. Blocks, corners, and jamming typify this solid route. The first ascent party found 25 pitches, some of which were short. A full day from base to summit; some parties may need to bivouac. (Ref: *CAJ* 1980, p. 14.)

RECOURSE PEAK 2100 m/6900 ft

A squat summit 0.5 km NE of Mt. Clarke.
Northeast ridge: *FA: P. Binkert and party—July 1972.* Gained from snowfield at the head of the cirque. Class 3.
Northwest face: *FA: J. Knight, D. Serl—July 26, 1976.* Approach as for Clarke's north ridge. The first ascent party began in a great cleft in the face and climbed out on the right several pitches up, to grassy grooves and walls. A better alternative may be to start right of the cleft. Several steep pitches lead to a snowfield and a final compact wall below the summit. Class 5.8. Somewhat mossy.
Southwest ridge: *FA: B. Fairley, H. Redekop—June 1979.* Gained from the Clarke-Recourse col. A short route of Class 3 difficulty. A couple of tricky moves near the bottom may require a rope.
Southeast face: *FA: M. Down, J. Howe—September 11, 1980.* Some bushy Class 4 and low Class 5 climbing leads to a final 5.7 arête.

VIENNESE PEAK 2130 m/7000 ft

A dark, blocky tower of rock 1.3 km NE of Mt. Clarke with an impressive wall fronting on the Clarke cirque and an even more spectacular face dropping to the N.
FA: P. Binkert and party—July 1972.
West ridge: Class 4. An exposed traverse onto the south face is made about a pitch and a half from the top of this route, which concludes in a short jamcrack.
Opus: *FA: P. Croft, D. Serl—July 21, 1984.* A large tongue of rocks juts out from the left side of the south face. From its top, scramble left and upwards 100 m/330 ft to a line of weakness through the steepest part of the wall. The first pitch features 10 m of overhanging cracks and blocks (5.10), followed by slightly easier climbing to the upper overhangs, where the climbing is again very difficult. The next 2 pitches take "dream-quality knobby slabs;" the remaining 100 m/330 ft are Class 3–4.
South face: *FA: B. Fairley, H. Redekop—May 22, 1980.* Begin on slabby rock immediately below the great corner on the face and pick a route up to the base of the corner. Follow it for a lead, then traverse right and move straight up for 3 pitches. A long traverse to the left leads to several possible variations for the finish. Twelve pitches to 5.7 and a full day's climb from bivy or camp on the upper snowfields of the cirque. (Ref: *CAJ* 1981, p. 64.)
East ridge: *FA: D. Serl, C. Styron, R. Wyborn—September 14, 1975.* This short route features one airy pitch of Class 5 climbing just below the summit and clean, blocky scrambling below. Gain the route most easily by traversing the undemanding

The south face of Viennese Peak   1.) West ridge   2.) Opus   3.) South face   Bruce Fairley

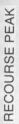

RECOURSE PEAK

VIENNESE PEAK

4

3

1

2

1980 m/6500 ft bump 0.7 km to the E or by scrambling up the south flank into the col between this peak and Viennese (Class 4). This is the common descent route from Viennese.

Crescendo: *FA: B. Kay, P. Berntsen—July 18, 1985.* The north face consists of a steep, relatively featureless eastern half and a series of hanging slabs, walls, and ribs in the higher western half. Traverse right across Class 4 rock from the upper snow bench at the extreme left of the face, then ascend to and climb the upper part of the rib dividing the face. Seven pitches to 5.9, plus considerable mid Class 5. A direct start is likely possible, but beware of falling ice.

Variazioni: *FA: C. Austrom, D. Serl—July 14, 1985.* Climb to the left side of a major rectangular snowfield well to the left of the rib followed by the original north face route. Walk right and climb the right edge of the snow and about 200 m/660 ft of rock to gain the ribcrest. Follow this about 300 m/1000 ft to the headwall. Begin on the left as for the north face route, then move right with difficulty to a right-angled dihedral. Climb this and a succession of slabs above until able to move up left to a major slab which leads to the top. 5.10 on the headwall.

North face: *FA: S. Flavelle, J. Howe—September 24–25, 1983.* Approach via Eagle Creek and Nursery Pass (*A3c*). From just left of the lowest rock, climb Class 3 slabby rock up and right to a point to the right of a prominent snowpatch, then climb straight up to gain the rib on its righthand side. Stay on or near the crest of the rib for 10 pitches of mid-5th till reaching the headwall, which is surmounted on the left wall of a corner leading to a ramp belay. One further pitch gains the slab above, which is followed for 2 leads to the summit ridge. Class 5.10; 700 m/2300 ft. Takes a full day. Some thin pegs are useful. (Ref: *CAJ* 1984, p. 31.)

GRAINGER GROUP

NURSERY PEAK 2070 m/6800 ft
A sharp rock tower located on the divide between the Clarke and Grainger massifs.
FA: D. Kasian—April 1978.
East side: Climb a shallow gully which in spring has 75 m/245 ft of steep snow. Approach via Eagle Creek (*A3c*). (Ref: *CAJ* 1979, p. 71.)

GRAINGER PEAK 2197 m/7207 ft
Highest summit in the Chehalis River drainage, located at the head of Eagle Creek (*A3c*).
FA: W. Cadillac, A. Dellow, T. Fallowfield, L. Harrison—August 1942.
East ridge and northeast face: The original ascent party traversed the high ridge above Eagle Creek (*A3c*). They encountered a series of towers on the ridge and traversed below them on the northeast slopes. This route remains the easiest way up Grainger.
East ridge crest: *FA: K. Kerestes, G. Seeklus, D. Serl, R. Tomich—June 30,*

The north faces of Viennese and Recourse peaks   1.) Crescendo   2.) Variazioni   3.) North face   4.) Northwest face   Scott Flavelle

Grainger Peak   1.) South ridge   2.) Southeast face   3.) South pillar   4.) Route 3

Don Serl

1985. Gain the crest up pleasant slabs several hundred metres E of the southeast gully, then traverse the complete ridge crest. Class 4 and easy Class 5. Recommended.

Southeast gully and east ridge: *FA: J. Bryceland, K. Dixon, N. Grainger—May 1977.* From the basin SE of the peak, gain the upper slopes by using a high ramp at the head of the cirque. Then climb up a steep snow gully to the upper east ridge, which is followed to the summit. Class 4. The gully and/or loosish ramps on its true right (W) side makes a reasonable descent route.

Route 3: *FA: D. Serl, R. Tomich—July 1, 1985.* Climb 2 pitches up dihedrals just left of the southeast gully (5.10 and 5.8 with one point of aid in each pitch). Scramble as far up and left as possible on a bench, then climb a pitch up cracks in a narrow face (5.7). A dihedral and overhanging wall (5.9) leads to easier ground on the left.

South pillar: *FA: J. Howe, D. Serl—July 15, 1984.* The route follows the rounded pillar on the right side of the south face. Begin on 5.10 cracks just right of the pillar crest (crux). When they end, move up and left across the crest. Continue upward near the crest for 4 pitches. The 6th pitch climbs onto the face to the left of a hanging, block-filled groove, then climbs up the overhanging chimney above. A final pitch ascends a second chimney with a very difficult exit left to the upper corners.

Exceptionally clean and solid, and easily worth the walk.

The J-Crack: *FA: F. Beckey, J. Nelson, K. Lewis—August 1985.* A rope-length to the right of the base of the south pillar, a long, prominent, left-facing crack leads up and then left as an undercling (5.9, large Friends). Two pitches higher, traverse right 1 ropelength on easy ledges, then climb an arête 1 pitch. The crux is a short 5.10 face-climbing section moving left. Two more pitches lead to easy ground.

Southeast face: *FA: S. Flavelle, R. Rohn—June 16, 1982.* A steep route on excellent, clean quartzdiorite. Route climbs almost directly to the summit. Begin on the right (E) end of a slabby platform. Climb straight up for 2 pitches then up cracks for 30 m; hand traverse right on a white flake (obvious from the ground) and up a short right-facing corner. On the next pitch move right (delicate) to gain the big right-facing dihedral which is followed to the top. Class 5.10; 230 m/750 ft.

South ridge: *FA: K. Balik, P. Bates, R. Bates, P. Kubik, E. Zenger—August 21, 1977.* This is a moderate climb of 6 or 7 pitches, mainly 4th and low 5th with one short harder section of about 5.6 difficulty. A favourite!

West face: A line on this face was soloed by F. Douglas while the south ridge was being climbed. Details unknown.

Northwest ridge: *FA: D. Serl, R. Tomich—June 30, 1985.* Scramble to a major ledge at the base of a steep wall. Nip around the corner to the left and ascend blocks and cracks back to the crest to avoid the difficulties. Climb slabs and cracks to the top. A pleasant hour for 200 m/650 ft of about 5.6.

EAGLE CREEK-DOCTORS CREEK AREA

In 1962, F. Arundel and L. Harrison climbed a summit, **"TRIO PEAK"** (1830 m/6000 ft), on the divide E of Eagle Creek. The location of this peak is poorly known. They approached from Trio Creek; the summit is a scramble. Farther N, **PEAK 6400** (1950 m/6400 ft) just W of the head of Doctors Creek was climbed in 1964 by E. Lance, who approached from Doctors Creek. The southeast ridge is Class 4.

TRETHEWAY CREEK AREA

A remote and seldom visited drainage NW of Grainger Peak. D. Kasian once again is the only climber to have recently entered this area; he traversed the chain of summits both to the E and the W of Tretheway Creek. (Ref: *CAJ* 1979, p. 29.)

EASTERN SUMMITS

To follow Kasian's route, approach via the south spur of the Tretheway Creek road, which leaves the main road about 6 km/4 mi from Five Mile Bay and climbs to 910 m/3000 ft in Coon Creek. Ascend the west side of the creek, then bushwhack up the ridge for 370 m/1200 ft to gain the divide. Exit via the west ridge of Peak 5800 (GR 619969) to Tretheway Creek road. Takes 2 days. Peaks are Class 3 or easier.

WESTERN SUMMITS

To follow Kasian's route, approach from the spur road about 5 km from Five Mile Bay; it climbs northward to 1070 m/3500 ft. Gain the ridge at Peak 5400, then follow the divide S to a tiny lake 3 km SE of Robertson Peak. Exit via the south flank of Peak 5800, S of the lake. Peaks are Class 3 or easier.

PEAK 6000 1830 m/6000 ft
Located between the forks of Winslow Creek.
FA: J. Roddick, O. Tokarsky—1954. Via the south ridge. Unlikely to be repeated for a long, long time.

ROBERTSON PEAK 2268 m/7400 ft
Highest summit in the Tretheway Creek drainage.
FA and FWA: D. Kasian, R. Lillie—February 1978.
Approach via Tretheway Creek (*B1*) on snowshoes. Ascend to a small lake 1 km S of Robertson's main summit and follow the south ridge to the col between west and east peaks. Either summit is Class 3 from this saddle. (Ref: *CAJ* 1979, p. 29.)

PEAKS NORTH OF TIPELLA CREEK
Three summits in this area were climbed in 1954 by J. Roddick and O. Tokarsky, who approached from Ironstone Creek.

Chapter 22

Coquitlam-Pitt

BOUNDARIES:
North: Garibaldi Park
East: Stave River and Stave Lake
South: Fraser River
West: Indian Arm and Indian River, Meslilloet Creek, Boise Creek, upper Pitt River

FOREST SERVICE OFFICES:

Maple Ridge Forest District
22747 Selkirk Avenue
Maple Ridge, B.C. V2X 2X9
467-6971

Squamish Forest District
P.O. Box 1970
Squamish, B.C. V0N 3G0
898-9671

LOGGING COMPANIES:

Empire Logging Division (Weldwood)
Box 280
Squamish, B.C. V0N 3G0 (Indian River)
683-3535

B.C. Forest Products
11641 - 224 Street
Maple Ridge, B.C. V2X 6A1 (Pitt River)
467-1511

Alvin Logging Camp
0711 (Vancouver Radio Operator and ask
for Forest Pitt N 627406, channel 15L)

District Municipality of Mission
8646 Stave Lake Street
Mission, B.C. V2V 4G4 (Mt. Crickmer)
534-1322

MAPS:
Federal:
92 G/7 Coquitlam
92 G/9 Stave River
Provincial:
92 G/SE

92 G/8 Stave Lake
92 G/10 Pitt River

92 G/NE

Introduction

   Despite their modest height, the peaks in this section are rugged. There are few glaciers today, but the evidence for past glacial activity is overwhelming. In particular, the series of north to south valleys debouching into the Fraser valley tell of large ice sheets which once flowed southwards across this landscape. The retreat and disappearance of the valley ice, combined with wet weather and a range of seasonal variations, have helped create conditions that make some of the climbs here coastal classics.
   The summits of the Golden Ears group are the most familiar in this area. They are serviced by good parks trails and offer some good rock, as well as various grades of

difficulty. Robie Reid and Judge Howay are striking, isolated summits. A new trail from the north end of Alouette Lake has vastly improved access to the former, but the latter is still notoriously difficult to reach. To have climbed "The Judge" is one mark of a dedicated Coast Mountain veteran.

Hiking in this area offers one evident advantage: it is close to Vancouver. Surprisingly, some of the trails do not see that much traffic, and one rarely seems to hear anymore of mountaineering parties setting out for the Coquitlam range. Once off the trail, travel below timberline tends to be arduous in this area, because of the heavy rainfall.

The Coquitlam-Pitt region is certainly not as popular today as it once was among mountaineers, but for the persistent, there are some climbs to be done here which are among the biggest alpine problems encountered anywhere in southwestern B.C.

Approaches

A. FROM INDIAN RIVER
You can reach the head of Indian Arm and the peaks W and E of the Indian River in either of two ways. The easiest is overland from Squamish. Turn right just before the Mamquam River bridge 1 km S of Squamish. After 4 km, the road starts up a hill; stay on the main road here but turn right immediately above. This road runs for 1 km to a bridge (posted watershed—keep out). The road then follows the Stawamus and Indian rivers to the head of Indian Arm (rough two-wheel drive condition). Avoid forks branching to the right. Alternatively, reach the head of Indian Arm by private boat or water taxi; Deep Cove Water Taxi (929-3011) and Harbour Ferries (687-9558) offer services to this point.

1. Meslilloet Creek roads: There is a bridge on the northeast side of the Indian River about 22 km/13.7 mi from the highway. Roads then climb E along the north side of Meslilloet Creek to 760 m/2500 ft.

2. Hixon and Brandt creeks roads: A complex of roads run between these two creeks. The main (Indian River) road crosses to the east side of the river about 32 km/19.9 mi from the highway, and continues 6 km/3.7 mi to the head of Indian Arm. A road branches N 1 km from the bridge. It crosses Hixon Creek and its north fork climbs into Brandt Creek and Norton Lake. The right fork climbs up the north side of Hixon Creek, eventually approaching Norton Lake. This is a popular four-wheel drive recreation area.

B. FROM PORT MOODY AND PORT COQUITLAM
1. Buntzen Lake roads: A road leading N from Ioco to Anmore climbs for 3 km along the east side of Buntzen Lake, passes through a Hydro gate, then continues to the north end of the lake. A gravel road begins 1 km from Anmore, where the pavement ends, and leads along the west side of the lake for about 1.5 km to the pipeline intake. The pipeline between Buntzen and Sasamat lakes, NW of Ioco, may be hiked. A system of hiking trails is being built on the west side of Buntzen Lake.

2. Cypress Lake and Eagle Ridge roads: Leave Highway 7 just W of Coquitlam River and travel N on good roads past Westwood Racetrack. There are double gates here. A system of logging roads leads NW to Cypress Mountain and Cypress Lake, just SE of Eagle Mountain. Alternatively, follow Maude Road from just E of Port

Moody to the powerline and transmission station. A four-wheel drive road (gated) leads from here along the powerline to intersect an old logging road complex climbing towards Eagle Ridge. This gate is controlled by B.C. Hydro.

3. Coquitlam Lake road: The Coquitlam Lake drainage area is the property of the Greater Vancouver Water District, and access is illegal. The Coquitlam Lake road goes up the west side of the Coquitlam River and ends at a gate shortly before the lake. Just beyond the gate, a reasonable road ascends Or Creek toward Coquitlam Mountain.

4. Burke Mountain roads: Turn off Highway 7 1.5 km E of Port Coquitlam onto Coast Meridian Road, which heads due N. After 4.8 km, turn right onto Harper Road which switchbacks (four-wheel drive) to 980 m/3200 ft and the site of an abandoned ski development. The road is sometimes locked in winter. From the end of the upper left fork, trails lead N to Dennett Lake. The right fork ends at a trail leading to Munro Lake. This area is heavily used by snowmobiles.

5. Munro Lake trail: Follow Coast Meridian Road from Highway 7 for 3 km and turn right onto Victoria Drive. Keep left where the road forks, and continue along it when it becomes Quarry Road. About 7 km/4.4 mi from Coast Meridian Road, a sign on the left indicates the trail to Munro Lake; there is a small parking area here. It is a 2 hour hike to the lake at 850 m/2800 ft.

6. Widgeon Lake trail: This trail has recently been upgraded, but is only accessible by boat. A private road leads N 7 km/4.4 mi from the end of the Quarry Road (gated) to a B.C. Forest Service picnic site on Widgeon Creek, where a recently rebuilt trail begins. For an alternative, public approach, cross the Pitt River by boat, skirting the north end of Siwash Island, and ascend the west channel of Widgeon Creek for about 2.5 km to the picnic site. From here, follow the trail up the west side of Widgeon Creek to Widgeon Lake. Where the trail forks about 4 km from the picnic site, keep to the left.

C. FROM GOLDEN EARS PARK

Drive E on Highway 7 to Haney, then turn N onto 228th Street. The route to the park is signposted from here, and ends at a large campground at the mouth of Gold Creek on the west side of Alouette Lake. There is a large network of trails in the south end of the park. Many are used for horse riding, and the only one of mountaineering interest is the "Incline trail" or "Alouette Mountain trail," which leads N along the divide from Mike Lake to Alouette Mountain. To reach this trail, drive W from the park headquarters and follow the signs.

1. Gold Creek trails: Trails extend N along both sides of Gold Creek from the campground. The one on the east side is the East Canyon (or Lower Falls) trail, which ends after 5 km. The West Canyon trail begins at the West Canyon parking lot and follows old spurs on the west side of the creek for 5 km, then turns left and climbs steeply up the north flank of the valley E of Golden Ears. The trail begins at the end of the highest spur and leads up a forested ridge to open country at 1370 m/4500 ft, NE of Golden Ears. There is a small shelter near this point. Takes 4 hours.

2. Evans Creek trail: A sketchy trail climbs up the south side of Evans Creek, beginning where the creek crosses the West Canyon trail, about 2.5 km from the parking lot. The trail ends at about 610 m/2000 ft, in a basin E of Edge and Blanshard, and N of Evans Peak. An obvious gully here can be used to gain the notch between

Alouette and Blanshard. Another good trail branches left from the West Canyon trail after 1 km, leading to a lookout above Viking Creek on the south side of Evans Peak. Takes 1 1/2 hours.

D. KEARSLEY CREEK WATERSHED ROAD

The area between Alouette and Stave lakes is largely a Tree Farm Licence of the District Municipality of Mission and has been heavily logged. From the dam at the outlet of Stave Lake, a good (gated) road leads up the west side of the lake. It forks just before Seventynine Creek, and after another gate the left fork leads high into the south side of the Kearsley Creek watershed. Mt. Crickmer is easily approached from here using a trail which heads NE. Keys for these roads are available from the Municipality of Mission.

E. ROBIE REID TRAIL

Access is from the NE end of Alouette Lake. A boat is required to reach this point. There are launching areas at the south end of the lake and at Gold Creek campground. Pick up the trail (unmarked) just W of the mouth of the upper Alouette River. It soon crosses the river by means of a Burma bridge, then climbs steeply to timberline on the southeast side of Robie Reid. Takes 4 hours.

Routes

MESLILLOET MOUNTAIN 2001 m/6565 ft

A large, rocky massif between Indian and Pitt rivers.
FA: F. Colbourne, P. Long, J. Selfe—1913.
From the south: From the end of Hixon Creek road (*A1b*), continue N up the valley to Anne Lake. Continue N up the south ridge from here over a minor summit to Meslilloet. Little difficulty.
West ridge: *FA: S. Grant, R. Tivey—1983.* From near the top of Meslilloet Creek road (*A1a*), cross the creek and bushwhack SE up a steep valley to a second lake, just above tree line. Climb a gully on the right side of the bluffs S of the lake to 30 m/100 ft below its top, then go right to a minor col. From here, follow the west ridge to summit. Class 3–4. (Ref: *BCM* 1984, p. 33.)
From the north: *FA: K. Haring—1981.* From the top of Meslilloet Creek logging roads (*A1a*), bushwhack E, then SE, up a creek valley. From its open upper basin, climb NE to gain a ridge trending NW/SE. It eventually leads to pocket glaciers NE of Meslilloet. These are crossed to the east ridge, which leads to the summit. There is a short detour into the south ridge near the top. Class 3–4.

MT. BONNYCASTLE 1740 m/5700 ft

Named for the engineer in charge of water surveys 1913-1914.
Located between the heads of Hixon Creek and Coquitlam River.
Reach Barnes Lake on the south side of Bonnycastle from Hixon Creek logging roads (*A1b*). Use the west side of the creek when approaching the lake. From here, either the southwest or the southeast ridge offers little difficulty. In 1974, K. Haring traversed the peak from S to N.

MT. FELIX 1320 m/4325 ft

A nondescript summit N of head of Indian Arm; incorrectly marked on 92 G/7 about 1 km S of actual location. Logging roads lead up Grand Creek from Granite Falls near the head of Indian Arm. From here, bushwhack NW up a side creek to the summit, which can also be reached directly from Indian River road (*A*). NTD. The 1430 m/4693 ft summit ENE of Felix is reached without difficulty from the lake at the head of Grand Creek. Strictly for desperate peak baggers.

EAGLE MOUNTAIN ("EAGLE RIDGE") 1050 m/3445 ft

Located in a heavily logged area N of Port Moody.

Approach via logging roads (*B2*) leading to Cypress Lake and Cypress Mountain, 1.6 km SE of Eagle Ridge, which is then easily reached. Logging road keys must be obtained from B.C. Hydro.

COQUITLAM MOUNTAIN 1584 m/5193 ft

All routes are bushy; best done as a ski trip.

FRA: P. James, D. Munday—1918.

From the south: Begin at the aborted Burke Mountain ski development (*B4*) and hike N to Dennett Lake, either directly or via Munro Lake. The latter can also be reached from Quarry Road via a trail (*B5*). Continue N along the divide for 2 km to the first col at 1120 m/3675 ft, then hike N over a shoulder and drop into the head of Or Creek (bushy). From here, ascend the southeast ridge directly. NTD; a full day return.

From Or Creek: Roads ascend Or Creek from near the outlet of Coquitlam Lake (*B3*). They lead to SW of Coquitlam Mountain, which is then easily ascended. This route is in the watershed and so is illegal.

From Widgeon Lake trail: Follow Widgeon Lake trail (*B6*) for 4 km from B.C. Forest Service picnic site. An overgrown spur leads W from here to the basin N of Widgeon Peak. Ascend NW to north ridge of a minor 1360 m/4460 ft summit 1.6 km ENE of Coquitlam. Follow the divide S, then W to Coquitlam Mountain.

WIDGEON PEAK 1431 m/4701 ft

FRA: T. Fyles, W. Wheatley—1933.

From the south: Approach as for the south side of Coquitlam Mountain (see above). Continue NE along the divide to the southwest ridge, which leads easily through broken forest to the summit. Alternatively, reach the ridge via old logging roads leading from Widgeon Creek (*B6*) into the valley SE of the peak.

From Widgeon Lake trail: Approach is the same as for Coquitlam Mountain. From the basin N of Widgeon Peak, bushwhack S to the top. NTD.

PENEPLAIN PEAK 1702 m/5572 ft

FRA: L. Harrison, R. Pilkington—1939.

Reach Widgeon Lake either via Widgeon Creek trail (*B6*) or by floatplane. From the northwest side of the lake, which is difficult to reach except when ice-covered in spring, climb W to the south ridge of Peneplain, which is NTD from here. Alternatively, from near the end of the Widgeon Creek road, climb the tributary NNW to the 1200 m/3900 ft col. An open ridge then leads NW to the peak. NTD.

OBELISK PEAK 1770 m/5800 ft
FA: L. Harrison, R. Pilkington—1939.
This peak is most easily approached along the divide N from Peneplain Peak. After about 2 km, bypass abrupt **"SHARKSFIN PEAK"** to the E, then continue to summit, which is NTD.

"FIVE FINGERS GROUP"
A group of spikey summits on Pitt-Coquitlam divide 6.4 km/4 mi north of Widgeon Lake. The fastest approach is to take a boat up Pitt Lake to the mouth of Debeck Creek. There is a short road here, and it is a day's pack beyond to Consolation Lakes at 1130 m/3700 ft. Keep on the south side of Debeck Creek, then on the north side of its third major tributary. Several of the summits may be climbed in a day from a camp by these lakes. (Ref: *CAJ* 1940, p. 154; *VOCJ* 1965.)

The highest peak is the **"MIDDLE FINGER"** (1890 m/6200 ft), standing between the Consolation Lakes on the west side. It may be reached directly from the southern lake and climbed without difficulty from the south side (*FA: L. Harrison, R. Pilkington—1938*). **"THE THUMB"** (1800 ft/5900 ft) is on a spur ridge about 0.3 km SE of Middle Finger. It is a scramble from the SE and may be traversed to reach the Middle Finger (*FA: R. Fraser, W. Mathews—1940*). The northeast spur ridge has the **"RING FINGER,"** immediately NE of the Middle Finger. Reach it by descending the ridge from near the summit of Middle Finger. From col at the base of Ring Finger, ascend until able to cross the major gully 30 m/100 ft below its head, then angle up and right to summit. Class 3–4 (*FA: J. Bryceland, A. Ellis, R. Woodsworth—1965*). **"THE FOREFINGER"** (1770 m/5800 ft) stands on the main divide to the SW of highest peaks. It is reached from southern Consolation Lake and climbed by a scramble from the S (*FA: T. Fyles and party—1924*). Finally, the **"LITTLE FINGER"** (1710 m/5600 ft) is about 1 km N of the other summits. It is approached by an ascending traverse from the lakes, and climbed on the south side without difficulty (*FA: J. Chamberlin, J. Roddick—1952*).

MT. CRICKMER 1340 m/4400 ft
Located in a thoroughly logged area between Alouette and Stave lakes. From logging roads in Kearsley Creek (*D1*) S of Crickmer, climb NE to summit. A good viewpoint. NTD; easy day.

BLANSHARD PEAK 1560 m/5113 ft
Southernmost of the Golden Ears group. The name is incorrectly placed on 92 G/7. See 92 G/8 for the correct location. Named after the first governor of the colony of Vancouver Island.
FA: P. James, D. Munday, M. Worsley—1918.
FWA: H. Davidson, D. Foster, G. Fraser, A. O'Connor, R. Worsely—March 1923.
From the Alouette Mountain trail: Follow the Alouette Mountain trail from Mike Lake (*C*) to the summit of broad **ALOUETTE MOUNTAIN** (a veritable plateau) at 1366 m/4481 ft. Takes 4 hours up. Alouette can be traversed to reach the base of Blanshard Peak; it is necessary to descend a gully or face to reach the base. Alternatively, reach this spot via Evans Creek (*C2*). Climb a Class 4 pitch directly up, then continue through easier bush and bluffs until able to traverse left without difficulty.

Ascend ridge to the right of the major gully (exposed Class 3) until level with the notch at the top. Cross this, then scramble to summit. A full day return.

North ridge: Descend the south ridge of Edge Mountain past a difficult section at a gap to Edge-Blanshard Peak col. Bypass a rock fin on W, then continue to summit. Class 3.

Northwest slopes: *FA: G. Fraser and companions—1925.* The party contoured around the west face and used steep snow to gain the summit.

West face: *FA: J. Archer, B. Moorehead—1973.* From the base of the Alouette Mountain trail route (see above), drop left down the gully to reach the centre of the face at its base. Climb up and left toward the prominent, white, overhanging pillars. Ascend their left side, then go up and right to a steep, short gully. Climb up and left to summit. About 10 pitches, with little bush. Class 5.5. Takes 1 day.

GOLDEN EARS 1706 m/5598 ft

A prominent, high double summit. Originally the "Golden Eyries" after the eagles in the area.

FRA: BCMC party—1911.

From the east: Approach via Gold Creek *(C1)*. This, the easiest route, is a walk starting above the col with Edge Peak.

Northeast face: *FA: B. Moorehead, J. Pinel, D. Wilkie—1972.* Same approach as regular route. An obvious, square gully runs from the lowest point on the face. Climb ridge to right of this to peak. Involves 6 pitches to 5.4. Other routes and variations may also have been done.

North ridge: From timberline E of Golden Ears *(C1)*, ascend to the north ridge of the Ears, which is followed (Class 3) to summit. Takes 2 hours up. Another, disused approach is from Raven Creek to the NW.

South couloir: From Alouette Mountain, contour into the creek basin W of Edge Peak. Climb the creek floor to a headwall, breached by a couloir leading to a col between the two summits. From here, join the regular route. Best in winter or spring.

"RAVEN PEAK" 1553 m/5095 ft

An unpleasant summit just E of Raven Lake. Climb its bushy, bluffy southeast side from Gold Creek.

EDGE PEAK 1645 m/5400 ft

A rugged massif southeast of the Golden Ears.

FA: possibly by S. Edge and companion—1876, otherwise by J. Irving, A. Lambert, D. McKee, and H. Sommerville—1929.

From the Gold Creek trail: Reach the saddle between Edge and Golden Ears from the end of Gold Creek trail *(C1)*. A series of steps on the divide leads to a small gap at the base of the final peak. These are Class 4–5 if climbed directly but can largely be avoided on the left. From the gap, go right into a gully which leads past a chockstone (Class 3) to summit. Alternatively, drop down from approach trail into the basin NE of Edge Peak. Cross it, then follow a prominent gully which swings under the north wall and leads to the previously mentioned gap. Class 3–4; avalanche danger in spring. More pleasant is a Class 3–4 white dyke to the right of the gully and parallelling it. Where the angle eases, traverse up and left into gap. All these routes take a full day return from Gold Creek.

North face: *FA: J. Bryan, B. Olson—1962.* Climb the major gully until it constricts beneath main wall of Edge Peak. Ascend the left of two corners until it ends against a small wall. Follow tree and heather ledges right for 60 m/200 ft beneath a wall of slabs. At the first break in this wall, climb up, heading for corner between the wall and the buttress to its right. Climb this corner, go right behind a gendarme, and climb another wall via a broken section. Above, angle right through a rotten gully to emerge right of apparent summit. Class 5. Takes 7 hours. (Ref: *VOCJ* 1962, 1963.) It is probably only possible to start this route when the gully at its base is snow-filled.

EDGE PEAK—EAST PEAK 1520 m/5000 ft
This peak is rarely climbed, as it is awkward to approach and descend. In addition to the west face route descent, it is also possible to downclimb the east ridge, rappelling to the NE where it steepens.
FA: T. Auger, R. Culbert, P. Thompson—1963.
West face: From the main summit of Edge, descend to the E, keeping to the right of the ridge, then rappel (double rope) into gap. Bushy rock (Class 3) leads to the summit. The main summit is regained by prussiking or jumarring up fixed rappel ropes, or by descending S until you reach the first side gully from W. Bushy Class 4 rock on either side of this gully provides escape.
North face: *FA: R. Culbert, D. Harris, B. Moorehead, J. Rance—1968.* Reach the northeast shoulder of the east peak by dropping from northeast basin (see west face route) and swinging around to gullies on the east side of the shoulder. The route goes up between the northeast corner (see below) and a shallow gully. The first pitch is bushy, but much is good gabbro. About halfway up the route becomes easier; from here, climb up either side of a major gully. Easy Class 5. (Ref: *CAJ* 1969, p. 79.)
Northeast corner: *FA: R. Dorling, N. Humphrey, B. Moorehead, J. Spencer—1971.* Reach the northeast shoulder as in north face route. Climb several leads (5.6) up the centre of a light-coloured, triangular slab at the base of a prominent corner; 3–4 pitches of A2 up this slab lead to a tree niche. Then traverse left to just below the summit ridge. Given the awkwardness of descent, a bivouac seems necessary.

OSPREY MOUNTAIN 1671 m/5482 ft
Located east of upper Pitt Lake.
FA: ACC party—1947.
Overgrown logging roads lead E for 3 km, starting from the mouth of Osprey Creek on the east side of Pitt Lake and ending on the north side of the creek. A broad ridge leads N into a large cirque on the south side of Osprey. Keep high on the right side of the cirque to avoid bush, then traverse left to a skyline notch just SE of summit. Complete the ascent on easy snow and rock.
From the east: *FA: D. Boekwyk, R. Craig, T. Jewitt, S. Tyldesley—1984.* Class 3–4 from the unnamed lake 1.5 km due E of the summit.

MT. ROBIE REID 2087 m/6847 ft
An impressive double summit located north of upper Alouette River. Named after a distinguished lawyer and historian.
FA: BCMC party—1925.
Reach timberline on the southeast ridge by one of three routes: (1) via the trail from

head of Alouette Creek (*E*); (2) by bushwhacking SW from Glacier Point on Stave Lake to the bump at 1100 m/3600 ft, then dropping W and ascending W then NW to timberline (original route); or (3) by bushwhacking W then NW from the abandoned logging camp opposite Deception Point on Stave Lake (1950s route). These last two routes are for moose only. From timberline to the SE, ascend NW to a steep area. Climb an obvious gully on the right side of this wall to the northeast ridge, which leads to the false summit. Traverse W to gain the true summit. Some loose rock on the final summit can be bypassed to the N. Class 3. (Ref: *CAJ* 1983, p.40.)

East face: *FA: ACC party led by C. Cooper—March 6–7, 1981.* Approach from the trail on the northwest side of Alouette Lake and follow it for 1 km to the North Alouette River, which is crossed on a Burma bridge. Stay on the east side of the river, following a trail. It is 3–4 hours to timberline. Gain the base of the east face N of a large, granitic tower, and ascend steep snowslopes, which end in a short, steep gully. Reportedly a nice line under winter conditions.

MT. ROBIE REID—WEST PEAK 1980 m/6500 ft
FA: D. Cowie, H. Rode—May 20, 1955.
Reach col between main and west peaks either by an intricate descent (one rappel) from the main peak or by a horrific bushwhack up from Tingle Creek to pocket glacier N of west peak. From the glacier, an easy gully leads to col (first ascent route). Traverse right from the col on a low series of ledges leading to a chimney on the north face; climb it past chockstones to the summit. Class 4–5.

MT. JUDGE HOWAY 2248 m/7376 ft
Steep twin summits located northwest of the head of Stave Lake in the obscure Mt. Judge Howay Provincial Recreation Area. Named after a judge and friend of Robie Reid. Due to its remoteness, this peak is seldom climbed. The northwest peak is the higher.
FA: E. Fuller, T. Fyles, H. O'Conner—1921.
From the head of Stave Lake: Reach the head of Stave Lake by boat, then continue up logging roads on the east side of Stave River about 7.2 km/4.5 mi. Cross the river by boat (or possibly by fording—chest deep) to reach the outlet of a creek draining the main cirque E of the summit. This steep, bushy Class 4 gully leads to a hanging valley. At 1070 m/3500 ft, climb to ridge to the N, following this and a snow gully above to the northeast ridge. Difficulties are then largely avoidable by climbing to the left, with the summit being Class 3. One party (V. Bauer, L. Patterson) approached via the valley to the NW, gaining the col between the two peaks by using a prominent couloir.

Judge Howay has also been climbed by bushwhacking up the creek to the S from Stave River. Keep W at forks, and from the creek head climb N to below the final peak about 100 m/300 ft below notch between summits. Ascent from here is Class 4, as described below. (Ref: *CAJ* 1950, p. 76.)
From the south: Begin at Clearwater Bay and follow the route as for Mt. Kranrod. Instead of ascending Kranrod, however, cross the basin east of Kranrod and either rap from the notch on its east ridge, or swing high around the arm of the east ridge (bluffs in part). Head NW across the basin to a lower lake mapped at 3000 ft. This lake is more than a day's pack from the bay for the average party. From the lake, head up the basin on the south side of Judge Howay, following a bouldery stream

bed and gully on the east side of the basin, and cross the ridge dropping S from the southwest peak. Do not climb to the col between the peaks, but climb the south face of the northwest peak, heading for the east ridge. Once on the ridge, cross a snowfield on the northeast face (ice axes necessary). Most parties will require a rope on this climb.

SOUTHWEST PEAK 2190 m/7200 ft
FA: T. Fyles—1920. From the notch between the peaks of Judge Howay, climb steep, broken Class 4 rock (loose in places) to the summit.

MT. KRANROD 1817 m/5961 ft
FA: J. Fyles, T. Fyles—1921.
This peak is not difficult from its northern side, reached via the creek which drain the north side of the mountain. Alternatively, the climb may be made from the outlet of Clearwater Bay (*FRA: K. Barnard, K. Kim—May 1983*). From the bay, ascend the broad, wooded ridge trending N, avoiding a prominent gully to the west, and gain the long, forested southeast ridge of Kranrod. Several wooded bumps must be traversed, and there is some easy rock. NTD; bush reportedly is not too bad.

Chapter 23

Chilliwack Valley

BOUNDARIES:
North: Airplane Creek, Foley Creek
East: Post Creek, Chilliwack Lake, upper Paleface Creek, Twin Spires
South: International boundary, Twin Lakes, Bear Creek
West: Cultus Lake

FOREST SERVICE OFFICE:
Chilliwack Forest District
P.O. Box 159
9850 South McGrath Road
Rosedale, B.C. V0X 1X0
794-3361

LOGGING COMPANIES:

Cattermole Timber
R.R. #1
Sardis, B.C. V0X 1Y0
823-8525
(Foley, Nesakwatch, Centre, Paleface and
Depot creeks)

Herman Sawmills
Box 3160
Mission, B.C. V2V 4J4
826-2771
(Tamihi, Borden creeks)

Pro West Logging
550 - 6th Street
New Westminster, B.C. V3L 3B7
(Slesse Creek)

MAPS:
Federal:
92 H/3 Skagit River   92 H/4 Chilliwack
Provincial:
92 H/SW
Outdoor Recreation Council Map #11: Chilliwack-Hope-Skagit
Recreation Map of the North Cascades (Beckey-Cardwell)

Introduction and History

The Chilliwack valley has long been celebrated for its challenging alpine routes, but it also harbours a surprising number and variety of hiking trails and much enjoyable scrambling. Logging in many of the valleys here has been voracious,[1] but one can still hike through the deep silence of mature fir and hemlock forests to havens of peace like Radium, Hanging and Greendrop lakes. The divide between Mt.

Corriveau and Mt. Lindeman offers some wonderful alpine rambling, sprinkled with all sorts of one and two pitch rock climbs, while the dark tower of Slesse and the clean, firm rock of Mt. Rexford or the Illusion Peaks have drawn increasing numbers of climbers in recent years.

Technical climbing is more developed in the Chilliwack valley than in any other area of the guidebook, with the exception of the Chehalis. There are some fine little climbs here for those who can manage from Class 4 to Class 5.6 or 5.7 in difficulty. All of the routes on Mt. Rexford fit into this category, and the lovely fractured rock of the east ridge is especially recommended, as is the traverse of the two Illusion Peaks from the north. Those with abilities in the 5.8 to 5.9 range have a fine variety of bold and dramatically situated routes to choose from, including several lines on the north side of Slesse Mountain with multiple pitches of Class 5 climbing, and some newer climbs in the rapidly developing Illusion group which are on even firmer rock.

One might think that an area which has been popular for so long would be ''climbed out'' by now, but in fact some of the lesser summits of the area, such as the pinnacles south of Slesse, still await extensive exploration, and there are some wall routes tucked away here and there which have yet to be tried. Although the deep, parallel structure of the valleys here makes the country unsuitable for longer alpine traverses, the Chilliwack valley has something to offer almost any level of alpine adventurer on weekend trips from Vancouver.

Lines of access are subject to very rapid change in this area, and winter storms have played havoc with bridges and road systems in the last few years. It is wise to check with the appropriate logging company on the current state of the roads before setting out. Also, a number of important roads in the drainage are generally gated.

Some of the ascents in this region have been historically important. The first ascent of Slesse Mountain in 1927 was one of the major climbs of the decade—the climb was made with only a short rope and no technical equipment of any kind. The first winter ascent of the peak, by Fips Broda and John Dudra, was perhaps the outstanding climb of the 1950s in southwestern B.C. Fred Beckey and friends made the first ascent of the northeast buttress, the most spectacular of Beckey's numerous Cascade routes. Ascents of the awesome east face and the ''Heart of Darkness'' couloir between the buttress and the north rib would likewise be considered landmark climbs.

The recent flurry of activity on the neighbouring Illusion Peaks has been largely propelled by Maxim de Jong, whose recent ascent of the northeast pillar on the south Illusion Peak caps his sustained and enduring love affair with the many hidden features of this alpine rock-climbing area. The Chilliwack valley, however, is one area where no one climber or group of climbers has been dominant, and if you look closely, you may see that almost all those mountaineers who have been active in establishing new routes in the hills have had a hand in this valley's development.

Approaches

A. FROM ELK MOUNTAIN TRAIL
Go S off Highway 401 on Prest Road for 4 km to Bailey Road. Follow it for 0.5 km and pick up Elk View Road, which goes E then S. Bailey Road can also be reached by turning E at the first stoplight in Vedder Crossing. Follow this road 12.5 km/7.5

mi to a small gravel pit, which serves as a parking lot. The trail is signposted from here. You can also reach this spot from Chilliwack River road, which intersects Bailey Road.

B. FROM CHILLIWACK LAKE ROAD

Heading E from Vancouver on The Trans Canada Highway, take the Cultus Lake/Sardis exit and drive 5 km S through Sardis and Vedder Crossing to the bridge over the Chilliwack River. Turn left before the bridge, and you are on the Chilliwack Lake road. All distances are measured from the first Chilliwack River bridge. The next bridge over to the south side of the Chilliwack River is at 10.4 km/6.4 mi.

1. Tamihi Creek road (10.4 km/6.5 mi): Turn right just after crossing the bridge over the Chilliwack River, and immediately go left up a well-used road past a gate at 3 km (impassable when locked). This road is completely washed out at 13 km/8 mi. At about 6.5 km, a very rough spur road climbs to about 1220 m/4000 ft in the valley S of Church Mountain.

1a. Church Mountain spur: Turn at the bridge and continue past the Tamihi Creek turnoff, then go left after 2.5 km and left again at 3.7 km. This road climbs in deteriorating condition to over 1450 m/4800 ft in the Little Tamihi Creek valley.

1b. Mt. McGuire spur: About 1.5 km before the gate on the Tamihi Creek road, turn left in a bend in the road, then immediately right. This "scruffy" road climbs to 400 m/1300 ft in two-wheel drive condition, then to 760 m/2500 ft in four-wheel drive condition.

2. Borden Creek road (20.3 km/12.6 mi): This road is gated at 0.7 km but climbs to over 1280 m/4200 ft on the east side of McGuire. It gives good access to the McGuire-Spencer-Border Peak area, and is two-wheel driveable to 0.5 km and four-wheel driveable all the way if the gate is open. The walk is pretty monotonous if you are stuck lower down.

3. Slesse Creek approach (21.2 km/13.2 mi): Access is changing rapidly in this drainage. After crossing Slesse Creek, the highway climbs a short, steep hill; turn right at the top of this into a clearing and follow the road 5.5 km to where an army bridge crosses Slesse Creek. Here you must decide whether to bush-crash up the east bank for 3 km (no trail or road) or cross the creek and make a serious ford higher up. There are bad bluffs on the east bank which make travel impractical. If you cross the bridge, turn left up the creek on a skid track which ends at a flagged trail. It rejoins the old road system after 1.5 km. A further 2.5 km along this road, you will come to a washout, and shortly beyond this, you will come to a Y intersection. Much of this area has been reclaimed by stream beds. The left (east) fork of the Y junction heads back to Slesse Creek in about 1 km. Formerly you could cross the creek on logs at this point. Now you will have to ford the creek, which is possible only at low water, and even then is tricky and dangerous. Once across the creek, go up a short hill (stay left at a junction) and find the steep trail, which begins near a creek by the remains of an old campsite and leads to the standard route on Slesse Mountain. There is no water on this trail.

3a. To reach Red Mountain mine and The Pleiades: At the previously mentioned Y junction, take the right (west) fork, which is presently stream bed, for about 250 m/825 ft. Beyond this section, a trail has been cut to the former minesite along the old road bed.

3b. To reach the Border peaks: Cross the army bridge (*B3*) and follow the main road about 250 m/825 ft. Go straight ahead at the switchback, and park. Follow the overgrown road up the valley and on a long southward traverse across the hillside. At the logged ridge where this trail ends (1070 m/3500 ft), drop into the bowl and traverse across it to gain the American Border Peak. To gain the north side of the Canadian Border Peak, continue westward up the ridge to 1700 m/5600 ft, where you can camp.

Alternatively, after parking, climb about 100 m/330 ft up the road and turn left into an overgrown logging track. Follow this for about 1 km, then cut uphill (cross country) through bush to rejoin the upper road. Markedly shorter, but bushy.

4. *Pierce Lake trail (22.9 km/14.2 mi):* Go S off the main road for about 0.7 km to a small parking lot; the trail is in excellent shape right up to the lower lake (about 3 hours). Somewhat vague beyond, but route finding is obvious.

5. *Foley Lake road (27.1 km/16.8 mi):* This road cuts off to the N (left) after a highway bridge across the Chilliwack River, then leads in 1.2 km to a bridge across Foley Creek. Head for Foley Lake (5.5 km). Slides shortly beyond the lake block auto traffic, but good bush-crashing is available farther up the valley for the hardcore. The Williamson Lake trail can be picked up by parking at Foley Lake and crossing the logjam at the outlet to the north side. See also Cheam Range chapter.

5a. *Mt. Laughington trail:* Go left immediately after crossing the Foley bridge, then right in 200–300 m/650–1000 ft. This road is impassable at present, but a trail goes up Mt. Laughington from the top of the highest spur. This mountain is also easily approached from roads in the Airplane Creek drainage, which climb to over 1220 m/4000 ft.

5b. *Mt. Mercer road:* Beyond the turnoff for Mt. Laughington trail, more roads branch off to the right; the next is Chipmunk Creek (see Cheam Range chapter). The third right (at about 6 km/3.5 mi from Foley Bridge) climbs onto the ridge between Mts. Thurston and Mercer (two-wheel drive to 600 m/2000 ft).

6. *Nesakwatch Creek route (27 km/16.7 mi):* Turn right immediately before a bridge which crosses the Chilliwack River and follow the Chilliwack River for about 2.5 km. The road is washed out after about 3 km, shortly before it reaches Nesakwatch Creek (there are two creeks here). Follow the Chilliwack River and then turn SE and hike along the Nesakwatch. Follow up the west side of Nesakwatch Creek until you can cross on logs—you may have to ford the creek. Bits and pieces of the old road can be picked up and followed on the east bank—brushy in spots. The road eventually climbs and switchbacks up onto the west side of the Illusion Peaks. The critical switchback is about 9 km/5.6 mi from the Chilliwack Lake road turnoff. Shortly after the first switchback to the N, head E into the bush to pick up the Mt. Rexford trail, which may be signposted. The first 200–300 m/650–1000 ft of the trail are obliterated, but it continues in fair condition higher up. Cross a stream gully, traverse through forest, then ascend the side of a narrow, steep basin between the Illusion Peaks and the Nesakwatch Spires (flagged) to a saddle. Make an ascending southward traverse to gain a flat area W of Rexford where camping is possible.

If heading for Slesse, a fork to the right cuts away from the main east side road shortly after you leave the creek bed (about 7 km/4.3 mi from the Chilliwack Lake road). A bridge here crosses Nesakwatch Creek to the W. Good roads climb the east flank of Slesse leading to the basin on the northeast side of the peak.

7. *Mt. Ford lookout (29.1 km/18.1 mi):* A track coming in from the left is likely four-wheel drive to its end (4.4 km), where a trail takes off to the Mt. Ford lookout.

The ridge to Williams Peak can be followed from here.

8. Williams ridge trail (32.5 km/20.2 mi): This steep but well-marked trail climbs up on the left (north) side of the valley onto the ridge between Mt. Ford and Williams Peak. Speed freaks have blitzed up Williams directly from the Chilliwack Lake road (35.6 km) in around 3 hours (little or no bush).

9. Centre Creek road (34 km/21.1 mi): This road goes S along the east side of Rexford as far as the American border. At the moment, a bridge is washed out right at Chilliwack Lake road; beyond this point the road is in good shape to Rexford. Logging spur roads climbing up to the N of the Illusions (first right at 4.5 km) and on the west side of MacDonald Peak (first left at 6 km/3.5 mi) are now impassable due to slides and erosion. Gates occasionally appear without warning on this road (Cattermole) and the second bridge (at 2 km) is chronically washed out. It takes 2 hours to reach the base of Rexford if hoofing it. The gully lying to the south of Rexford's south peak is an alternative way to gain the backside area of Mt. Rexford, or the south peak itself.

10. "Radium Lake" trail (38.4 km/23.9 mi): Turn right into a small housing development, and take the first left turn. Take the next right and go straight ahead, crossing the Chilliwack over two small bridges. Park in the lower sandy parking lot, from which a good trail is marked to the lake. The first crossing of Radium Creek is on logs and boulders, after which you should look downstream to pick up the trail. From Radium Lake, a rough trail climbs from directly behind the cabin to the Webb-MacDonald col. Recent work has apparently upgraded this trail.

11. Lindeman Lake trail (39.4 km/24.5 mi): A good, well-marked trail climbs from here past Lindeman Lake to Greendrop Lake, and rough tracks continue into the Hicks Creek drainage (see Skagit chapter).

12. Flora Lake trail (41.7 km/25.9 mi): This trail climbs steeply uphill to the E from this point (limited parking). The trail ends shortly before tree line. From here, traverse up and right to a col in the ridge above at 1760 m/5800 ft. Drop from here to the lake. It is inadvisable to try bashing down to the Lindeman Lake trail, as the bush is thick and steep.

13. Paleface Creek roads (48.3 km/30 mi): Drive down the east side of Chilliwack Lake to this point, where a spur road cuts left. A fork of this road goes left just before the 2 km mark (impassable); it climbs to 1310 m/4300 ft below Klesilkwa Mtn. The main road is two-wheel drive to 3.2 km, then four-wheel drive to 6 km at an elevation of 1400 m/4600 ft. Another road, which cuts off at 2.1 km and climbs high onto the north side of Mt. Edgar, completes the access routes in this logging moonscape.

14. Depot Creek road, spur, and trail (51 km/31.7 mi): The road is often gated (contact Cattermole Timber). It ascends Depot Creek toward the American border. About 3.4 km after the gate, an obscure but important spur to the left (undriveable) climbs toward the border slash. The Depot Creek trail begins at the end of this spur. It is in reasonable condition until it reaches a greasy headwall, which must be surmounted to gain the upper Depot valley—a marshy and poorly drained basin.

14a. Nodoubt spur: About 3 km from the gate, a spur to the right, in 4-wheel drive condition, crosses Depot Creek and climbs to about 1400 m/4600 ft on the slopes of Nodoubt Peak.

15. Hanging Lake trail: This steep, bushy, but well-marked trail climbs from Sapper's Park at the south end of Chilliwack Lake to Hanging Lake, at 1400 m/4600 ft.

The start of the trail is well signposted; the trail climbs up the drainage just N of the border slash. All routes above the lake are steep and bushy. Allow 3–4 hours to the lake.

16. Chilliwack River trail (54.7 km/34 mi): The trail begins just E of the bridge at the south end of Chilliwack Lake, follows the Chilliwack River, and eventually connects with the Whatcom Pass-Hannegan Pass trails and the Mt. Baker Highway. It is in excellent condition. Bear Creek shelter is reached after 7.2 km/4.5 mi, and the beginnings of a trail up Bear Creek can be found just E of the shelter. From the end of this trail, the climb to Ruta Lake is a bushwhack; the best plan is to gain the northwest ridge as soon as you can. It takes a day's bushwhacking to reach Bear Lake at the head of Bear Creek.

16a. Indian Creek (12 km/7.5 mi from Chilliwack Lake): The trail begins at Indian Creek shelter and runs along the north side of Indian Creek for about 5.5 km. From here, it is a bushwhack to the Indian Creek-Bear Creek col.

C. FROM MOUNT BAKER HIGHWAY
Head E from Vancouver on Highway 401, then S across the border at Huntingdon, B.C. into Sumas, U.S.A. From here, the highway is signposted to Mt. Baker.

1. Keep Kool Trail: Take the Twin Lakes road which leaves the Mt. Baker Highway 21.2 km/13.1 mi E of Glacier. This trail leaves the road at 3.8 km and climbs steeply into meadows above. This is a pleasant area, with nice flowers and impressive rock outcrops.

2. High Pass trail to Red Mountain mine: Follow the Twin Lakes road (*C1*) to its end at 1560 m/5120 ft; four-wheel drive. Follow the obvious Winchester Mountain trail for about 250 m/850 ft, then take the right fork over Low Pass to High Pass, 1800 m/5900 ft. About 1 hour. The Red Mountain mine (1740 m/5700 ft) is down to the NW. A trail is also stomped out to the base of The Pleiades.

Routes

MT. AMADIS 1522 m/4995 ft
A double summit on International Ridge just N of the border, and SE of Cultus Lake.

From Cultus Lake resort, drive 0.4 km along Sleepy Hollow Road, then turn S on a logging road and follow it around into Liumchen Creek valley. Shortly after entering the valley, the road is washed out. On foot, follow the road as it ascends beside the creek, then take the spur road which climbs the east flank of Amadis to just below its easy summit. The trip takes 4 hours. A more scenic alternative is to hike up older logging grades onto the nose of International Ridge. The highest spur here leads to over 910 m/3000 ft on the west side of the divide, but to avoid bluffs, swing onto ridge crest before the end of the road. The hike along International Ridge to Mt. Amadis is pleasant. **ISAR MOUNTAIN** (1585 m/5200 ft), just S of the border, is easily reached along the divide.

LIUMCHEN MOUNTAIN 1830 m/6000 ft
Located on the border 10 km/6.2 mi E of Cultus Lake, W of Tamihi Creek, and about 200 m/650 ft N of monument 48.

FA: Probably H. Custer—1859.
From the bridge across the Chilliwack River at 10.4 km/6.4 mi drive W down the south side of Chilliwack River past Tamihi Creek (*B1*). Pass two other creeks beyond Tamihi, then after about 2.5 km branch left up a logging road. After about 3 km you will come to a fork. Take the right fork for about 1.5 km then turn left and follow roads S, swinging right again onto the north ridge of Windy Knob. The road ends at 1430 m/4700 ft, and a trail continues onto **"WINDY KNOB"** (1693 m/5556 ft) on the main divide, about 30 minutes hike from the road. Continue S along the divide, climbing over **"OLD BALDY"** at 1726 m/5659 ft (at the junction of this divide and the Church Mountain spur ridge), and over other humps, until you reach Liumchen Mountain at the border. This is a lengthy but aesthetic day's return hike. Alternatively, take Sleepy Hollow Road from the Cultus Lake area, then turn right on Vance. At the fork reached after about 3 km, go left and descend to cross Liumchen Creek, then cut right, climbing old roads up the east side of the Liumchen Creek valley. Go right at all forks and you will eventually reach the same trailhead leading onto Windy Knob.

CHURCH MOUNTAIN 1686 m/5531 ft
Rises just E of the Baldy-Liumchen divide and is easily reached from there. It can be gained more directly by taking the left fork of the spur road at 880 m/2900 ft (see Liumchen Mountain), ascending through a logging complex to 1220 m/4000 ft, and then easily bushwhacking up the slopes on Church's north flank.

Both Liumchen and Church mountains have logging roads ascending their eastern sides from the Tamihi Creek road (*B1a*), and if unlocked these roads would be fast, though unattractive, approaches.

TOMYHOI PEAK 2271 m/7451 ft
Located 2.4 km S of the border on the west side of Tamihi Creek. Prominent from the Chilliwack area, Tomyhoi displays an unusually flat bench glacier at 1980 m/6500 ft.
Southeast side: Follow Keep Kool trail (*C1*) to tarns at 1520 m/5000 ft SW of Yellow Aster Butte, and then follow the divide NW to Tomyhoi. There is a notch isolating the final peak, which is a 45 m/150 ft steep scramble on poor rock. Takes 5 hours up from road.
Northeast side: *FRA: BCMC party—1968.* From Tamihi Creek road (*B1*) cross creek, boulder field, and moraine, bearing right along the timber's edge above glacier on the flank of Tomyhoi's northeast shoulder. Traverse left on snow and climb to the base of the bluffs, which may be avoided on the left or climbed directly (Class 3–4). Follow broken ridge system to summit. A 1 day return trip from road.
Northwest ridge: *FA: P. Stoliker and companion, September 1980. FWA: J. Bryceland, D. McAuliffe—March 5, 1983.* From about 760 m/2500 ft on the Tamihi Creek road (*B1*), ascend to camp at the forested shoulder (1770 m/5800 ft). Climb obvious ridge from here to summit, staying S if forced off the crest by cornices. Under winter conditions this climb takes 12 hours return from camp.

MT. McGUIRE 2018 m/6620 ft
FA: J.J. McArthur and party—1906.

Located above Chilliwack River, between Tamihi and Borden creeks. A pleasant winter objective.

East side: The Borden Creek road (*B2*) can usually be driven part way. Continue on foot along road, taking right fork after crossing Borden Creek and following this spur road to its end at 1460 m/4800 ft near timberline on McGuire's southeast flank. Ascend through forest and meadow to McGuire's easy east shoulder and scramble to summit. A pleasant 4 hours up from cars. The southern exposure is crowned by a series of massive limestone ribs.

North face: Route begins at a lake at 1415 m/4650 ft, involves 55° snow, and finishes left of summit. The route is gained via the McGuire spur (*B1b*). Described as attractive. This was the normal route before Border Creek was logged.

Northwest ridge: Gain from McGuire spur (*B1b*). NTD except for a Class 5 step below the summit.

The Border Peaks   1.) Southeast face   2.) East buttress   3.) Illegal Entry Buttress   4.) Northeast side   5.) Northeast rib   6.) Standard route

Maxim de Jong

CANADIAN BORDER PEAK 2255 m/7400 ft

A steep rock peak just N of the border on the west side of Slesse Creek. On map 92 H/4, the name ''Border Peak'' is positioned on a minor peak about 0.5 km E of the summit.

FA: T. Fyles, S. Henderson—1932.
FWA: T. Hall, R. Wyborn—March 21, 1971.
Northwest ridge: Approach via Slesse creek (*B3b*). From shoulder below north face, cross into the wide, shallow cirque between the main summit and a spur shoulder on the N. There is avalanche danger here in spring. From part way up the cirque, cut to the right, scrambling up onto shoulder and up this to the main northwest divide. A major, steep step where this divide abuts against the peak is bypassed to the W by a steep gully which is very loose and Class 3. The final summit pyramid is slightly more difficult. A long day return trip from Slesse Creek; many parties prefer to camp higher. (Ref: *VOCJ* 1983, p. 26.)
Northeast rib: *FA: R. Culbert—1963.* Approach via Slesse Creek (*B3b*). From shoulder below north face, traverse S under walls to a prominent rib dropping from the divide just S of the summit. Ascend this, starting on the left, but following near crest most of the way. Upon reaching the divide, gendarmes may be traversed or bypassed to the W, and the summit pyramid climbed just to the right of the divide. A long climb, mostly Class 3 or 4 and loose in some places.

AMERICAN BORDER PEAK 2446 m/8026 ft
A rotten, discoloured summit located W of Slesse Creek and immediately S of the border.
FA: A. Dalgleish, R. Fraser, T. Fyles, S. Henderson—1930.
FWA: H. Mathers, H. Starr—March 1958.
Southeast face: From Twin Lakes follow High Pass trail (*C2*) over south ridge of Mt. Larrabee and descend about 300 m/1000 ft toward Tomyhoi Lake. Swing under the west buttress of Larrabee and ascend over rockslides to the base of American Border's south ridge. This point can also be reached in two hours, over heather, slab, and glacier, by climbing E from Red Mountain mine (*B3*). The summit is climbed by a series of gullies and ledges, mostly loose, on the south ridge's east side. The final lead is up a narrow, gritty gully and is a stiff Class 3. Takes 7 hours up from Twin Lakes.
East buttress: *FA: M. Gardiner, S. Oates—July 28, 1984.* This is the buttress on the far left side of the east face. Its toe is enclosed by glacier ice. Enjoyable Class 4 climbing and scrambling leads to a junction with the southeast face route. Some loose rock.
Northeast side: *FA: D. Baker, F. Beckey, J. Dudra—September 21, 1952.* From the shoulder beneath the north face of Canadian Border Peak, drop SE into the basin and skirt below Canadian Border's walls. Once past the walls, ascend up small bluffs and snow patches (Class 3, minor Class 4) for about 300 m/1000 ft to the col northwest of American Border Peak. Final summit is climbed on face to left of the divide, up 45° snow gully and Class 3 rock. Takes 5 hours from camp. This complex route involves a lot of scrambling on loose rock. There may be more interesting lines on the west side of the col. (Ref: *Cascade Alpine Guide: Rainy Pass to Fraser River* p.45, 137.)
Illegal Entry Buttress: *FA: B. Griffiths, D. Jones, R. Nichol, D. Serl—May 23, 1982.* This rounded buttress bounds the east face in its right side. Approach via Slesse Creek (*B3b*). It is best to follow the old and overgrown road and traverse along it back across the hillside, dropping into the bowl E of Canadian Border Peak, then traversing or climbing to a camp or bivy. There is a good campsite at 1220

m/4000 ft. The route ascends steep snow couloirs and runnels, stepping across to the right onto the boundary of the northeast face about 600 m/2000 ft up. The summit block requires some delicate mixed moves. Class 4–5.

MT. LARRABEE ("RED MOUNTAIN") 2398 m/7868 ft
A large, reddish mass of rotten rock E of the head of Tamihi Creek.
FA: Likely by survey party—1906.
FWA: H. Mather, E. Pigou—March 1958 (via east buttress).
Southwest ridge: A trail leads from Twin Lakes around the northeast side of Winchester Mountain to High Pass (*C2*) and to 2070 m/6800 ft on Mt. Larrabee. Ascend fairly easy southwest rib and face or scramble up southeast ridge from trail end. Takes 5 hours up from Twin Lakes. Alternatively, from the Red Mountain mine (*B3a*), climb to the ridge between Larrabee and American Border Peak, then traverse the west face. Likely tedious.
North face: *FA: F. Douglas, J. Douglas—1968.* This face is reached from the Red Mountain Mine (*B3a or C2*) by traversing the glacier and is marked by a band (dyke) of lighter coloured (and firmer) rock leading to the upper east ridge. There is a tricky moat crossing at the base and the first few leads are Class 4, becoming easier above.
East buttress: Climbed in winter after a traverse over the Pleiades. There is significant exposure and fairly continuous climbing to Class 4–5. A fine ridge climb.
East face: *FA: S. Jones, S. Oates—August 13, 1983.* Approach via the High Pass trail (*C2*) to col SE of Mt. Larrabee, then traverse around the southeast ridge to gain the face, which is climbed on steep snow and Class 3 rock. Somewhat firmer than other routes.

THE PLEIADES 2240 m/7360 ft
A ridge of sharp peaks W of Slesse Creek just S of the border.
FA: D. Baker, F. Beckey, J. Dudra—September 20, 1952.
FWA: H. Mathers, E. Pigou—March 1958.
Southwest route: From Twin Lakes, follow the trail to High Pass (*C2*) and traverse across basins to base of The Pleiades. A loose gully gives access to the main notch between the eastern and western peaks. Either group is Class 3 from here. The eastern peaks are reached from the notch via the narrow, loose gully of the south side of the divide.
Northeast ridge of easternmost peak: From the Red Mountain mine (*B3a, C2*), ascend the ridge of the easternmost summit and continue on to the higher peak via the shattered, Class 3 connecting ridge. The two western summits are beyond a larger gap, and parties wishing to continue the traverse should use a loose, Class 3–4 gully on the south face to get down into the gap. Usually the traverse is done from the W when this gully is ascended.
North ridge of westernmost peak: *FA: R. Culbert, B. McKnight, G. Woodsworth—September 17, 1961.* Approach from the Red Mountain mine (*B3a, C2*). Most of this ridge is Class 3 on good rock, but there is one stiff Class 4 pitch. Some snow may be encountered. This route, when combined with a W–E traverse of the Pleiades and descent of the northeast ridge of the easternmost peak, offers a full day of alpine climbing.
North face couloirs: The three snow and ice couloirs on the north side are all feasible lines. The snow tongue dividing the eastern and western summits has ice cliffs

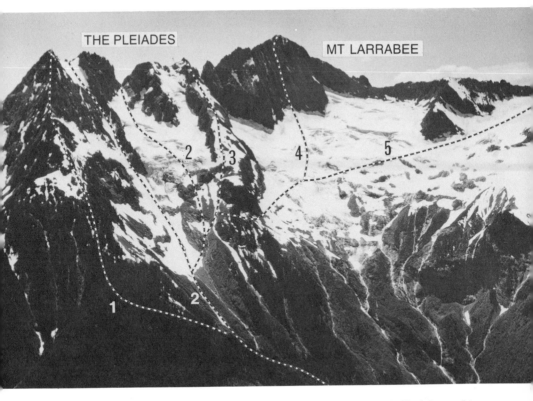

The Pleiades 1.) Northeast ridge   2.) Northern couloirs   3.) North ridge   4.) North face   5.) to
the south ridge of American Border

Maxim de Jong

which can be bypassed over rocks on the left. The area is sometimes used to practice
ice climbing.

MT. PIERCE 1959 m/6426 ft
Located E of Pierce Lake on the divide 5 km N of Slesse Mountain.
From the upper Pierce Lake (*B4*) at 1770 m/5800 ft ascend Mt. Pierce's easy south-
west ridge. This is a pleasant day trip from cars, with altitude gain mainly on trails.
Potentially a nice winter climb.

MT. MacFARLANE 2099m/6885 ft
Located on the divide 1.5 km SW of Mt. Pierce. Approach via the Pierce Lake trail
(*B4*). NTD via the rocky northwest spur.

CROSSOVER PEAK 2186 m/7172 ft
The main summit on the divide 2 km N of Slesse Mountain.
FWA: D. Serl, J. Wittmayer, G. Yavorsky—March 5, 1978.
Crossover Peak is most likely to be met by people traversing the divide between
Slesse and the Pierce Lake trails. This is a fine trip, but route finding is tricky. Head
N from the base of Slesse along the divide, swing W around **MOUNT PARKES**

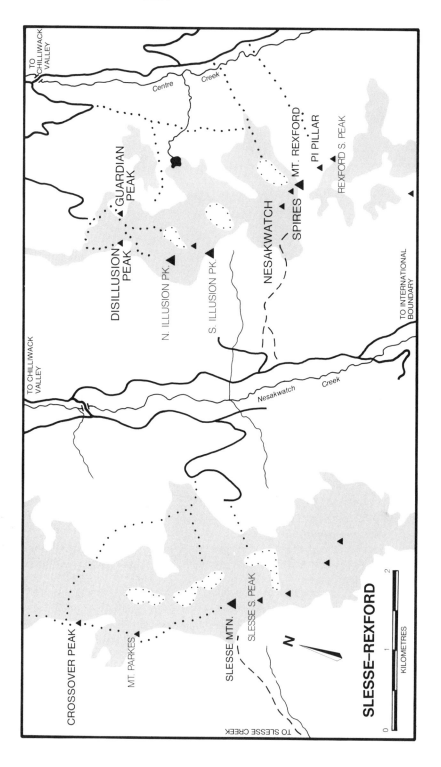

SLESSE–REXFORD

(2130 m/7000 ft) and E past the pinnacle beyond. A minor summit on Crossover's south ridge is avoided to the W. Traverse Crossover (Class 2–3) on poor rock and descend the slopes beyond to upper Pierce Lake (*B4*). Alternatively, you may make a descending traverse over Crossover's southeast flank to its easy east ridge (which may also be gained over steep scrub, etc. from the cirque NE of Slesse). The view from here is spectacular and Pierce Lakes may be gained by traversing NW under bluffs to a pass at 1920 m/6300 ft.

North ridge: *FA: P. Binkert, V. Moore—September 19, 1971.* Ascend the east ridge, then scramble to saddle N of summit. The summit ridge is an exposed class 3–4.

The northwest side of Slesse Mountain   1.) Northwest face   2.) Regular route   3.) West Pillar

Maxim de Jong

SLESSE MOUNTAIN 2375 m/7800 ft

A dark rock tower rising from the divide E of Slesse Creek, about 3.2 km N of the border. Slesse Mountain is an inspiring peak and a popular climb. Its great northeast buttress is a classic. All routes require roped climbing.

FA: S. Henderson, F. Parkes, M. Winram—August 10, 1927.
FWA: F. Broda, J. Dudra—1955.

The usual approach to the standard route is a steep trail which leaves a fork of Slesse Creek road (*B3*) about 140 m/450 ft after it crosses to the east side of Slesse Creek 0.8 km N of the border. Unfortunately, the trail is difficult to reach because the bridge across Slesse Creek has disappeared. The trail, sketchy near the 1220 m/4000 ft level, leads to an open shoulder at about 1770 m/5800 ft, W of Slesse. Strong parties have climbed Slesse in a day return from the road, but most prefer to camp near the shoulder. Water is scarce here late in the season.

In 1956, an airplane struck the south peak of Slesse, killing all 62 people aboard. Parts of the wreckage can still be found, especially in the cirque to the E.

West side: The easiest routes on Slesse head first to a notch high on the mountain's southwest shoulder. The most popular way to gain the notch is to climb a gully leading to the area between Slesse and a minor spike on the divide to the N, then traverse an ascending, cairned ledge system (Class 4) on the west face to a major gully (marked by a prominent gendarme) which leads to the notch. There is a tricky move into this gully. Immediately above the notch, a short lead of Class 5.6 is unavoidable. Following this lead, move left (easiest) or follow the ridge crest over easy ground to the summit. Beware of falling rocks. Most parties take about 3 hours up from the base. It appears that before the trail was put in, parties on Slesse gained "the notch" area by following a great gully straight up the southwest face from Slesse Creek, which heads for the south peak before cutting back to reach the regular west side route at the notch. The gully begins south of the large tributary of Slesse Creek coming off Slesse and was the variant used on the first winter ascent of the mountain. The first winter ascent of the west side route as it is climbed today was made by P. Piro and D. Serl on January 8–10, 1977.

West pillar: Route goes straight up, beginning where the west side route goes into the gully below the gendarme. Class 5.8; 5 pitches.

Northwest face: *FA: F. Beckey, E. Cooper, D. Gordon—June 21, 1959.* Several nice crack systems in this face may be reached directly from its base or by traversing out from the notch on divide to N (see photo). Routes tend to take about 4 hours. Good rock (mid Class 5) deteriorates near the summit. A recommended line.

Northwest face variation: *FA: C. Cooper, G. Morris—July 28, 1980.* Begin to the N of the west pillar (see photo). Cracks and face climbing to Class 5.7 on generally good rock. Finish on the west pillar.

Northeast buttress: *FA: F. Beckey, E. Bjornstad, S. Marts—August 1963. FWA: K. Lewis, J. Nelson—March 1–8, 1986.* This sweeping buttress is one of the finest alpine rock routes in the Cascade Range. Begin at the highest logging spur (*B6*) beneath the east face. Ascend to a wooded ridge, then traverse right (beneath the east

Slesse Mountain from Mt. Rexford   1.) Southeast buttress-south peak (and variations)   2.) East buttress   3.) Northeast buttress
Don Serl

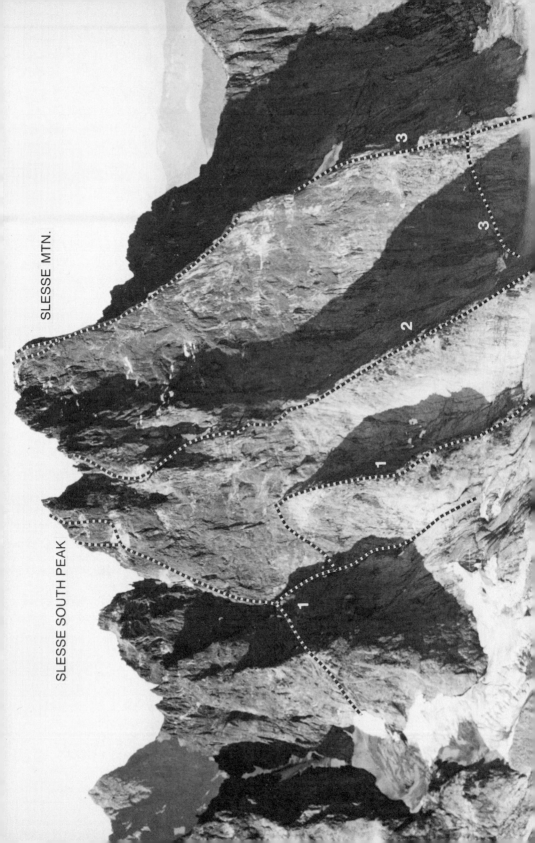

SLESSE MTN.

SLESSE SOUTH PEAK

buttress; beware of falling ice) and up onto the hanging glacier. Cross the hanging glacier below the east face, then climb a bushy diagonal ledge leading onto the buttress. The hanging glacier is usually well broken by midsummer (though rarely impassable); most parties stay near its upper edge. Crampons can be useful. This start avoids danger of falling ice on the approach to the dirty, polished lower third of the buttress which no one climbs any more. If you are a total purist, this lower third of the buttress can be reached from the logged basin directly below it; once again, beware of falling ice. The section is fairly low in angle and has been done free, although it is reportedly not too pleasant. It intersects the bypass route in a treed area. About 15 pitches lead from this treed area to the summit. Stay on or near the crest, although "ramps" to the right at half-height can be used to avoid a steep (crux) section. Ledges at two-thirds height have good bivouac sites, as well as snow until late in the year. The final steep section offers 7 pitches of superb climbing, with some loose rock near the summit. Small, wired nuts are very useful.

Climbing is to Class 5.9, with much mid Class 5. The route is all free; no pitons are needed for the upper two-thirds. The full buttress requires 1 1/2 days, or 1 day if you use the bypass. Approach takes about 5 hours. Descend via the regular route (southwest face), then retreat back to northeast cirque, as described for Crossover Peak, or descend via trail (*B3*) to Slesse Creek. Note that if you descend the trail, you must either ford Slesse Creek or bushwhack down the east bank of the creek to the road. (Ref: *CAJ* 1971, p. 66, 1965, p. 152; *VOCJ* 1970, p. 120; *Cascade Alpine Guide: Rainy Pass to Fraser River*, p. 132.)

North rib: *FA: R. Kiesel, J. Lowe—July 1972.* The north rib route climbs the rib and face to the right of the northeast buttress; the two routes are separated by a horrific gully (the "Heart of Darkness"). Reach the north rib route, and the two routes that follow, from the logged basin below the northeast buttress. Bushwhack up and to the right through bluffs and jungle to reach the hanging glacier. Climb through this sometimes broken glacier to the base of the rock. The route leads directly to the notch below the upper northwest corner, and then up cracks to the left of the crest. Stay to the left at the prominent snow patch. Fine rock; 27 pitches to Class 5.8 (mostly 5.6 and 5.7); good bivy at base. P. Croft soloed this route in 1983. The upper section is a worthwhile route in its own right; approach as for the northwest face.

North face couloir: *FA: P. Beckham, D. Serl, J. Wittmayer—January 27, 1980.* Route climbs the gully between the north rib and Fraser Ribber. About 21 pitches with a difficult exit and slopes to 70°. The route ends at the notch below the upper northwest corner. Few good belays, but little objective danger. First ascent party took 12 hours up from bivy at base of route.

Fraser Ribber: *FA: H. Fraser, P. Ourom—August 1982.* Begin on the north rib (see above), then switch to the prominent rib to the right of the north rib, once you get above the snow patch. About 15 pitches up to Class 5.8 on the rib. The route ends at the basin below the northwest side of the main peak.

East buttress: *FA: D. Mullen, J. Stoddard—August 1977.* Located about 200

Slesse Mountain in winter   1.) East buttress   2.) Northeast buttress   3.) North rib   4.) North face couloir   5.) Fraser Ribber   Jim Haberl

m/650 ft S of the northeast buttress, across the pocket glacier. This buttress steepens into the face in the upper half. Approach as for the northeast buttress. There is some fairly thin aid on this route and the occasional section of poor rock. The route angles slightly to the left across the side of the first small snowpatch and to the right around the second to finish on the skyline crest. Takes 2 days. Class 5.9, A3.

SLESSE MOUNTAIN—SOUTH PEAK 2345 m/7700 ft
FA: F. Beckey, J. Dudra, H. Staley—1952.
Northwest side: From the notch on the southwest shoulder of the main summit (see Slesse, west side), climb SE down a gully to gain saddle in the main divide which isolates the south peak. This point may also be gained directly up loose gullies from base of walls between the two peaks. Climb 1 lead up the divide, then keep to the right. Climbing to Class 5.4; 3 leads on fairly good rock.
South ridge: *FA: P. Binkert, J. Bryan, F. Gechter, E. Kafer—1961.* Swing under the west face of Slesse's main summit to base of the south peak, and start up a broad gully. Always take the right forks in the gully, and gain a prominent notch in the divide. Ascend steep, 12 m/40 ft pitch to scree cirque, then traverse left and climb wall and slanting chimney back to ridge, which leads to summit. Class 4; 5 hours up from base.
Southeast buttress: *FA: S. Flavelle, K. Nannery—June 1977.* The obvious buttress on the south peak. Approach via Nesakwatch Creek (*B6*). Climb headwall of cirque to right, traverse left into couloir, and ascend 3 pitches to where buttress rises to right. This point can also be reached by a traverse in from S. Climb near crest, first on left, then right. Below upper wall, cross left and finish by climbing up face, or angle back onto upper ridge. About 20 pitches to Class 5.7.

SLESSE MOUNTAIN—SOUTHEAST PEAKS
These are a succession of craggy summits trending SE from the south peak. They are not difficult to climb and may be reached from the west side of Slesse's main peak by traversing.
Labour Day Buttress: *FA: R. Culbert, F. Douglas, P. Starr—September 1, 1969.* This is the northeast buttress of the triangular east summit (GR 035305). Traverse to the base from the cirque below the east face of Slesse (*B6*). About 300 m/1000 ft of Class 5.4 on good rock. A striking line.

THE ILLUSION GROUP
All major lines from the Centre Creek side (*B9*) are gained in one of three ways:
1. From the highest logging spur to the W of Centre Creek (beginning 4.5 km from Chilliwack Lake road), gain "Disillusion Notch" between Guardian and Disillusion peaks. Climbing is up to Class 5.8 on greasy rock, but there may be fixed ropes. For descent, rappel from the notch using two fixed stations. Only a single rope is needed. Protection is poor on the climb to the notch if ropes are not in place.
2. From the second highest spur on the same road system, gain the northeast ridge of Guardian via an obvious draw. Climb to the summit (low Class 5) and descend to the notch.
3. Follow a route from the valley as indicated on the photograph. A couple of short Class 5 steps must be overcome.

NORTH ILLUSION PEAK
SOUTH ILLUSION PEAK
DISILLUSION PEAK
GUARDIAN PEAK

"Illusion Peaks"   1.) Northeast pillar   2.) Giant's Causeway   3.) Northeast buttress   4.) East ridge

Maxim de Jong

"GUARDIAN PEAK" 1800 m/5900 ft

A squat peak at the northeast end of the Illusion cirque, overlooking Centre Creek (*B9*), and featuring immense, clean slabs on several exposures.

FRA: D. de Jong, M. de Jong—August 1982.

Traversed from Disillusion Notch up the west ridge and down the northeast ridge. Class 5.7.

The Slabs: *FA: D. Harris, D. Mitten—1983.* Follow the bushy ledge which cleaves the southern slabs of Guardian. Where the ledge necks down, take slabs on the lefthand side. About 6 pitches to Class 5.7.

East ridge: *FA: M. de Jong, J. Roddan, G. Stead, J. Weaver—June 1985.* Leave the Illusions logging road spur (*B9*) at the first switchback and contour S around the toe of the northeast ridge to gain the base of the east ridge. The east and northeast ridges are separated by a gigantic cleft. Follow brushy ledges up the crest of the route and rope up at the end of the bush. From this point there are thirteen pitches of mainly slab climbing to 5.8 with generally poor protection. Take knifeblades, shallow and small angles. Exit from the route is difficult until you reach the top. Descend via the northeast ridge.

"DISILLUSION PEAK" 1985 m/6500 ft
Located on the divide immediately N of the Illusion Peaks.
Northeast face: *FA: J. Howe, B. Robinson—July 1982.* This climb goes up the centre of the face and involves 10 pitches (5 good ones). One slimy corner at mid-height was nut-aided. Class 5.8, A1.
East ridge (Ignoramus Ridge): *FA: M. de Jong, B. Kippan—December 7, 1982.* Approach via Disillusion Notch, then climb east ridge 365 m/1200 ft to the summit. The route in winter consists mainly of snow on steep granite steps and "upside down tree climbing." In summer, a Class 4 line (minor bush) with short, difficult class 5 steps. Take 6 or 7 chocks.

"ILLUSION PEAKS" 2100 m/6900 ft
Two steep granite summits on the divide N of Mt. Rexford. The massive, slabby faces on these peaks have become popular objectives.
FA: R. Culbert, R. Hatch, M. Lasserre, A. Shives—September 1961.
Northwest route: To climb both peaks from Centre Creek, climb to the summit of Disillusion Peak and descend to the gap beyond. Drop right and climb bushy Class 4–5 draw to ridge beyond gap, and walk along this to summit of northern (lower) Illusion Peak. Continue S down ridge in abrupt steps, then rappel into the gap which isolates the south summit. Drop to right down gully, then take the prominent ledge out onto the face beyond. From here it is 3 leads on steep granite. Difficulty need not exceed a stiff Class 4, but most parties get well into 5th class. The line goes up and slightly to the left for 2 leads, then back to the right behind protruding finger to easy summit ridge. On the return, there is one low 5th class lead out of the gap between summits—climb up, then left around corner from this col. This is a great traverse and an aesthetic route; a long day return from cars.

"ILLUSION PEAKS"—NORTH PEAK
West buttress: *FA: R. Culbert, F. Douglas, P. Starr, R. Wyborn—1972.* From the road on Nesakwatch Creek (*B6*), a gully leads to the gap N of Illusion Peaks. Ascend gully, then climb right on steep ramp under west face until on crest of nose. Route goes up this nose, involving several leads of Class 4 and 5, largely crack climbing. Tree ledges make the line less than classic but it is fun and rock is good. The one nasty-looking wall is turned by sneaking to right over a flake and around corner (Class 5.6). A full day's climb. Descend by the gully.
Northeast buttress: *FA: M. de Jong, H. Kim— August 9, 1981. FWA: D. Canton, B. Kay—March 1986.* Gain the base via Disillusion Notch. The climb is 10 pitches, up to Class 5.8, and involves both easy and interesting climbing. Begin at the toe of the buttress at 1675 m/5500 ft. An easy pitch leads to the base of a corner which is climbed, exiting to the right. Climb a broken face to the "Giant Slabs" at mid-height, gained by climbing the crest left of a large amphitheatre. From the top of the slabs, take bush ledges left to the rock crest adjacent to the "Giant's Causeway," a large, diagonal fault line (Class 4) which ascends to 2010 m/6600 ft on the north ridge. Follow this crest to ridge and summit. A recommended line.

"ILLUSION PEAKS"—SOUTH PEAK
South side: From the campsite W of Mt. Rexford (see below), go to the col one

bump S of Illusion Peaks, cross this bump and climb down ledges beyond. From here, the higher Illusion Peak is only Class 2–3. There is some exposure.

North face: *FA: P. Ourom, C. Thompson—July 1982.* A wall climb with 12 pitches; 5.9, A3. Much aid on knifeblades. Descend to E by rappels (now fixed) from notch between north and south peaks.

Memorial Pillar (Northeast pillar): *FA: M. de Jong, R. McLeod—July 1984. FWA: B. Kay, C. Zozikyan—February 14, 1986.* From "Pika Pond" at the base of the small "Illusion Glacier," a prominent gut cleaves the face. Route ascends the left edge of this cleft. Begin right of the gut, but move into it for the second pitch. Traverse left out of the gut onto an escape ramp, then climb straight up, heading towards a chimney behind prominent gendarme. From top of the gendarmes, climb a corner to "a spectacular hemlock," then take a loose gully to the base of a 40 m/130 ft off-width crack (aided, 6 bongs in place) which widens to a chimney. From here 3 pitches of face climbing followed by much Class 4 lead to the summit. Class 5.9, A3. The easiest lead is 5.7. Many fixed pins, but additional 4–8 inch bongs will be needed for the off-width, which is almost a full pitch long. An unusual and nicely situated climb with exciting variety.

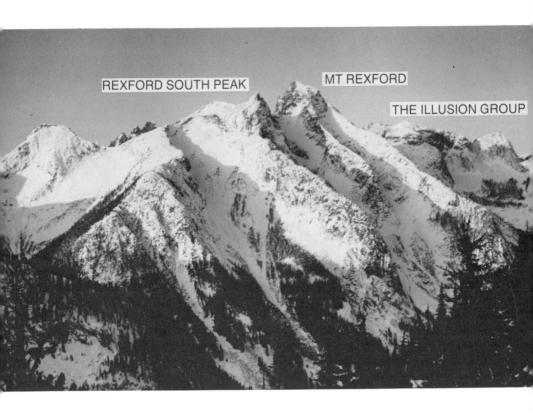

Mt. Rexford in winter   Harold Redekop

THE REXFORD GROUP

"NESAKWATCH SPIRES" 2255 m/7400 ft; 2195 m/7200 ft
Two sharp granite towers on the divide just N of Mt. Rexford.

"NESAKWATCH SPIRES" — SOUTH SPIRE
FA: H. Burton, T. Rollerson — August 1969.
The south ridge is most easily reached from the Rexford campsite via the easy gully leading to the col between the south spire and Rexford. From the col, several pitches of Class 4 lead to the top and an awkward 5 m summit block. The col can also be reached by climbing a prominent Class 4 ice gully on the NE (*FA: R. Coupe, L. Priest — 1970*).

"NESAKWATCH SPIRES" — NORTH SPIRE
Southwest ridge: *FA: M. Down, J. Howe — September 1982.* Six pleasant pitches to Class 5.8, beginning from Rexford basin. Descend via the ridge leading to the south peak (Class 3), then descend on broken ledges into basin. (Ref: *CAJ* 1982, p. 69.)
North ridge: *FA: K. Cover, B. Fairley, A. Ourom, R. Schneider — July 1984.* About 8 pitches to low Class 5, with difficulties avoidable on either side. Mostly Class 3, but a rope and a few slings and nuts are advisable.
Nesakwatch Notch: *FA: N. Jones, K. Sellers — July 7, 1984.* This is the large rib dropping NE into Centre Creek. Approach as for the northeast ridge of Rexford (see below). Climb couloir on the east side of the peak. Eight pitches to the top of the notch. From there, descend 60 m/200 ft, ending on blocky terraces. Climb a 2-pitch corner (5.9+) to the summit ridge, which is Class 4–5. To descend, rappel the east face at the point where the ridge is gained (5 double rope-lengths).

MT. REXFORD 2320 m/7600 ft
A prominent massif dominating the area E of Slesse Mountain; the highest point on the Centre-Nesakwatch divide. This granitic summit is characterized by cracks, slabs, pillars and buttresses, and provides some of the cleanest and finest climbing in the area. On map 92 H/4, the summit is incorrectly positioned about 0.5 km NW of the correct location.
FA: H. Genschorek, W. Sparling — 1951.
FWA: J. Arts, S. Flavelle, D. Mitten — January 1, 1978 (via northeast ridge).
West ridge: *FWA: S. Fuller, B. Griffiths, B. Kandiko, D. Serl — March 11, 1979.* About 5.5 km beyond the main creek crossing in Nesakwatch Creek valley (*B6*), a spur road climbs sharply uphill (about 880 m/2900 ft). A marked trail starts here, and ascends steeply into the meadowy basin NW of Rexford. Here you will find good campsites. Cross the basin to the toe of the west ridge. Ascend this (Class 3 and scrubby) to a steep section. (Alternatively, reach the ridge via an obvious but sometimes awkward snow gully.) Traverse left on a rising ledge system on the northwest face, then climb straight up a broken area to a false summit. Cross a Class 4 gap beyond to the main peak. Good rock and 3 hours up from camp. The upper west ridge itself may be ascended directly to false summit (*E. Hansen, B. Howard — 1967*), climbing cracks and ledges on the left side of ridge to jamcrack near the top. Ascend this, laybacking last pitch to summit. Class 5 and aesthetic.

Southwest side: From the shoulder on Rexford's west ridge, swing around to routes on the south side of the mountain. From the col SE of main summit, climb up and left through gully systems to a broad couloir which is followed to summit. This is a Class 3 climb, but on poorer rock than the other Rexford routes. The col can also be reached from the E via a steep, narrow couloir 300 m/1000 ft in height, and 50–55° in steepness (*M. Bitz, D. Jones, D. Serl—January 1980*).

Northeast ridge: *FA: H. Burton, J. Burton, C. Oloman, S. Saba—May 1969. FWA: J. Arts, S. Flavelle, D. Mitten—January 1, 1978*. Cross Centre Creek (*B9*) S of a bushy area and ascend through forest, traversing right into a gully at the first set of cliffs. Climb the gully and bluffs at its head to reach a second, heathery gully. Open slopes above this lead to a small moraine which offers good camping. From campsite, gain ridge crest via a prominent ledge and chimney and follow crest until ridge steepens, then complete climb on east face. Route is mainly Class 3–4. Most breaks can be avoided, but the odd Class 5 move should be anticipated. Alternatively, to gain the ridge from the south side, approach as for the east ridge, and gain the northeast ridge via a gully (actually a dyke), which lies directly across from the start of the east ridge climb. Class 4.

East ridge: *FA: J. Bryan, W. McNeil—July 1973*. This ridge may be approached directly from the Centre Creek road (*B9*). The climb starts slightly above and to the right of toe of ridge. Follow diagonal line up and left, heading for prow of ridge (easy Class 5). From prow there are 5–6 leads of Class 3–4; use the ridge crest and avoid difficulties to the right. Follow the ridge to summit, which is 2–3 leads above a flamelike pinnacle, or cross to S and traverse to slightly easier ground, scrambling final 100 m/350 ft to summit. Climb involves 10–12 leads of Class 4 or 5 without getting above a low 5. It will take at least a day from base. A classic moderate climb.

MT. REXFORD—SOUTH PEAK 2225 m/7300 ft
FA: A. Ellis, G. Woodsworth—September 1963.

West side: This summit may be reached from the camp on the west side of Rexford by crossing the ridge to the S and the basin beyond. From a point 120 m/400 ft below and N of the south peak, traverse S across the ledge system to gain the west ridge, which is followed to summit. NTD.

East ridge: *FA: B. Fairley, H. Redekop—September 15, 1980*. You reach this climb by ascending the steep and sometimes bushy gully lying S of the peak. The toe of this ridge is bushy and offers no obvious line. The first ascent party traversed the base of the ridge into the basin to the S (some bush) where a prominent green dyke was followed (low Class 5 and ugly) to the crest of the ridge. From here, a pleasant walk, a rappel, and some Class 3 climbing lead to the summit.

Pillar of Pi: *FA: J. Buszowski, J. Howe—August 1–2, 1981*. This route ascends a prominent pillar which rises from the gully between the east ridges of Rexford and the south peak. Begin on the crest of the pillar at the lowest tongue of rock, down and to the right of a prominent white scar. Follow the pillar for 5 leads of A1 and Class 5 until you gain a ledge system. Climb a further 2 pitches and a blank section (requiring pendulums to the left), and you will gain an upper corner system, which leads in turn to a spacious ledge. The angle lies back above the ledge and the climb can be finished free. Class 5.8, A2; 19 pitches (some short). Some thin pegs should be carried. (Ref: *CAJ* 1982, p. 30.)

"PI PILLAR" 2010 m/6600 ft

An immense block supported on two pillars and mounted on the north ridge of Rexford's south peak.

FA: R. Cuthbert, G. Mellor—1967.

Reach the Pillar either by rappelling from the south peak or by descending from the west shoulder of Rexford to the basin to the south side. Scramble up the west face beneath the pillar until you feel like roping up. One roped pitch of varied climbing to 5.7 leads to the crown of a block. From here it is one exposed step across to the summit. Descend by rappelling.

MT. COPE 2010 m/6600 ft

FA: Likely the Boundary survey.

An infrequently visited summit located on the international boundary at the head of Centre Creek. A scramble from the divide to the S.

MT. CORRIVEAU 1950 m/6400 ft

A forested ridge E of Centre Creek. Of little mountaineering interest, but pleasant ridge-top walking.

MT. WEBB 2163 m/7097 ft

Located immediately E of Radium Lake, 4 km N of Mt. Lindeman.

From Radium Lake (*B10*), ascend to the Webb-MacDonald saddle, and from there walk south ridge to summit. Good views of Chilliwack Lake. The northwest ridge can also be scrambled from the Radium Lake basin.

West face: *FA: K. Haberl, A. Ourom—July 1984.* Reach the centre of the bottom of the face from Radium Lake (*B10*). Climb 5 pitches up and somewhat to the right on decent rock to end just below summit. Mid Class 5. There are longer, more difficult possibilities further left.

MacDONALD PEAK 2225 m/7300 ft

FWA: H. Haberl, D. Serl, R. Tomich—January 6, 1980.

From the highest spur on the east side of Centre Creek (*B9*), ascend through bush, then over talus to the 1800 m/5900 ft saddle between MacDonald and Mt. Lindeman. From here, MacDonald is a pleasant scramble via the south ridge. You can also easily reach this peak by climbing around to the W from the Webb-MacDonald saddle. A third, popular, possibility is to approach along the pleasant, broad ridge from Radium Lake (*B10*).

East ridge: *K. Haberl, A. Ourom—July 1984.* Traverse from the Webb-MacDonald col (*B10*) to the base of the route. The ridge involves about 5 pitches of pleasant climbing on blocky, solid rock of up to low Class 5 difficulty. Its companion ridge on the south summit is bushy, except for the last 2 pitches, which require a short pendulum or rappel just below the summit.

MT. LINDEMAN 2310 m/7578 ft

A massive granite peak W of the south end of Chilliwack Lake. Its steep, complex northeast face is one of the most impressive sights in the Chilliwack River valley.

The north face of Mt. Lindeman   1.) North face   2.) North edge   Kevin Haberl

Named for an isolated trapper who was the sole resident at Chilliwack Lake in the 1930s.

FA: Likely by surveyors.

FWA: B. Fairley, H. Redekop—December 29, 1982.

From Centre Creek: Follow logging roads as far as possible up Centre Creek valley (*B9*), then follow steep, timbered slopes to gain the basin on the southwest side of the mountain. It is best not to cross the creek; stay on the north side. There will usually be some moderately steep snow on this route. Class 3; a day return.

From MacDonald Peak: To climb both MacDonald and Lindeman from the Radium Creek trail (*B10*) makes for a very long day. Descent from MacDonald is straightforward but if you don't want to lose a lot of elevation, climb 1 pitch of Class 5 (rappelled on descent) to gain the west ridge of Lindeman at about the 1800 m/5900 ft level. The entire west ridge can then be followed to the summit (Class 3, 1 possible rappel) on good rock. Alternatively, you can drop into the southwest bowl and complete the ascent by hiking up easy slopes and scrambling up a short ridge.

North edge: *FA: R. Driscoll, B. Fairley—August 1982.* Begin from the

MacDonald-Lindeman col. About 7 pitches of varied rock climbing from Class 3 to 5.6 lead to the west ridge.

North face: *FA: R. Culbert, F. Douglas, A. Purdey—October 1971.* This is a 1070 m/3500 ft climb on granite, but is not particularly aesthetic. The toe of the buttress is reached most easily by descending from the south ridge of MacDonald, approached by Centre Creek (*B9*). The lower portions are Class 3 and 4. Where the buttress fades into the face, transfer left into far gully and climb this until it ends in a chimney. Swing to the right around a big, white boil and continue to ledge above. Involves 5 leads of Class 5, minor aid, and poor rock in gullies. (Ref: *CAJ* 1972, p. 72.)

East ridge: *FA: B. Fairley, J. Manuel—September 1982.* The ridge was gained from Centre Creek (*B9*) by dropping over the south shoulder of MacDonald, crossing the basin below the north face, and ascending a steep, loose and obvious gully—one move of aid required. The ridge begins as a scramble, steepening to Class 5.8. The final, blank headwall is avoided by traversing left. Good rock. (Ref: *CAJ* 1982, p. 72.)

From Hanging Lake: A brushy ascent can be made first to the upper lake (*B15*) then to the southwest bowl. This route takes longer than climbs from the Centre Creek side.

MIDDLE PEAK 2276 m/7464 ft
Located 0.5 km S of the border near monument 60, 2 km SW of Mt. Lindeman.
FA: H. Custer, Mitchley, and an Indian friend—1859.
This peak can be approached from the west side of Lindeman (*B9, B10*) or from Hanging Lake (*B15*). The southwest ridge offers pleasant scrambling and the north snow slopes are reportedly NTD.

PALEFACE MOUNTAIN 1760 m/5800 ft; MT. MERONUIK 1800 m/5900 ft
Located 2 km due E of Chilliwack Lake. Both peaks are hikes from the desolate, ugly valley of Paleface Creek (*B13*).

MT. EDGAR 1980 m/6500 ft
Located between Depot and Paleface Creeks. A bushwhack from either Depot Creek (*B14*) or Paleface Creek (*B13*).

MT. REDOUBT 2730 m/8956 ft
A high, conspicuous summit E of Chilliwack Lake.
FA: J. Cherry, R. Ross—1930.
South face: Approach via Depot Creek (*B14*), swing around on Redoubt Glacier from the head of the creek, or climb a glacial couloir (badly crevassed late in season) to cross the divide NE of Redoubt. Ascend the steep, narrow cirque in Redoubt's south face, then scramble left onto snow and scree shoulder. (This shoulder may be

Mt. Redoubt, northeast face

Austin Post

THE PICKET RANGE

MT REDOUBT

DEPOT CREEK VALLEY

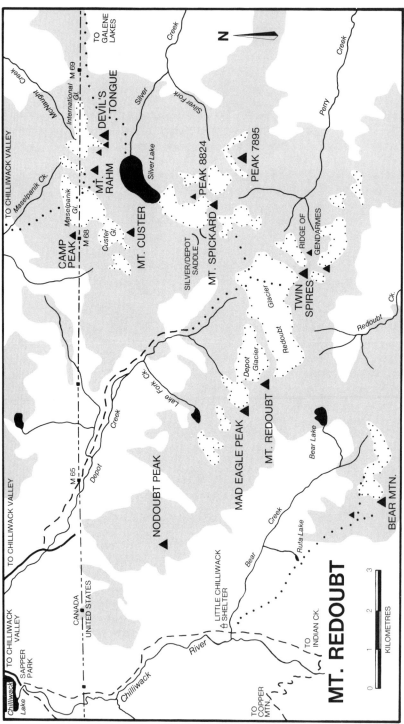

TO GALENE LAKES

DEVIL'S TONGUE

International Gl.

M 69

McNaught Creek

TO CHILLIWACK VALLEY

Silver Creek

Silver Fork

MT. RAHM

Maselpanik Ck.

Maselpanik Gl.

Silver Lake

Silver

PEAK 8824

PEAK 7895

Perry Creek

N

CAMP PEAK

M 68

Custer Gl.

MT. CUSTER

SILVER/DEPOT SADDLE

MT. SPICKARD

Glacier

RIDGE OF GENDARMES

TWIN SPIRES

Redoubt Ck.

Redoubt

TO CHILLIWACK VALLEY

M 65

Depot Creek

Lake Fork Ck.

NODOUBT PEAK

Depot Glacier

Redoubt Glacier

MAD EAGLE PEAK

MT. REDOUBT

Bear Lake

BEAR MTN.

CANADA
UNITED STATES

TO CHILLIWACK VALLEY

SAPPER PARK

Chilliwack Lake

Chilliwack River

LITTLE CHILLIWACK SHELTER

Bear Creek

Ruta Lake

TO INDIAN CK.

TO COPPER MTN.

MT. REDOUBT

0   1   2   3
KILOMETRES

gained directly from the W by parties crossing from Depot Creek.) Several gullies lead up from shoulder. Start on the righthand part of an obvious ledge, but before the gully here, cut back on a steep Class 3 rock ramp or break; follow this into an easier gully leading to a notch beside the main peak. Scramble to the top. Rock is extremely rotten.

West flank: Easily reached from Bear Lake (*B16*) or from Depot Creek (*B14*) via the glacial couloir mentioned in the south face route above. The route runs to the upper part of the northwest ridge, which it follows. It is Class 3–4 except for one annoying Class 5 notch. Rock is poor.

Northeast face: *FA: F. Beckey, J. Rupley—1971. FWA: R. Barley, P. Rowat—February 1977 (to the east ridge only).* The most popular line today. Route ascends the obvious ice tongue on the face, continuing on steep snow to a final couloir leading to a notch in the summit ridge or to easy Class 5 rock to right of the couloir. Take ice gear for this deserved classic. (Ref: *CAJ* 1978, p. 81.)

"TWIN SPIRES" (MOX PEAKS)

Two dark rock towers located 3 km SE of Mt. Redoubt. The southeast summit is the higher. Approach via Depot Creek (*B14*).

"TWIN SPIRES"—NORTHWEST SPIRE 2535 m/8320 ft
FA: F. Beckey, H. Beckey—June 21, 1941.
North ridge: Climb to the low point in the ridge from the small glacier; Class 4. Follow ridge until about 60 m/200 ft below the summit, then traverse left until directly below the summit. A steep pitch straight up to the notch, then another to the summit complete this historic route. Class 5. Takes 5 hours from the Depot Creek divide.

West ridge: *FA: D. Hendricks, S. Jensen, M. Loranger, W. Van de Graff—August 12, 1964.* From the glacier on the west side, ascend to the top of a snow finger and traverse (Class 3) across the north face of the tower to the notch on the west ridge. Climb ridge to summit. Class 4–5; takes 5 hours.

Southeast face: *FA: D. Adams, D. Goodman—July 28, 1980.* From the notch between the two spires, climb up the obvious gully 10 m to a ledge. Carry on up the loose Class 5 gully to the left of a prominent gendarme. Gain a gully to the left and climb it to the northeast ridge, from which the regular route can be gained.

"TWIN SPIRES"—SOUTHEAST SPIRE 2585 m/8480 ft
FA: F. Beckey, H. Beckey—June 22, 1941.
Gain the notch in the "Ridge of the Gendarmes" immediately below the summit, and beside an overhanging gendarme, by ascending a gully on the west side. The base of this gully can be reached from the col between the spires by going S along ledges and crossing a rib running W from the ridge. From the notch, descend 30 m/100 ft in a steep gully, then traverse right another 75 m/250 ft. From here, climb straight up, keeping to the right of a white overhang, then continue up a steep white groove (Class 5.6) to the top. Takes 6 hours return from the col. Variations of this route have been done, including an ascent from the notch higher up the Ridge of Gendarmes via a "whitish horn." This is a steep and exposed route, also mid Class 5.

MT. SPICKARD 2706 m/8879 ft
Highest peak in the ''Chilliwacks.''
FA: Boundary Survey—1904.
From Depot Creek: Ascend Depot Creek (*B14*) valley toward Twin Spires, then swing E up easy terrain to gain an obvious 40o snow couloir on the southwest face which is followed to its head. Steep Class 3–4 scrambling for 60 m/200 ft leads to the summit.
From Silver Creek: Reach the glacier on the northeast side of Spickard from Depot Creek (*B14*) or from the south fork of Silver Creek (Skagit chapter, *A16*). The ascent from here is not very difficult. Takes 5 hours up from camp. A long snow couloir on the mountain's southeast face has also been used, but the approach to this via Perry Creek has fallen into disuse.
North face: *FA: BCMC party led by P. Binkert—1959.* Approach via Galene Lakes (see Skagit Chapter [*A13*]) or the Silver-Depot saddle (*B14*) to this attractive snow face above Silver Lake. Make an ascending traverse across the north face to gain the north ridge about 60 m/200 ft below the summit or, if conditions are favourable, just crampon right on up to the top. Steepness may reach 50°. Great for skis.

PEAK 8824 2690 m/8824 ft
Located N of Mt. Spickard.
FA: R. Culbert—1961.
From the southeast side of the lake at the head of Silver Creek (*B14* or Skagit chapter, *A16*), scramble to scree and slabs above the first line of bluffs. Traverse toward the peak until able to climb ice to the col at base of the north ridge. This ridge is Class 3 on shattered rock.

BEAR MOUNTAIN 2421 m/7942 ft
A steep rock ridge with a huge north face rising S of Bear Creek and W of the Chilliwack River.
FA: C. Bressler, W. Thompson—August 1939.
Northwest ridge: About 200 m/660 ft beyond the Bear Creek shelter (*B16*), the trail turns right; pick up an obscure side trail on the left here. This quickly peters out, but rather than following it to its end, continue up the divide from where the trail swings S, and gain the northwest ridge as soon as possible. Ruta Lake (1536 m/5040 ft) makes a good campsite. From here, climb up the divide to the summit. Class 3 with some minor Class 5 near the summit.
North face (west buttress): *FA: A. Kearney, S. Kearney, E. Newville, J. Thomas—September 11, 1977.* Approach by descending from the saddle beyond Ruta Lake. The first ascent party bivvied 120 m/400 ft up, then climbed up and left into a chimney. The route generally follows the left edge of the buttress. It is 17 pitches; Class 5.9.
North face (north buttress): *FA: F. Beckey, M. Fielding—July 14–15, 1967.* Approach as for the north face (west buttress), traversing scree and snow to a small glacier below the face. This is a very steep wall of about 760 m/2500 ft. The route runs up a pocket under the main summit, then onto the buttress on the right. Climbing is mainly free, but there is a section in the upper part requiring A4 and then a difficult traverse (pendulums) off the crest to the right. Takes 2 days. (Ref: *AAJ* 1968, p. 67.)

East ridge: *FA: R. Fahy, D. Hendricks, S. Jensen, M. Loranger, J. Stout, A. Tatyrek, W. Van de Graff—August 14, 1964.* Reach the long east ridge from upper Indian Creek (*B16a*). At the notch between the highest summits, the route meets the south ridge. Class 4.

South side: Class 5 rock routes have been done on the south face of Bear, and there seem to be several possible lines on the gullies and ribs here. Rock is loose in places. Probably best approached via Ruta Lake (*B14*).

NODOUBT PEAK 2222 m/7290 ft
A rugged, pyramidal summit 5 km NW of Redoubt.
FRA: D. Fraser—1935.
From the east or west: NTD; offers good views on the northern Silver Lake peaks. The south ridge is also reported to be easy.
North face: *FA: M. de Jong, G. Manning, J. Roddan, G. Stead—March 2, 1985.* From the basin beneath the face follow the main couloir up and right, then switch to a second, steeper couloir on the left which leads directly to the summit.

MAD EAGLE PEAK 2463 m/8080 ft
A twin-summited rock peak 1 km NW of Mt. Redoubt. The east summit is higher and easier to climb.
FA: S. Allabach, J. Medlicott, J. Roper—August 1979.
North ridge: Make a descending traverse from the col NW of the summit to ascend slab and scree to the ridge, which is a Class 3 scramble.
East face: *FA: D. Campbell, M. de Jong, M. Evans, D. Houtman, D. Kinischuk, D. Owen, Q. Pham, J. Wheelan—1984.* Ascend the "West Depot Glacier," taking the highest tongue on the right before the Redoubt-Mad Eagle col. From the top right corner of the icefield, climb a 5.6 crack 1 pitch to the summit ridge, then scramble over horrible rock to the summit.

WILLIAMS PEAK 2123 m/6965 ft
A rock horn located above the Chilliwack River 6 km/4 mi NW of Chilliwack Lake.
FA: Canadian Boundary Survey—1908.
Normal route: You can reach this peak from the top of the trail (*B8*) by following the long west ridge to the base of the southwest slopes. Ascend heather and Class 3 rock on this side. About 5 hours up, and pleasant. The southwest side has also been gained by climbing directly to the base from the Chilliwack Lake road (*B8*). A gully and chimney on the west face have also been used—rope required.
East buttress: *FA: J. Howe, D. Serl—October 9, 1980.* Approach via a traverse across the south face from the normal trail. A grassy ramp provides access to the base of the buttress. After 1–2 pitches of Class 5.7, you will reach several more pitches of mainly Class 4: "short walls, a bit of bush, mostly steep but moderate." About 10 hours return.
Northeast ridge: *FA: M. Down, J. Howe—September 1982.* The companion ridge to the east buttress is of similar length and difficulty.

"GOAT PEAK" ("PORCUPINE PEAK") 1980 m/6500 ft
A bulky, granitic summit 2 km E of Williams Peak.
FRA: W.E. Ricker and a hunting companion—about 1933.

Gain the ridge from Post Creek campsite (*B11*). A long and easy ridge walk leads to the bald summit. Descend via "Marmot Creek," ENE of summit, down to Lindeman Lake trail (*B11*). "Marmot Lake" (1480 m/4850 ft) is a beautiful spot. In descending, stay in open timber, well away from creek gorge where terrain steepens at 1220 m/4000 ft. For an alternate route, see Mt. Nowell (Skagit chapter).

GOETZ PEAK 2010 m/6600 ft
Located 2 km N of Williams Peak. Climbed by traversing over Williams Peak on the west side, or by hiking E from spur on Foley Creek road (*B5*).

MT. LAUGHINGTON 1770 m/5800 ft
An open ridge between Chipmunk and Airplane creeks.
Take the Foley Creek road and follow it for 1.4 km, to the bridge across Foley Creek. Cross the bridge and turn left. After about 100 m a switchback to the right heads uphill. Take this switchback and continue up, taking the highest logging spur to its end, where a trail begins. Follow the trail and open ground to the summit, which is pleasant terrain and has an excellent view. An easy, 1 day return hike. Mt. Laughington may also be reached via Airplane Creek (see Cheam Range chapter); this route takes 3–4 hours up from cars.

ELK MOUNTAIN 1430 m/4700 ft; MT. THURSTON 1625 m/5335 ft; MT. MERCER 1710 m/5500 ft
Three minor summits at the west end of the ridge between Chilliwack and Fraser rivers. All these summits are served by a hiking trail, which is marked from a small gravel pit by Elkview Road, 12 km/7.5 mi S of Bailey Road above Vedder Crossing (*A*). Takes 2 1/2 hours to Elk, 4 hours to Thurston, and 5 1/2 to Mercer. Thurston also has an extension of the Mt. Mercer road almost to its summit on the northeast side (*B5b*).

Chapter 24

The Cheam Range

BOUNDARIES:
North: Wahleach Creek and Wahleach (Jones) Lake
East: Foley Creek and Foley Lake Road
South: Airplane Creek and Chipmunk Creek basin
West: Trans Canada Highway

FOREST SERVICE OFFICE:
Chilliwack Forest District
P.O. Box 159
9850 South McGrath Road
Rosedale, B.C. V0X 1X0
794-3361

LOGGING COMPANIES:

Herman Sawmills
P.O. Box 3160
Mission, B.C. V2V 4J4
826-2771
(Chipmunk Creek, Airplane Creek)

Cattermole Timber
R.R. #1, Sardis, B.C. V0X1Y0
Sardis, B.C. V0X1Y0
823-6525
(Foley Lake Roads)

MAPS:
Federal:
92 H/4
Provincial:
92 H/SW
Recreation Map of the North Cascades (Beckey-Cardwell)
Outdoor Recreation Map of British Columbia #11, Chilliwack-Hope-Skagit

Introduction and History

Despite having some pretty detestable rock, the "Cheam Range" remains a popular climbing area. Ease of access and a conspicuous location no doubt have a lot to do with this. Cheam Peak itself is the most striking of all summits visible from the Fraser Valley, and with 2100 m/6800 ft of relief from the valley floor, the mountain is a prominent and imposing landmark from as far away as 50 km/30 mi. The four eastern peaks of the range are known as the "Lucky Four Group," after the old mine site of that name, and early access into the area was provided by the first mine road, built during the First World War. This road ran up Wahleach Creek past Wahleach (Jones) Lake, from where stunning views of the big northern and eastern faces, many of them glaciated, may be obtained. Any peak in the Cheam Range can be climbed in a day by fast parties.

Despite the popularity of the area, few big routes have been established. The shattered volcanic rock tends to demoralize the big wall crowd, who have found the challenges across the valley in the Chilliwack area more to their liking. The Cheam group is rapidly gaining popularity, however, as a winter mountaineering mecca. All the summits have now had winter ascents.

The most outstanding climbs completed to date have been on the north face of Cheam Peak. The route was first attempted in the 1920s by Stan Henderson and Fred Parkes, a team which bagged the first ascent of Slesse Mountain. The route exists now in two versions. The first, climbed during a July long weekend in 1975 by Don Serl, Doug Herchmer, Don Hepner, and Kurt Ulmer, was Serl's first new route in the Coast Mountains. The second line, which takes the centre of the face, was put up as a winter climb by Maxim de Jong and Robert McGregor in March of 1981. The pair was minimally equipped for the challenges encountered and endured a stormy summit bivouac before making a forced retreat in whiteout conditions down the unknown ground of the east face. Their climb took 32 hours to complete. A fine couloir route on the east face of Lady Peak was recently climbed in winter.

The Cheam Range is not as well contoured as it might be on maps, and not all of the ridges and buttresses that seem prominent from the ground are shown on the sheets. An effort has been made in this guide, however, to match route names with features shown on the maps, so that a route formerly called the northwest ridge may now be called the north ridge if the map indicates that this is the more appropriate name.

The range has been traversed in both directions. The first traverse by Jack Bryan and Jim Craig, from Cheam Peak to Foley Peak, was made in the summer of 1961.

Approaches

A. FROM THE NORTH
All routes diverge from the Trans Canada Highway E of Chilliwack.

1. The Cheam Peak road: Take the Bridal Veil Falls turnoff on the right at Popkum. About 1 km past the unspeakably monstrous "Bedrock City," turn right up the Cheam Peak road, a gravel road (usually signposted) which begins beside an old wood-frame cottage. This road climbs the north flank of Cheam Peak, and forks at 760 m/2500 ft. The east fork, guarded by a small stream, leads to "Killarney Valley" or "Spoon Valley," where the standard (flagged) trail up the west ridge of Cheam begins. The west fork of the road switchbacks up the north flank of Cheam and crosses the divide to the W, eventually joining roads in Chipmunk Creek. This west branch is completely blocked by slides. You will need a four-wheel drive vehicle to reach the fork.

2. The Cheam Peak trail: Use this trail to approach Cheam's north face and northeast ridge. An obscure spur road leaves the Trans Canada Highway 4.5 km E of Popkum exactly where the powerlines cross the highway. Follow this spur for 1 km and park at a faint creek bed (GR 949518). From here, the beginning of the trail is hard to find; look for occasional markers leading S, away from the highway. Once found, the trail is well marked and easy to follow. It climbs to 1280 m/4200 ft on slopes E of the summit.

3. Popkum road: This road climbs to 1370 m/4500 ft on Four Brothers Ridge and was once used to gain Cheam's northeast ridge. It is now very overgrown and parties should use the trail (*A2*). The road itself leaves the highway just before the Hydro power house on the Trans Canada Highway.

4. Wahleach (Jones) Lake roads: You can approach all peaks in the range from these roads. From Laidlaw on the Trans Canada Highway, take the road which climbs to Wahleach Lake ("Jones Lake") at 640 m/2100 ft. The road forks 3.5 km from the north end of the lake. Follow the left branch for 3 km; it climbs the east side of "Flat Creek," which flows down from the Welch-Foley basin, and ends at a washout (1070 m/3500 ft). From here, a route using old roads climbs SE to Conway Peak. Foley Peak can be easily approached from this point. It may now be faster to take the right branch of the road, which heads along the valley floor for 2 km and ends about 2 hours (easy cross country) from the base of Foley.

To approach the east side of Lady or Cheam, follow the road that runs along the southeast shore of the lake (right branch) and park at the washed-out bridge. Follow the road for another 0.5 km, then cut onto the lake shore. Regain the old road about 0.5 km from the south end of the lake, and then follow game trails into moderate bush. Traverse the heavily forested slopes to the S (left) of the prominent stream gully running from the Lady-Cheam col, and enter the gully when the bush becomes unbearable.

B. FROM THE SOUTH

All routes diverge from the Chilliwack Lake road. From the Trans Canada Highway, take the turnoff for Cultus Lake/Sardis (southward) at Chilliwack and drive S along Vedder Road to Vedder Crossing. Before crossing the bridge over the Chilliwack River, turn left onto the Chilliwack Lake road. Distances are from this point.

1. Foley Lake road: A bridge crosses the Chilliwack River at 27.4 km/17 mi. Turn left immediately after crossing the bridge. The road crosses Foley Creek after 1.5 km, where it then forks.

1a. Chipmunk Creek road: Take the left branch and follow it back along the north side of the Chilliwack River for 1.4 km. A road here climbs N along Chipmunk Creek to the basin south of Cheam Peak. It is usually gated and currently is in fine condition.

1b. Mt. Laughington trail: Take the left branch, as for Chipmunk Creek, and switchback right immediately onto the old Mt. Laughington road, which is now washed out.

1c. Foley Lake road: Take the right fork after crossing the bridge. This fork ascends Foley Creek to Foley Lake (800 m/2600 ft).

1d. Airplane Creek road: This road turns steeply uphill off the Foley Lake road about 1.3 km before the lake and 4.2 km from Chilliwack Lake road. The gate has been removed, and the bridge rebuilt. If walking, parties can save time by using an old skid trail which cuts off the first long switchback and is picked up about 1 km up the road at the first bridge. Takes 2–2 1/2 hours to the head of the basin. Good access to the central peaks of the range.

1e. Williamson Lake trail: About 6.4 km/4 mi from the Chilliwack Lake road, a flagged trail climbs very steeply from the Foley Lake road to the attractive Williamson Lake. Cross Foley Lake on a logjam to gain the trail, which begins on the north side of the lake. About 3 hours up.

Routes

CHEAM PEAK 2107 m/6913 ft

Tourist route: From the end of the Cheam road's east fork (*A1*), an obvious trail ascends to the southwest ridge. Hike up the ridge (well flagged) avoiding minor difficulties (steep rock) to the right. There is one exposed area. A long day return if you walk the Cheam road.

Via Chipmunk Creek: Ascend from the end of the road (*B1a*) up easy south slopes. NTD. A reasonable ski trip under good conditions, although the road itself is a fairly boring ski.

The north face of Cheam Peak   1.) North face direct   2.) North face   Don Serl

Northeast ridge: *FA: J. Baldwin and companion—1957.* Approach by Cheam Peak trail (*A2*). The ridge is Class 4, but much of the climbing does not actually follow the ridge but is done on the face (Class 4), about 30 m/100 ft below it. Use an obvious gully to surmount the cliff band at the top. Rope advised.

North face direct: *FA: M. de Jong, R. McGregor—March 21, 1981.* Approach by the Cheam Peak trail (*A2*). A challenging alpine route most feasible under winter conditions. From the trail's end, proceed to an obvious wooded knoll at the base of the large snowfields. Ascend steep snow ramps left of the centre of the face, then move right to the rocky crest directly above the knoll. From the highest end of the ramps, move right around a corner, then straight up to a "perched boulder belay." Turn cliffs above to the right, gaining the obvious cleft left of summit. Snow and ice to 75°, rock to 5.7. Take some thin pins and don't expect to be back for tea. (Ref: *CAJ* 1982, p. 60.)

North face—right side: *FA: D. Serl, D. Herchmer, D. Heppner, K. Ulmer—June 30, 1975; FWA: M. de Jong, G. Manning, J. Roddan, G. Stead—March 9, 1985.* This is a serious mixed climb involving a variety of challenges and made more dangerous because of falling stones. From the top of the Cheam Peak trail (*A2*), take avalanche runouts to a wooded knoll in the centre of the base of the north face. Ascend a pocket glacier here, then cut back left across a rock band for 1 lead. In winter, a 100 m/330 ft couloir (50°) on the right may be used. Another 1 1/2 leads on snow then take you to the upper rock wall. Traverse right along the base of this wall for 3 leads to a corner, then follow easier snow and rock up to a point where the southwest ridge blends into the face. About 100 m/300 ft of scrambling on poor rock then lead to the northwest ridge. The first ascent party made their exit about 100 m W of the summit. Knifeblades and horizontals are recommended for belay stations. The climb takes 8 hours up from the knoll. Under good conditions, a classic winter line.

LADY PEAK 2164 m/7100 ft

FRA: I. Henderson, E. Knight, J.R. Smith—1889.
Approach via Cheam Peak (*A1*) or via Chipmunk Creek (*B1a*). The west face of Lady can be gained by either of the above approaches; the climb from the Cheam-Lady col is a scramble, while the route from Chipmunk Creek makes a feasible ski ascent.

Northeast couloir: *FA: P. Cooper, W. Noble, K. Sellers—December 27–29, 1985.* This was once a much sought after first ascent. As you approach from Jones Lake, the route is clearly visible. There is some bad bush at the end of the lake. The lowest section above a broad avalanche fan is the crux. It may vary from steep rock to very steep ice, depending on season, and is about 1 pitch long. Beyond, the couloir is mainly moderate snow climbing, but there is a "thin" steep section 2 rope lengths from the summit ridge. It is probably not very feasible to avoid the crux by ascending flanks either side of the couloir and rappelling in, despite appearances.

KNIGHT PEAK 2237 m/7340 ft

FA: E. Knight—1892.
The easiest peak in the Cheam Range, Knight Peak is also the least visited.
Via Airplane Creek: Ascend from the Airplane Creek road (*B1d*) as for Baby Munday, which may be bypassed either to the W or E. You can then saunter up the easy slopes to Knight Peak's broad summit ridge. It is also possible to follow Airplane Creek to its headwaters in a narrow, south-facing basin, and from there, to climb the northwest ridge—likely a steep scramble. This basin can also be reached via Lady Peak (possible rappel) or from Chipmunk Creek road by ascending from the road over the south shoulder of Lady.

BABY MUNDAY PEAK 2190 m/7200 ft

This sharp rock peak, named for Edith Munday, looks like a miniature version of Slesse when viewed from Airplane Creek. Although routes are somewhat exposed in places, it is not a particularly difficult climb.

FA: W. Dobson, W. Henderson—1933.

FWA: J. Bryceland and party—1978.

From the Airplane Creek road (*Bld*), drop into the creek valley and ascend the gully which drops southward from the peak, keeping to the lefthand side when the gully divides. The true summit is hidden from view until you traverse around the south buttress of the peak.

South ridge: Ascend to the col between the main summit tower and the south shoulder. This can be accomplished either from the E or W. The ridge is Class 3–4 on loose rock and requires a rope. Under winter conditions, this route can provide an enjoyably exposed and corniced Class 4 climb.

North face: *FA: J. Bryan, J. Craig—1961.* Make 1 rappel from the lower middle peak of Baby Munday to a gap between Baby Munday and the higher southern summit. Two Class 4 pitches on good rock lead to the top.

STEWART PEAK 2230 m/7300 ft

FA: Believed to be by E. Knight, D. Walker—September 1884.

FWA: H. Redekop—February 1982.

Approach as for Baby Munday. The southeast and southwest ridges are both scrambles. In winter, you can ski up this side almost to the summit.

North buttress: *FA: A. Bitterlich, H. Mather—July 1967.* At present, the approach from Wahleach (Jones) Lake (*A4*) to the base involves striking through several hours of bush. Begin in a prominent snow gully, transferring right at the midway point to gain the face and buttress. Reportedly good rock, but few other details are available. A very full day, and one of the biggest routes in the area. Likely unrepeated.

THE STILL 2286 m/7500 ft

FA: A. Cooper, F. Smith, F. Spouse—1925.

FWA: K. Dixon, H. Redekop, R. Snutch—1977.

An easy ascent from the W or NW. The peak is gained as for Baby Munday or Stewart Peak.

WELCH PEAK 2440 m/8000 ft

Highest peak in the Cheam Range. On Map 92 H/4 the name is incorrectly placed on the lower south peak.

FA: A. Cooper, F. Smith, B. Spouse—1924.

FWA: D. Serl—February 25, 1978, via the south ridge.

After Cheam Peak, Welch is the most popular mountaineering objective in the Cheam Range. Glaciers cover much of the mountain's northern and eastern flanks. The peak is an impressive sight from beautiful Williamson Lake (*Ble*), and this is

The northwest face of Welch Peak   Harold Redekop

now the preferred approach, although the climb can also be done from Wahleach Lake (*A4*) or Airplane Creek (*Bld*). A winter traverse of the mountain was completed in early March of 1981, after several attempts, by Bob Stair and Harold Redekop; they ascended the west face and descended via the east ridge.

East ridge: Gain the col between Welch and Foley directly from Williamson Lake (*Ble*), or by traversing the crevassed Foley Glacier from a camp below Conway Peak. Climb Welch's east ridge on loose rock, bypass the prominent gendarme by making a 15 m descent, and traverse on the south face. Class 3. Takes 3 hours up from either camp.

Southeast face: This face, which stands above Williamson Lake (*Ble*), is an easy Class 3 climb. The usual line runs to the south ridge just below the summit.

South ridge: *FA: E. Kafer, M. Kafer—1965.* Rises above Williamson Lake (*Ble*). Class 3–4 on reasonably firm rock.

West face: *FA: H. Redekop, B. Stair—March 1981.* Approach via Airplane Creek (*Bla*). Ascend the huge gully which drops from the Welch-Still col into Airplane Creek. At about 1520 m/5000 ft, turn right into a broad snow face and follow gullies to a point between the main summit of Welch and the south summit (2357 m/7733 ft). Class 3 and 4. If you are making a S-N traverse of the range, this route can be used for descent.

Northwest face: *FA: M. de Jong, B. Fairley, H. Redekop—February 7, 1982.* Approach as for the west face, but ascend almost to the Welch-Still col (a beautifully exposed gap), and take the last major chute on the right before entering the col. The line involves about 275 m/900 ft of steep snow to about 50° and a couple of tricky mixed moves (they may require a rope) just below the summit. This climb takes 13 hours return from the Foley Lake road (*B1*). (Ref: *VOCJ* 1981, p. 87.)

FOLEY PEAK 2307 m/7570 ft

A steep pyramid of loose, rusty rock located at the east end of the Cheam Range.

FA: B. Cayley, D. Foster, E. Fuller, D. Munday, P. Munday, H. O'Conner, B. Wheatley—May 1924.

FWA (via southeast ridge): P. Berntsen, K. McComber, P. Stoliker—December 1974.

Southeast face: Approach via Wahleach (Jones) Lake (*A4*). The original route apparently ascended the "Lucky Four Glacier" on the east face to the northeast arête about 100 m/300 ft below the summit. This glacier is not shown on current maps. There is likely to be snow on the face early in the season; rock scrambling may be involved later on.

Southeast ridge: Approach via Wahleach Lake (*A4*). Traverse under the east face, then ascend to a broad notch in the ridge. Once gained, the route stays to the left of the crest in short gullies and easy Class 3 terrain.

Southwest face: Approach via Williamson Lake (*Ble*). Gain the Welch-Foley col, then ascend slopes (possibly snow) to cross a gap in Foley's southwest ridge. Descend to the south face and take your pick of various nondescript lines wandering up from this side. Ropes are advised as a rappel may be necessary to regain base on descent. Class 3 but could be Class 4 if your route finding's off.

Southwest ridge: *FA: G. Walter, E. Zenger—1971.* This is a steep ridge with climbing to 5.5 and some loose rock. A dramatic challenge.

North ridge: *FA: D. Jones, D. Serl—1979.* The top few leads of this route were climbed by J. Fairley, T. Fyles, and E. Otten in the 1930s, who gained it on early season snowgullies from the W. The full ridge is 5.6 on "uncomfortably loose rock."

CONWAY PEAK 2000 m/6560 ft

The high point of a ridge running northwest from Foley Peak. A walk from all sides. Best approached from Wahleach Lake (*A4*).

Chapter 25

Skagit

BOUNDARIES:
North: Highway 1
East: Highway 3, Skagit River, Ross Lake road, Mount Hozameem
South: Lightening Creek
West: Chilliwack Lake, Depot Creek, Wahleach Creek and Lake

FOREST SERVICE OFFICE:
Chilliwack Forest District
P.O. Box 159
9850 South McGrath Road
Rosedale, B.C. V0X 1X0
794-3361

LOGGING COMPANIES:

G and F Logging Co. Ltd.
P.O. Box 99
Hope, B.C. V0X 1L0 (Maselpanik Creek)
869-9032, 869-2030

Herman Sawmills
P.O. Box 3160
Mission, B.C. V2V 4J4 (Klesilkwa Creek)
826-2771

Cattermole Timber
R.R. #1
Sardis, B.C. V0X 1Y0 (Yola and Depot
creeks) 823-8525

Whonnock Lumber Div.
Whonnock, B.C. V0M 1S0
(Silverhope Creek)
462-7111

MAPS:
Federal:
92 H/3 Skagit River
92 H/6 Hope
Provincial:
92 H/SW
Outdoor Recreation Map of B.C. #11: Chilliwack-Hope-Skagit.
U.S. Maps:
Mt. Challenger 1:62,500
Mt. Spickard 1:24,000
Hozomeem Mountain 1:62,500
Washington Green Trails series:
WA-NO 15 Mt. Challenger
WA-NO 16 Ross Lake
Recreation Map of the North Cascades (Beckey-Cardwell)

Introduction and History

This region contains a great many summits of moderate elevation which are seldom climbed, as well as several higher uplifts which are reasonably popular. On the whole, rock quality in this area cannot compare with that of adjacent areas, such as the Chilliwack valley or the Chehalis. Consequently, the region has not proven popular in the 1980s among climbers who are pushing the big routes in the mountains. The most challenging lines in the Skagit region were established in the 1970s. The knowledge gained in that period has brought almost all climbs here now within the ability of a moderately experienced mountaineer. This is not to say that some are not challenging, since poorer rock may make it harder to find protection, or require more careful route finding. Also, anyone who completes one of the more serious routes on Rideout, Hozomeen, Redoubt or the Twin Spires can feel satisfied that they have been out on a big face.

A few of the climbs in this area are classics in their own way. The northeast face of Redoubt is an outstanding alpine climb, involving all the elements that make general mountaineering such a joy: steep snow and ice, the need for route finding through the preliminary icefall, serious length, and a finish on reasonable rock. Any climb of the Hozomeen peaks is an exhilarating experience, for they stand as isolated and fierce towers, visible from much of the Skagit region, and a long, steep climb is required before any of the three summits can be topped. The Sumallo Valley can be recommended as a fine spot for winter mountaineering, as the approaches are easy and the weather often a little drier than in the country farther to the west.

There is still some room left to explore the nooks and crannies of the Skagit Range. Roads radiate from the Ross Lake road (the principal line of access) up almost every side valley now, and some of the peaks tucked away up some of these creeks have had very few recorded ascents. Washington State authorities have decided recently not to raise Ross Lake and flood the Skagit valley as had been planned, so future generations can continue to enjoy this region.

Approaches

A. FROM THE ROSS LAKE ROAD (SILVER-SKAGIT ROAD)
Runs from the Trans Canada Highway (Highway 1) to the American border. All distances are measured from Highway 1. Turn right off the Trans Canada Highway onto the Ross Lake road at the Riviera Motel sign shortly before Hope and immediately before the bridge across Silverhope Creek (signposted). The road crosses the creek near Silver Lake, crosses to the north side of the Klesilkwa River, then finally joins the Skagit River, which it follows down to Ross Lake (63 km/39 mi).

A government campground on the American side of the border swarms with campers and motor homes on popular weekends. The following roads and trails branch from the Ross Lake road and give access to mountains in the Skagit area.

1. Sowerby Creek road (6.4 km/4 mi): A road branches to the right, passes over a bridge and leads eventually to a ratty campsite on the west side of Silver Lake. Popular among gorbies on the weekends. Two spur roads climb W.

1a. Eureka Mine road: Gated. This road is in good repair (two-wheel drive). It climbs to about 1680 m/5500 ft on the north flank of Silver Peak and is the best approach to Silver and Isolillock peaks.

1b. Sowerby Creek, south side: This spur road is four-wheel drive and is washed out after 3 km. It continues up the valley and can be used as a southern approach to Isollilock Peak.

2. Eaton Lake-Eaton Peak trail (16.5 km/10.25 mi): Turn left and follow a short, steep road to a small parking area, where you will find a Forest Service recreation site. The trail from here is obvious and well maintained.

3. Swanee Lake trail (17.7 km/11 mi): A few years ago the Forest Service supposedly cut a trail up Swanee Creek, but if it existed at all, it is now apparently sketchy and difficult to follow. Another difficulty is that to reach the trail you have to ford Silverhope Creek.

4. Yola Creek and Cantelon Creek roads (20 km/12.4 mi): Several old four-wheel drive roads branch W and climb up the south side of Cantelon Creek for about 4 km. Don't let the initial intersection confuse you; all spurs eventually lead to the main line. Roads used to extend to within a few kilometres of the heads of the Yola Creek and Cantelon Creek valleys, and much of the upper stretches can still be walked. The moment logging ceases in this creek, the road is demolished by slides.

5. Hicks Creek road (24 km/15 mi): A good two-wheel drive road ascends Hicks Creek almost to Greendrop Lake, where it connects with the Centennial Trail from the Chilliwack valley. Waterbars are the only problem. Peaks on either side of the creek are seldom climbed.

6. Silverhope Creek road (28.2 km/17.5 mi): Gated; contact Whonnock Lumber. A good two-wheel drive road ascends the creek to its headwaters at 1400 m/4600 ft.

7. Klesilkwa Mountain roads (30 km/18.6 mi): Gated; contact Herman Sawmills. New roads here extend to about 1370 m/4500 ft on the east side of Klesilkwa Mountain, but there is a major washout after 1.5 km.

8. Maselpanik Creek roads (35.5 km/22 mi): Gated; contact G and F Logging. A major series of roads extends to the head of Maselpanik valley and enters major side valleys to the W. Roads run up both the east and west sides of the creek for about 8 km/5 mi, where they rejoin and continue up the east bank. The road on the west side is the most driveable at present. Superb access to the "International" cirque.

9. Skagit River trail and Centennial Trail (43 km/26.8 mi): This trail connects the Ross Lake road with the Hope-Princeton Highway. It basically follows the east bank of the Skagit River at a gentle gradient. The Centennial Trail parallels the Ross Lake road, eventually joining the Skyline Trail (A12) to the S. It is somewhat bushy at present.

10. Shawatum Creek spur road (46 km/28.5 mi): A short spur leads up the creek for about 1 km. Old roads further up are now totally bushed in.

11. McNaught valley viewpoint (49 km/30.5 mi): You can get a good view of the peaks in the unlogged McNaught Creek valley from this point on the Ross Lake road.

12. Skyline Trail (55.5 km/35.4 mi): Signposted at present, but often not so. This wide and well maintained trail climbs to the high divide N of Hozomeen and continues on into Manning Park.

13. Galene Lakes trail (58 km/36 mi): A new footbridge across the Skagit River, installed by the Parks Branch, has reopened this route to the attractive "Galene Lakes" area. The generally excellent trail follows the Skagit River upstream for 3 or 4 km. Just after crossing Galene Creek, pick up an excellent trail which switchbacks up the hillside S and E of Galene Creek to the lakes at 1750 m/5750 ft, E of the Devil's Tongue.

14. International Boundary (61.2 km/38 mi): A large swath cut along the International Boundary has been used as the fastest access to the north and west sides of Hozomeen. It is now so overgrown that parties usually ascend through the forest on either side of the swath. No water and brushy in parts.

15. Hozomeem Lake-Willow Lake trail (62 km/38.5 mi): This well maintained, well signposted Forest Service trail leaves from a ranger cabin in the campground. It runs for 5.6 km/3.5 mi to Hozomeen Lake (the southern approach to the north and central summits of Hozomeen) and a further 4.8 km to Willow Lake (the best approach to the south summit).

16. Silver Creek: You need a boat to reach the mouth of Silver Creek on the west side of Ross Lake. A rough trail runs up the north side of the creek. At about 880 m/2900 ft, the trail ends. Ascend well above the creek until it forks at 975 m/3200 ft, then drop down to the main creek again. This is a rugged and involved alpine approach. The Galene Lakes approach (*A13*) is longer but more pleasant.

B. FROM THE HOPE-PRINCETON HIGHWAY (HIGHWAY 3)

All distances are measured from the junction at Hope with Highway 1 (Trans Canada Highway).

1. Hope Mountain trail (4.5 km/2.8 mi): Just beyond the "S" bend and the bridge on the Hope-Princeton Highway, 4.5 km beyond Hope (at the point where Alexander Creek from the S intersects the highway), park in the pullout and find a blazed route, which runs up and right from the gravel cut.

2. Wells Peak roads, or "Four Mile Creek" roads (6.4 km/4 mi): These roads climb high into the basin N of Wells Peak and provide good access to the northwest ridge of the mountain.

3. Berkey Creek and Wray Creek roads (11.3 km/7 mi): You can reach the roads that run up both of these creeks from a single spur which leaves the highway to the S. After about 1.5 km, a switchback to the NW leads to Berkey Creek, and the road climbs the east side of the creek before crossing higher up and continuing up both forks to 1250 m/4100 ft. The old Wray Creek roads climb even higher, to 1460 m/4800 ft just N of the Eaton Lake divide. Both roads are 4-wheel drive but recent cutting of cedar blocks has somewhat improved access in both drainages. Higher up the roads are bushy.

4. Ferguson Creek roads (19 km/12 mi): The roads in this valley were built during mining activity some years ago, and probably are not driveable now. Formerly they climbed to almost 1310 m/4300 ft into the area N of Eaton Lake. They leave the Hope-Princeton Highway at the east end of the Hope Slide.

5. Sumallo River road (21.7 km/13.5 mi): This road leaves the Hope-Princeton Highway at the Sunshine Recreational Development and follows the river S to the base of Silvertip Mountain. The road branches E to a ski development after 3 km, and the southern portion is often not driveable beyond this point. After a further 2 km, the road branches again, and the righthand forks lead into the basin below Mt. Forddred and Mt. Rideout.

6. Skagit River trail (36.2 km/22.5 mi): The trail leaves the highway to the S just before a bend to the N leads past Rhododendron Flats. It is in excellent condition.

Routes

HOPE MOUNTAIN 1837 m/6026 ft
Rises immediately S of Hope townsite.
The Hope Mountain trail (*B1*) heads E, parallelling the highway for about 1 km before turning S and switchbacking up the east side of Alexander Creek. It gains the bowl at the head of the creek and eventually climbs the southeast ridge of Hope Mountain. Follow the ridge to the summit; NTD. Allow 10 hours return. The once magnificent bowl at the head of this creek has now been destroyed by the most short-sighted and destructive logging methods practiced anywhere today outside the Third World.

WELLS PEAK 1830 m/6000 ft
Located E of Silver Lake.
Walk up the Four Mile Creek road (*B2*) to its highest spurs at 1130 m/3700 ft, then hike up the eastern slopes to the summit. NTD and not very interesting. The peak can also be climbed by following the crest from the Hope Mountain trail (*B1*).
"Silver Bluffs": *FA: R. Culbert, A. Purdey—1966.* These are the white walls rising above and to the E of Silver Lake. They may be reached from the Silver-Skagit road by ascending a creek bed from near the northern end of the lake. The route follows the prominent shoulder or buttress, which proved to be Class 4–5 and is not recommended. Cracks up the main wall farther right appear to offer more difficult, and more enjoyable, lines.

MT. COULTER 2000 m/6563 ft
A pleasant summit 4 km NE of Eaton Lake.
Easily climbed through open forest from Ferguson Creek (*B4*).

MT. POTTER 1890 m/6200 ft
Located 3 km SE of Mt. Coulter.
From Ferguson Creek road (*B4*), cross the creek and climb through forests, heading for the shoulder W of the peak. Summit area is meadowed and pleasant.

"CRESCENT LAKE PEAK" 2172 m/7126 ft
Located N of Eaton Lake.
FRA: P. Binkert, J. Booth, R. Chambers, J. Irving, D. Montgomery, J. Teevan—June 16, 1951.
From the outlet of Eaton Lake (*A2*), climb NW through timber and follow the ridge above to open meadows and the broad summit. NTD.

EATON PEAK 2105 m/6900 ft
FA: J. Butcher, E. Jenkins, F. Rogers—October 15, 1950.
South ridge: From Eaton Lake (*A2*), ascend steeply to S over bushy, boulder-strewn terrain. At the base of the north ridge, traverse the long east face (on snow) to the south ridge, which is Class 3. Takes 4 hours up from lake.
North ridge: The first ascent party apparently gained the upper reaches of this ridge by skirting the toe of the route and making an ascending traverse up its west flank.

An exposed rock climb of Class 3–4 difficulty leads to the summit. The entire north ridge would be Class 5.

East face: *FA: P. Hinkley, J. Schmiesing—October 12, 1969.* A number of variations are possible on this short face, most of which are 2–4 pitches in the mid Class 5 range.

MT. FORDDRED 2160 m/7100 ft

Located N of the head of Klesilkwa River.

FRA: R. Culbert, P. Plummer—1964.

South side: From the end of the road (1430 m/4700 ft) which runs up the second to last western fork of the Sumallo River, ascend scrubby gullies and meadow (spring snow helps) to the col S of Forddred. From there, climb to the summit. NTD; 3 hours up from the road. From the col, you can also scramble up the slightly higher summit to the S. Meadows cover much of the divide around Mt. Forddred.

East ridge ("Stegosaurus Ridge"): *FA: R. Boyce, M. De Jong, B. Fairley—May 24, 1981.* An entertaining variation on the standard route. Ridge is gained as for south slopes route. Crux is a 5.6 jamcrack on loose rock. The route is somewhat spoiled by its close proximity to easier terrain. A full day's outing.

MT. PAYNE 2470 m/8100 ft

The westernmost of the three summits in the Rideout group; located on the Klesilkwa-Sumallo divide. Named for Father Damasus Payne, a climber from the Benedictine abbey in Mission, killed on Edge Peak in October 1978.

FA: J. Bussell, H. Genschorek, I. Kay, A. Melville, W. Sparling—1950.

Southeast ridge: From the Ross Lake road, the southeast ridge is a very uninviting and bushy proposition.

Southwest ridge: *FA: J. Holmes, R. Mason—1956.* From 30.6 km/19 mi on the Ross Lake road (*A*), ascend the steep, narrow ridge through bush, meadows, and small bluffs to summit. Takes 6 hours up.

From the Sumallo River: The west fork of the Sumallo River (*B5*) is now the logical approach. Likely a bluffy Class 4 ascent.

North face: *FA: M. de Jong, J. Roddan—November 24, 1985.* Approach via the west fork of the Sumallo River (*B5*). Climb up and right to the base of a gigantic rock cliff, then move up and left into an obvious 40° couloir which exits on the summit ridge. In early season you will have to contend with short sections of steep ice. The crux, Class 5.9 rock with poor protection, is the last pitch leading to the summit. Be wary of cornices!

MT. RIDEOUT 2447 m/8029 ft

Located 3 km W of Silvertip Mountain.

FA: J. Bussell, H. Genschorek, I. Kay, A. Melville, W. Sparling—1950.

FWA: J. Bajan, J. Buszowski, D. Serl—January 1983.

East side: From the end of the Sumallo road (*B5*), gain the saddle E of Mt. Rideout by ascending a prominent gully (best with spring snow). From the saddle, scramble up the east flank in an ascending traverse. The direct east arête is Class 3 and somewhat greasy when wet. About 4 hours up.

North face: *FA: R. Culbert, F. Douglas—1970.* This is a 900 m/3000 ft face with rather poor rock. You can easily reach the base by making an ascending traverse over rockslides from the end of the road at the head of Sumallo River (*B5*). The route starts on the left side of the wall, and goes up and right to the left side of a small shoulder in mid-face (water here). It continues up the indistinct buttress, avoiding major difficulties first to the right, then to the left. Climbing need not exceed Class 5.3, but the ascent is a full day. (Ref. *VOCJ* 1969, p. 99.)

North couloir: *FA: J. Bajan, J. Buszowski, D. Serl—January 1983.* Follow the most prominent couloir on the north face for 200 m/660 ft to where a rock step forces an exit to the right; then make a tricky traverse back into the couloir. Climb finishes on many leads of 50° snow. Takes 6 hours up from bivy at base.

SILVERTIP MOUNTAIN 2610 m/8500 ft

Located at the head of the Sumallo River.

FA: N. Kellas—September 1, 1940.

FWA: B. Fairley, H. Redekop—March 1981.

West ridge: Approach via the Sumallo River road (*B5*). This route is enjoyable only when spring snow fills the approach gully and covers the obnoxious slide alder. Follow branches of the Sumallo River road to the base of the northwest flank of Silvertip, where an obvious gully descends from the basin above at 1680 m/5500 ft. Ascend the gully; it is very steep at the top and is very tricky to downclimb. Scree and rock to the right (W) are safer in late season. The rock in this area is poor and the route on the wall to the left is not recommended. The actual west ridge itself is blocky Class 3 and pleasant.

From Klesilkwa River-Ross Lake road: A gully drops to the Silver-Skagit road near a gravel pit 5.6 km/3.5 mi W of the Skagit River crossing. This gully offers a good line of attack when snow covers bush. Climb slopes E of the gully for about 460 m/1500 ft until above the gorge, then follow the gully, keeping right at the first fork and left at the second. Leave the gully at 1980 m/6500 ft, and ascend to Silvertip's west ridge. A longish day return from the road. When the main gully, which drops from just E of Mt. Rideout, is filled with snow, it can also be used to reach the west ridge. This was the original line of ascent.

Northeast ridge: *FA: Alpine Club party—1950.* Approach via the Sumallo River road (*B5*), traversing through slash and bush to large couloirs descending from the lower reaches of the northeast ridge. A reasonable approach. The ridge has also been reached from Silvertipped Creek to the E. If you use this approach, gain the ridge to the N of the creek, and follow it the the base of the route. This is a rock climb, with Class 5 on the last 2 pitches of the crest. Good rock.

North face: *FA: B. Fairley, H. Redekop—March 21, 1981.* Approach via the Sumallo River road (*B5*). Ascend the gully farthest to the W on this face—ice to 45°. From there, endless snow leads to a series of steep gullies several pitches below the summit. First ascent party made their exit about 2 leads to the W of the summit, on the west ridge. Not difficult, but a long day in winter. (Ref: *CAJ* 1982, p. 38.)

MARMOT MOUNTAIN 2072 m/6800 ft

Situated 4 km SW of the Sumallo-Skagit confluence. Marmot Mountain, **MT. TEARSE** (1925 m/6315 ft), and **MT. McCONNELL** (1920 m/6300 ft) make up the northeast corner of this region. Approaches to some peaks look difficult, and no climbs have been reported, although Tearse should be an easy ski ascent from the Silvertipped ski area.

MT. BARR 1898 m/6228 ft
Located 4 km E of the end of Wahleach Lake. An easy hiking objective reached via logging roads from Wahleach Lake (Cheam Range chapter, *A4*).

ISOLILLOCK MOUNTAIN 2076 m/6810 ft
A prominent summit 8.9 km/5.5 mi SW of Hope.
The Isolillock-Silver col can be reached from the end of the Eureka mining road on the north side of Silver Peak (*A1a*), although the road is totally brushed in up high and recent parties have found direct approaches through forest from the last open section on the road preferable. An easy rock scramble from the col. A 240 m/800 ft snow gully leading to the north ridge has also been climbed; scramble up the ridge over the false summit to the crest. **SILVER PEAK** (1950 m/6400 ft), immediately E of Isolillock, is an easy scramble from the col.

MT. STONEMAN 1720 m/5600 ft
An unexciting summit rising SW of Silver Lake. Probably best approached directly from the Ross Lake road (*A1*) or from spurs in Sowerby Creek (*A1*).

MT. NORTHGRAVES 2100 m/6900 ft
A steep summit between the heads of Yola and Cantelon creeks.
FA: A. Armour-Brown, R. Culbert, B. McKnight—1960.
Southwest ridge: From the end of the Yola Creek road (*A4*), hike through forest on the northwest side of the valley, swing across the rockslides at the mouth of the cirque below Northgrave's impressive south face, and ascend into the basin beyond. From there, you can easily gain a pass at the head of Yola Creek. Follow the divide through tanglefoot and heather to the summit, avoiding difficulties to the left. NTD and pleasant; 5 hours up.
South face: *FA: J. Bryan, R. Culbert, F. Douglas, P. Starr—1972.* The cirque under the south face is a 2-hour pack from the Yola road (*A4*). It is about 370 m/1200 ft high and made of metaconglomerate—a good climbing rock but hard to protect in places. The route goes up the lower portion of the wall on the left edge, then out onto the prominent central nose. Ascend this on cracks and corners for 7 leads of stiff climbing. Here, an obvious, large, white corner required an aid pin; 1 lead higher, another large corner is avoided on the left. Climbing is to 5.7; the route is a fairly long day. (Ref: *CAJ* 1973, p. 62.)

JEFFREY PEAK 2051 m/6729 ft
Located SW of the Yola-Cantelon junction.
A spur of the Yola Creek road (*A4*) cuts across the mouth of the basin which holds the lake at 1250 m/4100 ft SE of Jeffrey. From here, you can climb to the divide and traverse on the far side to Jeffrey Peak, or you can approach more directly from the lake through meadows and bluffs.

MT. NOWELL 1830 m/6000 ft
Located on the E end of the divide between Hicks and Yola creeks.

A logging spur from the Yola Creek road (*A4*) climbs the west face of Nowell and swings up to a lake at 1550 m/5100 ft, to the W of the summit. Continue for half an hour through heather and light forest; pleasant. Another spur farther up Yola Creek climbs almost to the divide between Nowell and the 1830 m/6000 ft summit above Greendrop Lake. "Goat" or "Porcupine" Peak (1980 m/6500 ft) S of the head of Yola Creek might be reached by traversing along this heathery divide (see Chilliwack chapter).

MT. WITTENBERG 1860 m/6100 ft
Located N of Flora Lake between Post and Silverhope creeks. Likely bushy but NTD via Greendrop or Flora lakes (see Chilliwack chapter).

MT. HOLDEN 2010 m/6600 ft
Located between the mouths of Hicks and Silverhope creeks.

Thrash up the north slopes from the bridge over Silverhope Creek (*A6*). Hicks Creek (*A5*) is an alternative and equally bushy approach.

CUSTER RIDGE 2130 m/7000 ft
The divide between Maselpanik Creek and Chilliwack Lake.

This is a fine area of high meadowland, suitable for hiking and ski touring. Best access is now from the Klesilkwa Mountain road (*A7*), but the area has also been approached from the Maselpanik system (*A8*). **THOMPSON PEAK** (2130 m/7000 ft) is the high point; it is a very steep ski trip from Maselpanik Creek and is best approached from the divide itself. (*FRA: D. MacLaurin, R. Mason—1961.*) **MT. DALY** (2130 m/7000 ft), 2 km SSE of Thompson, is a pleasant hike from the valley to the SE; approach via Maselpanik Creek (*A8*). **KLESILKWA MOUNTAIN** (2070 m/6800 ft) forms the northern buttress of Custer Ridge. It is easily climbed from Paleface Creek (see Chilliwack chapter) or from the head of Silverhope Creek (*A6*). **MT. LOCKWOOD** (2042 m/6700 ft), located N of Custer Ridge, is an easy hike from all directions.

WHITWORTH PEAK 2294 m/7525 ft
Located E of lower Maselpanik Creek.

FRA: T. Riggs—1905.

From spur roads in Maselpanik Creek (*A8*), ascend to the ridge NW of **FINLAYSON PEAK** (2205 m/7236 ft). Contour under Finlayson to the col between Finlalyson and Whitworth; scramble on poor rock to the summit. The peak has also been climbed from the N using snow couloirs (*K. Hunt, T. Scratchley and party—1954*).

"MT. CUSTER" 2630 m/8630 ft
A reddish summit located W of Silver Lake at the head of Depot Creek.

FRA: F. Dawe, R. Mason, K. Teichman—1958.

The best approach now is via Maselpanik Creek (*A8*), although parties have also approached from Depot Creek (see Chilliwack chapter) and from Silver Lake via Galene Lakes (*A13*).

South ridge and south face: From the col between the head of Depot Creek and the lake at the head of Silver Creek, climb N, bypassing gendarmes, and scramble up the south face. Class 3 on loose rock.

Southeast face: *FA: G. Rice, J. Roper, R. Tindall—August 1971.* Ascend from the lake over mixed ground to a notch in the east ridge, just below the summit. Mainly a scramble. In July 1979, D. Cagle and R. Crocker traversed the east ridge to Mt. Rahm.

From the north: *FA: E. Zenger and party—about 1983.* Approach as for the northwest slopes of Mt. Rahm, climbing the "Maselpanik Glacier" to the W of Rahm to its upper west edge, then descend a steep slope to the W to gain the "Custer Glacier" (facing NW). Ascend to col W of the peak, and then to the summit.

"CAMP PEAK" 2350 m/7700 ft
Located 1.6 km N of Mt. Rahm.
FA: Boundary survey.
This peak is actually the western buttress of Mt. Rahm, fronting on the headwaters of Maselpanik Creek (*A8*). NTD along the south ridge.

North buttress: *FA: A. Greer, K. Haberl, M. Rigby—July 1984.* Ascend buttress on the left side of the face, left of the prominent couloir. Some loose rock; Class 4 and an easy day.

MT. RAHM ("INTERNATIONAL PEAK") 2584 m/8478 ft
FRA: J. Hutton, P. Hutton, R. Mason—1955.
Northwest slopes: Ascend the east fork of Upper Maselpanik creek (*A8*) into a snow basin. Climb to the head of the basin, then follow steep snow beside the north ridge to the summit. Rock on the ridge itself may be Class 4 and poor quality.

PEAK 8200 2500 m/8200 ft
Mounted on the ridge between Mt. Rahm and the Devil's Tongue.
FA: J. Bryceland, G. Longmuir—1965.
From Mt. Rahm: The original ascent party traversed the intervening ridge from Mt. Rahm to gain the summit. Exposed and delicate Class 3 climbing.

North face: *FA: J. Manuel, H. Redekop—August 14, 1983.* Approached via Maselpanik Creek (*A8*) and a traverse over the north ridge of Mt. Rahm. There are several possible lines of descent into the McNaught Creek basin; all are best when spring snow fills the gullies. Begin to the right of the lowest point of rock, following an obvious dyke for 3 pitches. Traverse left to a gully and climb the adjacent lefthand edge. Mainly Class 4 with minor 5th, but belays and protection are poor. Takes 10 hours. (Ref: *CAJ* 1984, p. 73.)

DEVIL'S TONGUE 2453 m/8048 ft
A rock tower just S of the border at the head of McNaught Creek.
FA: D. Cowie, D. Thom—1957.
From Galene Lakes (*A13*), follow meadowed ridges SW to the border. Traverse SW under the next bump on the ridge, and follow ridge to a sub-peak at 2160 m/7100 ft, beneath the final peak. There are small ponds of water here. Descend to the gap beyond, then angle up and left to the southeast ridge, which is ascended to the summit. Class 3, and more difficult if your route finding is off. Takes 4–5 hours up from

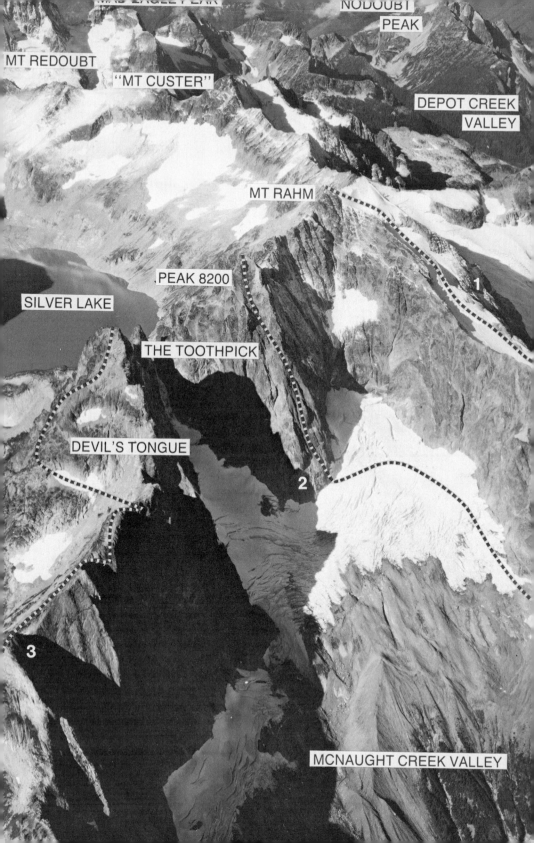

MT REDOUBT

"MT CUSTER"

NODOUBT PEAK

DEPOT CREEK VALLEY

MT RAHM

PEAK 8200

SILVER LAKE

THE TOOTHPICK

DEVIL'S TONGUE

1

2

3

MCNAUGHT CREEK VALLEY

a camp near Galene Lakes. The **"DEVIL'S TOOTHPICK"** (2355 m/7720 ft) is a narrow, steep, rock tower just W of Devil's Tongue. No recorded ascents.

WRIGHT PEAK 2040 m/6700 ft

Located 4 km S of the mouth of McNaught Creek, and mainly an easy hike N from Galene Lakes (*A13*). The final summit requires a Class 3 scramble up a gully partly hidden by a large fir tree.

MT. RAEBURN 2092 m/6863 ft

Located on the west side of Ross Lake just S of Silver Creek.
FRA: BCMC party led by F. Dawe—June 5, 1960.
Cross Silver Creek near its mouth and ascend through forests to NE of Mt. Raeburn. Spring snow helps with bush. The northeast ridge of the final peak is a steep scramble and the northwest ridge appears longer but easier. An easy 1 day return trip from cars.

DESOLATION PEAK 1860 m/6102 ft

Located between Lightning Creek and Ross Lake.
The Desolation Peak trail leads from the Lightning Creek campground, climbs to Desolation's south ridge, and from there ascends to a lookout. About 9.7 km/6 mi; NTD. The mountain has also been reached in a long day from the Willow Lake trail (*A15*) by following the divide southward. Good viewpoint.

MT. BRICE 2164 m/7099 ft

A meadowed summit N of the head of Shawatum Creek.
Hike from the end of the Shawatum Creek road (*A10*). Bush is reasonable if you stay on the north side of the creek.

SHAWATUM MOUNTAIN 2158 m/7081 ft

A prominent double summit above the Skagit Valley.
FA: H. Custer—1859.
FWA: D. Kasian, B. Rundle—November 11, 1977.
Take the (likely impassable) spur of the Shawatum Creek road (*A10*) which crosses to the south side of the valley. Ascend the northwest ridge through forest and continue to the summit on Class 3 rock.

SHAWATUM MOUNTAIN—EAST PEAK 2135 m/7000 ft

FA: K. Keats, H. Rode—1951. A short Class 3–4 climb from the col with the west peak. This col has been reached by ascending the gully between the two summits. You can also reach it by descending from the west peak.

NEPOPEKUM MOUNTAIN 1938 m/6357 ft

A gentle summit above the Skagit River valley, S of Nepopekum Creek.

The Skagit Range   1.) Mt. Rahm, northwest slopes   2.) Peak 8200, north face   3.) Devil's Tongue, regular route
Austin Post

The north peak of Hozomeen Mountain   1.) Southwest buttress   2.) Standard route

Harold Redekop

FA: American Boundary Survey—1859.
An easy 1 day return trip via the Skyline Trail (*A12*) and the long connecting south divide. The peak has had a winter snowshoe ascent (*D. Kasian, B. Rundle—December 1977*).

THE HOZOMEEN GROUP
A dramatic triad of peaks rising immediately S of the border and E of Ross Lake. They may be viewed to advantage from Manning Park and from many other parts of the Skagit valley. The rock is metamorphosed basalt or greenstone, commonly quite firm but usually difficult to protect.

HOZOMEEN MOUNTAIN—NORTH PEAK 2459 m/8066 ft
The highest peak in the group, located at the N end of Hozomeen Lake.
FA: Boundary Survey—1904.

The Hozomeen group from the north   Peter Jordan

From the north: Ascend the border swath (now rather overgrown) (*A14*) from the Ross Lake road. Where the swath gets deep, swing right through light forest, cross the divide, and gain the basin N of the north peak. This may also be reached in a day's march by following the largely open divide down from the Skyline Trail (*A12*). Snow and rock on the north face of the final peak give a low Class 3 route to the top. The northeast buttress is slightly more difficult, but on firmer rock, and most problems may be avoided on the right. This is a rather strenuous day's return trip from the road.

From the south: From the Hozomeen Lake campground (*A15*), a rough trail runs around the east shore of the lake. From the end of this trail, make an ascending traverse through timbered slopes until you can drop into the great gully. This runs under the southern walls of the north peak to the col between the north peak and the southwest peak. It is best to descend into the gully at a low elevation (between 1220 m/4000 ft and 1370 m/4500 ft) as there are bluffs higher up. Climb up the gully to the col, then follow loose, broken ground to the summit. Very poor rock on the last pitch; a taxing Class 3 climb. Fast parties could do this route in a day in summer.

Southwest buttress: *FA: R. Culbert, A. Purdey—1968.* An outstanding alpine climb which has not had a repeat ascent. It is easiest to approach the buttress from Hozomeen Lake (*A15*) by angling gently upward from the end of the lake and crossing the major gully (used to gain the south-side route) at about the 1220 m/4000 ft level. Route begins at about 1520 m/5000 ft at the base of the wall. Scramble through initial bluffs near buttess crest, then climb left into the prominent chimney; exit required minor aid. At the 1830 m/6000 ft level, major walls are turned by 5 leads (to Class 5.4) up the right fork of the prominent gully system to the right of the nose. Traverse easy slabs around the right side of the "Untouchable Tower" group mounted on a shoulder of the buttress and ascend gully against face to the gap behind the towers. After 2 Class 4 leads up the nose, traverse left into a gully leading to the south ridge 1 pitch below the summit. Difficulty need not exceed Class 5.6. No water, but there is usually snow in gully behind the Untouchables. Rock is unusual but not bad climbing. (Ref: *VOCJ* 1968; *CAJ* 1969, p. 81.)

HOZOMEEN MOUNTAIN—SOUTHWEST PEAK 2277 m/7471 ft
Located immediately E of Hozomeen Lake.
FRA: J. Dudra, H. Rode—1951.
From the southwest: The summit has no great relief above the east rib which adjoins the southwest and the south peaks of Hozomeen (see below) and is a loose, unpleasant Class 3 from there. The saddle has also been gained by a long, loose scramble from the pass between the north and south summits of Hozomeen, reached by ascending gully from Hozomeen Lake. Keep in the forests to the left of the gully until you are well up.
South ridge: *FA: R. Culbert, G. Johncox, W. Sharpe—1958.* Ascend the ridge adjacent to the campground at Hozomeen Lake (*A15*) and follow this to the southwest peak. There is one Class 4–5 lead on loose rock, dramatic exposure, and some scrambling. No water late in the season; good views of the south peak from the ridge.
West face and buttress: *FA: J. Oswald, G. Walter, E. Zenger—1969.* This route does not actually ascend the dramatic buttress visible from Hozomeen Lake. Ascend the gully which drops from the north side of the southwest peak, until you reach the base of the walls. Here a ledge cuts across the northwest face, rising to a point about halfway up the ridge crest. From here, obvious face climbing provides several leads of good Class 5 to the summit; the first lead is the most difficult. Takes 5 hours up.

HOZOMEEN MOUNTAIN—SOUTH PEAK 2439 m/8003 ft
This imposing summit was the last major peak in the Cascades to be climbed. It has probably had less than ten ascents, but is not particularly difficult.
FA: F. Beckey, M. Marcus, J. O'Neil, K. Prestrud, H. Staley, C. Welsh—May 30, 1947.
From the south: From Willow Lake (*A15*), ascend forests to the N and gain the south ridge of the southwest peak, which is followed to just above tree line. A steep wall here forces you to descend a hidden gully into the basin to the E; a few moves of steep downclimbing are necessary. Alternatively, in early season, you can ascend a bushy gully from the forest; this gully descends from the aforementioned basin and is best climbed when snow is still present. Next, traverse the basin well below the lesser peak to the E to gain the south ridge of this lesser peak. Descend from here to where a prominent cleft on the gully opens out into the second basin. Cross the mouth of this cleft (this is one spot where there may still be patches of snow in late season) and scramble up the steep headwall of the basin to the main ridge. Final ascent remains near the ridge crest and is mostly Class 4. The crux is a small vertical wall of about 4 m which the first ascent party overcame with a shoulder stand

—unprotected Class 5.6. A long day from Willow Lake; probably best done as a bivy. Most parties will wish to rappel 2 or 3 pitches to regain the second basin. The downclimb of the headwall is fairly tedious and very exposed; great caution is needed. (Ref: *CAJ* 1948, p. 105.)

North ridge: *FA: F. Douglas, P. Starr—1974.* This steep and spectacular route was first climbed as part of a traverse of the Hozomeens; approach was via the southwest peak. A long, exposed, and sometimes loose rock climb, taking 6–8 hours up. Although rated only 5.4 by the first ascent party, this is a serious alpine climb because of the difficulties in arranging protection. It has not been repeated.

Chapter 26

Manning Park

by Rob Driscoll

BOUNDARIES:

North: Tulameen River
East: Similkameen River, Chuwanten Creek
South: Boundary Trail (Northern Pasayten Wilderness)
West: Skagit River, Sumallo Creek, and western boundary of the proposed Cascade
     Wilderness area.

FOREST SERVICE AND PARKS OFFICES:

Chilliwack Forest District
P.O. Box 159
9850 South McGrath Road
Rosedale, B.C. V0X 1X0
794-3361

Princeton Ranger Station
P.O. Box 818
Princeton, B.C. V0X 1W0
295-6988

Manning Provincial Park
Park Headquarters, Highway 3
Manning Park, B.C. V0X 1R0
(road information) 929-2358
840-8836

Parks Branch
1019 Wharf Street
Victoria, B.C V8W 2Y9

Winthrop Ranger Station
Winthrop, WA 98856
(509) 996-2266

Okanogan National Forest H. Q.
P.O. Box 950
Okanogan, WA 98840
(509) 422-2704

LOGGING COMPANY:

Balco Industries
P.O. Box 39
Merritt, B.C. V0K 2B0
378-2224

MAPS:

Federal:
92 H/3 Skagit
92 H/7 Princeton
Provincial:
92 H/SE

92 H/6 Hope
92 H/12 Manning Park

92 H/NW
Outdoor Recreation Council of B.C. Map #8: Princeton-Manning-Cathedral
Ministry of Environment map: Manning Park and Skagit Valley Recreation Area

U.S. Maps:
Concrete (1955) 1:250,000   Hozameen Mountain (1969) 1:24,000
Skagit Peak (1969) 1:24,000   Castle Peak (1969) 1:24,000
Frosty Creek (1969) 1:24,000
Okanogan National Forest map:
Pasayten Wilderness Area (1978)
1:100,000 (metric) (available at all their offices)

Introduction

There is a discontinuity in the trend of the coastal ranges in the vicinity of the international border, and south of this, the high mountains extend eastward almost to the Okanogan River. The resulting terrain is largely open, well suited to hiking and wilderness backpacking trips. This friendly terrain is represented in Canada by the areas of Manning and Cathedral Parks, but is much more clearly developed in the U.S., where it is largely included in the Pasayten Wilderness, a remote and lovely region with many trails. The fastest access to much of the area is from the north.

The climber is offered little in terms of technical routes and spectacular peaks in this area; however, the trails in Manning Park are among the best alpine hiking routes in this guidebook. In the area of the proposed Cascade Wilderness (northwest of Manning Park), the historic pack trails are being restored largely through the efforts of H.R. Hatfield and the Okanagan-Similkameen Parks Society and the Okanagan Historical Society. These trails date back to the fur-trading and gold rush days of the mid-nineteenth century. They include the Hudsons Bay Brigade Trail (1849) and the Dewdney Trail of 1861. The fight for the wilderness seems to be something of a losing battle presently, with extensive logging planned for 1985–90, particularly in the eastern half of the region. The following books (referenced in the introductory chapter) are recommended for those who wish to explore the area more thoroughly: *Old Pack Trails in the Proposed Cascade Wilderness* (excellent for historic pack routes), *103 Hikes in Southwestern British Columbia* (good maps and photos of the area), *Cascade Alpine Guide: Rainy Pass to Fraser River* (excellent historic detail), *Hiking the North Cascades* (the best for the complex U.S. trail system), and *Exploring Manning Park*.

Approaches

A. FROM THE HOPE-PRINCETON HIGHWAY
The Hope-Princeton Highway (Highway 3) bisects Manning Provincial Park. Park headquarters and the Manning Park Lodge are located on this highway 66 km/41 mi east of Hope (SE of the 1352 m/4436 ft Allison Pass).
1. Gibson Pass road: From the park headquarters, a road runs to a ski development at Gibson Pass (1370 m/4500 ft).
1a. Lightning Lake trail: Take the first left off the ski area road onto a short road which leads to Lightning Lake. A hiking trail passes around the north side of

Lightning Lake and on down Lightning Creek, past Flash and Strike lakes, to Thunder Lake at 1190 m/3900 ft (21 km/13 mi from the road).

1b. Poland Lake trail: Shortly before reaching the ski area, an 8 km/5 mi fire-access road branches to the right and leads to Poland Lake at 1740 m/5700 ft. This locked spur road is open to foot travel only. **GRASSY MOUNTAIN** (1888 m/6194 ft) and **BOJO MOUNTAIN** (1898 m/6227 ft) are located N of the trail and are easily ascended on the approach to Poland Lake. A panabode shelter sits at the north end of Poland Lake, and a trail from the east side leads down the north side of Mamaloose Creek to the highway at Allison Pass.

2. Skyline Trail: The Skyline Trail provides a fine ridge traverse between the area of the park headquarters and the Silver-Skagit (Ross Lake) road. On the eastern side there are two beginnings to the Skyline Trail. The first starts from the trail N of Lightning Lake about 3.6 km beyond the parking lot and climbs N to the divide, which it follows westward; the second leaves Gibson Pass road at a fire-access spur about 8.9 km/5.5 mi (Strawberry Flats) from the park headquarters. Where the spur road (which is used to reach Shadow Falls) branches from the Gibson road, a trail heads S, and this is followed until it intersects the Skyline Crest at Despair Pass (1710 m/5600 ft). The route then continues W over the shoulder south of easy **SNOW CAMP MOUNTAIN** (1975 m/6479 ft) and **LONE GOAT MOUNTAIN** (2004 m/6575 ft) before descending to the 1680 m/5500 ft pass at the head of Mowich Creek. **RED MOUNTAIN** (2022 m/6633 ft), to the north of the divide, is easily gained from here. The trail crosses one more ridge before descending W into Skagit Valley. To find the present western end of the Skyline Trail, see the Skagit area chapter.

3. Heather Trail: The very beautiful Heather Trail is reached from the Manning Park headquarters by a public road (open in summer) climbing northward to a parking lot beside the summit of **BLACKWALL PEAK** (2063 m/6768 ft). A jeep road (not open to vehicles) goes 4.8 km farther N to a campsite and shelter near the 1830 m/6000 ft pass between the heads of Buckhorn and Goodfellow creeks. Heather Trail climbs N from here and traverses NW over meadowland beneath the summits of the Three Brothers divide. It then crosses Nicomen Ridge and drops to meet the Grainger Creek trail at Nicomen Lake, which is about 22.5 km/14 mi from the road by the Grainger Creek trail or Heather Trail.

3a. Three Brothers meadows routes: The meadows may also be approached by an old road running up ''Cambie Creek'' from the highway about a mile E of the campground near Allison Pass. In winter there are several cross-country ski loops up Cambie Creek and, with reasonable snow cover, the route to Three Brothers meadows is quite pleasant. The skiing potential in the area is superb.

3b. Upper Similkameen River: In addition, a locked logging road (not shown on park maps) on the upper Similkameen River runs to the edge of the meadows at 1830 m/6000 ft on the ridge southwest of Three Brothers Mountain. This route is not pleasant in summer, but in winter it is used frequently to make a ski loop to Blackwall Peak.

3c. Bonnevier trail: This trail runs up Bonnevier Creek from the eastern park entrance 16.1 km/10 mi from the park headquarters. It starts just W of the gravel road near the park entrance and follows the divide from the head of Bonnevier Creek to join Heather Trail near the summit of **BIG BUCK MOUNTAIN** (2143 m/7031 ft). This junction is about 21.7 km/13.5 mi from the highway. There is water at the

8.5 km/5 mi point, but otherwise the route may be dry.

4. Friday Mountain roads and trail: A mile N of where the highway crosses Sunday Creek, a road complex climbs to about 1520 m/5000 ft on the ridge, and a trail leads on up the ridge to near the summit of **FRIDAY MOUNTAIN** (1950 m/6400 ft).

5. Microwave station road: A rough road branches N from the highway at Allison Pass and climbs to the microwave station at 1680 m/5500 ft. From here, you can hike along the attractive Similkameen-Skagit divide to several minor summits, 2010 m/6600 ft. Good views.

6. Hope trail (Skaist River trail): The trailhead is located 46 km/28.6 mi past Hope, some 35 km/21.75 mi W of the park headquarters on the north side of the highway. Park here, or try driving the 2.5 km up the old fire-access road. Alternatively, reach this trail from the start of the Dewdney Trail (*A8*) via a horse trail which runs parallel to the highway. At 6.4 km/4 mi, the Parks Branch Grainger Creek trail forks E to join Heather Trail at Nicomen Lake. From Nicomen Lake, Heather Trail runs N 9.3 km/5.8 mi to Hope Pass. From Grainger Creek, the Hope trail runs for 3 km up the south side of the Skaist River before crossing to the north side, where it remains until it reaches Hope Pass. The cattle trail continues down the north side of Whipsaw Creek before joining the 1861 Dewdney Trail E of Fortyseven Mile Creek (see below).

7. Whipsaw Creek road: The Whipsaw Creek road exits W 8.8 km/5.5 mi S of Princeton and runs up the north side of the valley. (Note: Hope Pass is wrongly placed on map 92 H/7. It is actually 1.5 km farther S.) The road deteriorates into a four-wheel drive road past Fortyseven Mile Creek and eventually becomes a cattle trail leading to Hope Pass, a distance of about 28 km/17.5 mi. The road has completely obliterated the original Hope-Dewdney Trail. A rough track heads across open country, passing over **GRANITE MOUNTAIN** (1890 m/6200 ft) and dropping to Wells Lake, before continuing over **LODESTONE MOUNTAIN** (1895 m/6218 ft) and down to the town of Coalmont (a total distance of about 75 km/46 mi). The Dewdney Trail goes up the right bank of Fortyseven Mile Creek some 32.2 km/20 mi from Princeton via Highway 3 and the Whipsaw Creek road.

8. Dewdney Trail (Snass Creek trail): This historic trail starts at the Snass Creek bridge on Highway 3 as for the Whatcom Trail (*A8a*) and continues up past Dry Lake via the north fork of Snass Creek. About 8 km/5 mi after passing the Cascade divide (1480 m/4850 ft), the trail branches right and leads to a fork of the Tulameen River. Cross the divide between Tulameen and Holding Creek and ford the latter to the east side before continuing up the north bank of Hubbard Creek. From the pass at the headwaters of Granite Creek, the trail continues over the next divide, crossing Frenchy Creek below Hudson Bay Meadows before continuing down the northeast bank of Fortyseven Mile Creek.

8a. Whatcom Trail—1858: Originally, this trail ran from Bellingham Bay to the Hudsons Bay Company Brigade Trail on the Tulameen Plateau (and on to Kamloops). This trail starts from a gravel parking area complete with horse hitching-posts. Go 100 m/330 ft E from the point where Highway 3 crosses Snass Creek and turn left up an unmarked logging road. This point is just beyond Rhododendron Flats (11.5 km/7 mi E of the western entrance to Manning Park). After 3 km, the trail takes the east fork of the Snass. This is somewhat more overgrown than the Dewdney Trail. Climb to Punch Bowl Pass and then drop into the Punch Bowl. Below the Punch Bowl, the trail crosses the Tulameen River (left bank) and follows this side for some 11.3 km/7 mi down Paradise Valley (as for Dewdney Trail). Ford the Tulameen River about 2 km N of the crossing for the Dewdney Trail. Then ford Holding Creek, before heading NE towards Wells Lake. The H.B.C. Brigade Trail is met 8 km/5 mi S of Lodestone Lake. Distance from the Hope-Princeton Highway to the H.B.C. Brigade Trail is 27 km/17 mi.

8b. Skagit River trail/Silverdaisy Creek trail: This southern portion of the old Whatcom Trail follows the Skagit River. The trail begins at Rhododendron Flats, 10 km/6.3 mi E of the western entrance to Manning Park, at the junction of the Sumallo and Skagit rivers, and just where the highway makes a sharp turn to the N. The trail follows the east bank of the Skagit down to the Ross Lake road, and is in excellent shape.

To reach the trail up Silverdaisy Creek, follow the Skagit River trail for about 1.5 km, then turn E and follow switchback up the north side of Silverdaisy Creek. The trail climbs to 1800 m/5900 ft, reaching the pass 1 km S of Silverdaisy Mountain.

9. Hudsons Bay Company Brigade Trail (1849): This ancient trail from Tulameen to Hope has been upgraded recently, primarily through the efforts of volunteers. The route travels 22.5 km/14 mi by logging roads which are currently washed out from Hope to the head of Peers Creek (see Anderson River chapter). The largest washout occurs where Peers Creek road crosses back to the N. Follow the creek for about 1 km (the road is nonexistent). Once back on the "road," follow cairns and sketchy flagging to the end of the logging block. Generally, you want to end up on the highest spur on the lefthand (east) side of the valley, looking up. Overgrown and tough going. From the end of Peers Creek logging road, head SE up Manson's ridge to a saddle at 1447 m/4750 ft and then drop into Fool's Pass. The trail traverses down to cross Sowaqua Creek, just above Matthew Creek. E of Sowaqua Creek, the trail winds up the slopes of **MT. DAVIS** (2008 m/6590 ft) to the second night's rest spot, Campement du Chevreuil (Deer Camp) at the head of Chevreuil Creek. This is some 30.6 km/19 mi from the head of Peers Creek. From here, the trail climbs onto the north shoulder of gentle Mt. Davis, before dropping to Palmer Pond. Continue down Podunk Creek, past Jacobson Lake. The Vuich trail intersects here *(9b)*. Travelling 11.3 km/7 mi down the left bank of the Podunk will lead you to the Tulameen River. Ford the river at Horseguard meadows (Horseguard 3rd camp is on the east bank).

The trail crosses Packers Creek and heads E up the spur between Packer and Squakin creeks. Cross Squakin Creek and continue heading E onto the Tulameen Plateau (1830 m/6000 ft). **DEAR MOUNTAIN** (1950 m/6400 ft) can be climbed by heading NW on the broad ridge. After travelling 1.2 km on the plateau (posted as "Stocktrail #452"), the trail intersects the Granite Mountain jeep road (which obliterates the Blackeyes-Whatcom Trail). From the intersection, 8 km/5 mi of travel to the NE leads to camp number 4 at Lodestone Lake. The original trail continued to the NE and dropped via Collins Gulch to the Tulameen River.

9a. Ghost Pass trail: Start 1 km E of the western park entrance. The trail starts on the north side of highway on a stretch of old road. Follow Eighteen Mile Creek 8 km/5 mi to a pass at 1400 m/4600 ft, then drop to Ghostpass Lake. From here, travel N on the west bank of the Sowaqua and join the H.B.C. Brigade Trail at the Sowaqua crossing (a further 8 km/5 mi).

9b. The Vuich trail: Intersects the H.B.C. Brigade Trail at Jacobson Lake. To the N, it follows the east fork of Vuich Creek (see Coquihalla chapter). To the S, it crosses Podunk Creek and follows the north side of Sowaqua Creek before joining the Ghostpass trail where Ghostpass Creek and Sowaqua Creek meet.

9c. Granite Mountain: The Granite Mountain jeep road is the effective end of the H.B.C. Brigade Trail. The trailhead is about 8 km/5 mi S of the Badger Creek branch. The 1490 m/4900 ft **HAMILTON HILL** can be ascended easily from the road. The right fork of the road takes you to Tanglewood Hill rising above Blakeburn Creek.

10. Tulameen River roads: From the town of Princeton, a road runs W on the north side of the Tulameen River. At 19 km/11.8 mi, the Granite Creek road crosses the river S of Coalmont. Take the major left fork 1 km past the ridge. Further on, the road forks, with the left branch swinging past Tanglewood Hill and over to Lodestone Lake. The right fork continues up Granite Creek. Branches reach 1370 m/4500 ft in Arrastra Creek and connect with the Whipsaw Creek-Lodestone Lake road. The condition of these roads is unknown, but they are probably in extremely rough, four-wheel drive condition.

The Tulameen River road continues to the Tulameen townsite at 26.9 km/16.7 mi. About 7.5 km/4.7 mi past Tulameen, a road crosses the river and heads up the west side of Hines Creek to 1580 m/5200 ft. The Tulameen River road continues up Vuich Creek before branching up Amberty Creek and looping back down Sutter Creek. The road climbs to 1490 m/4900 ft south of **TREASURE MOUNTAIN** (1710 m/5600 ft). At present, Balco Industries has pushed the Illal Creek road from the N to the Tulameen River road. In 1984 this road was upgraded to the south end of Vuich Creek canyon. Balco is also currently building a road up the Tulameen River so that they can log the historic Podunk Creek valley. The road will run to Jacobsen Lake at the head of Podunk Creek. Balco also intends to log Paradise Valley within the next 6 years, and yet another glorious wilderness sanctuary will be devastated.

11. Pacific Crest-Monument 78 Trail: The route starts 1.7 km E of the park headquarters as the fire-access road up Windy Joe Mountain. At 4.2 km, a trail branches right from the road. The road continues a further 1.2 km to the summit of Windy Joe. From where it leaves the road, the trail runs for 1 km before it forks, with the right fork heading to Frosty Mountain, and the left fork dropping southward into Castle valley to cross the border at Monument 78, 12.1 km/7.5 mi from the highway.

B. FROM THE AMERICAN SIDE

On the U.S. side of the border, the country adjacent to Manning Park and westward towards the Okanagan is usually referred to as the Pasayten Wilderness. It is an area of high, friendly mountains served by a network of good trails (many are horse trails) which spread northward from the North Cascades Highway, and from roads in the watersheds of Methow and Chewack rivers.

The main trails are laid out on the U.S. Forest Service map of the Winthrop Ranger District, and a major chunk of this wilderness is most easily accessible through Canada.

There are two connections southward from Manning Park itself, the best of these being the Monument 78 trail (*A11*). Monument 78 was once reached more directly by a trail up the southeast side of Castle Creek itself, which goes 4.8 km up from the

highway to a logging area on Castle and Chuwanten creeks and is used by snowmo-
bilers in the winter. The Castle Creek trail has not been maintained and is in poor
condition.

1. Monument 78 trail: Monument 78 is the traditional connection with the Cascade
Crest Trail system (Pacific Crest Trail-Trail 2000) of Washington. From here, the
trail swings SE up Route Creek to Castle Pass (1600 m/5250 ft), which is an easy
day's pack from the highway. Frosty Pass (1980 m/6500 ft), which is reached by
taking Trail 453 E from near Castle Pass, may also be gained in a day from the highway. The long trek of 51.8 km/32.2 mi down the Crest Trail from Manning Park to
Harts Pass on the North Cascades Highway can be done in 3 strenuous days, but at
least 4 are recommended. Ice-axes should be carried, and there are some steep, tricky
spots when snow is hard.

Hiking the North Cascades, and *Cascade Alpine Guide: Rainy Pass to Fraser
River* cover the trails in this section in far more detail.

2. Boundary trail: From Castle Pass, the Boundary trail (Elbow Basin-Three Fools
Creek branch trail #749) heads W, arriving at Ross Lake after 43.5 km/27 mi. The
scenic **TWO BUTTES** (1992 m/6534 ft) can be climbed from the trail before it
drops into Big Face Creek after 10 km/6.2 mi. By 14.6 km/9.1 mi, the trail ascends
to Elbow Basin. It then descends S to the Three Fools Creek trail and follows this W
before joining up with the south fork of the Lightning Creek trail, which leads to
Ross Lake.

2a. Lightning Creek trail's north fork: The north fork of the Lightning Creek trail
eventually leads E to reach 1550 m/5100 ft in the north fork of Freezeout Creek.

3. Ross Lake trail: A trail runs N up the east side of Ross Lake to Hozameen Campground on the Silver-Skagit road (see Skagit chapter).

4. Monument 83 jeep track: The second southward route from Manning Park is the
Monument 83 jeep track or fire-access road (locked) which leaves the main highway
4 km E of the park headquarters. It goes up Chuwanten Creek, and then up its tributary, Monument Creek, to a fire lookout on the main divide at Monument 83. This is
a good day's return hike in itself. Monument 83 is near the departure point for the
Manning Park-Cathedral Park trail system (see Cathedral Park chapter). The main
trail southward drops down the ridge past the campsite by a spring at 1860 m/6100 ft
and joins the Boundary trail.

5. Boundary trail (from Monument 83): The west trail branch (Trail #482) does a
descending traverse into Chuchuwanteen Creek (American name for Chuwanten
Creek), which is forded 4 km from the junction. Shortly after crossing Frosty Creek,
the trail splits. The right fork (Trail #453) goes up Frosty Creek valley to beautiful
Frosty Pass and Frosty Lake; the left fork (Trail #482) continues SW down the
Chuchuwanteen, climbing to meet the Cascade Crest Trail near Hopkins Pass. The
wilderness trail between monuments 83 and 78, via trails #482, #453, and #2000,
may be incorporated in a scenic 3 day loop from the Hope-Princeton Highway. The
east fork of the Monument 83-Boundary Trail intersection heads to the Pasayten
River in Cathedral Park (see that chapter).

Routes (Canadian Side)

MT. OUTRAM 2440 m/8000 ft
A major summit rising above the west entrance to Manning Park.
Normal route: Begin on the Eighteen Mile Creek trail to Ghost Pass (*A9a*), which leaves Highway 3 1 km inside the Park boundary. After a few hundred metres the Mt. Outram trail forks from the Eighteen Mile Creek trail up and N to a small lake at 1890 m/6200 ft. The broad south ridge to the summit is pleasant from here. The higher north summit requires a short, careful scramble. (Ref: *VOCJ* 1983, p. 52.)
Northeast ridge: *FA: S. Heiberg and companion—September 6, 1954.* The base of the route may be gained by using the approach for the normal route. The ridge is mainly Class 2, but there is one Class 5 chimney on the route containing two chockstones, which may be bypassed on the right.

MacLEOD PEAK 2160 m/7100 ft
Located 6 km/3.7 mi NW of Mt. Outram. It is an unpleasant bash onto MacLeod's west ridge from Highway 3 about 2 km NW of the Hope slide. This ridge is Class 3 near the top. Allow a full day return.

JOHNSON PEAK 2027 m/6630 ft
The infamous Hope slide tumbled from the northwest end of this peak. The summit has been climbed several times by geologists; a direct south buttress approach may be the most efficient.

PEAK 7200 2200 m/7200 ft
Located 2 km E of MacLeod Peak. *FRA: J. Hutton, R. Mason—1956.* Probably best via connecting ridges from Outram or MacLeod.

SNASS MOUNTAIN 2310 m/7580 ft
Snass is the highest summit on the Snass-Skaist divide, N of Manning Park.
FA: Boundary survey party—1859.
From the Punch Bowl (*A8a*), ascend S to the 120 m/400 ft col above, and then follow the west ridge over subsidiary summits to the main peak. NTD. In the spring, hike SE up a small valley to the subsidiary col, then cross the snow basin beyond and climb steep snow to the base of the final peak.

"SNAZZY PEAK" 2225 m/7300 ft
The sharp southeastern peak of Snass.
FA: D. Cowie, H. Rode—1955.
From the summit of Snass, drop 60 m/200 ft from the main summit and scramble up over talus. The west ridge is Class 3 on good rock.

WARBURTON PEAK 1800 m/5900 ft
Located about 7 km/4.4 mi N of Snass Mountain, between Paradise Valley and Podunk Creek. Presently, it is easiest to approach along the Dewdney Trail (*A8*). In the future, it will be simpler to take logging roads in Paradise Valley (*A10*).

MT. DEWDNEY 2246 m/7368 ft
A gentle summit W of Snass Creek. Visible from where Snass Creek crosses the highway.
West ridge: From Ghost Pass (*A9a*), ascend Dewdney's west ridge to the pleasant shoulder above timberline, and from there, ascend to the summit. Not difficult. Although longer than the northeast ridge, this is more aesthetic.
Northeast ridge: Follow the west side of Snass Creek (*A8a*) for 2.4 km, then ascend the gully which descends from the ridge north of Mt. Ford. Dewdney is reached by hiking NE along the ridge. Its final summit is climbed either directly up the ridge or more easily by first traversing W. Takes 1 day return from highway; bushy after snow leaves the gully. (Ref: *BCM* February 1985.)

MT. FORD 2100 m/6900 ft
Located 3.1 km SSW of Dewdney. From the gully mentioned above, head S along the ridge. (Ref: *BCM* April 1958; February 1972.)

SILVERDAISY MOUNTAIN 2042 m/6700 ft
Located S of the Hope-Princeton Highway, between Silverdaisy Creek and the Skagit River.
Approach via the Silverdaisy trail (*A8b*). The south ridge is a scenic meadow ramble, and the east ridge is also pleasant and attractive. Old roads associated with past mining exploration climb the west flank of Silverdaisy. They begin 18 km/11 mi from the western park entrance and follow the Skagit River for 3 km before cutting SW up to the pass 1 km S of Silverdaisy. However, the road is gated at the highway and there is no bridge across the Skagit River.

HATCHETHEAD MOUNTAIN 1948 m/6391 ft
Hatchethead is an easy summit which may be gained from the head of the Silverdaisy trail (*A8b*). **"THE MOLES"** (1670 m/5500 ft) are twin pinnacles mounted on its west ridge (*FA: J. Dudra, H. Rode—1952*). Approach via the Skagit River trail (*A8b*), which you should walk almost to Twentysix Mile Creek (about 4 km), then pick a route up the west ridge through brush and bluffs. The higher pinnacle requires one Class 4 lead on the south face or west rib. For the lower, western Mole, traverse from between pinnacles to a gully on the south face, which is low Class 5. Scree gullies dropping to the southwest make a good exit route to Twentysix Mile Creek.

OLIVINE MOUNTAIN 1800 m/5900 ft
Located S of the Tulameen River and E of Olivine Creek.
The best approach is probably from old logging roads up Hines Creek, which branches from the south side of the Tulameen River (*A10*).

SKAIST MOUNTAIN 1920 m/6300 ft
Rises N of Hope Pass. Ascend this gentle summit from Hope Pass (1820 m/5970 ft) or from the Skaist Mountain road (*A6*).

KETTLE MOUNTAIN 1860 m/6100 ft

This broad summit can also be climbed from the Hope Pass area. NTD.

THREE BROTHERS MOUNTAIN 2272 m/7453 ft

All three summits of this group are easily ascended from Heather Trail (*A3*), which traverses high on their southwest slopes. The ascents are a 1 day return trip from the parking lot near Blackwall Mountain (*A3*) and highly recommended during alpine flower season. Also a fine ski-touring area.

BIG BUCK MOUNTAIN 2143 m/7031 ft

Heather Trail almost crosses the summit of this gentle peak, which is located SE of Three Brothers Mountain.

FOURTH BROTHER MOUNTAIN 2153 m/7064 ft

Located several kilometres NW of Three Brothers Mountain. A stroll from Heather Trail (*A3*).

LONE MOUNTAIN 1800 m/5900 ft

Located just S of Thunder Lake. *FA: Early survey team.* Best approach is probably NE from Thunder Lake.

MT. ANGUS 1475 m/4840 ft

A low summit rising N of junction of the Pasayten and Similkameen rivers. Presumably easy.

FROSTY MOUNTAIN 2423 m/7950 ft

Located above Castle Creek 8 km/5 mi SW of the park headquarters.

From the east: At 0.8 km E of the Manning Park headquarters, a locked road breaks to the right and climbs to a lookout on the 1822 m/5978 ft summit of **WINDY JOE MOUNTAIN**. Walk 4 km up this road, then take a good trail which breaks to the right. Keep right again, where the trail forks 1 km farther on, and follow the pleasant divide, finally ascending over meadow and scree to the east summit of Frosty. The slightly higher southwest peak is about an hour further; loose and steep. This is a fairly long 1 day return trip from cars.

From Lightning Creek: Cross the Lightning Creek dam (*A1a*) and take the trail which climbs to S beyond. This leads up the ridge NNE of Frosty and joins the route from the E on the shoulder of the east summit. This route is shorter than the Windy Joe approach and can be linked with it as a circle tour.

CHUWANTEN MOUNTAIN 2148 m/7048 ft

A bald summit 4 km N of Monument 83.

FA: Boundary survey party—1904.

A gated fire-access road (*B4*) leaves the main highway 4 km E of park headquarters. It runs up Chuwanten Creek, then up its tributary, Monument Creek, to a fire lookout on the main divide at border monument 83. From this point it is a long cross-country ramble to the summit.

Routes (American Side)

FREEZEOUT MOUNTAIN 2360 m/7744 ft
Located 3.7 km S of the International Boundary and 2.4 km SW of Castle Peak.
Freezeout can be climbed from the end of the Freezeout Creek trail (*B2a*) by con-
tinuing to the head of Freezeout Creek and climbing **PEAK 7647** (2331 m/7647 ft),
2.4 km N of main summit, en route. It can also be climbed via the Boundary trail
(*B2*) over high, open ridges. The peak is NTD.

SKAGIT PEAK 2073 m/6800 ft
This summit has a long E-W ridge which is the divide between Three Fools and
Freezeout creeks. The easy west slope is approached from the Lightning Creek trail
(*B2a*). The south slope, also easy, approached via Boundary trail (*B2*) from Three
Fools Creek.

JOKER MOUNTAIN 2317 m/7603 ft
Located 4 km SW of Castle Peak and N of Welcome Basin. *FA: L.
Wernstedt—1925*. The west ridge is easy from the Freezeout Creek trail (*B2a*).

MT. WINTHROP 2393 m/7850 ft
A sharp, isolated peak located 1.6 km NE of Castle Pass (*B2*) and just S of the In-
ternational Boundary. *FRA: E. Darr, H.L. Frewing—1940*. The south ridge from
Frosty Pass is a scramble. See the Boundary trail (*B2, B5*).

BLIZZARD PEAK 2323 m/7622 ft
Located 1.6 km SE of Frosty Pass (*B2, B5*). May be ascended over steepish snowslopes on its north side or from the Cascade Crest Trail (*B1*) S of Castle Pass.

CASTLE PEAK 2540 m/8306 ft
An impressive summit located 2.4 km S of the International Boundary on the Castle-
Freezeout divide.
FA: U.S. Geological Survey party—1904.
South slopes: Ascend gentle south slopes by leaving the Pacific Crest Trail (*B1*) in
Castle Creek E of Castle Peak and climbing through bush to the south side scree
slopes. Another easy route is from upper Freezeout Creek (*B2a*).
North face (west side): *FA: F. Beckey, P. Leatherman, G. Markov—1973*. From
the Crow Creek fork of Castle Creek (*B1*), climb via the broad, blocky buttress to
the W of the main face. Climb just W of the main glacier; aim to finish on west
ridge. Largely Class 4, some Class 5. (Ref: *AAJ* 1974, p. 144.)
North face: *FA: F. Beckey, R. Nolting, R. Tindall—1979*. Approach from Crow
Creek fork (*B1*) to start at lowest rock toe of central buttress. Class 5.8, A1. Takes
15 hours return from camp in Crow Creek. (Ref: *Cascade Alpine Guide: Rainy Pass
to Fraser River*, p. 168, good photo.)

Chapter 27
Cathedral Park

BOUNDARIES:
North: Highway 3
East: Similkameen River
South: Pasayten Wilderness (north of Boundary trail)
West: Eastern boundary of Manning Park

FOREST SERVICE OFFICE:

Penticton Forest District
1643 Carmi Road
Penticton, B.C. V2A 6Z1
869-9961

Princeton Ranger Station
P.O. Box 818
Princeton, B.C. V0X 1W0
295-6988

Early Winters Visitor Information Center
Highway 20, near junction with Methow
Valley Highway
(509) 996-2534

Winthrop Ranger Station
Winthrop, WA 98862
(509) 996-2266

Twisp Ranger Station
Twisp, WA 98856
(509) 997-2131

Okanogan National Forest Headquarters
P.O. Box 950
Okanogan, WA 98840
(509) 422-2704

RESORT:
Cathedral Lakes Resort
1333 Balfour Street
Penticton, B.C. V2A 4Y7
499-5848

MAPS:
Federal:
82 E/4 Keremeos
92 H/2 Manning Park
Provincial:
82 E/SW
Outdoor Recreation Map of B.C. #8:
U.S. Maps:
Frosty Creek (1969) 1:24,000
Ashnola Mountain (1969) 1:24,000
Baverman Ridge (1969) 1:24,000
U.S. Forest Service map:
Okanogan National Forest

92 H/1 Ashnola River

92 H/SE
Princeton-Manning-Cathedral

Tatoosh Buttes (1969) 1:24,000
Remmel Mountain (1969) 1:24,000

Pasayten Wilderness Area (1978)
(metric) 1:100,000

Introduction and History

Cathedral Park is a unique and intriguing area, very popular with hikers and back-packers. It has topographic characteristics unlike any other region in the guidebook area: massive, mesa-like summits, bouldery valleys, wide open vistas. This is an alpine area which conveys a great feeling of spaciousness, and once you have reached Quiniscoe Lake there are many possibilities for rambles along the trail network or hikes along the broad ridges on either side of Lakeview Creek.

The access situation in Cathedral Park is curious, to say the least. The only road into the park is controlled by Cathedral Resorts, which runs a private lodge at Quiniscoe Lake and which presently charges a hefty fee for a drive into the lake area. The alternative hiking trail takes three to six hours of hiking to reach the same point.

Despite frequent use by the Outward Bound school located at Keremeos, the climbing available in the park is not widely appreciated and is difficult to document. Many of the routes which exist have been put up by Outward Bound instructors, who do not make a point of recording their achievements. Some years ago this situation resulted in a controversy over who had made the first complete traverse of the Grimface massif. Outward Bound maintains a log book of their climbs and the friendly staff seem happy to make it available to visitors who drop by the school seeking information.

The outstanding formation in the park is Cathedral Ridge, which includes the entire Grimface massif as well as extensive outriders. Most of the climbing on the southern end of this group has been done from the Wall Creek side, because the approach from that direction is free, and because the rock tends to be fractured into great fissures and chimneys. The northern exposures, facing the Cathedral Lakes, feature some very steep and blank-looking walls. The rock in the area is predominantly granodiorite.

Controversy concerning the name Grimface continues to smoulder, with some people (including both Outward Bound and the Lodge personnel) referring to the peak (incorrectly) as "Mt. McKeen". This controversy is but one aspect of the thoroughly confused nomenclature situation within the Park. Virtually every map of Cathedral Ridge tells a different story, with the Parks version seeming to be about the most accurate at present. However, once you find your way around, there is scenery here to amply reward just about any type of visitor. A recommended reference is Fred Beckey's *Cascade Alpine Guide: Rainy Pass to Fraser River*.

Permits for camping are required in the Okanogan National Forest and the Pasayten Wilderness Area. They are available from U.S. Ranger Stations, as well as from the Parks Branch in Manning and Cathedral Parks.

Approaches (Canadian Side)

A. FROM ASHNOLA RIVER ROAD
This road heads S off Highway 3 3.2 km W of Keremeos and extends to within 3 km of the American border. The road ends about 4 km past Wall Creek. A trail heads S into the U.S. on the east side of the Ashnola River (*G2f*). Distances are measured from the turnoff on Highway 3.

1. Ewart Creek trail (15.7 km/9.8 mi): A branch road crosses the Ashnola River at this point and runs SW along the Ashnola River for 3.5 km, where it ends beside an old cabin. Ford Ewart Creek to an old roadway (the Ewart Creek trail) on the opposite side. Continue up the west bank for 4 km, then cross to the east side; here the trail joins the Susap Creek trail (*B2*). After about 8 km/5 mi, the trail crosses Ewart Creek again and heads W, becoming the Centennial trail (see the Cathedral Lakes trail [*C3*]). From this point, a faint trail heads S (along Ewart Creek and Haig Creek) to Scheelite Pass just south of the international boundary (*G1*). A trail in poor condition continues SW from the Haig-Ewart confluence through a large burn area to the head of the Ewart Creek valley.

2. Quiniscoe Lake road (22 km/13.7 mi): A gated bridge crosses the Ashnola River to the Cathedral Lakes Resort's private road. It is signposted. From here, you can either pay the exorbitant fee of $35.00, return, and get a lift to Quiniscoe Lake at 2040 m/6700 ft, or you can use the Quiniscoe Lake trail (*A3*).

3. Quiniscoe Lake trail (23 km/14.2 mi): A hiking trail climbs 14.4 km/9 mi and 1190 m/3900 ft to the lake. It leaves the Ashnola River road about 1 km past the gated bridge mentioned above and crosses the river on a foot bridge. The trail crosses the road at several points, then climbs to the W. It branches when it breaks out of the trees. The right branch climbs towards "Scout Mountain," then continues on to Quiniscoe Lake; the left branch leads directly to the lake. Hikers are requested to stay on the trail. Don't drink the water on the trail—it is contaminated. The fastest way to Quiniscoe Lake is actually to walk the road from where it intersects this trail, although the route is less aesthetic. About 4 hours to the lakes.

4. McBride Creek road (44 km/27.5 mi): About 0.5 km N of McBride Creek, a road branches N. It climbs to almost 2130 m/7000 ft, just S of **PLACER MOUNTAIN** (2190 m/7200 ft), which you can easily climb from this point. The road continues in a northwestern direction, eventually intersecting Highway 3 just N of Copper Creek (9 km/5.6 mi E of Manning Park's eastern entrance). Condition unknown.

B. FROM SNOWY MOUNTAIN ROAD

Head S from Keremeos on Highway 3 for 19.3 km/12 mi. Turn W onto a bridge which crosses the Similkameen River, and drive to a T junction.

1. Roberts Creek road: Take the south fork at the T junction. After 0.2 km, a mining road heads W up the south side of Roberts Creek, until eventually the road swings S into the 1400 m/4600 ft saddle. A spur road branches SW and ends at 1740 m/5700 ft (above Shoudy Creek). Here a trail starts. It heads S towards Snehumption Creek then turns due W towards Snowy.

2. Susap Creek trail: Take the north fork at the T junction. Shortly after this, follow the road which heads up the north side of Susap Creek (not labelled on map) to 1520 m/5000 ft. At this point, cross to the south side of the creek, and you will meet the Susap Creek trail. It heads generally W until it comes to Joe Lake at 2160 m/7100 ft; then it heads NW, climbs to 2350 m/7700 ft, and descends and contours W around the north side of easy **FLATIRON MOUNTAIN** (1890 m/6200 ft). Finally, the trail drops down a fork of Juniper Creek to Ewart Creek (*A1*).

If you follow this trail, the Skyline trail of Manning Park, and the regraded Centennial hiking trail westward to Vancouver, you can hike continuously across the southern rim of B.C.'s coastal ranges.

3. Joe Lake-Snowy Mountain road loop: From Joe Lake (*B2*), another trail heads S. After reaching Harry Lake, this trail swings SW across Juniper Creek, then rises to some small lakes 3.2 km N of the border. The trail crosses a pass to the E, descends from upper Snehumption Creek, and heads SW to come out on the south fork of the Snowy Mountain road.

C. FROM MANNING-CATHEDRAL TRAIL (CENTENNIAL TRAIL)

1. Centennial Trail to Cathedral Park: This trail system, running just N of the border, links Manning and Cathedral parks. A locked fire-access road leaves the main highway 4 km E of Manning Park headquarters. It runs up Chuwanten Creek, then up its tributary, Monument Creek, to a fire lookout on the main divide at border monument 83. From monument 83, the trail has been cut eastward to cross the Pasayten River less than 1 km N of the border. This trail is also called the Cathedral Lakes trail. About 0.4 km E of the bridge over the Pasayten River, a trail branches N to the Pasayten River roads (*E5*). Cross the river on a suspension bridge (good camping at its east end) and head up through the Pasayten burn (partially on skid track). The trail parallels the border and follows Peeve Creek to monument 88, where it swings N out of Peeve Creek and heads towards Trapper Lake. At 17.7 km/11 mi from the Pasayten River, a trail splits to the SE and heads towards Border Lake. Trapper Lake is only 1.5 km from this junction. A cattle trail runs from Trapper Lake down the north side of Easygoing Creek to join the Ashnola River road at about 51 km/31.6 mi from Highway 3. From Manning Park to the Ashnola River road is a 2–3 day trek.

2. Centennial Trail through Cathedral Park: Runs from the Ashnola River road to Ewart Creek. At 50.1 km/31.3 mi from the highway, ford the Ashnola River and head N until you can log-walk across Wall Creek. A trail follows the north side of the creek, then branches S and climbs up to Cathedral Ridge at 2290 m/7500 ft. It curves back, passes S of Scout Lake, and approaches Quiniscoe Lake from the S 20.1 km/12.5 mi from the Ashnola River road. If you continue up Wall Creek until you are 1.6 km N of the Cathedral fork, you can pick up a trail heading N and follow it across Cathedral Ridge to Glacier Lake. From this point, you can easily pick up the Centennial Trail at Quiniscoe Lake. The trail descends E from Quiniscoe Lake to Lakeview Creek, then climbs high onto the north shoulder of Lakeview Mountain. It then continues S of Twin Buttes and drops down Mountain Goat Creek to join the Ewart Creek trail (*A1*).

2a. Wall Creek: Start as for the Centennial Trail but continue on the north side of Wall Creek to the Wall-Ewart Creek pass at 2320 m/7600 ft. You can continue through windfalls in upper Ewart Creek to pick up the Ewart Creek trail (*A1*).

3. Cathedral fork: From the junction with Wall Creek, this trail heads SE to cross the border E of monument 93. It descends across the border, joins a fork of Cathedral Creek, climbs this creek, then swings high on the west flank of Cathedral Peak to upper Cathedral Lake. It continues past Lower Cathedral Lake and joins the Boundary trail (*G1*) just W of Cathedral Pass. Probably the best access to U.S. Cathedral Lakes and to Orthodox Mountain and The Deacon. A long day's pack from the Ashnola River road.

D. FROM CATHEDRAL PARK TRAILS

1. Cathedral Ridge: The peaks from Peak 7772 (mapped as Red Mountain on 92

H/1) S to Grimface Mountain can all be climbed easily via a cairned trail. Begin this ridge traverse from either branch of the Centennial Trail coming out of Wall Creek, or gain the ridge from many points on the lakes to the E.

2. *From Quiniscoe Lake:* Trails connect with Pyramid, Glacier, Ladyslipper and Goat lakes. From these trails, the previously mentioned southern traverse along Cathedral Ridge can be gained N of Stone City Mountain via Ladyslipper Lake. From Ladyslipper Lake, a route climbs to Cathedral Ridge. A more sporting route is the Class 3 rock ridge on Pyramid Mountain between Glacier and Ladyslipper lakes.

3. *Grimface route:* From points N of the Goat Lakes area you can climb into the narrow basin on the north side of Grimface. From this point the pass between Grimface and Ovis may be gained by scrambling. Once through the pass a route continues SE to the Ewart-Wall Creek divide.

4. *Haystack Lakes:* The Haystack Lakes can be reached from Goat Lake by circling around the Boxcar or from the Centennial Trail (*C2*) or the upper Ewart Creek valley (*A1*).

E. FROM PASAYTEN RIVER ROADS

Take the turnoff on the south side of Highway 3, 88 km/54.7 mi from Hope, 2.7 km E of the eastern entrance to Manning Park. Drive to the millyard of Pasayten Forest Products. You must get permission here to continue. The road crosses the Similkameen and heads uphill. Take the right fork 2.4 km from the bridge. At present, the road ends at a washout at 19.3 km/21 mi. After another 1.6 km, a bridge crosses the Pasayten River. The border is only another 3.2 km away (*G2c*). About 0.5 km beyond the bridge there is a second span crossing Peeve Creek, and 0.5 km beyond this is a junction. Take the right fork at the junction and head 0.5 km along an old logging road until you reach a clearing. Head SW to intersect the Centennial Trail.

F. FROM PASAYTEN RIVER-TRAPPER LAKE AREA TRAILS

Exit to the S from Highway 3 95.5 km/59.3 mi from Hope, and drive a short distance through a private resort to the bridge. Get permission to leave your car at the campground (for Similkameen Falls). The 24 km/15 mi trail to Trapper Lake begins just S of the bridge. At 4.8 km, the trail crosses an old logging road and becomes a skid track. About 1 km further, take the right fork to avoid swampy and buggy ground. Continue S towards Calcite Creek. Here the trail swings E and climbs through a burn to open alpine country at 2070 m/6800 ft, approximately 1.5 km S of Placer Lake at 1650 m/5400 ft. The trail continues E and climbs to 2350 m/7700 ft just W of **FLAT TOP MOUNTAIN** (2265 m/7430 ft). This peak is easily ascended from the trail and provides a good view of the area. A rough trail heads N to intersect roads to Placer Mountain. Descend 2.5 km to the S to Trapper Lake at 1950 m/6400 ft. Good campsites are available here as well as in the alpine terrain at 15.6 km/9.7 mi, 2070 m/6800 ft elevation, and in Calcite Creek (10.5 km/6.5 mi from bridge). From Trapper Lake, the Centennial Trail drops 12.1 km/7.5 mi down Easygoing Creek to Ashnola River road or heads W back to the Pasayten River (*C1*). To the S, 9.7 km/6 mi of fairly easy hiking lead to Border Lake.

Approaches (American Side)

The best source of information for access S of the border is Fred Beckey's *Cascade Alpine Guide: Rainy Pass to Fraser River*. A sketch map on p. 181 of Beckey's guide covers this area.

G. FROM UNITED STATES TRAILS

1. Boundary trail-monument 83 east: From 1.6 km S of monument 83 (*A3*, and Manning Park Chapter *B4*), the Boundary trail heads E. It travels past Rainy Camp and drops some 640 m/2100 ft down Harrison Creek to its low point at 1190 m/3900 ft, where it joins the Pasayten River. It then heads N.

Not far N of Trail Creek it crosses to the east side of the river and heads N on this bank before swinging E up Bunker Hill Creek. The trail passes over **BUNKER HILL** (2234 m/7329 ft) after 12 km/7.5 mi, and stays high on the ridge while continuing E, then drops down to cross Dean Creek near its head. It next contours under the south and west faces of **QUARTZ MOUNTAIN** (2295 m/7530 ft) and finally reaches Peeve Pass at 2070 m/6800 ft. It is about 13 km/8 mi from Bunker Hill to Peeve Pass, and enjoyable.

From Peeve Pass, the trail heads E and N to descend Martina Creek to the Ashnola River (7.5 km/4.6 mi). It crosses the river just N of Timber Wolf Creek and heads E onto the enormous, broad west ridge of **BALD MOUNTAIN** (6.5 km/4 mi).

The trail next works E and N to Cathedral Pass, contouring around the head of Tungsten Creek before continuing E to Scheelite Pass. From the pass, it contours S of Baverman Ridge and the Teapot Dome, to Dome Camp, S of Haig Mountain.

2. Branch trails from the Boundary trail: west to east

2a. A trail heading SW in the Pasayten River valley (west side) connects with the North Cascades Highway near Harts Pass.

2b. Soda Creek trail: Near the end of the Pasayten River airstrip at the Pasayten River-Soda Creek junction, a trail heads W up Soda Creek and then NW past Dead Lake to join the junction of the monument 83 and the Boundary trail in Chuchuwanteen Creek.

2c. Pasayten River border trail: A trail continues N up the west side of the Pasayten River to the border (*A3*).

2d. Boundary trail-Sheep Mountain detour: Shortly before Peeve Pass, the trail forks. The left fork continues N past Sheep Mountain, swings around into Ramon Creek, then traverses into Martina Creek and rejoins the Boundary trail.

2e. Trails also continue S down the Ashnola River and E into Spanish Creek, S of Bald Mountain.

2f. Ashnola River border trail: From the east side of the Ashnola River, the Ashnola River trail #500 heads N to join the Ashnola River road in Canada (*A1*).

Routes (Canadian Side)

RED MOUNTAIN 2225 m/7300 ft

Northwesternmost bump of the Cathedral Ridge. Easily approached and climbed from all sides (*A3, D1*).

CATHEDRAL RIDGE

The ridge from Point 7772 (labelled Red Mountain on 92 H/1 but "Scout Mountain" by other authorities) to Point 8570 (generally agreed to be Stone City Mountain), is the subject of much disagreement in nomenclature. All points on the northern portion of this are easily ascended (*A3, D1, D2*).

QUINISCOE MOUNTAIN 2470 m/8100 ft

Rises S of Red Mountain and is an easy hike from there.

PYRAMID MOUNTAIN 2530 m/8300 ft

An outcropping of the ridge to the NE. The peak rises between Glacier and Ladyslipper lakes (*D1, D2*).

STONE CITY MOUNTAIN 2612 m/8570 ft

Easily climbed from N or S along the ridge (*D1, D2*).

East face: *FA: J. Halliday, P. Kubik—1975.* This 240 m/800 ft face route starts N of the northernmost gully of the Stone City-Smokey the Bear massif. The route angles up and left from the centre of the broken regions on cracks and ledges for 3 pitches. From the edge of the face, climb 1 lead up a left-facing flake edge right onto an obvious narrow chimney. From its end, traverse right. A ledge leads to a 45° snow gully which exits near the summit. Class 5.7, A2; standard rack including some larger pieces. A few pins (knifeblades) will come in handy. Takes 8 hours; good rock.

OVIS MOUNTAIN 2620 m/8600 ft

A walk from the N or S along Cathedral ridge, which can be gained using the trails from Ladyslipper Lake or Lakeview Creek (*D1, D2*). Erosion of a basalt dyke has formed an abrupt and photogenic notch, "The Giant's Cleft," to the N of Ovis Mountain.

Giant's Cleaver: *FA: B. Koen, I. Pragnell—August 1984.* This climb follows the rock rib on the north side of the Giant's Cleft. Approach via Ladyslipper Lake (*D2*). From the base of the cleft, move right on a large ledge 30 m, then climb straight up and work right into a groove which is followed till near the end of the second pitch. Cross a steep, grassy area on the right to gain the farthest of several chimney/crack systems. Follow cracks and a slab/crack system on the left to the top. An interesting and moderate climb—5.4.

GRIMFACE MOUNTAIN 2630 m/8620 ft

While mapped at the above height, Boundary Survey parties triangulated the height at 2652 m/8701 ft. Located on the divide between Lakeview and Wall creeks. *FA: K. Carter, N. Carter—1932.*

Approach from the notch to the NE of Grimface via Cathedral Ridge or Goat Lake (*D1, D2, D3*), then traverse SE on the west side of the massif. Other approaches are from the Wall-Ewart Creek pass and from Wall Creek itself (*C1, C1a*).

Neal Carter reportedly named the peak because a subsidiary rock formation had the profile of a human face when viewed from the W. The peak has been climbed by many routes, but the extensive crack and chimney systems on the south and north faces still offer possibilities. There have been some shorter, but unrecorded rock

GRIMFACE
MOUNTAIN

MACABRE TOWER

MATRIARCH MOUNTAIN

DENTURE RIDGE

routes in the area as well. (Ref: *CAJ* 1932, pp. 189, 191; 1975, p. 66; 1976, p. 57; 1977, p. 45; 1978, p. 59.) You can also check the route book at Outward Bound for up-to-date details.

Northwest ridge: The standard route, climbed by the first ascent party. Route starts from the notch at the base of the ridge. Notch can be gained from Wall Creek (*C2, C2a*), from the Lakeview Creek side (*D3*), or by following a cairned trail S of Ovis Mountain from the Cathedral Ridge (*D1, D2*). Climb is up solid Class 3 rock on the left side (looking up) of a major gully. About 25 m/80 ft up, move into the gully, and ascend it through a narrow section (large chimney), or bypass this by working to left, then passing through a cleft in the rock to the right to regain the crest of the ridge. An exposed Class 3 pitch of about 20 m/65 ft leads to easy scrambling and the summit.

North buttress: *FA: R. Driscoll, B. Fairley—June 30, 1985.* This is the longest and most difficult route on Grimface. Ascend snow on the left side of the toe of the buttress and begin in a short, obvious crack which leads to a sloping ramp. Move straight up from the end of the ramp (5.9 crack) and gain a hand crack at the west end of a ledge. Follow the crack, making a couple of hard moves where it trends left, then climb a crack and blocks to gain a ledge. A large wall with moss-filled cracks shoots upward from this ledge, but instead of climbing these, the route traverses left, down a few moves, then ascends a cleaner 5.9 crack to a roof. Undercling the roof to the right and step around onto a smooth wall, following a strenuous 5.10 crack to an arête. The sixth pitch then follows a curving crack and traverses right, below overhangs. Some Class 4 gains the notch, where a short rappel is necessary. Above the notch, traverse out to the right on ledges and blocks, then follow cracks to the summit, keeping to the right of the buttress crest. If you get lost en route, some hard variations are no doubt possible. Excellent rock; 11 pitches, with most climbing in the 5.7 to 5.9 range. Recommended.

Northeast face: *FA: S. Barnett, F. Beckey, D. McCarthy—1973.* Route begins about 60 m/200 ft N of the southeast notch. Climb 2 pitches towards a small fir tree. A rock tower (a sub-summit) E of the main summit can be reached in 2 more pitches. Class 5.7; 2 hours.

Southeast notch route: *FA: Outward Bound party—1972 or 1973* (probably during a traverse of the peak). Reports are that the climb is varied and enjoyable. Climbing to 5.7 on good rock.

Southeast chimneys: *FA: R. Cuthbert, D. Nichol, R. Mansey—1973.* This line goes up the chimney system on the left side of the gully which divides the main and southern summits. From the base of the rock on the east side of the divide, climb chimney to rubble pocket where the gully widens, then climb cracks up the left wall to a deep cleft. Ascend this, passing behind massive chockstone to ledges. An overhang and squeeze chimney follow, leading to top of the mountain's south shoulder. The line is 180 m/600 ft in total, 120 m/400 ft of chimney. Strenuous 5.7; 4 hours. Excellent rock.

"Mother Of Invention": *FA: D. Burbank, P. Comean, P. Gauthier—1975.* Starts as for southeast chimney route of main buttress S of the true Grimface summit.

The Grimface massif from the north   Bruce Fairley

Grimface Mountain from the north   1.) Northeast buttress   Bruce Fairley

Excellent cracks in sound rock. Good belay stations. At the end of the 1st pitch (at aramp), head right onto the wall and climb jamcrack and flake. Continue up through a chimney choked with chockstones and some Class 4 scrambling to a belay at a dark dyke (90 m/300 ft). Here it is possible to descend a gully back to southeast chimneys. The route, however, continues up and right past a free-standing pinnacle to a belay on a large platform. Climb 30 m/100 ft crack (Class 5.7) and traverse left on slabs below an overhang. Climb crack to semi-hanging belay under next overhang.

Again traverse left, lower and pendulum into chimney. Class 4 to summit. Class 5.8; 9 pitches. Take some larger hexes. A topographical map is available in the Outward Bound climbing book.

South southwest wall ("Stemgrinder"): *FA: G. Clarkson, S. Hamilton—1980.* Approach as for normal route until about 60 m/200 ft vertically below the col. To the E is a wall which is divided in half by a 60° corner, up which runs an obvious, large, vertical crack system (off-width). At the bottom of this corner, a horizontal dyke runs 1 m or so off the ground. The climb starts at the western end of the dyke and follows the line of least resistance. Some large blocks are loose. Class 5.8; 120 m/400 ft of worthwhile climbing. Easy half day.

Southwest face: A short face of between 120 m/400 ft and 150 m/500 ft. A large and obvious "cubby hole" can be seen in the wall. It seems that there are 4 routes up the face; they are listed here as they would appear from Wall Creek, looking from left to right. Information is based on Fred Beckey's *Cascade Alpine Guide*.

Southwest face, route 1: *FA: R. Mansey and party—1973.* A 4-pitch chimney route starting on the extreme left corner of the cubby hole. Class 5.8.

Southwest face, route 2: *FA: S. Barnett, F. Beckey, D. McCarthy—1973.* The route starts on the left side of the cubby hole and aids a dihedral crack. From the large ledge, climb up and right to a crack in the groove (Class 4 with aid), and climb left past a large block before gaining a system of steep cracks. Climb past blocks and up a chimney before the last lead up a strenuous crack. Tops out on west ridge. Class 5.8; A2.

West face, route 3: *FA: D. Anderson, J. Brugger, F. Folsom—1973.* This line drops down a right-facing corner system 30 m W of the summit. Involves 4 pitches mostly in jamcracks. Class 5.8.

West face, route 4: *FA: Outward Bound Staff—1975.* This 5-pitch chimney route starts near the far right side of the cubby hole and provides climbing to Class 5.8.

MACABRE TOWER 2620 m/8600 ft

A rock tower located just SE of Grimface.
FA: F. Baumann, P. Macek, M. McPhail, K. Ricker—1975.
From the Wall Creek valley (*C2a*), use a major gully between rock buttresses (second gully SE of Grimface) to gain the ridge crest. Low Class 5 climbing and a rappel leads to summit. First ascent party used several large hexes. Descent to the Macabre-Matriarch notch involves several rappels.

MATRIARCH MOUNTAIN 2620 m/8600 ft

FA: Outward Bound party—1972 or 1973.
The first ascent party traversed summit from the Wall-Ewart Creek divide (*C2a*). Easiest route is from the pass to the W of Grimface (*D2, D3*). Traverse slopes above Wall Creek towards the pass to S of Matriarch and scramble talus slopes on the southwest ridge. Some parties may prefer to use a rope to tackle several minor routes on the ridge crest. Can be climbed from the Matriarch-Macabre notch via a gully to the W.

DENTURE RIDGE 2590 m/8500 ft

An enjoyable scramble from Goat Lake via the east ridge (*D2*).

ORTHODOX MOUNTAIN 2507 m/8224 ft

Located 1.8 km NE of monument 94 and 1 km W of The Deacon. It has a steep north face and, like The Deacon and Mt. Ewart, a gentle south side. Probably first climbed by J. Hill and the Boundary Survey party in 1935 when the peak was used as a triangulation station. Most easily reached by the Cathedral Forks trail (*C3*). This peak can be reached from Cathedral Lakes (Canadian) through the pass to the W of Grimface (*D2, D3*).

THE DEACON 2560 m/8400 ft

Located on the Wall-Ewart Creek divide.

The peak is easily climbed from the Wall-Ewart divide via the northeast ridge. Contour lines indicate a steep climb awaits on the east face. Approach as for Orthodox Mountain.

MT. EWART 2440 m/8000 ft

Located less than 1 km N of the border at the head of Ewart Creek. Located NNW of Snowy Mountain between Susap, Gillander and Hunter creeks. Approach from the Susap Creek trail (*B2*) or, more quickly, from the road which branches W from the north fork of Snowy Mountain road (*B2*), N of the Susap Creek roads; it travels to 1950 m/6400 ft in the saddle 2 km E of **PEAK 7970** (2430 m/7970 ft) Both Ewart and Peak 7970 are easily climbed from this point.

North face: *FA: D. Anderson, S. Barnett—1974.* The lower part of this steep, 8-pitch climb was done largely on aid. Route ascends centre of face. After the 5th pitch, the route can be freed. Class 5.9; A3. Approach using Wall or Ewart creeks (*A1, C2a*).

CRATER MOUNTAIN 2293 m/7522 ft

Located SW of the Ashnola-Similkameen junction.

A rough road runs to the summit of this mountain via its northeast ridge, breaking from the Ashnola River road (*A*) 11.5 km/7 mi from the Highway 3 turnoff. Another road starts from the Ashnola at Crater Creek (17.5 km/11 mi) and climbs to 1980 m/6500 ft. The summit can be reached from this point through light bush and meadow. This mountain features extensive meadows and cliffs of columnar basalt.

Somewhat farther up the southwest side of the Similkameen River, a road runs up Paul Creek, and from this a well maintained spur road climbs to an important microwave relay station on the gentle 1980 m/6500 ft summit N of this creek.

LAKEVIEW MOUNTAIN 2628 m/8622 ft

An open dome rising E of the head of Lakeview Creek.

FA: E.C. Barnard and Boundary Survey team—1904.

Ascend easily from where the Twin Buttes trail (*C1*) crosses the divide to the N. You can also reach the summit from Quiniscoe Lake (*A2, A3*) by following the trail beyond Ladyslipper Lake down into the head of Lakeview Creek and then ascending through the forest. Takes 5 hours return. NTD.

Both The Boxcar and Lakeview mountains are easy scrambles from the intervening gap. Gain this via Goat lake (*D2*).

THE BOXCAR 2590 m/8500 ft

A massive double summit 2.1 km S of Lakeview. Impressive east and west faces, but easily climbed from N and S.

West face ("The Jobbie"): *FA: B. Beattie, D. Cohen—1975.* An easy 240 m/800 ft route put up somewhere on the west face for Outward Bound students. Hardest climbing is first pitch of 5.6 on a slab above a snowpatch start. Traverse right past loose flake and work up a corner before angling left on easy slabs. Climb past a large block at the righthand side of a light-coloured section of wall. Continue up past a flake. Two pitches of 5.3 go straight up from here, then Class 4 to summit. Class 5.6. Descend via gully to S. Approach from Goat Lake (*D2*). If anyone finds out exactly where this route is located on the mountain, the author would be interested in hearing from you.

TWIN BUTTES 2280 m/7486 ft; 2275 m/7464 ft

The Centennial Trail (*C1*) passes within 90 m/300 ft of the summits before dropping into Mountain Goat Creek (or Lakeview Creek).

HAYSTACK MOUNTAIN 2603 m/8541 ft

Located SE of the head of Billygoat Creek E of Cathedral Park.

From the trail on Mountain Goat Creek (*C1*), a poorer trail climbs to Haystack Lakes at 2190 m/7200 ft. It stays N on the flank of the valley which drains these lakes. A good day's pack from Ashnola road. Haystack Mountain is NTD by its north ridge. It can also be approached either from The Boxcar (*D4*) or by traversing around the rim of Mountain Goat Creek valley and along the divide over Haystack's western summit.

SNOWY MOUNTAIN 2593 m/8507 ft

A gentle summit W of where the Similkameen River crosses the U.S. border. Ascend directly to summit after about 2 1/2 hours on the trail from the spur road (*B1*). This is NTD and the fastest way to the summit of Snowy. From the point where the trail crosses Susap Creek (*B3*), you can follow ridges southwest directly to Snowy or you can take the trail up the creek to an attractive campsite by Joe Lake (2160 m/7100 ft). Snowy's summit is 6.4 km/4 mi from Joe Lake over easy terrain. Ascents via Joe Lake require at least 2 days.

Routes (American Side)

The routes listed here are generally more fully documented in Fred Beckey's *Cascade Alpine Guide: Rainy Pass to Fraser River*.

THE POPE 2519 m/8264 ft

A craggy complex just S of border monument 95, 1 km S of The Deacon. You can approach The Pope through the U.S. by using the Boundary trail (*G1*) or by traversing over The Deacon from Wall Creek (*A3b*). Some rock climbing endeavours have been undertaken on these towers, but details are sketchy. Appears pleasant.

CATHEDRAL PEAK 2622 m/8601 ft

A large, conspicuous granite summit located 1.5 km SSE of The Pope. This peak, which boasts some excellent climbing routes, forms the north rampart of Cathedral Pass (*C1*). (Ref: *Cascade Alpine Guide*, pp. 183–187.)

West ridge: From Cathedral Pass, ascend to gap in skyline ridge about 60 m/200 ft below the summit. The scramble to the peak is not difficult, though somewhat exposed.

Northeast ridge: *FA: E. Brown, P. Doorish—August 1973.* This route basically follows the crest, and is reported to be an enjoyable low Class 5 climb.

Southeast buttress: *FA: P. Doorish, G. Wilson—July 1973.* This climb follows the buttress rising from behind the prominent block (The Monk) on the southeast side of Cathedral. Start left of the gully well below the notch (almost on the south face) and ascend straight up onto the rounded buttress. This route is 10 pitches long, the 8th being the summit headwall (5.9 if taken directly via cracks, 5.8 if bypassed to the left). Chocks only; bring a couple of big ones.

South face: *FA: F. Beckey, J. Brotten, D. Leen, D. Wagner—September 1968.* An aesthetic climb up a 300 m/1000 ft face of vertically jointed granite. Class 3 up to the centre of the face, then a left-leading slabby ramp allows you to reach the bottom of an obvious "Y" on the steep, white face. Go up the first crack to the right, and carry on upwards via steep free-climbing plus a little aid. Climb is 7 pitches. Class 5.8; A1. Has since been done free and clean via some minor route variations.

THE MONK height unknown

This is the massive granite tower on the southeast side of Cathedral. Pete Doorish and friends have put a few 4–5 pitch rock climbs up the southern face. All these routes are well protected with chocks; descend via northeast gully (3 short rappels). From W–E these are:

West cracks: *FA: P. Doorish, D. Leonard—July 1975.* Left crack is Class 5.8; right crack is Class 5.7.

Ondine: *FA: P. Doorish, R. Odum—September 1974.* A single, prominent crack; chimney and jam are Class 5.8.

Le Gibet: *FA: P. Doorish, G. Wilson—July 1973.* Start from the low point of the face; go left around prominent roof at mid-height; Class 5.8.

Scarbo: *FA: P. Doorish, K. Hanson—August 1973.* A winding route on the right side of the face; Class 5.9.

AMPHITHEATRE MOUNTAIN 2548 m/8358 ft

This sprawling ridge forms the southern rampart of Cathedral Pass, 3 km S of The Pope. The nicest climbing is on the north face, which rises directly above Upper Cathedral Lake.

FA: Calkins and Smith—1901.

Southwest route: The easy way. You can traverse around the west side from the Cathedral Pass area, or directly up from trails on the southwest side. NTD, but pleasant ridge walking.

North ridge: *FA: E. Brown, P. Doorish—August 1973.* This ridge rises out of Cathedral Pass, leading directly to the north peak. It involves a series of good rock steps (to Class 5.5) with scrambling in between. Takes 2–3 hours from the pass.

North buttress (Middle Finger buttress): *FA: D. Anderson, D. Harder, D. Hel-*

ler—*August 1971.* The largest and westernmost of the 3 major buttresses above Cathedral Lake. The route is obvious, directly up clean chimneys and dihedrals on the left side of the buttress. Class 5.7; A1.

Middle Finger buttress, right side: *FA: E. Brown, P. Doorish, G. Wilson—July 1973.* Start on a steep slab with a thin finger crack part way up the right side of the buttress. Class 5.9.

North rib: *FA: J. Howe, B. Robinson—August 1981.* Ascends the obvious rib to the right of Middle Finger buttress. Mainly Class 3–4 with an unavoidable 5.9 face-crack on the final headwall.

BALD MOUNTAIN 2417 m/7931 ft
A large, rounded summit 5.6 km/3.5 mi S of the border.
Easily ascended from the Boundary trail (*G1*) which contours to N of the summit.

SHEEP MOUNTAIN 2522 m/8274 ft
Located 2.7 km S of the international border on the divide between Peeve and Martina creeks. This mountain can be approached directly from the Ashnola River trail (*G2f*) and can also be ascended from the Peeve Creek area (*G1, G2d*).

QUARTZ MOUNTAIN 2298 m/7539 ft
Located 3.2 km SW of Sheep Mountain.
FRA: L. Wernstedt—1926.
The south slope is easily ascended from the Boundary trail (*G1*) which passes high on the south slope.

ARNOLD PEAK 2462 m/8076 ft
Rises above the northeast part of Horseshoe Basin, 0.8 km S of the border. Ascend from the basin (*G1*).

ARMSTRONG PEAK 2471 m/8106 ft
Located 7.7 km SW of Snowy Mountain on the international border. This double summit, unnamed on maps, is marked by boundary monument 103 (2471 m/8107 ft) and monument 104 (2469 m/8100 ft).
Approach from Horseshoe Basin from S (*G1*) for an easy walk-up. Also possible is the route from the trail (*B3*) running beside Snehumption Creek, which drains to the E.

ROCK MOUNTAIN 2322 m/7617 ft
Located NW of Horseshoe Basin and easily ascended from there (*G1*). *FA: Boundary Survey party—1860.*

TEAPOT DOME 2319 m/7608 ft
Another insignificant summit, this rocky peak rises at the head of Haig Creek. Ascend from Horseshoe Basin (*G1*). Southern slopes should present no difficulties.

HAIG MOUNTAIN 2397 m/7865 ft
Located 1.9 km S of the border, E of Baverman Ridge. Slopes to the S are NTD from the Boundary trail (*G1*).

BAVERMAN RIDGE 2452 m/8044 ft

A long, high ridge which affords excellent views of the Okanogan Range. The ridge high-point is S of Scheelite Lake and is located W of Horseshoe Basin (*G1*).

WOLFRAMITE MOUNTAIN 2480 m/8137 ft

Located 1.6 km S of the international border, and N of the Tungsten Mine. An easy ascent from any side. Climb from the Boundary trail (*G1*).

Vancouver Island:
Introduction and History

by Bob Tustin

Mountaineering interest in Vancouver Island centres on a small number of outstanding peaks. Most of these peaks, all well known, are located within the boundaries of Strathcona Park, although Mount Arrowsmith, outside of Port Alberni, has a long mountaineering history and is one of the most popular Island objectives. It plays host to mountaineering schools and snowcraft training sessions every year.

North of Strathcona Park lie those regions which have seen the least exploration to date for mountaineers. The opening of the North Island Highway has prompted several exploratory probes, but it is unlikely that further exploration will yield a finer massif than Rugged Mountain, lying between Tahsis and Zeballos. The rock in the Hahte Range, culminating in Rugged Mountain, is very good and there is much scope here for general mountaineering. Unfortunately, many of the summits on northern Vancouver Island are not very high, and usually this means that routes are bushy with perhaps only a few hundred feet of clean rock at the top of the climb. Strathcona Park still offers a chance to explore wilderness areas, often unvisited for a generation. As Ferris Neave wrote in 1942, "its peaks offer rich gifts of graceful line and solid rock to the climber. Its trailless valleys will still test the patience of his soul." Quiet yet popular, most of the mountains in Strathcona Provincial Park were climbed before the First World War, despite the pronouncements of guidebooks.

Interest in the wilderness of central Vancouver Island started when John Buttle, a surveyor and naturalist, was commissioned by Governor Kennedy in 1865 to explore the unknown regions of Vancouver Island north of Barkley Sound. He returned and wrote newspaper articles about the magnificent mountains and lakes he found. Years later, in 1892, another surveyor named William Ralph, while locating the boundary of the Esquimalt and Nanaimo Railway land grant, climbed most of the peaks east of Buttle Lake. This survey was no easy task. Ralph established a post on each mile of the boundary in this rugged terrain. One of the points on the boundary often highlighted in old maps was Crown Mountain, because it was the north end of the boundary.

The next explorers to visit the mountains of central Vancouver Island were led by Rev. W.W. Bolton in 1896. Their trip was a continuation of the *Province* newspaper expedition to explore Vancouver Island, which had started two years earlier. In his journal, Bolton tells of leaving a Union Jack flying on a 7500 ft peak in the "very centre and heart of the Island." From the description in the journal of the route up the mountain from Buttle Lake, it appears that this summit was Mount McBride. The *Province* newspaper expedition wandered 315 miles while covering the area from Woss Lake to Alberni in July and August of 1896. Although the group did not climb many mountains, they did have amazing weather—only three wet days out of forty-six.

Between 1900 and 1912, many write-ups of mountaineering adventures on Vancouver Island appeared in newspapers. Mount Arrowsmith and the Comox Glacier were popular. About this time, prospecting in the remote wilderness mountains was also carried on in high gear, this again fostering exploration.

In 1912, nine members of the Alpine Club of Canada, led by A.O. Wheeler, reached the summit of Elkhorn Mountain. The account in *CAJ* for 1913 is full of interesting problems the expedition had to overcome, since access was a challenge all the way from Campbell River.

Also in 1912 and 1913, topographical surveys were done of most of the area that had been set aside by the Legislature in 1911 for B.C.'s first provincial park, Strathcona Park. The government commissioned Reginald H. Thompson to plan the park. He hired two surveyors and mountaineers, W.W. Urquhart and W.R. Kent, to explore and map the area for him. The result was an excellent and accurate 1:100,000 topographic map with 200 foot contour lines.

Urquhart and Kent covered 1170 miles and took 564 photographs during 1912 and 1913. The photographs were often taken from the summits of mountains and indicate that the surveyors climbed almost every mountain west of Buttle Lake in Strathcona Park. Altimeter readings are given for the higher peaks such as Elkhorn Mountain, Mount Colonel Foster and the Golden Hinde, Vancouver Island's highest summit.

In the mid 1930s a new survey of the area to produce new maps was undertaken under the direction of Norman C. Stewart. In 1936, Alf Slocomb and a friend, who were working on the survey party, reportedly climbed the highest summit of Mount Colonel Foster and left a white T-shirt on a small cairn. The only two mountains not climbed during this survey were Elkhorn Mountain and Rambler Peak (known as El Piveto to these surveyors).

Since that survey, some land features have undergone changes that are especially interesting to climbers. Photos taken during the survey show some summits as solid rock that have now broken up from the 1946 earthquake. The Golden Hinde is a good example.

More recent climbing endeavours on the Island have parallelled developments elsewhere, and a small group of enthusiasts have put up a number of fine technical climbs. The east face of Colonel Foster, climbed by Culbert, Starr and Douglas in 1972, was an important contribution and the first really big technical climb on the Island, although this ascent was preceded by some impressive solo mountaineering on the part of Mike Walsh, who made solo ascents of four of Colonel Foster's six summits, including the highest. Walsh also traversed the massif in both directions, once with Joe Bajan and once with Bill Perry.

Other technical achievements have, not surprisingly, occurred around the higher summits of the Island. Joe Bajan emerges every few years or so to claim a different new line on Elkhorn, the Golden Hinde, or Colonel Foster.

Meanwhile exploration continues, with lots of potential still available in places such as the MacKenzie Range. Of late, the team of Rick Eppler and Rob MacDonald have been most active at unearthing new information on the hidden corners of the Island, and their rambles around Cats Ears Peak and vicinity have yielded some fine new climbs in a promising area.

Chapter 28

Southern Vancouver Island

BOUNDARIES:
All country south of Highway 4

FOREST SERVICE OFFICES:

Duncan Forest District
5825 York Road
Duncan, B.C. V9L 3S2
746-5123

Port Alberni Forest District
4227 Sixth Avenue
Port Alberni, B.C. V9Y 4N1
724-5786

LOGGING COMPANIES:

MacMillan Bloedel, Chemainus Division
(Cowichan Lake and Chemainus River
roads)

Crown Forest Industries
21B - 2220 Bowden Road
Nanaimo, B.C. V9S 1H9
(Nanaimo Lakes roads)
758-2475

MacMillan Bloedel,
Northwest Bay Divison
Nanoose Bay, B.C. V0R 2R0
(Englishman River)
468-7621

MacMillan Bloedel,
Cameron Lake Division
P.O. Box 550,
Port Alberni, B.C. V9Y 7N4
(From Highway 14 and Port Alberni)
723-3585

MacMillan Bloedel, Sproat Lake Division
Port Alberni, B.C. V9Y 7N4
(Sproat Lake, Kennedy River)
724-4433

MAPS:
92 F Alberni (1:250,000)

92 F/3 Effingham River

Approaches

The access situation on Vancouver Island is extremely complex, changes rapidly, and is difficult to completely document. The best that can be done is to outline the main logging road systems and provide contact numbers of logging operators for specific regions. Generally the Forest Service is less well informed about road systems than the companies themselves. Printed maps are no longer available from most private firms, but many will provide copies of their own masters for public use. Most of these roads are closed weekdays between 6 a.m. and 6 p.m.; a few of the main line roads, however, are always open to the public and these are signposted. As usual, gates appear and disappear and all access roads are closed during periods of fire hazard.

A. FROM LAKE COWICHAN AND CHEMAINUS RIVER ROADS

This excellent road system unfortunately does not give access to very many interesting hikes or climbs. For more information, contact MacMillan Bloedel, Chemainus Division.

1. Cottonwood Creek roads: Take the Highway 18 exit N of Duncan and proceed past Cowichan Lake and 2 km past the lumber yard of Youbou. A road system into Cottonwood Creek valley starts here and ascends N onto the west side of Mt. Landalt, but it is usually barred by a locked gate. The key is available from MacMillan Bloedel in Youbou. The road is in two-wheel drive condition right to the end at the present. Take this fork (four-wheel drive) to a creek crossing, and then switchback where the road swings back along the west side of Landalt. From this point, a marked trail leads NE to scenic Lomas Lake—a uniquely beautiful spot. Lower portions of this trail are likely to be logged shortly, but the trail can be picked up at the top of slash by ascending one switchback higher on the road. From gate to trailhead is 7.7 km/4.75 mi.

2. Chemainus main line: This two-wheel drive road leaves Highway 1 about 1 km S of Chemainus and follows the north side of the Chemainus River 50 km/32 mi to the pass between Mt. Whymper and El Capitan Mountain. Gated, but keys are available from MacMillan Bloedel. It is not necessary to go to the pass to reach either peak. Whymper can be climbed from logging spurs (four-wheel drive) which leave the main line 20 km/12.5 mi from the MacMillan Bloedel gate; El Capitan and Mt. Landalt can be reached from roads branching to the left shortly after the gate.

B. FROM NANAIMO LAKES

A road runs up the north side of the Nanaimo River to Nanaimo Lakes and beyond. Virtually every major creek in the drainage now has a road up one or both sides. The main line leaves Highway 1 to the W at the Nanaimo River crossing, which is 9 km/5.5 mi S of Nanaimo, and it is signposted just N of the airport. The road is paved for 22 km/14 mi where there is a gate. Branches include:

1. Branch C (9 km/5.5 mi from the gate): Ascends Dash Creek. Parking spot for ascending the south ridge of Mt. DeCosmos.

2. Branch K (26 km/16.5 mi from the gate): Ascends Green Creek to the Green Mountain ski area. K30 crosses the creek and climbs to 1130 m/3700 ft; four-wheel drive.

3. Branch L (27.5 km/17 mi from the gate to crossing): Follows the west side of Fourth Lake and the north side of Sadie Creek (four-wheel drive). You should park about 8 km/5 mi from the Sadie Creek crossing at the south end of Fourth Lake. Higher up the creek an elk trail can be picked up which leads to alpine lakes E of Mt. Hooper. This peak now overlooks the wasteland of the Nitinat River—devastated by logging.

4. Rockyrun Creek (17 km/10.5 mi from the gate): Branch right onto this four-wheel drive road about 2 km after Third Lake. After about 9 km/5.5 mi, a trail running NW leads to Labour Day Lake.

C. FROM THE ENGLISHMAN RIVER

This road system leaves Highway 19 5 km N of Nanoose Bay and 7.25 km/4.5 mi S of Parksville. The only important branch road (marked "A40") crosses the river after 19 km/12 mi and again several km further on. This way of gaining Mt.

Arrowsmith has never been popular. A spur (marked "146") of this road runs 6.5 km/4 mi S up Moriarty Creek and is a good approach to the northeast side of Moriarty. In four-wheel drive condition in the upper section.

D. FROM HIGHWAY 14 AND PORT ALBERNI

1. Cameron Lake trail, also called "Pipeline Creek trail" (23 km/14.5 mi from Parksville): Well signposted and in good condition. Trail leads S up Pipeline Creek to Mt. Cokely ski area. Takes 4 1/2 hours.

2. Cameron main road (36 km/22.5 mi from Parksville): Leads to Mt. Arrowsmith and Labour Day Lake. The road is signposted "Mt. Arrowsmith Ski Area" and leaves the highway at Loon Lake. The first 3 km are actually called "Summit Main Road;" it joins the Cameron main leaving from MacMillan Bloedel's Cameron Lake division yard S of Port Alberni, then follows the Cameron River to Labour Day Lake, with an important branch (the Pass main road) crossing the river 10.5 km/6.5 mi from the highway; two-wheel drive.

3. China Creek road (6 km/3.7 mi from Port Alberni): Leads to McQuillan Creek. Take Third Avenue in Port Alberni S to a Y junction and bear left on the Ship Creek road, which is signposted for Bamfield. The road shortly turns to gravel. Follow it 6 km to a T junction; MacMillan Bloedel's Cameron Lake division yard is on the right. The China Creek road begins here, following the north side of China Creek; two-wheel drive.

4. Franklin River road (18 km/11 mi from Port Alberni): Gives access to Father and Son Lake. From the Ship Creek road T junction (see above), turn right past the Cameron division yard and office, drive 6.5 km/4 mi to China Creek Park (signposted), then another 6.5 km to the Thistle Mine road—18 km/11 mi total from Port Alberni. This two-wheel drive road climbs the north side of Franklin River to Father and Son Lake at 1070 m/3500 ft. Stay left at the major fork after 3.5 km, and avoid spurs leading away from the river.

4a. Museum Creek road (leads to "Reft Creek"): At 3.5 km up the Thistle Mine road (see above), this road branches right and crosses the Franklin River road. It follows the west bank of Museum Creek and is two-wheel drive to 1070 m/3500 ft, where it swings E into Reft Creek. Gives access to Mt. McQuillan from the S.

E. FROM SPROAT LAKE/KENNEDY RIVER (HIGHWAY 4)

1. Nahmint River road (22.5 km/14 mi from logging camp to the new bridge): Take Third Avenue in Port Alberni N to Roger Street. Turn left for one block, then right onto Victoria Quay. After three blocks, bear left onto River Road, then take the bridge left across the Somass River to a T junction. Turn left again and follow the road to MacMillan Bloedel's Sproat Lake division office. From here, a good road leads W toward Nahmint Lake. The Nahmint River has now been bridged above the lake, and current plans are to push roads up the south side of the river and the west shore of the lake; this will open access to Nahmint Mountain.

2. Klitsa Mountain roads (26.5 km/16.5 mi from Sproat River bridge): Follow signs N from Port Alberni to Sproat Lake. At the west end of the lake, bear left, cross the Taylor River, go right for 0.3 km, left up a logging spur for 0.5 km, then switchback left and follow road to the top. A trail from the top of the road leads to Klitsa Mountain.

3. Taylor River road (31 km/19 mi from Sproat River bridge): The main road now goes up the south side of the river, branching after about 4 km. The right branch crosses the river and climbs to over 760 m/2500 ft—it might be considered as access to alpine country S of Nine Peaks. The left branch climbs to the divide between the Taylor and Kennedy rivers.

4. From the Kennedy River section of Highway 4: Most of the access into the Clayoquot Forest Region E of Highway 4 is by routes rather than trails or roads.

4a. Fifty-Forty trail; Marion Creek road (about 48 km/30 mi from Port Alberni): From highway 4 at a point 2 km W of Sutton Pass the Marion Creek road, newly graded, heads left and connects with the Fifty-Forty trail, the old road grade formerly used. The 1480 m/4850 ft peak to the NE is known as Adder Mountain. The road goes up the east side of the creek valley to the W of Adder Mountain.

4b. Cats Ears Creek (60 km/38 mi from Port Alberni): This is the name given to the creek which drains a small alpine lake 3 km WNW of Effingham Lake. A two-wheel drive road ascends the south side of this creek for 4 km.

Routes

MT. ARROWSMITH 1817 m/5962 ft
The Mt. Arrowsmith group marks the southernmost point of mountaineering interest on Vancouver Island. Although numerous minor summits further S are frequent hiking objectives, none are difficult enough to involve serious technical climbing. Arrowsmith is a prominent summit from many points on Highway 4, and looking E from Port Alberni, it dominates the skyline. It is the most popular training ground on Vancouver Island, and offers great potential for winter climbing because of its "Scottish" conditions and reasonable access.

Normal route: Via Cameron main road (*D2*). From this road, swing left across the bridge crossing Cameron River and ascend switchbacks for about 9 km on the pass main road. Bear right at the first switchback about 4 km from the bridge, avoiding the steep hill. An old road intersects the new road shortly after a sharp switchback to the right. Park here. Ascend the old road until you reach the creek; then follow the left side of the creek to the end of the logged-out area, where a flagged trail leads to the saddle between Arrowsmith and Mt. Cokely. Parties have also climbed a prominent gully to this saddle. Descend from the saddle to traverse snow across the east side of Arrowsmith, until you reach a prominent gully, which may require a rope. Some Class 3 scrambling completes the ascent.

"The Nose": Approach as for the normal route. The Nose route ascends rock to the left of the gully and is Class 3. A sporting line in winter.

West side ("Judges Trail"): From the Cameron main road (*D2*), take Pass 32 branch road to the right and follow it to its termination at a large ravine. Head left through the woods, climbing bushy ledges, etc. to summit. Fun in winter.

Via Cameron Lake trail: This trail (*D1*) is basically an alternative start to the standard route.

Rock routes: A couple of rock routes have been put up on the wall to the left (S) of the gully used on the normal route. Both are 4-pitch climbs. The first ascends an obvious groove which divides the summit buttress from top to bottom; the second goes unbroken between two grooves to the right of the buttress. Both routes are in the mid-5th range, but protection on the second is nonexistent. Rock is solid metavolcanic conglomerate.

MT. MORIARTY 1610 m/5283 ft
Located at the head of the Cameron River, N of Labour Day Lake.

Approaches are from the Cameron main road to Labour Day Lake (*D2*), the Nanaimo Lakes road (*B4*), and the Englishman River road (*C*). Best climbed in spring to keep bush-thrashing to a minimum. NTD from most angles, although the north ridge offers a pleasant Class 2–3 climb. Fairly popular as a ski objective from the S. All routes an easy day.

MT. WHYMPER 1541 m/5056 ft
The main Chemainus River logging road (*A2*) crosses the pass between Whymper and El Capitan mountains. By climbing up the south side of a creek from the road about 1.5 km S of this pass, Whymper's west ridge is easily ascended. Alternatively, drive 20 km/12.5 mi past the MacMillan Bloedel gate, then turn right onto branch road C29. This road deteriorates quickly into four-wheel drive condition. Ascend for 4.5 km; about 0.5 km beyond, and to the right of a gully, trail markers may be picked up which lead through mature forest to alpine area. Still another alternative is to drive C29 to its end and hike up through mature timber (flagged trail), then through a short bluffy section to alpine country. Follow the southeast ridge to the summit.

EL CAPITAN MOUNTAIN 1493 m/4897 ft; MT. LANDALT 1540 m/5042 ft
The traverse of these two peaks is recommended. El Capitan may be reached from the pass between it and Mt. Whymper (*A2*). Mt. Landalt is usually ascended via the southeast ridge from branches F5 of the Chemainus River road; go left 21 km/13 mi after the MacMillan Bloedel gate. There is some possibility for 1–2 pitch rock routes on El Capitan, but they may be somewhat grubby. A more aesthetic approach to Landalt is via Cottonwood Creek roads (*A1*) and the major gully S of the lake. Take gully direct in winter; in summer ascend ledges to either side.

MT. SERVICE 1490 m/4887 ft
Located 2.5 km WNW of El Capitan.

Approach via the Chemainus main line (*A2*). This peak can be climbed from El Capitan via the broad ridge that connects the two. Roads also climb up the north slope of Service from Jump Lake (Nanaimo River system). The shortest approach is now from Cottonwood Creek (*A1*) via south slopes.

HEATHER MOUNTAIN 1345 m/4412 ft
Located N of the head of Cowichan Lake. Mainly of interest as a ski ascent. A logging road climbs to 760 m/2500 ft on the south side, and from its end a trail leads to the summit.

MT. DeCOSMOS 1355 m/4444 ft
A hiking objective N of Second Lake. The currently favoured approach is directly up

the south ridge of the west peak from Nanaimo Lakes road (*B1*) then E along the ridge to the main summit. There are some good cliffs, just below the summit, which offer some fine 1–2 pitch climbs.

GREEN MOUNTAIN 1470 m/4808 ft
An alpine hiking and skiing area S of Third Lake. Approach via Nanaimo Lakes (*B2*).

MT. HOOPER 1491 m/4982 ft
Logging roads lead up from the Nitinat River to about 1100 m/3600 ft (four-wheel drive). Hike up the west ridge; there is some scrambling near the top. You can also ascend Sadie Creek (*B3*) to the alpine lakes. Gain the east ridge and follow it to the summit block, which is climbed by a gully on its south side. Features views of the new moonscape.

MT. McQUILLAN 1575 m/5168 ft
Located at the head of the Franklin River.
Via King Solomon Basin: Approach via the China Creek road (*D3*). From McQuillan Creek, hike to King Solomon Basin at 760 m/2500 ft, then follow an old mining trail on the east side of the basin to 1100 m/3600 ft. Ascend a gully to the S and scramble the west ridge to the summit. Some exposure. A good spring climb.
Via Father and Son Lake: Approach via the Museum Creek road (*D4a*). Faster but less aesthetic. From where the driveable portion of the road ends, head up switchbacks to the E. Hike N from their end to McQuillan. Limestone bluffs have been reported to the S of Father and Son Lake, but no one knows yet if they are good for rock climbing.
Via Nitinat River roads from Cowichan Lake: A short hike through timber leads to the long southeast ridge. It is a scenic hike over two minor summits to the peak. A long day return.

MT. KLITSA 1340 m/4397 ft
Approach via Mt. Klitsa roads (*E2*). From the end of the road, follow the stream across the cirque and climb the prominent snow gully beyond to the divide W of the summit. A trail also follows the ridge to the right of the gully; it is a good alternative once snow has left the gully. This climb is a popular and reasonably attractive day trip. Starting from the summit, this gully also offers about 900 m/3000 ft of excellent steep downhill skiing.

MT. GIBSON 1332 m/4369 ft
Located 2.5 km NW of Mt. Klitsa. Gibson can be easily ascended from the Mt. Klitsa roads S of the Taylor River using the above-mentioned trail on Mt. Klitsa.

NAHMINT MOUNTAIN 1568 m/5144 ft
An isolated summit located S of the head of the Nahmint River.
Nothing is known of its climbing history. It may be more feasible to ascend once the roads being developed in Nahmint Creek can be used. A long alpine ridge connects Nahmint with Peak road to the W.

ADDER MOUNTAIN 1480 m/4860 ft
FA: Jackson-McGraw survey party—1941.
West ridge: *FRA: R. Eppler, B. McGregor—1980s.* Ascend through bluffs and bush to the summit. Best with spring snow.

"FIFTY-FORTY PEAK" 1540 m/5040 ft
FA: Jackson-McGraw Survey party—1941.
Approach via the Marion Creek road and Fifty-Forty trail (*E4a*). From the end of the road, cross the creek and ascend the broad bushy northwest ridge to an open summit.

Cats Ears Peak   Rob MacDonald

CATS EARS PEAK 1480 m/4860 ft
FA: R. Eppler, D. Hobil, K. Johnson, R. McDonald—1980.
Approach via Cats Ears Creek (*E4c*). At about 3 km, take the right spur (washed out) to its end. Ascend steep timber to W of the main avalanche chute on the north side of the creek, then climb a smaller gully to the W. Gain the west ridge, which is followed over the west summit. Two pitches of Class 4 beyond complete the ascent. A nice line. Takes 6 hours to west peak; 1 1/2 beyond to the main summit. The north bowl looks like it might be a pleasant approach on spring snow.

"NEEDLESS PEAK" 1440 m/4720 ft
Located 1 km S of Cats Ears Peak. Likely unclimbed.

TRIPLE PEAK 1525 m/5000 ft

Located 3.5 km SE of Cats Ears Peak.

FA: R. Eppler, R. MacDonald—1984.

Approach from the end of the logging road on Cats Ears Creek (*E4b*) and follow a miner's trail to the 730 m/2400 ft gap. Ascend bush S to the lake at the head of Cats Ears Creek. Contour around north side of the massif, ascending snow to divide. The northwest ridge of the main summit is Class 3, while the east ridge of the west peak offers Class 4 difficulty.

MT. HALL 1440 m/4720 ft

Located 6.2 km/3.9 mi NW of the head of Effingham Inlet. No recorded ascents.

WITCH HAT · FLATTOP · MACKENZIE PEAK · REDWALL PEAK · SHADOW BLADE

The Mackenzie Range   Bob Tustin

THE MacKENZIE RANGE 1360 m/4450 ft

A ridge of rocky summits 2.5 km SW of Cats Ears Peak.

The recommended approach is to take the road SE from Highway 4, 2.5 km S of Canoe Creek. From here, it is a 6 hour pack directly up the bushy, bluffy ridge due W of the main group of towers. A trail is presently being cut up this ridge. The highest peak is in the centre of the group and is a scramble from this side (*FA: P. Guilbride, S. Watts—1968; FWA: B. Perry, M. Walsh—1972*). The northwest peak is "**REDWALL**," a Class 4 climb from its col with the main summit (*FA: R. Culbert, T. Stevens—1960*). The easternmost summit is "**THE CENTAUR**," and may be reached by a Class 4 gully to the S between it and "**THE WITCH HAT**," a spike immediately to the W. Both are Class 3 from the divide at the top of the gully (*FA: R. Facer, M. Walsh—1969*). The next summit W ("**FLATTOP**") may have been climbed in 1975; the pinnacle ("**SHADOWBLADE**") between it and the main peak is Class 4 (*FA: B. Perry, M. Walsh—1972*).

Chapter 29

West-Central Vancouver Island

BOUNDARIES:
North: Highway 28, Muchalat Inlet
East: Buttle Lake, Price Creek, Drinkwater Creek
South: Highway 4
West: Pacific Ocean

FOREST SERVICE OFFICES:

Port Alberni Forest District
4227 Sixth Avenue
Port Alberni, B.C. V9Y 4N1
724-5786

Campbell River Forest District
231 Dogwood Street
Campbell River, B.C. V9W 2Y1
287-2194

MAPS:
Federal:
92 F/3 Effingham River
92 F/12 Buttle Lake
Provincial:
92 F/SW Kennedy Lake

92 F/5 Bedwell River
92 F/13 Upper Campbell Lake

92 F/NW Buttle Lake

Approaches

A. FROM HIGHWAY 28 TO GOLD RIVER

1. "Cervus Creek" trail: This creek is located at the north end of Buttle Lake, 17 km/10.5 mi from the Campbell River bridge crossing. An excellent elk trail follows the creek. At the mouth of the creek, the trail is supposedly high on the valley flank, but it descends to follow about 60 m/200 ft above the creek on the west side clear to the lake near the valley head. Cervus Creek is the summer range of a depleted elk herd; if travel by this route is unavoidable, please take care to avoid disturbing these animals.

2. Elk River trail: Begins 23 km/14.3 mi from the Campbell River bridge crossing. This is the key access trail for much of the best climbing available on Vancouver Island. Take Highway 28 past the mouth of the Elk River valley and turn S onto the Elk River Timber Company logging road. Turn left at the T junction (well signposted) and left again onto a small spur. The trail begins here and is well marked up the west side of the Elk River valley. (Its location is shown incorrectly on 92 F/13.) The trail crosses the creek which drains Landslide Lake 1 km N of the lake and swings toward the SE, ending at a pleasant cirque 1 km SE of the lake and E of Colonel Foster. To reach Landslide Lake, continue straight up the west side of the creek, crossing to the east side about 200 m/650 ft before the lake. This section is rough in places.

3. Kings Peak route: Continue E from the Elk River trail turnoff on the Elk River